Noël Browne

To the memory of
Bill Hyland and Matt Kingston

Noël Browne
Passionate Outsider

John Horgan

Gill & Macmillan

Gill & Macmillan Ltd
Hume Avenue, Park West, Dublin 12
with associated companies throughout the world
www.gillmacmillan.ie
© John Horgan 2000
0 7171 2809 1
Index compiled by Helen Litton
Design by Identikit
Print origination by Carole Lynch
Printed by ColourBooks Ltd, Dublin

This book is typeset in Bembo 11pt on 13.5pt.

A CIP catalogue record for this book is available
from the British Library.

1 3 5 4 2

Contents

Preface

In Ireland, we tend to take our heroes neat; our villains also. This is why a biography of Noël Browne is, of necessity, a risky undertaking. No book could replace or supplant his extraordinary autobiography, *Against the Tide*, published in 1986 and still in print. This undertaking has a different ambition and, in a sense, is an attempt to take up the challenge laid down by Noël Browne himself when he made it clear that his own work was not 'a definitive history'. Of course, as Noël would have been the first to recognise, the business of what is, and what is not, 'definitive' raises many questions. So much of human history has been written by the ideological victors that any claim to 'definitive' status needs to be closely scrutinised for any political baggage it may carry.

Perhaps there is no such thing as definitive history. Biography, like history generally, is an art form that is continuously in flux. The modest task of the biographer is not to help the reader like his subject more (hagiography) or less (deconstruction) but to understand him better and, through him, the times in which he lived. This process, if we are lucky, is a mutual journey of discovery, as well as a narrative which tries to put flesh on the bare bones of chronology.

It is a work of selection. Noël Browne lived to be over eighty, and had a political career of over three decades. In any account of such a life, many more things will be excluded than included, and this work of choice and rejection inevitably shapes the final product. Fair-mindedness — an old-fashioned virtue, perhaps, and unfashionable in an age of contested visions of the past as well as of the future — is the often elusive objective.

It is also a work partly of imagination: whether the biographer himself lived through all, part or none of the times in which his subject flourished, he has to try to envision, in his mind's eye, the motives as well as the milestones, the feelings as well as the facts. But at the end of the day, no matter how much he has uncovered, no matter how close he thinks he may have got to his subject, his assessment is always in a sense provisional; the final verdict is the reader's alone.

On this journey I have had many helpers. Some friends and colleagues have read various parts of the manuscript; their comments have always improved it. The book could scarcely have been written at all without the positive support for research at Dublin City University, where I work. Many people who knew Noël Browne at one stage or another of his tempestuous career — inevitably, they include his critics as well as his adherents — have been more than generous with their time and their memories; their modest appearance in footnotes is poor enough recognition of the many insights which have been incorporated into this study.

The work of other researchers has also been of rare value. Ruth Barrington, whose own superb book on the health services of Ireland is the starting point for many an exploration, generously made available to me original notes of her own interviews, and original research notes given to her by the late John Whyte, including his notes of his interview with Dr J.C. McQuaid — the first interview ever granted to a historian by this prelate. Gerry Gregg and Martin McGovern, two near-contemporaries at UCD, dug out of their attics copies of their MA dissertations — one on Clann na Poblachta, the other on Noël Browne himself — which read extraordinarily well despite the passage of years, and which contain much original material.

Staffs at every grade in the public and private archival institutions and libraries in which I carried out this research contributed immeasurably to whatever qualities it possesses, with their indefatigable energy in meeting requests for more and more documentation. In particular, I should thank David Sheehy of the Dublin Diocesan Archives, a sure-footed guide to that extraordinary collection; Tom Quinlan of the National Archives, who filled innumerable gaps; Dr Bernard Meehan, Keeper of Manuscripts in Trinity College, Dublin, who made some of Noël Browne's manuscript material available for this study; Séamus Haughey in the Oireachtas Library, who patiently checked wayward references to Dáil debates; Marion Boushell, assistant general secretary of the Labour Party; and Seosamhín Ní Chadhain, steward of the invaluable Fianna Fáil archives. Nor, in this technological age, should I omit the contribution of Eoin Campbell and Genevieve Quinn, each of whom administered the kiss of life on more than one occasion to a computer which had suffered cruel and unusual punishment.

Although I did not know Noël Browne well, the creation of this book has afforded me the opportunity to get to know members of his family, not least his wife, Phyllis, and his daughters, Ruth and Susan. They could not have been more helpful in sharing their unique perspective on — and deep pride in — his multi-faceted life. This book, and the judgments in it, are not in any way their responsibility; but it could not have been as complete without their help. Noël Browne's youngest sister, Ruth, who now lives in Tennessee, has as fierce a pride in her beloved brother's political record, and has a special position as his only surviving sibling. She and her husband, David Wick, have welcomed me into their home, and both Ruth and Lois Coy, who was a devoted friend and companion for many years to her sister Kitty, have helped enormously with memories, copies of letters, and unique photographs. I owe a debt of gratitude too, to Clem Walsh, a cousin of Noël Browne from east Galway, who with his wife, Mary, helped me to explore one of the least well-known aspects of Noël Browne's childhood and background.

Above all, my wife, Mary, and our two children, Jane and Jack, have been my unseen support, the payers of the invisible price that is exacted by the work of research, composition and revision that sometimes seems never-ending. Their patience in the face of my too-long absences, and their encouragement, has been the bedrock of the whole enterprise.

John Horgan
March 2000

CHAPTER ONE

'Memory is the Place Where We Live'[1]

At the height of the Mother and Child controversy in April 1951, a short paragraph in a small west of Ireland newspaper, in the inimitable way of local newspapers everywhere, drew its readers' attention to the local background of the man in the news. Dr Noël Browne, Minister for Health, it noted, had 'close links' with Co. Mayo. The nature of those links was specified: the father of the embattled minister had served in the county as a member of the Mounted Division of the Royal Irish Constabulary.[2]

This in itself was not exceptional. In the nature of things, many young Irishmen who were born in the first two decades of this century had fathers who were RIC men; Jack McQuillan, later Noël Browne's comrade-in-arms in politics and a lifelong friend, was another. The father of Jack's wife, Angela, was an RIC man. So was Noël's uncle Jim, who served in Moate, Co. Westmeath.[3] What is surprising, however, is that Noël's own account of his early years makes no mention whatsoever of this, and is brief to the point of opacity.

> *We had moved from Waterford, where I was born on 20 December 1915. My father, unemployed and the unskilled son of a small farming family in Co. Galway, brought us shortly after my birth to Derry, where we lived for a time in the Bogside. He obtained work in one of the shirt factories.*[4]

The omission is surprising because Noël himself knew that his father had been a policeman, and referred to it in passing from time to time, in private conversations with friends and in at least one radio interview carried out not long before his death.[5] When his autobiography was being prepared for publication in 1986 the editor became aware of this fact and wrote to Noël suggesting that it should be included. His reply was telegrammatic: a curt

'No' written on the margin of her letter. This shows that it was a positive decision on his part, not a lapse of memory or an editing error.[6] The fact that he chose to exclude it from the first page of his autobiography speaks, at the very least, of mixed feelings, of a certain ambivalence towards a fact that had a political resonance in the Ireland of the 1920s and indeed for many years afterwards. The alternative explanation — that he considered it irrelevant — is impossible to accept.

Noël may not even have known that his grandfather, too, was an RIC man. Although he was described as a subconstable of police on the birth certificate for his son Joseph — it was common for sons who followed their fathers into the RIC to rise higher in the ranks than their parent — and as a police pensioner on his death certificate, he was described as a deceased farmer on Joseph and Mary Browne's marriage certificate six years after his death.

At one level, to focus on an omission like this can seem pedantic. But there are at least two possible reasons for his decision to exclude this part of his history from his personal testament, and each of them is relevant to the search for the other Noël Browne — the Noël Browne whose complexities are often obscured by the vivid brush-strokes of *Against the Tide*, the Noël Browne, in a sense, he wasn't sure about, or the Noël Browne he himself was trying to forget. His own account of his life, in *Against the Tide* and in countless press, radio and television interviews, has been extraordinarily influential, particularly on people whose political sensibilities were honed by the events of the second half of the twentieth century. But it is far from complete. Some of his interpretations are open to question. There are occasional factual inaccuracies. Altogether, these suggest that a re-evaluation of the events he describes, and his role in them, is timely.

One of the reasons why the suppression of the information about his father is significant relates to Noël Browne's adult Republicanism, of which the readers of *Against the Tide* would remain totally unaware. From about 1957 onwards, Noël Browne's attitude to the Northern issue was resolutely anti-Republican, or at least anti-paramilitary; he endorsed the Republicanism of Wolfe Tone in its ideological dimension, but not in its military one; and he referred frequently and with increasing asperity to the activities of armed Republicans in the North of Ireland. Before that date, however, his utterances on this topic, though rare, were indistinguishable from mainstream Republican sentiments, and indeed mirrored those of his Clann na Poblachta party leader, Seán MacBride.[7]

The other relates to the fact that during the 1948–59 period Noël's principal opponent, Seán MacEntee, did his best to play politics with Noël Browne's parentage. Noël never responded publicly to MacEntee's jibes, but he was often present when they were uttered, and they were as wounding as MacEntee could make them. There is an indirect reference to the fact that at some election meetings MacEntee 'vilified [Noël] up and down the constituency'.[8] Hearsay suggests that MacEntee on these occasions, safely out of reach of parliamentary reporters, could have used the traditional jibe: 'RIC man's "get"'.[9]

He certainly used the more genteel version of the insult not long after the 1948 election, when he barked across the floor of the Dáil at Browne's colleague, the new Clann na Poblachta TD Jack McQuillan, that he had been 'bred, born and reared on an Article 10 pension'.[10] He needled Browne about it in the Dáil, too. When the new Minister for Health remarked disparagingly about the condition of the county homes, many of whose buildings had been there for the best part of a century, MacEntee described them waspishly as 'an inheritance from a regime with which the Minister is very intimate'.[11] A year later, he accused Browne of being hostile to the erection of the planned memorial to those who had died in the War of Independence on a site in the Rotunda Gardens, which Browne was taking over on a temporary basis for a childcare clinic.[12] In 1959, when Noël Browne was pursuing de Valera relentlessly on his ownership of shares in the *Irish Press*, and referred tellingly to the Fianna Fáil leader's decades of free publicity in the newspaper, MacEntee retorted with a reference to another publication in which de Valera had also figured prominently — *Hue and Cry*, the RIC bulletin which regularly featured photographs and descriptions of wanted Republicans in 1920–21.[13] Noël's sensitivity to this aspect of his heritage is perhaps part of the key to a life that was long, eventful, and characterised by strong passions, deep emotions, and a belief in himself and in his mission that took no prisoners.

Noël Browne was not even Noël Browne. According to his birth certificate, he was Noël Brown. He was born on 20 December 1915 in 38 Bath Street, Waterford city, a small street of one-storey labourers' cottages. No. 38 was a four-room house, with three windows to the front and (uniquely in the street) a chicken house at the rear.[14] His parents are named on the birth certificate as Joseph Brown, who is described as a sergeant in the RIC, and Mary Theresa[15] Brown, formerly Cooney. In itself, the absence of the final 'e' is probably not of any real significance; when Noël's father, Joseph, was born on 23 May 1872 at Barrack Street, Loughrea, Co. Galway, his father James Brown's surname was also spelt without the final 'e'. James Browne lived at Kilchreest, a little village between Loughrea and Athenry, and was stationed at the RIC barracks in Loughrea when his son was born. The maiden name of James Browne's wife, Mary Anne, was Serridge — so unusual a name that it must have been an Anglicisation; Noël himself believed that this particular branch of the family was part-Spanish.

The registrars who took down the details in both cases probably did not even bother to ask how the surname was spelt, and it is spelt 'Browne' on

James Browne's headstone in the small graveyard of Kilconieran, halfway between Athenry and Loughrea. Noël himself discovered the discrepancy only when he first applied for a passport many years later.[16] More surprisingly, given the meticulous nature of the record keeping evident in their archives, the National Society for the Prevention of Cruelty to Children, which later employed Joseph Browne, also recorded his name without the final 'e'. An early official minute of a meeting of the cabinet of which Noël was a member recorded his name without the final 'e' — no doubt a reflection of the fact that he was still in some respects a political unknown — but this was later corrected by a different hand.[17]

Noël's mother was the daughter of Patrick Cooney, who served with the RIC in Co. Mayo and spent much of his time in service in Hollymount, where she was born. The Mayo connection was to be a strong one in Noël's childhood, and even later; one of the first foreign journalists to interview Noël after he became Minister for Health was Marje Cooney, a radio reporter from the United States and the daughter of one of his mother's cousins who had emigrated many years earlier.

The Waterford into which Noël Browne was born was his father's last posting. The young Joseph Browne had joined the RIC in February 1891. Its official records[18] noted that he had no trade or occupation, and that he had been recommended by the local district inspector. Noël remembers his father as a tall man;[19] in fact, he was only five feet nine inches, and his son, despite a lifetime of recurring illnesses, was to exceed that height comfortably. Joseph was an accomplished athlete, and won numerous trophies. Noël's contemporaries at the English public school he later attended also remember his prowess as an athlete,[20] although he sometimes preferred not to compete; he would set out with apparent dedication for scheduled long runs with a group of boys, but would duck out of the exercise to hide — encouraging others to join him when possible — and rejoin the throng at a later stage, pretending that he had run the full course.[21]

After initial training, the young Joseph Browne, as was the custom for young single RIC men, was moved frequently. His first posting, to Waterford, was in November 1891. In September of the following year he was assigned to the ranks of mounted RIC men. Again, there was nothing unusual in this; most RIC men were trained to ride and handle horses as part of their ongoing training.

In August of 1894 he was transferred to Wexford and in May of the following year to Hollymount, Co. Mayo. Mary Theresa Cooney of Hollymount, whom he was later to marry, was then aged only eleven. She would have been sixteen when Joe Browne left for his next posting — to Derry, where he was stationed from the first year of the new century. There were two RIC barracks in Derry at the time, a small one at Creggan Road and the large one at Strand Road. Browne, as an unmarried constable, lived in Strand Road with thirty-five other RIC men. The majority of them (twenty-four) were Catholic, and the head constable was an Irish-speaker from Donegal. Even then, security considerations evidently played a major part in Irish policing; in the official returns for the 1901 census, from which the above information has been drawn, the denizens of RIC barracks were identified only by their initials and by a number of other characteristics — their age, linguistic ability and county of origin. The census return for the 28-year-old 'J.B.' from Co. Galway records additionally that he could both read and write.

In December 1904 Joe Browne was posted back to Mayo. He was now aged thirty-two; Mary Theresa Cooney was twenty. They were married there on 8 September 1905, by which time she had turned twenty-one. Joseph Browne was posted to Waterford at the end of the year, but his wife returned to Hollymount for the birth of their first child, Eileen, which took place on 26 June 1906. This puts into a somewhat different perspective Noël's contention that both families had disapproved of the marriage and had effectively cut all links with the young couple.[22] There is evidence that the Cooney family may have been initially unhappy; the only close family member to act as a witness at their wedding the previous year had been Isabella Browne, Joseph's sister. But at least some form of relationship had been restored, otherwise Mary Theresa Browne would hardly have returned to her parents' village for the birth of her first child. Additionally, when the 1911 census was taken, Joe Browne was on his own in the Bath Street house, suggesting that his wife and the baby may have been away on a visit to Hollymount at the time. Eileen was the first of eight children; she was followed by Jody, who was born on 30 August 1912; Kitty, born in 1913; Noël, born in 1915; Martha, born in 1917; Una, born in 1918; and Ruth, the youngest, who was born in December 1923. One child, Annie, born in Athlone (the year is not specified in *Against the Tide*), died soon after birth from tuberculosis.[23]

Noël's position in the family is worthy of some comment. His father had little time for his older brother Jody, who suffered dreadfully from tuberculosis of the spine, and was deformed; for a fine, upstanding RIC man, this was not progeny to be proud of and Noël became, by default, the eldest son. There is some scientific evidence that younger children — perhaps because they have to compete harder for attention and even for resources — tend to do disproportionately well in later life. One psychological study has noted[24] that high achievers almost invariably hold special family positions, in that they have been treated as special by the family as a whole, or by key members of it, early in their development. It is certainly the case that after their parents' death, and Jody's death, Noël's sisters put his welfare and his needs before their own in a truly self-sacrificing way.

His place in the birth order is also significant. The study already mentioned observes that the middle position in the family is not the disadvantage it is sometimes assumed to be; middle children accounted for 15 per cent of all US presidents and a quarter of all British prime ministers up to 1980. A more impressionistic study[25] suggests that position in the family is a better predictor of social radicalism than class, and that later-born children are more risk-oriented than their first-born siblings, more likely to empathise with downtrodden individuals and to support radical innovations. Looked at in this light, the young Noël Browne can be said simultaneously to have enjoyed, paradoxically, the privileges of the eldest son (emotionally speaking) and the cultural and political preparation for battle which is the inheritance of the younger child.

Joseph Browne was evidently a straightforward, competent policeman. His RIC file notes that he incurred no punishments, and was allocated no rewards. Promotion was to follow. In November 1911 he was promoted to acting sergeant and in February 1913 full sergeant; few Catholics achieved a higher rank in the RIC. Five years later, days before his forty-sixth birthday in May 1918, he retired on a pension of just under a pound a week (or approximately £34 weekly in 1998 terms).

Noël, unsurprisingly, had no childhood memories of Waterford; the few references he makes to it are hazy. For example, he once alluded to his father's resignation from the RIC as having taken place in 1916, the year of the Easter Rising.[26] As Noël was then less than a year old, this may be a reflection of something he picked up later about his father's political views, but in fact Joseph Browne continued to serve for another two years after that seismic event. Another version, in an article on Noël Browne published during his lifetime by a long-time admirer, Michael McInerney, then political correspondent of *The Irish Times*, says that Joseph Browne resigned from the RIC 'as a protest against his work during the Anglo-Irish War'.[27] Presumably this information came from Noël himself, who was interviewed several times by McInerney in September 1967 while the article was being prepared, but the somewhat haphazard approach to the dates and facts of Browne's family history in the article does not engender confidence. Joseph Browne's resignation was in fact more than six months before the 1918 election in which Sinn Féin won a majority of the Irish seats and used that mandate to establish the first Dáil, and eight months before the shooting at Soloheadbeg in January 1919 which launched the War of Independence. All that can be said is that, as family lore has it,[28] political factors of some kind may have played a part in his decision.

Noël's earliest childhood memories are from his sojourn with his family in Derry. He remained incurious about Waterford. On one occasion, he even drove down Bath Street with his wife without realising where he was; Phyllis, who had noticed the street name, thought the houses so impoverished that she decided not to bring it to his attention in case it might upset him.[29] His father had already served in Derry for four years, and this evidently had something to do with his decision to return there — Noël thought that there were some family connections there too, but these have been impossible to trace. But there is — apart from the inference that political factors were in some way involved — no detail available about when or why the family left Waterford, and when they arrived in Derry.

This unexplained gap in the Browne family history, between May 1918 and December 1919, is only very partially filled by the section of *Against the Tide* which deals with Derry. The gap is of more than passing interest because of a number of stories, current in Dublin during his period as Minister for Health, which suggest that the link between Noël Browne and the Chance family, who effectively adopted him and paid for his university education, may go back to that early period in his life.

T.C.J. O'Connell, the surgeon who was later to play a major role in the Irish Medical Association's campaign against Noël Browne's Mother and Child Scheme, and who knew the Chance family, told an interviewer in 1983 that after Joe Browne resigned from the RIC he had taken a job as gamekeeper to the Chance family on an estate they owned in Waterford, and that this was the source of Lady Chance's interest in the young Noël.[30] The closely linked nature of the medical network in Dublin suggests that there may be some truth in this story. Dr James Deeny, the medical civil servant who was first a collaborator and later a critic of Noël Browne's during his period as minister, had another gloss on it. He believed that there had been a shooting incident on the Chance estate in which either Noël's mother or his sister Eileen had inadvertently been put at risk, and that this was the source of a sense of obligation on the part of the Chance family which went back long beyond 1934, when Noël and Neville Chance first met at the Jesuit public school Beaumont.[31] If any of this is true, it would not be surprising that Noël, then barely three, should not have remembered it; equally, it may have been part of an inventive attempt to explain the mystery of the Browne/Chance relationship, which would certainly have been the subject of gossip in Dublin in 1948–51, but about which Noël did not speak in depth until the publication of his autobiography. Either way, it remains a tantalising story, impossible of verification.

Life in Derry was undoubtedly hard. The income from his father's work in a local shirt factory, although obviously supplemented by his RIC pension, was simply not enough. His mother was an outworker, possibly for the same factory, but their housing quality was poor and the young Browne, as he recounted it more than half a century later, experienced it as a childhood of deprivation and even danger.

The only occasion on which Noël is on record as having returned to the city in later years was in 1969, during the so-called battle of the Bogside, when a Labour Party delegation (he was then a TD) went North to find out for themselves what was happening. There were five of them, travelling in one car: Noël, Conor Cruise O'Brien, Justin Keating, Barry Desmond and Michael O'Leary. Conor Cruise O'Brien's recollection of the expedition is that Noël had become particularly emotional during the visit to Derry — so much so that he made effectively no political contribution to the discussions that took place on that occasion.[32]

During his Derry childhood he contracted persistent deafness in one ear, apparently because of a poorly treated case of measles. This disability would have been accentuated by the doses of streptomycin he received for his tuberculosis while Minister for Health. This deafness, unknown to all but close family and friends, contributed in no small way to a manner that was sometimes described as aloof or even arrogant, although it may not have entirely explained it. Certainly some political associates in later years, who knew of his disability, noticed that whereas he was comfortable in one-to-one conversations, he became withdrawn in groups or at meetings, as he patently was not always aware of everything that was being said.[33] Indeed, one of his principal adversaries, Archbishop John Charles McQuaid, was also partially deaf; but whether any of the misunderstandings between them were aural rather than ideological is, many years later, impossible to ascertain, and in any case, given the evidence which will be adduced later, unlikely.

At this point, a biographer has to voice a note of caution. Noël Browne's autobiography is sometimes an unreliable guide, at least on certain factual matters which can be verified from public records. This is particularly true of the first twenty-five pages or so, dealing with his earliest childhood memories. A few examples may indicate the nature of the problem. His father's income is stated with great clarity, but is inaccurate. He gives two different years for his father's death (1923 and 1925), both of them mistaken. He has a vivid memory of the plate on his father's coffin giving his age at death as fifty-four; Joseph Browne was fifty-five when he died (but this could well have been an undertaker's mistake). Two different causes of death are given for his infant sister Annie. He says that his brother Jody never attended school because of his ill health, but it is clear that he did. He writes that Ruth was born after his father's death, whereas she was born four years earlier, when Noël was almost eight. He misstates Eileen's age by four years, which becomes significant in the later context of the decision to move from Mayo to London. His mother, according to his account, was forty when his father died in 1927, but in fact she was forty-three. The target of the ambush outside his family home in Athlone was not Seán Mac Eoin, as he believed, but Brigadier George Adamson, the first victim of the Civil War in that district.[34]

Some of these errors of recollection are more significant than others, and given that Noël was in his seventies when he put down his memories on paper, few of them are surprising. When he was being pressed, during the writing of *Against the Tide*, for more specific biographical details, he demurred, offering the excuse that 'our pet dog Butch eat [*sic*] my Curriculum Vitae in a moment of frustration'.[35] What they indicate, however, is that the early pages of his autobiography are a better guide to feelings than to facts; and that, from his earliest years, Noël Browne was someone to whom emotion was deeply, even critically important. On a public as well as a private level, emotion informed many of his actions, and was an important ingredient in much of the strong loyalty towards him that developed in the Ireland of the 1950s and 1960s.

The emotional map he draws of his early childhood is one of strong contours and striking contrasts. Waterford is non-existent. Derry is darkness; rats, poverty and danger. Athlone, by contrast, is like the sun coming out from behind storm clouds; it was where he knew 'real happiness for the first time'.[36] Right up to his father's death, this period of his childhood is treated almost lyrically. Visits to the circus, playing around the Shannon, delivering milk, fair days and country rituals filled young Noël's life to the brim with memories that, even six decades later, have an extraordinary vividness and immediacy.[37] Some incidents, seemingly insignificant in themselves, burned themselves into his memory and could be recalled later with pin-sharp clarity. In an unpublished manuscript, he recounts the story of a piece of wood which he had found in one of the big demesnes bordering Athlone, which he was promised would be turned into a hurley for him. Before this could be done, it was taken away by mistake and chopped up in the demesne sawmill. The sense of loss with which he invests this incident is palpable. Later, in Trinity, he found that the son of the big house which owned the demesne was a fellow student. In the same manuscript, he records with evident fondness the company of a child of his own age named Maura, and the fact that he 'spent [his] time more with girls than with boys at that time'.[38]

After Athlone, the darkness descends again in Mayo, although even here there is a hint that, despite his straitened circumstances, life was pleasant enough for Noël. It was, on the other hand, undoubtedly difficult and unhappy for Jody, who is not even recorded as having attended the local school at this time.[39] London is next, chaotic, wounding, as the family confront first the death of their mother and then a desperate search for somewhere to live. Things do not return to an even keel until luck, his own intellectual ability, and his older sisters' unremitting efforts on his behalf pluck him from this desolate landscape and ensconce him, first, in an exclusive primary school, and then in one of England's most prestigious Catholic academies.

The circumstances of the family's move from Derry to Athlone need some elucidation. It would certainly have been unusual for an unemployed labourer to be employed as an inspector by the National Society for the Prevention of Cruelty to Children (the institution did not become the ISPCC until 1956), as Noël's account has it. On the other hand, it was entirely appropriate that an ex-sergeant in the RIC should have been so employed, and the ranks of the Society's inspectorate were frequently filled in this way. Such officers would already have had a basic knowledge of the law, would be familiar with courtroom procedures, and would have had the degree of physical fitness and training required for a job that was often demanding, with long hours and many journeys around the countryside on a bicycle.

The NSPCC was founded in 1889 in London. An earlier attempt by a Cheshire vicar in 1881 to establish such an organisation (Britain already had a society for the prevention of cruelty to animals) was rebuffed, with an evident sense of regret, by the liberal Lord Shaftesbury on the grounds that 'the evils you state are enormous and indisputable, but they are of so private, internal and domestic a character as to be beyond the reach of legislation'.[40] Its guiding light in its formative years, a Yorkshire Congregational minister named Benjamin Waugh, was specific about the character of the inspectorate. The 'Cruelty Man', as he became known (or, in rural Ireland, 'The Crewlty Man'), 'needed to have a cheerful disposition to put children at their ease, with a natural courtesy towards family members, but with strength of character to act wisely on the children's behalf. Married men were preferred because of the support their wives could give them.'

The available records suggest that Joseph Browne may actually have emigrated to Britain in search of better employment. NSPCC archives show that he joined the organisation as a temporary probationer not in Ireland but in Shrewsbury, on 6 December 1919.[41] The Shrewsbury and Shropshire branch, where he briefly worked in 1919–20, was a particularly large one, covering most of Shropshire, an area of some 1,060 square miles with more than 200,000 people at that time (the intended average size of an NSPCC branch was 100,000 people). The branch helped an average of about 450 children a year.

Joseph Browne was appointed inspector to the Society's Athlone branch on 1 January 1920 in succession to another ex-RIC man, Jeremiah Daly, and the family moved into a fine, double-fronted house at the end of a terrace of similar houses in Irishtown, on the eastern side of the Shannon. The house went with the job, and a brass plate on the side of the door proclaimed the occupant to be the District Inspector of the NSPCC.[42]

Noël Browne remembers his father's salary variously as £5 a week or £11 a fortnight. In fact Joseph Browne's starting salary was £2 a week, which, with the pound a week pension he received from his RIC service, would be the 2000 equivalent of some £112. By the end of his service his basic salary was £3 per week, with an extra seventeen shillings and sixpence added as a 'war bonus',[43] giving a total, with his RIC pension, of some £4 17s 6d, or approximately £195 per week in today's terms.

His income, in other words, although no doubt modest to begin with, had increased by almost three-quarters over a period of some seven years. It is difficult to establish any meaningful basis for comparison with other occupations, but the salary payable to national school teachers may provide some illumination. The teachers were paid under a salary agreement struck in November 1920, which provided for an annual salary for trained male teachers of £170, rising by seventeen annual increments to a maximum of £370.[44] A national school teacher appointed in 1920 would by 1927 (providing he was not teaching in a small school, and received no special merit increments) have been in receipt of an annual salary of £254, almost the same as Joseph Browne's total income of £253 10s.[45]

In the Athlone of the 1920s, such an income was undoubtedly significant, probably sufficient to allow its owner to consider himself as a member, however lowly, of that middle stratum of society which was slowly coming into existence in the new Irish State. It was an undernourished middle class, certainly (the national teachers had to accept a 10 per cent salary cut from Ernest Blythe, the Minister for Finance); but there is no way in which it could be confused with the landless cottier at one end of the social spectrum, or the wealthy merchants, professionals and landed gentry at the other.

What happened in Derry, and in Mayo, appears to have coloured to some extent Noël Browne's memories of his social origins. His grandfather, as an RIC subconstable, was undoubtedly working-class, although he lived to draw his pension, and acquired or inherited a farm. His father's rise through the ranks of the RIC, and eventually into the NSPCC inspectorate — the Derry hiatus apart — marked him as upwardly socially mobile, at the very least. There were, of course, seven children to feed, but Noël's sister Eileen had a bicycle, which Athlone's working-class teenagers could rarely have aspired to in the 1920s.

There is also evidence, in the family photographs, that Joseph Browne carried himself with a certain flair. That his marriage portrait[46] should show him dressed to kill in white tie and tails is perhaps to be expected, but a later, though undated, portrait[47] shows still more clearly his sense of self-possession, and his delight in good clothes. He is wearing a fashionable tweed suit, a waistcoat and a fob, and is posed (possibly in a photographer's studio) with his hand resting carelessly on a pile of books, every inch a man of the world — a dandy, even. Phyllis Browne's gloss on the photograph is instructive: 'You can see where Noël got it from.'[48] Noël, by her account, used to love fine clothes whenever he could afford them, which was not often. On occasion, he would even pick out a piece of cloth for her, and advise her to make something for herself from it. (An accomplished seam-stress among her many other talents, Phyllis would sometimes make clothes both for Noël and for herself.)

The background detail about the Browne family's life in Athlone, scanty though it is, throws at least some new light on Noël's assertion that his 'class instincts [were] deeply rooted'[49], and on his reference to 'many poor peasant families of our class'.[50] Elsewhere, he described his background as 'sort of working class — middle working class'.[51] Some commentators have been openly sceptical. A memoir of Athlone by James Spollen, a local journalist, printed and published but never distributed (for legal reasons), includes a chapter entitled 'Doctor at the Wailing Wall', which takes issue with Noël Browne's recollections.

> *I was born in Irishtown in 1915 and my family lived a few hundred yards from the Browne home, but at a lower social scale. I was a classmate of Dr Browne and his brother, Jody, in the Marist Brothers National School with a difference that I wore a patch on the arse of my pants . . . There was consolation in the fact that other pupils were more adorned with patches than I and that other snotty-nosed youths trotted to school in their bare feet, even in the depths of winter, they being even bereft of the traditional 'hand-me-downs'. In contrast the Browne entourage had all the trappings of high respectability as their father's situation in life would have dictated . . . The family, according to Dr Browne, lived a life of 'precarious survival' on a weekly wage of £5. I was a member of a family of eight and my father was a railway worker. Had we had that income we would have been regarded as millionaires.[52]*

Although Spollen was driven primarily by a desire to defend the good name of the religious, who he felt had been treated in Noël Browne's auto-biography with 'antagonism and cynicism',[53] the memoir has a certain rough-hewn authenticity about it in this respect. In defending the Athlone Marist Brothers against Noël Browne's strictures, however, the author is certainly overreacting; Browne's comments on his early childhood edu-cation there are brief and not unfriendly, apart from two passages. One is an account of an incident of sexual abuse by a visiting member of the religious order which ran his primary school. This vividly prefigures, both in style and in substance, a similar passage in the 'Bishop John' story which occasioned so much controversy many years later.[54] The other is a complaint that, as a left-handed child, he was forced to write with his right hand — surprisingly, no substantial research has been done into the possible psychological or other effects of a forced change from left-handedness to right-handedness, possibly because this is no longer a common practice.

Fragmentary school records survive, both for Noël and Jody. Both boys entered the school on 12 January 1920, Noël into infants' class (his age is wrongly given as three and a half; he was in fact four). Jody, who was then seven, went into first class. Jody's attendance at school was only occasionally better than Noël's; from January to June 1920, Noël was at school for only 62 days, Jody for 76. Later on, the positions were reversed. In 1925 alone, Jody missed 132 out of 289 school days; in an eighteen-month period between 1924 and 1927, Noël missed only 16 days in total. Jody was, however, evidently a backward child; by fourth standard, both brothers were in the same class, along with forty other children. The list of the parents' occupations gives a strong flavour of an urban national school in a garrison town in the 1920s: six of the parents were soldiers, three were railwaymen, and there were no fewer than seven widows. Jody left school finally in May 1927, a few months before his fifteenth birthday.

Possibly the only school companion of Noël and Jody's still alive is John Bracken, who was born in the same year as Jody, and whose mother is mentioned frequently by Noël in the portion of his autobiography dealing with Athlone. Mrs Bracken used to frequent the Browne house, which was adjacent to her own, to help out and give advice about the children; both mothers were constantly aware of the dangers of TB, which was rampant at the time. John remembers Noël as a bright child, eager to learn and fond of play. Jody, however, was small and stout, with a hunchback, and prone to illness.[55]

The school Noël attended is now a licensed social club operated by and for the members of the Knights of St Columbanus, who numbered among their members at least some of Browne's colleagues in the 1948–51 inter-party government. In the 1920s, however, all this was a long way in the future, and Noël's childhood in Athlone, which he later described as 'idyllic',[56] was heading towards a crisis of which he and his siblings were, as yet, completely unaware.

Both his parents were infected by tuberculosis. When and where they became infected cannot be ascertained, but their housing conditions in Athlone were good, and the greater likelihood is that the onset of the disease in one or both parents had taken place in the squalor of their Derry house, briefly but graphically remembered by their son. In later years, Noël returned, restlessly, to an unanswerable question: who had infected whom? His diagnosis in *Against the Tide* was that 'my father's hard-working conditions had led to the infection in the first place' and that 'he slowly destroyed himself working long and late hours'.[57] While not saying so explicitly, this at least implies the possibility that, in his view, his father had been the original carrier. This suggestion is buttressed by a passage recounting the way in which one particular father, suffering from the disease and a patient in the sanatorium at Newcastle, Co. Wicklow, had been sent home while still a carrier and had — Browne assumed — infected the remainder of his family with the disease.[58]

However, in an earlier, unpublished draft of his autobiography he had dealt with the problem in greater depth, and had come to a much firmer diagnosis, based in part on his study of his father's case notes, which he discovered when he went to Newcastle as assistant medical superintendent after the war. This diagnosis again referred to the hard physical nature of his father's work but, instead of implying that this was what had 'led to the infection in the first place', used the same evidence to come to precisely the opposite conclusion: his father could not have worked so hard, for so long, if he had been the original carrier, and therefore it was 'likely that it was my mother who infected and innocently caused the death of the man for whom she had such a deep love, my father, as well as her infant daughter, Annie . . . through ignorance my mother was unaware of her role in all this dreadful sequence of sickness and death in our family'.[59]

A decade after the publication of his autobiography, and not long before his own death, Noël Browne showed that the problem was one which had not ceased to preoccupy him. 'I have often wondered who was the original carrier . . . it was possibly my mother who infected my father, but it's useless to speculate now.'[60]

Useless it may have been; but the fact that the speculation had endured for nearly seven decades, as the physician who was also the child of the patients attempted a posthumous diagnosis, speaks for itself. To waver between identifying first his father and then his mother as the immediate cause of the infection which devastated the family reflects an indecision which must have been influenced by strong emotions about the implications of coming down on one side or the other. The unpublished manuscript version is, in its own terms, by far the more persuasive, and clinically detailed.

Noël Browne had very few memories of his father, although their family existence in Athlone, from just after Noël's fourth birthday to some months before his twelfth, was in many ways a settled one. 'When I could, I stood beside him, watching and following him like the tail on a high-flying kite'.[61] Yet another memory, surprisingly, is of guns. His father owned two, one of them a single-barrelled shotgun which he took out to shoot game birds. For any private individual to own a gun during or immediately after the Civil War was unusual; Noël recalls that, on one of these expeditions, the firearm was carefully concealed.[62] Even more unusually, Joseph Browne also owned a revolver. His son came across it 'innocently by accident in a press in his room, and twirled the barrel. It had a musty sweet smell, so distinctive I can still recall it.'[63]

He evidently remembers more of his mother, and although he remarks with some surprise that she 'never kissed or fondled me',[64] he judged her 'fragmented love . . . sufficient'.[65] She was also a proud woman. On one occasion, when the innocent young Noël had been invited by the teachers to partake of a First Communion breakfast — he was still in infants' class at the time — he returned home full of the good news, to be astonished by his mother's angry reaction; she thought that he had been invited to the meal because the teachers felt that he needed nourishment.[66] An autobiographical piece in his private papers gives more detail: 'She tried to beat me, poor pet, but because she had never done that before or afterwards in her life, she got a stick that wasn't very strong, and it broke.'[67]

The first overt sign of the disaster that was to befall the family came when his little sister Annie, only just born, succumbed to a particularly virulent form of tuberculosis, known colloquially as 'galloping consumption'.[68] The young Noël was wakened, in the bedroom which he shared with his parents and his infant sister, by the sound of a muttered conversation between the adults.

> *In the wispy, shadowy indistinction of the night, under the window a square boxlike roofless structure. Out, from inside, a purple violet glow threw patterns on the ceiling. A soft sighing whispering sound, overlaid by a minimally harsher spasmodic bobbling gasping sound of an infant's troubled breathing. At seven tall enough to look over the tight safety pinned Odlum flour sack cotton walls of the square, in turn, supported and framed by the sides of Marie Therese's[69] infant cot. Mild surprise at the unprotected flame under a small thin straight sided flat bottomed tinker's kettle, its short straight spout, a funnel stuck in its mouth . . . Pillowed in the shadowy depths an apple-sized head of the tormented infant, twisting and turning, uselessly fighting for life-supporting air, that wouldn't come. Wildly sucking in the warm moist steam filled mixture, generated by the tin kettle steam engine, her fate already decided, she fought out her hopelessly one-sided struggle with death.[70]*

The adults were soon to follow. Joseph Browne was the first to seek medical help, although Noël remembers his mother had 'an incessant and productive cough'[71]. An initial visit to a specialist in Dublin revealed that he had an advanced case of pulmonary TB, and he was subsequently hospitalised in Newcastle from 30 March 1926 to 22 May.[72] He continued to receive his salary during his illness. Noël implies that his eventual return to Athlone may have been because of his inability to pay,[73] but TB treatment was free, and had been since 1911. It is much more likely that he was sent home because the doctors in Newcastle felt that his illness was terminal and there was no point in keeping him in. This probability is supported by the fact that in the case notes, he found that his father was given no chance of survival.

When Joe Browne returned to Athlone, he had no more than fifteen months left to live. The account of his death on 23 August in the following year, 1927, as recorded by his son, is written like a scene out of a novel by Zola. Less than a month later, the annual meeting of the Westmeath branch of the NSPCC was held in the Greville Arms Hotel in Mullingar. The temporary NSPCC inspector, Miss Munnelly, gave a report which indicated clearly that Joe Browne had been effectively out of action since September 1926, and a vote of condolence was proposed to his widow.[74]

There does not seem to have been any special gesture from the NSPCC towards the young family in such difficult circumstances; Sir Robert J. Parr, one of the senior administrators in the Society's London headquarters, sent a personal message to the family but it was not accompanied by anything more tangible.[75] Joseph Browne's will, leaving everything to his widow, was probated on 21 October. The value of his effects amounted to £218 10s 0d,[76] of which, presumably, £100 was accounted for by the insurance policy referred to in Noël's autobiography. In 2000 terms, the £218 is the equivalent of approximately £8,754, or almost a year's salary for Joseph Browne. It hardly represented security; but neither was it destitution. To some extent, therefore, Noël's assertion that on his father's death 'we children were left homeless and penniless, as were and are so many unwanted children of primitive peasant societies such as ours was'[77] was one informed by powerful emotions, recollected in tranquillity.

A few months later the young widow, with her surviving children, had to vacate the NSPCC house in Athlone to make way for Joseph Browne's successor — as it happened, another ex-RIC man. It is impossible to establish this date with any accuracy. Noël says that she applied unsuccessfully for a local authority house in the town, but the family, realising that Athlone had no more prospects for them, decided to move back to Mayo and the hoped-for support of the Cooneys, Mary Therese Browne's family.

After a journey that has echoes of the Flight into Egypt,[78] the clearly distressed Browne family arrived at Hollymount. It was wintry,[79] and in all probability just before Christmas 1927. Having once again applied without success for a local authority house, they moved into rented accommodation in Chapel Lane. It is possible to pinpoint with relative accuracy the time the family moved, because the Marist Brothers' records in Athlone note that Noël left the school on 10 December 1927, while the records for his next school, the Christian Brothers-run national school in the neighbouring town of Ballinrobe, note that he was first enrolled in that school on 4 January 1928. (Interestingly, when Una entered school in Hollymount on 26 October 1928, her last previous school was given as Roscommon, indicating that she may have been boarded out there with relatives prior to the family's move from Athlone. Also, in the school roll there her mother's occupation is given as 'dressmaker' rather than 'widow'.)

Now aged twelve, the young Noël Browne finished his fifth standard at the end of June 1928. He was at the older end of the class, which included pupils born a year or two after him. The fact that his contemporaries entered in the same month suggests that it was what was called a 'primary top', i.e. a separate section of a national school which was created for older children, and which effectively followed at least part of the secondary school curriculum. Under the heading 'Position or Occupation of Parent or Guardian', the school register notes starkly: 'É marbh'.

In his autobiography, Noël has given us detailed portraits of many of his Ballinrobe teachers, not all of them flattering. Three elements in that period of his education stand out. The first was Irish nationalism, the second corporal punishment, the third sexual abuse. Although he is sharply critical of the Brothers' brand of nationalism, it is clear from later passages in *Against the Tide* that some of it, at least, had stuck. He was aware of sexual abuse, and shared the general feeling of powerlessness that most children of his age would have experienced in the face of such appalling behaviour, but was not directly affected by it. Similarly with corporal punishment; although he watched, with horrified awe, the beatings that were handed out, often for no reason that he could discern, he never suffered himself. 'I got approval by being a good boy,' he confessed many years later.[80] Both his parents harboured the hope that he might go to Mungret, in Limerick, to finish his secondary education and train for the priesthood.[81] In time, the quiet, obedient and studious child, who might under other circumstances have become a priest, matured into the rebellious, uncompromising public man.

The school roll also provides at least a partial answer to his immunity from the regime that affected other children harshly. He was at school on 117 days between January and June 1928 in Ballinrobe, and 179 days in the following school year. His marks for the teacher's examinations in fifth standard in June 1928 record two of ten out of ten, in arithmetic and algebra, a nine in reading and two eights, in geography and history. His lowest mark — a five — was in grammar, but this was hardly typical.[82] In other words, he was close to being a model pupil. Unusually, there is no section on the roll for attainment in Irish, although it was undoubtedly taught.

This academic promise was to be seriously jeopardised by what happened next. The school roll records Noël Browne's sudden, unscheduled departure on 24 May 1929, before the end of the school year and before taking his sixth standard examinations. In the section headed 'Destination of Pupil', the roll notes tersely: 'Londún'. A later hand has added 'Minister for Health, 1948 (Feb)'.

There are two versions of the circumstances surrounding the family's hurried departure for London. Noël's own version is bleak. The family had run out of money; spurned by relations and friends, they had no option but to leave, taking their by now invalided mother with them, to join his older sister Eileen, who had already been there for some years. His younger sister

Una had already been sent to the United States, on the boat from Galway, to live with her mother's sister Martha, who had emigrated some years previously.

The bleakness of Hollymount is to some extent hindsight; Noël himself records that, until he saw the yellow and black notices announcing the auction of the family's effects, he 'did not know of the impending tragedy . . . school was tolerable, the pleasures of boys in rural Ireland were enjoyable'.[83] He was possibly mistaken in attributing the problems experienced by his family to a latent local hostility towards his mother based on her marriage. The Brownes were a tubercular family. Even if the neighbours in Hollymount had been unaware of the circumstances of his father's death, his mother's condition was unmistakable. Tuberculosis had all the connotations of plague. Neighbours and friends alike avoided sufferers if possible. Sixteen years later, that sense of fear found dramatic public expression in the Public Health Bill of 1945, with its draconian provisions for forced seclusion of sufferers and even, it was hinted, for banning people suffering from infectious diseases from travelling on buses; a CEK cartoon in *Dublin Opinion* the following year shows a bus conductor applying a stethoscope to a prospective passenger's chest.[84] In the rural Mayo of 1928–9, the combination of fear and rumour would have been lethal to a family like the Brownes, but perhaps not always for the reasons that the young Noël suspected.

There is, as it happens, another version of events, containing details of which Noël may have been unaware as he was writing *Against the Tide*, at a time when he had by and large forgotten the existence of a cohort of east Galway cousins. He assumed that most of his mother's family had emigrated to the United States.[85] In fact, as he discovered when his cousin Clem Walsh from Craughwell introduced himself to Noël in Eyre Square in Galway shortly after the publication of the book, there was, and remains, a strong network of Cooney cousins in the area between Loughrea and Athenry, where his Browne aunts also lived. Lack of communication between the two families is at least a partial explanation for his unfamiliarity with this branch of his family tree. It may also be relevant that, after he became a minister, his rare visits to the area were, by and large, policed by the Brownes, and the Cooneys sometimes found out about such a visit only after he had left.[86]

The Cooney connection is important in this context because of Noël's assumption that his mother's family would do nothing to help them in their straitened circumstances in Hollymount. This is bound up with another key fact — his mistake about Eileen's age. In his autobiography, Noël says that his mother 'in desperation, decided to take us to our eldest sister, Eileen, who had emigrated to London in 1926, aged sixteen'.[87] The problem about this is that Eileen, if she emigrated in 1926, would then have been either nineteen or twenty, not sixteen. By the summer of 1929 she was twenty-three, and had been a wage-earner in London for some time. She was now a young women of independent means, with a strong sense of responsibility for her ailing mother and her threatened siblings. Another, equally important factor may also have been involved. Before she left Mayo Eileen had also been engaged to a local man, Robert Harty, but she had broken off the relationship.

The Cooneys' recollection is that Noël's mother — she was known as 'Sissy' in the family — came to her first cousin, Patrick Cooney, in some distress, saying that her daughter Eileen was pressing her to go to London with the children, but that she was not keen to go and was looking for advice. Patrick Cooney told her, according to his daughter, Biddy Kelly, that as far as he was concerned, she was family, and whatever could be done for her would be done. The Cooney version of events, therefore, is that Eileen Browne's insistence that her mother and family should join her in London, rather than any coolness towards the family locally, was the critical factor in the decision that was finally taken.

The central and verifiable element in all of this is Mary Theresa Browne's distress, compounded by an illness which was approaching its climax. It is also important to remember that she was undoubtedly still devastated by grief at her husband's death. Psychologist Peter Marris, who studied the bereavement in 1950s England of young widows who had young children to raise, expected that they would have money problems and problems with having to go back to their families for help, but found that their biggest concern was not money but meaning. 'Losing someone you love is more like losing the crucial premise which sustains a vital set of beliefs than like losing[even] a very valuable and irreplaceable possession.'[88] Bereft not only of financial support but of meaning, torn between the perils of leaving her native place and the urgings of her apparently strong young daughter, what was Mary Browne to do?

Her decision to yield to her daughter's persuasion — if this is what happened — undoubtedly hastened her own death and that of her eldest son, Jody. The family went to London by train and boat. It is a journey which no Irish emigrant has ever undertaken without deep emotion, but it is interesting that Noël gives it little space in his autobiography — a mere three and a half lines. This is an absence at the heart of his narrative which is, in its own way, as striking as much that is included.

Eileen had found a place for the family to stay at 333 Croxteth Road, in the London suburb of Lambeth.[89] Less than a month after Noël's last day in the Christian Brothers' School in Ballinrobe, Mary Browne was taken away from Croxteth Road in an ambulance, never to return. Noël, then thirteen and a half,[90] remembers kissing her goodbye in the hallway. She died in

Lambeth Hospital, of uraemia and acute nephritis, on 18 June 1929. She was buried, according to her son, in a pauper's grave; after Eileen's death from tuberculosis some years later, nobody could recall where their mother's burial place was located.

But the desperate journey she had made with her family was also, and paradoxically, an essential link in the chain of events which saw her second son, Noël, set on an extraordinary road. It led to an education, and a future higher and more productive than even she could have hoped for when, in her fondness, she imagined his passage through a seminary and out into the wider world.

There was a continual search for somewhere to stay; at one point, Kitty was reduced to carrying her crippled brother Jody, now in the final stages of his own tubercular illness, on her back.[91] But the break with Mayo, while it had been dramatic, was not complete; the networks had not been entirely fractured. A Mrs Steere, who was a second cousin of Noël, took Jody in for a time.[92] Another network, referred to by Noël as the 'medical mafia', also played its part. These doctors, with Mayo connections, sometimes took Noël during school holidays, as he really had no permanent home throughout his period in England.

Eileen's efforts on their behalf eventually brought them to Worthing, on the south coast, where she had secured employment in a holiday home owned by a Miss Salter at 8 Winchester Road.[93] Miss Salter's sister was joint proprietor of St Anthony's, an exclusive Catholic preparatory school, and Eileen managed to get Noël admitted to the school without payment of fees. Here Noël mixed not only with young English Catholic boys but with a cross-section of foreign children who had been sent by their wealthy parents to be educated in England. He had some catching up to do, notably in Latin, for which Ballinrobe had not prepared him, and accordingly he went to a local girls' school, the Notre Dame Convent (now Our Lady of Sion School), where he was given additional tuition in that subject and in mathematics by an Irish nun named Sister Rachel. Sister Rachel died in retirement at Bellinter, near Navan, in 1997 at the age of 102.

Noël's youngest sister Ruth, now living in Tennessee, recalls Miss Salter as 'terrible . . . she was strict, but I guess she had to be.'[94] Nonetheless, she provided a home for the family. It was a relatively brief respite. Miss Salter died shortly afterwards, and the holiday home was closed. This was followed rapidly by Jody's death, although the exact date of this is unknown.

Into his old age, Noël Browne was 'tormented' by the thought of his mother's death.[95] He was also obsessed by Jody and his fate.[96] His emotions about it often emerged as anger, but they also included guilt; as in a passage in *Against the Tide* recounting an occasion on which, comfortably ensconced in a cart pulled by a donkey, Noël passed his brother hobbling along a road in Athlone without stopping to help him. 'From out of all those early deaths', he declared two years before his own death, 'there is one message. Of that family of Brownes, there were thousands of our kind in the Republic, I was the sole survivor. The reason for my survival was so unjust and so wrong.'[97] This sense of the unfairness of fate, common among survivors of family tragedies or other disasters, often imbues those who experience it at any level of intensity with strong, sometimes even incoherent desires to right the wrong they feel has been done. It is a sense of guilt which impinges particularly on people who feel that they have better lives than their parents or siblings, and the greater the discrepancy, the greater the empathic distress. 'And always the nagging questions: were you chosen or did you look after yourself too well? Is your life stolen? How can you enjoy a life that isn't really yours?'[98]

It is tempting, and perhaps not entirely fanciful, to see in Noël Browne's sense of loss, his sense of the unfairness of fate and his deep attachment to the memory of his mother some similarities with the persona of another political figure who could not have been further removed from him on the ideological spectrum, but whose career had almost as many twists and turns: Enoch Powell. Powell was, like Browne, in many respects a loner, although on the political right rather than on the left. Once a British cabinet minister, he fell into disfavour and later turned on his former colleagues, finally migrating into the Ulster Unionist Party. He was a thinker who returned, over and over again, to the vagaries of a fate which had taken so many of his family and friends in World War II, but which had spared him. And, where Noël Browne wrote prose with a novelist's eye for detail, Powell wrote poetry, most tellingly about his mother.

> *Mother, with longing ever new*
> *And joy too great for telling*
> *I turn again to rest in you*
> *My earliest dwelling.*[99]

Sixty-five years after his mother's death, and less than three years before his own, Noël Browne spoke at the unveiling in Hollymount of a plaque to the memory of his mother. His speech was delivered as if in a trance — 'he was lost in himself . . . crooned the words almost' — as he told the story of his mother's life and death. 'God love him,' said a woman in the crowd. 'He's not over it yet.'[100]

The older sisters were by now working, but Ruth knew no other home but the Our Lady of Sion convent until she left school. Noël's star, however, was in the ascendant. St Anthony's, or 'Patton's', as it was known (its other proprietor was a Mr Patton), frequently sent boys on to Beaumont, a small

Jesuit public school near Windsor, now an IBM training centre. Noël was to be one of them. Beaumont's size — there were generally fewer than 200 boys in the school, and some 70 in its associated preparatory school, St John's — did not denote any feeling of inferiority; legend had it that when the headmaster of Eton, which was close by, once enquired about Beaumont, he was told that 'Beaumont is what Eton once was — a Catholic school for the sons of gentlemen.'[101]

The estate of which it formed a part had once been owned by Warren Hastings, and although Hastings' house had been destroyed, a magnificent mansion, modelled on the White House, had been built in 1798 in its place. The Jesuits acquired it as a noviciate in 1854. It had been opened as a school in 1861. It played rugby against Eton, the matches held on Runnymede. The social class of its pupils can readily be deduced from the self-confident missives sent back from foreign parts to the editors of the *Beaumont Review* on tea planting in Assam and volcano climbing in Uganda.[102] It was hardly a punishment station; an anonymous writer in the *Review* suggested that 'it must be a very pernickety type of epicure who would say that the Beaumont boy of today is not abundantly well fed'. Nor was it a nursery for nonconformists; in October 1930, just before Noël Browne made his way up from Patton's for his first term, the school debating society, which was organised on parliamentary lines, agreed by twelve votes to three that 'a socialist government is not conducive to the welfare of the Nation'.

Its fees in the 1930s were £150 a year — almost £6,150 annually in 2000 terms — and plainly far beyond the reach of the young Irish orphan. Noël Browne was awarded a scholarship, but this would appear to have been on the grounds of need and potential rather than on those of achievement. No details of the scholarship schemes for Beaumont survive but Dr T.C.J. ('Bob') O'Connell, the Dublin surgeon who knew the Chances well, believed that Noël had been the recipient of support from a school fund quaintly entitled the 'Distressed Loyalists Fund'.[103] The initial entry for him in the Beaumont register records that he entered the school on 15 January 1931, after a year at Patton's, and that he had come 'from Athlone, where he had no Latin or French'. He was further described as 'backward' and put into the Lower Third.

Almost immediately, he was promoted to the Upper Third, indicating that his educational deficiencies were now judged to be environmental rather than intellectual. He was to stay in the school for just over three years, until July 1934, and his career was evidently a chequered one. It would not have been easy for a boy of his background to blend unnoticed into the social milieu of Beaumont, and he would have had to fight his corner. Some, at least, of the references to him in the *Beaumont Review*, have a certain asperity about them.

This is particularly true in relation to his early activities at scrum-half for his year's rugby team. At first he shone, in partnership with his out-half, Harold Bidwell, who was plainly the star of the team, but towards the end of 1932 he was coming in for increasingly unfavourable attention. 'Our scrumhalf had a very "off" day and was quite outplayed by his opponent,' the anonymous commentator observed after one match. Following another, he was even more critical: 'When we began to attack, our movements broke down — sometimes in fact they never began, for Browne had an erratic day and sometimes bowled the ball hard straight behind him towards our goal, giving some easy chances to our opponents to chase through.'[104] Shortly afterwards, the hapless scrum-half found himself translated into the front row, where as hooker he was to redeem his reputation as a conspicuous player who 'headed many rushes'.[105]

He had a regular if undistinguished career in the cricket Second XI, but his particular prowess appeared to be at throwing the cricket ball, an event he won at three successive sports days, his longest throw being eighty-seven yards, two feet and two inches. He was also a keen, though less successful, member of the boxing team in both 1933 and 1934; his only recorded inter-school bout, at a match against Aldershot in March 1933, was stopped in the third round, 'Browne being outclassed'.[106] He was once a finalist in an internal boxing competition, in which boys from various 'houses' competed against each other. The other finalist was Derrick Walker, a boy from his own house. As both winner and runner-up points would go to their house regardless of the result of the contest, the two boys agreed that there was no point in trying to hurt each other and boxed three rounds almost without landing a blow. The referee, considerably displeased, declared the bout void, but Browne's house still won the competition. He maintained his enthusiasm for boxing right up to his Trinity days, when he turned suddenly against it after knocking out his opponent in a club bout.[107] As late as the eve of the 1948 election, his membership of the TCD Boxing Club was being advanced by the editor of *The Irish Times* as yet another reason why the electors of Dublin South-East should support him.

Away from the field of play, Noël Browne's school career, while academically steady, had its twists and turns. He was not averse to going on stage, playing the minor roles of Donalbain and Seyton in a senior school production of *Macbeth* in December 1932, and even blacked his face to sing 'Coal-Black Mammy' in the school's concert at Shrovetide 1933. He appeared as St Peter in the senior school dramatic production of November 1933, a play about the trial of Jesus, which subsequently relapsed into no doubt well-deserved obscurity.

In March 1933 he was admitted to the Higher Line Sodality. In an unpublished section of his memoir, Noël Browne recalled that, like James

Joyce at Clongowes, he and his companions had been subjected at this time to the 'weird and wonderful rhetoric of a Jesuit sermon'.

> *There was a sermon on the theme that 'the wages of sin is death'. I wondered about the kind of sin we children could commit which would merit death, and what kind of God would think that our death was a just reward for those sins . . . I cannot say that I was frightened. I was moved in admiration by the clarity and diversity of the visions fabricated by the words, as they tumbled from the remote dark figure of the priest in the pulpit.*[108]

His orthodoxy was obviously not sufficiently trusted for him to be sent out to speak at open-air meetings organised in London by the Catholic Evidence Guild, at which young Jesuit students were 'blooded' in public controversy on religious topics. This may in turn have had something to do with his participation in a debate about the political relationship between Ireland and England, which took place in October 1932 in the wake of de Valera's accession to power in Dublin. The *Beaumont Review* does not record his contribution but we have his own word for it that he castigated English Catholics for their attitudes towards their Irish co-religionists in a speech which later was described as 'anarchic' by the headmaster, Fr Weld, in a letter to Eileen Browne. It is certainly of note that the motion — 'That this House disapproves of Mr de Valera's policy of separating Ireland from the British Empire' — was defeated.[109]

A contemporary remembers Noël as a quiet, uncommunicative boy who 'could easily be aroused to fury by any misplaced humour concerning Ireland and the Irish'.[110] Even as a teenager, the anger which was to be commented on by friend and foe alike in his later years, and which had its roots in personal trauma, was becoming a hallmark of his personality. His rebelliousness in this area did not preclude more intellectual activity, however; he became, according to his own account, something of an authority on the New Testament, simply by exploring the resources of the school library.

Even more problematic was his relationship with the Officer Training Corps, where membership was compulsory. At first, things appeared to be going well. He joined with others as a cadet, was promoted to Junior Lance-Corporal on 17 October 1932, and to Junior Corporal in February 1933. Thereafter, his name is conspicuous chiefly by its absence from the quarterly list of promotions (although he attended all the summer camps organised during his stay at the school, possibly in part because effectively he was homeless). In his own account of his time in uniform, he says that he managed to avoid promotion by deliberately failing the necessary examination on twelve separate occasions. He was presumably among the twenty-five candidates who all — mercifully cloaked by anonymity — finally passed the examination in February 1934. None of this prevented him from being recorded in the school review as a first-class shot.

In another unpublished section of his autobiography, he added a level of class analysis to his rejection of militarism, which seems to have been based initially on a profound humanitarianism as much as on any residual Irish nationalism.

> *Not alone were we prepared to use our military tactical techniques against other colonial powers, but even within the British class system itself. We were prepared for battle against that other great but disorganised, never armed, never trained, working class.*[111]

The warning to Eileen about his heterodox views had its effect; he was a dutiful acolyte for the remainder of his time at the school. It was perhaps one of the last occasions on which any institution managed to instil in him such a sense of conformity, and corporal punishment — one of the essential adjuncts to public school education across the board — was in its own way also instrumental in encouraging the young Browne to keep his head down. His detestation of this practice lasted throughout his adult life. At the same time, not all of the Jesuit educational experience passed him by; he was to leave the school with an unusual mix of 'archaic Irish and public school snob values',[112] which was not to be seriously challenged until he began medical work in Britain in the cauldron of World War II.

A link with Ireland was sustained. A cousin recalls that Noël would come back to east Galway for school holidays as a teenager, aged between fourteen and fifteen, with his sisters Kitty and Martha. They would be collected by an uncle, Jack Browne, from the railway station in a pony and trap, and play with their cousins and with older children. Noël was particularly adept at devising plays for the children to perform. He was also a compulsive reader, and would spend hours in the woods with a book. He was noted for his impeccable manners; on one occasion, one of his aunts was in charge of a gaggle of children who darted across the road after they came out of a church, leaving her to fend for herself. Noël stayed behind to see her across, leading her to comment: 'I hope that one day you'll be President of Ireland — you have manners, unlike all those ones.'[113]

He sat for his Schools Certificate twice during his time at Beaumont, in 1933 and 1934. At his first attempt, he passed in Religious Knowledge, English, Latin, French, History (with a distinction) and General Science. For his second sitting the following year, he repeated these subjects, with the exception of Religious Knowledge, and evidently passed them all without difficulty. Almost at the end of his Beaumont career, however, Noël was asked by Fr Weld to take under his wing a slightly younger boy from

Dublin, Neville Chance, on the basis that Browne, as another Irish boy, was best equipped to show the newcomer the ropes. Neville, who had up to then been at school in Clongowes, arrived in the school in March 1934, only four months before Browne left.

Neville's father was Sir Arthur Chance, his mother Lady Eileen Chance, Arthur Chance's second wife. Sir Arthur, despite his knighthood, was a nationalist, and during the 1916 Rising he defied the curfew by driving around Dublin in his carriage, hoping to be arrested; the authorities declined to give him the satisfaction. He was perennially short of the sort of money required to sustain a fairly lavish lifestyle, but this problem was resolved in a most unexpected manner after the death of his first wife, with whom he had four children. His second wife, Eileen, was a daughter of William Martin Murphy, the west Cork builder who had become a newspaper proprietor before the turn of the century, had been a Nationalist MP at Westminster, and had enhanced the already substantial family fortunes with the establishment of the *Irish Independent* in 1905. This marriage helped to provide Arthur with the necessary degree of financial insulation, and they had no fewer than seven children of their own, four sons and three daughters.

The large house in which they lived, Nullamore, is now a centre for the Opus Dei organisation. In the 1930s, however, it was home not only to the Chance family but to their friends, and Noël, having fortuitously become one, was invited to spend the summer holiday with them in 1934 after he had been 'minding' Neville at Beaumont. The invitation introduced him to a household which was to provide the foundation for an education, and a professional career, to which otherwise he could not have hoped to aspire.

Of Eileen Chance's four stepchildren by her husband's first marriage, three had not married, and decided with their married sister to support Noël through medical school. When Noël wrote from England after the holidays to thank them for their hospitality, they wrote back to him — they would not have had his address if he had not written his polite letter — to suggest that he attend Trinity College, Dublin under their auspices. Accordingly, he went to Trinity for his first term in the autumn of 1934.[114]

The family's generosity showed itself in many ways. The fees were not the only problem. Noël had assumed that he would, during his student days, be able to stay with his father's sister, Isabella, who was married and living in Phibsborough. To his surprise, he was told that this was not possible, as she did not take students in as a matter of policy. Many years later, Noël was to discover that she in fact had taken in students as paying guests for at least part of the time that he was at Trinity; the inference is that her family could not do without the money that a paying student would have brought in, and could not, in addition, afford the expense associated with a non-paying, impoverished relative.[115]

His experience with the Chances surfaced again towards the end of his life, when, working in semi-fictional form on some of his childhood memories, Noël Browne wrote a number of versions of a short story about a dinner party in a Dublin professional household — the details suggest it was the house of a medical family in Merrion Square. It is a dinner party from hell. The father is absent — may even be dead. The two main characters are the son of the house, a young man who had once been a member of the IRA and had been interned in the Curragh, and his mother, a society hostess with hidden political depths. Although the son now maintains only a veneer of his original Republicanism, the mother is strongly committed, and her political views emerge at the end of the party when, very much the worse for drink, she insists that her embarrassed and decidedly non-Republican guests rise to toast 'The Republic'. The dating suggests 1936 or 1937, and it is a powerful cameo of some of the political tensions of the day.[116]

Noël had a car, or the use of a car, for at least part of his time as a medical student,[117] which would have been a rarity. And his early years at Trinity, at least, were marked by a number of carefree, though impoverished, expeditions to the Continent. One of them was a trip down the Danube in 1938, which is recorded in his autobiography. The trip had originally been planned by two female students, Anne Dowds and Moira Mallagh. When Noël and Peter Denham heard of their idea, they asked if they could accompany them. Anne Dowds' father was anxious about the students' safety, however, and Noël and Peter set off on their own ahead of the two girls.[118] The trip was to be in two parts — the first part down the Elbe, the second down the Danube. The canoe was bought in Germany, but the flat German lowlands held little charm for the intrepid pair, who loaded their canoe onto a passing barge for the initial, featureless part of the journey.[119] Mallagh and Dowds followed them, coming across their names in guest house registers as they travelled south.

To make such a journey in 1938 was not without risk, and indeed had some political connotations as well, but at this time Noël's political sensitivities, at least in relation to international events, were relatively undeveloped. He was to tell the Dáil many years later, when he was advocating the banning of a projected trip to South Africa by an Irish rugby team, that 'during the thirties many of us sought to close off the fascist countries by cutting down on trade and other relationships with them in the social and recreational sphere', and that he and Peter 'were advised not to go to Hitler's Germany . . . because we would be spending money and supporting a racialist and anti-semitic society'.[120] What he neglected to inform his fellow TDs was that in the 1930s he and his companion had done precisely the opposite of what they were advised to do, and what he was now earnestly advising the Irish rugby team to do. That is, they had ignored the advice and gone to Germany. Even at this stage, Noël Browne was evidently unwilling to have anyone else make up his mind for him.

Life as a medical student at Trinity was both hectic and pleasant for a student who, in his own words, was 'neither serious nor self-financed'.[121] He was serious about only one thing: his medical vocation. That apart, he lived life to the full, talking through the night, drinking in the back room of the Bailey or in Davy Byrne's, going to bed at six in the morning and getting up in time to catch a train down the country to play a football match.

Students who were contemporaries of his — especially women — remarked on his handsomeness.[122] His dark hair fell forward over his forehead in a Yeatsian manner; later he tended to comb it back, so that he looked more severe. He enjoyed women's attention and was an enthusiastic party-goer, often playing a small accordion to entertain other guests. It was an innocent time, and few emotional relationships between students were sexually consummated. Noël once complained to a fellow student that on a journey home by car after a party, when he had been at close quarters with a girl in the back seat, his activities had been serially interrupted because she insisted on blessing herself whenever the car passed a church.

Underneath the gaiety, though, was a certain seriousness. One female contemporary, who met Noël at a party in the Trinity Boat Club, went on for a meal with him at a taximan's café in the centre of the city. Noël spoke passionately about the plight of the poor, and what could be done for them. The couple eventually had to leave as the regular clientele, aware of the intensity of the conversation but not of its content, began to make disparaging remarks about 'Trinity students'.[123]

Some of his contemporaries noted a certain reserve; it could also become hauteur. It was observed by Dr William Pike.

> *What really irked him was that he had to accept charity. The Chances dressed him, paid his fees, gave him pocket money; but he was very rude to her. I spent an occasional night out at Nullamore with him; he would complain about the breakfast; summon the butler and give him a telling off. He couldn't accept authority from anyone.*[124]

The Boat Club in 1936 was the scene for another meeting which was to change his life. Phyllis Harrison, a quiet young woman who had already seen him on the student promenade in Grafton Street, attracted his attention, and he asked her to dance. She was sixteen, five years younger than Noël, but was given an unusual amount of social liberty by her parents, perhaps because she was, she felt, 'an unwanted addition to an already too large household'.[125] Phyllis's family was Church of Ireland. Her grandfather had been a musician, who had eked out a precarious livelihood playing in the

Protestant 'Big Houses'. Her father worked in a clerical position in one of the railway companies, and they lived on the Cabra Road in Dublin. The rapport was immediate; it was the beginning of a relationship which was to survive for some six decades, through numerous vicissitudes and twenty-nine changes of address, and which provided both of them with an unrivalled companionship, solidarity and love.

Phyllis remembers seeing, as a child, a newspaper photograph of Noël's father breasting a tape at an athletics meeting, under the caption: 'Joe Browne Does It Again!' The memory remained dormant until Noël mentioned his father's background. She was to suffer from TB even before Noël, being diagnosed in 1938.[126] When she was in hospital, Noël wrote to her every day; later, when he was in hospital, he again wrote every day. The letters, to her regret, were mislaid in the course of one of their many moves.[127]

It was an era famous for the so-called 'chronic meds' — medical students unencumbered by later rules about the maximum number of times they could fail examinations, and on occasion supported by legacies from doting elderly relatives to support them for as long as they were in medical school.

> *A number of these, possibly the wiser ones, remained on and on, and on, for years. There was Bunny Ellecker, Jammie Clinch, and Dick Sandys. They lived pleasantly on during those last few lotus years at university, before the awesome bloodletting of world war two.*[128]

That bloodletting was approaching fast. In the summer after his Danube trip, Noël Browne and others went on a sailing trip to Brest in a classic yacht, the *Samphire*, which had been built on the Clyde in 1904 for Lord Lloyd. In his autobiography, he emphasises the poor weather they experienced and — understandably — his persistent ill health, which was to be diagnosed on his return as tuberculosis. It was a journey that had its high spots, although Noël principally remembers, in *Against the Tide*, the dangers of a near-shipwreck and a narrow escape from a torpedo fired by a submarine on a training exercise. One crew member from the trip survives, Dr William Pike, now living in retirement in Blackrock. He recalls that it got off to a bad start when a launch on which they were going out to the yacht in Dún Laoghaire harbour upended, consigning some of their provisions to the bottom: 'the "supplies" we were loading was a crate of whiskey. He blamed me, I blamed him. When the dinghy tipped, he went to grab me rather than the crate. If he had grabbed the crate we would have been all right.'[129]

Noël was a good crewman, ready to do anything that was asked of him — although occasionally, when Dick Clements, the skipper, required a particularly unpleasant job to be done, he and Pike would retire below to play cards, the loser destined to do the work. There were times when the card game went on so long that Clements, in desperation, did the job himself.

When they went on shore in Brest, Pike and Noël both bought Breton smocks and berets, the sort the sailors wore; Pike's was red, Noël's was blue, and they wandered around the town in them. Noël picked up a few girl-friends on the way — he spoke in broken English, pretending to be Spanish. He tried to enlist Pike's support but his friend demurred, not being particularly good at affecting a foreign English accent. It was all 'very innocent'.

The boat was a forty-foot yawl with a lot of brasswork, difficult to keep shined up while they were at sea. So when they were in Brest, Noël and Pike hired someone to do the polishing for them — a very small man, almost a Caliban figure, who in addition to his skill in polishing brasswork could ascend the leech of the mainsail, hand over hand, while the boat was under way. He slept on deck at night, with a tarpaulin thrown over him. They paid him a shilling a day. Then, for some supposed infraction or other, he was fired. An hour later, a small boat loaded with gendarmes made its way out to the *Samphire*; it appeared that Caliban's father was head of the local dock workers' trade union, and the entire crew of the yacht were hauled off and clapped into gaol. Luckily, Clements spoke French and some time later, to their relief, they were all released and presented with invitations to a party thrown by the mayor.

By the time they got back to Weymouth, it was the end of August, days away from the declaration of war. British warships were being assembled in Portland harbour, and the Irish crew got back to Dublin by train and ferry — in Noël's case, to face his final year in college with the daunting prospect of treatment for tuberculosis also ahead of him.

Noël followed the normal six-year medical course in Trinity without interruption. The only blip was in 1939 when, shortly after Phyllis had herself been hospitalised with TB, the first symptoms of the illness appeared in him, and he was hospitalised in Dr Steevens' Hospital in Dublin. Although he had completed his courses in all the relevant subjects (including a number of special courses), he did not sit the necessary examinations at the end of the academic year. He was nevertheless awarded credit for the year, and subsequently sat and passed the necessary exams.

He qualified as a doctor in December 1940.[130] Contemporaries recall him as quiet and reserved,[131] and not an outstanding student — roughly in the middle of his class.[132] More relevant, in view of his later career, was that he was no great respecter of authority. In his autobiography, he gives a number of instances of his attempts — rarely successful — to take on higher authority on behalf of nurses and other employees, but another incident not recorded in *Against the Tide* secured him a reputation even among final year medical students, who are notoriously difficult to impress.

This involved one of the consultants in Steevens', Dr Solomons, a some-what flamboyant gynaecologist. Every time there was a birth in the British royal family, he would disappear ostentatiously for some time, leaving the housemen to suppose that this was where he was engaged. He also took up hunting, and used to go out with the Ward hunt on Saturday mornings. On his way to the meet, he would turn up at the hospital, resplendent in hunting pink.

Noël Browne was his house surgeon. One Saturday morning, attired as usual, Solomons told Browne off for wearing a dirty housecoat. Browne, he said, looked 'worse than a painter'. The reproof was not unusual, nor was it particularly unjustified: there was a laundry in the hospital, and Noël could have picked up a clean housecoat at any time, but he never believed that there was any necessary relationship between the quality of care and sartorial standards. Browne rounded on Solomons: 'And you look like a broken-down jockey in that ridiculous gear.'[133] History does not record Solomons' reaction — if any — but the incident provides, at the very least, evidence of Browne's sharpness of tongue, which in different contexts later was to under-mine others' support for many causes to which he was passionately attached.

The slight confusion about his qualifying date (in his autobiography he says he completed his qualifying examinations in 1942) is related to the fact that the obligatory final stage in training was hospital internship, which he undertook in Dr Steevens' Hospital between January 1940 and January 1941.[134] He had begun his medical experience in the same hospital in October 1936.

There is a gap in his employment record here of some sixteen months, which corresponds to his first major hospitalisation for his recently diag-nosed tuberculosis. This, paid for by the ever-generous Chance family, was at the King Edward VII Sanatorium in Midhurst in Sussex.[135] It was wartime, but the facilities there were as good as could be provided any-where, and although some of the techniques were highly experimental and dangerous, the risk appeared to be worth it. After losing almost two stone, Noël underwent an especially dangerous operation on his right lung, under local anaesthetic. The operation was successful inasmuch as he did not die from loss of blood, but unsuccessful in that the space left in his lung which should have been filled by air became filled by blood. Almost a decade later, after he became Minister for Health, he was medically examined by his Clann na Poblachta colleague Dr Michael ffrench-O'Carroll, who found that effectively he was functioning on only one lung, and not a particularly good lung at that.[136] The lengthy hospitalisation had its own, unexpected bonuses; he listened avidly to the radio, and read widely: 'There was certainly the advantage for those of us who survived the ordeal — we became satisfyingly well read.'[137]

Restored to health, after a fashion, Noël Browne went to Newcastle Sanatorium as a house physician in April 1942. Newcastle — to give it its full name, the Royal National Hospital for Consumption in Ireland — had been established in 1896 by a committee led by Florence Wynne, whose mother, one of the Galway Blakes, had died of TB. Initially, the hospital could accommodate only 24 patients, but by 1914 the bed complement had risen to 125, at which level it remained until 1950.[138]

This period of employment was brief, lasting until April 1943, when Noël emigrated to take up a position as assistant medical officer at Cheshire Joint Sanatorium in Shropshire. He was by now deeply involved in the care of TB patients, his energy and dynamism fuelled by his own experience of the disease, particularly at Midhurst; he had also begun the work which was to secure him his medical doctorate, which he was awarded by Trinity in 1946, for original research into the blood sedimentation rate of tuberculosis sufferers.

There was, however, even more to his emigration than medical curiosity and a career move. In the early 1970s, when he was no longer in the Dáil but, as a senator, still a national political figure, he was approached by the Independent newspaper group with the suggestion that he should write a regular opinion column for one of its titles. He replied, with the insouciance for which he had long been well known, that he would be delighted to do so as long as there was no attempt at censorship, and that he would feel free to write material critical of the Independent's principal shareholder (since 1973), Dr A.J. F. O'Reilly.[139]

The staff member to whom he was speaking on this topic told him, with feeling, that it would be more than her job was worth to relay that message to her superiors, but, undeterred, Noël set out to write an article in the form of an open letter to Dr O'Reilly, which is now with his papers in Trinity. The relevance of the article to this period of his life is that, in accusing Dr O'Reilly of being indifferent to the trauma caused by involuntary emigration, Browne maintains strongly in his manuscript that his departure for England in 1943 was voluntary, motivated by political conviction: 'As a medical doctor, later, I volunteered to emigrate so as to play my part in the second world war against fascism. You have favoured emigration, Dr O'Reilly.'[140] His conviction, as it happened, went even deeper than medical service; he actually applied to join the British armed forces — possibly the Royal Army Medical Corps — but was turned down, inevitably, on health grounds.[141] This raises the interesting question of whether — knowing his own medical history — he seriously thought he might have been passed fit for service. It also suggests that the nationalism engendered in Ballinrobe was by then fairly dormant, although it was to re-emerge later in a quite unambiguous form.

He found the generally relaxed but businesslike approach to medical care in the Cheshire sanatorium a refreshing change from the hierarchical oddities of Dublin hospitals. This was followed by further work at Harefield County Sanatorium, near London, which was staffed in part by senior medical personnel who had been evacuated from London, and where a wide range of war wounded were treated. It was a learning experience in top gear. Allied to the fact that no charges were payable by the patients, it endorsed the convictions of the young Noël Browne, still not yet thirty, that medical care and private medicine were on some fundamental level incompatible, or at least inappropriately conjoined. Thereafter — although he briefly operated a voluntary, pay-what-you-can-afford system when he was working in Co. Wicklow, which was rapidly discontinued — he never charged a fee for any medical service he provided, and declined a number of potentially lucrative offers to go into private practice.

Harefield was on the German bombers' flight path to the capital. This — and well-founded concerns about his own health — suggested that his marriage to Phyllis should not be put off for too long. Phyllis, for her part, accepted the idea with her eyes open; she was told, by a friendly doctor who had examined Noël, that he had at best six months to live. The wedding, when it took place on 14 January 1944 in a church in Uxbridge, near Harefield, was a chapter of accidents from beginning to end. The registrar failed to turn up on the day originally chosen; the best man — a Scots doctor who was a friend of Noël's — drank the bottle of Irish whiskey which Phyllis had brought over from Dublin for the celebration, and was nowhere to be seen the following day, when the ceremony actually did take place;[142] and there was neither the time nor the money for a honeymoon. However inauspicious the beginnings, it was the inauguration of an extraordinary marriage.

It was, of course, a Catholic ceremony. Noël had been brought up a Catholic and had certainly developed a sense of intellectual curiosity about religion, but had given up its practice at least by the time he was operated on at Midhurst.[143] He was to return intermittently to the practice of religion later, but for the time being, at any rate, agnosticism was in the ascendant. In the 1940s, for non-practising Catholics to shun a church wedding would have been unusual, to say the least, whatever their private convictions. There was, however, a straw in the wind. Under the regulations then (and for many years afterwards) operational in the Catholic Church, Phyllis would have been required to sign a written pledge that she and her husband would ensure the Catholic upbringing of any children of the marriage. Although Phyllis was, by general agreement, a quiet, even shy person, her inner determination came to the fore; the promise was never signed. In the confusion of wartime Britain, and the mixed-up dates for the ceremony, nobody noticed or, if they did, they chose not to make an issue of it.

As the war wound down, Noël and Phyllis decided to return to Ireland. It was difficult for Noël to acquire a public post; his status as a Trinity graduate created substantial employment problems for him, foreshadowing similar problems later in his career which also affected Dr Michael ffrench-O'Carroll. So it was back to the eleemosynary atmosphere of Newcastle Sanatorium. Here he was given free accommodation in a gate lodge and a salary of £21 monthly (about £122 per week in 2000 terms). He set to work again, treating patients, completing his doctorate and looking after his young family; Ruth was born in January 1945, Susan in April 1947. The next phase of his life had begun, but at this stage nobody could have guessed how tumultuous it would be.

CHAPTER TWO

The
Angry Young Man

T he Ireland to which Noël and Phyllis Browne returned had, in
at least one respect, begun to change from the Ireland they had
left. Public health was, however slowly and belatedly, becoming
a matter of major public concern. Noël Browne was to become
an integral part of that process. It was an area which his future adversary,
Archbishop John Charles McQuaid of Dublin, had already staked out as his
territory. The government, for instance, regularly sent Dr McQuaid horri-
fying reports from the Health Embarkation Scheme, one of which noted a
lice infestation rate of 60 per cent among male and 82 per cent among female
emigrants; one nineteen-year-old girl had an estimated eight thousand lice
on her body, 'exclusive of nits'.[1]

Venereal disease was an even more urgent threat, especially in the altered
circumstances of the war, and the incidence was no doubt increased by the
high participation rate of Irish males in the British armed forces during the
conflict. McQuaid, whose sister Helen specialised in treating venereal
diseases in her medical work in London,[2] sent a large cheque to Jervis Street
Hospital in 1944 for the establishment of a clinic for venereal disease cases,
whose work was carried out with great efficiency and discretion. He had an
ally, later to become an opponent, in the editor of The Irish Times, R.M.
(Bertie) Smyllie. The newspaper was carrying on a more public campaign,
in respect of which McQuaid offered Smyllie his support. Smyllie replied,
thanking him for his letter: 'Your public-spirited action in the "VD" problem
has set an inspiring example to the nation, and I hope earnestly that it will
yield badly needed results.'[3]

The single health problem which affected most people, however, was
tuberculosis, which had become a major issue at least by 1943. Seán MacEntee
was the Minister for Local Government and Public Health (then combined
under one minister). Although he was, according to a contemporary critic,

'much more concerned with local government than with public health — it was not vote catching',[4] he wrote to McQuaid in that year to outline his plans for dealing with a disease that was devastating urban and rural poor, and extending its ravages even into the comfortable middle classes.[5] Although the incidence of the disease was disproportionately high among poorer people, the popular stereotype of the urban slum as its main location was inaccurate; some of the blackest disease spots in Ireland were in rural areas, and even after death rates began to fall in Dublin and Belfast, they continued to rise for a decade in the northern and western counties.[6]

Even as MacEntee took his first steps, however, battle lines were already being drawn elsewhere. Judge Wylie, who was closely associated with the Royal Dublin Society, and Professor R.J. Rowlette, Professor of Materia Medica at Trinity College and a member of Seanad Éireann for the Dublin University constituency, had begun to convene meetings of doctors to set up a national association to combat the disease.[7] McQuaid, alerted to this threat to his hegemony, moved swiftly to counter-attack. His preferred vehicle was the Irish Red Cross, which was effectively under his control, and which he felt was the appropriate body to launch an anti-tuberculosis campaign. Unaware of the machinations going on behind the scenes, Wylie and Rowlette went ahead with their organisation, only to find it hijacked at the inaugural meeting on 15 February 1943 when the parish priest of Donnybrook, Fr Daniel Moloney, acting on McQuaid's behalf, declared that the campaign should be more properly carried on under the auspices of the Red Cross.

The chairman of the Red Cross central committee, Mr Justice Conor Maguire, who was also present at the meeting, intervened to say that although the archbishop's suggestion had not been made at the instance of his organisation, the Red Cross would willingly take up the work. He was being disingenuous; the correspondence in the Dublin Diocesan Archives indicates quite clearly that, although the initiative had not come from the Red Cross (it had come from the archbishop), Maguire had secretly and enthusiastically co-operated to frustrate the ambitions of the multidenominational group. Later the same year, McQuaid wrote to Moloney with an air of quiet satisfaction: 'The anti-TB [sic] would still be in the wilderness only for the Church.'[8] In his autobiography, Noël writes about this episode as if he had played an active part in it, noting merely that he had not been a member of the steering committee. He may well have been in touch with members of it, but he was still working in Britain and did not return to Newcastle until after the war at the earliest,[9] so his involvement would necessarily have been minimal at the time of McQuaid's decisive intervention. Later on, this was to change dramatically.

The archbishop was not the only person to interest himself in the welfare of TB sufferers. A group of former sanatorium patients convened a public

meeting at 6 Gardiner's Row, Dublin on 26 July 1944 to establish an organ-
isation called the Post-Sanatoria League, designed to secure an immediate
improvement in the conditions of those suffering from TB. Patrons included
Professor T.W.T. Dillon, MD, the businessman George Findlater, and
Alderman Michael O'Sullivan, TD, the carpenter and mayor of Dublin, who
was reputed to have been the model for Fluther Good in Sean O'Casey's
The Plough and the Stars. The honorary secretary was Charles O'Connor, a
TB sufferer who had already been in Newcastle and who was to return
there as a patient of Noël Browne's.[10]

Harry Kennedy was another committee member, and — even though
he was to die before Noël Browne entered public life — was the hinge on
which much of Noël's future was to turn. This was because he was the link
between Noël and two of his friends, key actors in the close-knit world of
medicine and politics: Noel Hartnett and James Deeny. All three shared
with Browne a belief in the need for radical methods to deal with TB; but
they played hugely different roles in the drama that was to follow.

Kennedy, born in Ballymena in 1906, was a journalist with *The Irish
Times.* He was more than just another journalist, however, and his career
had a touch of brilliance about it. Educated at Queen's University, Belfast
and Oxford, he then became a journalist for the London *Times* in the Far
East and in America, returning to the *Irish News* in Belfast, and thence to
Dublin and *The Irish Times* in 1938. Deeply but unostentatiously Catholic
in his religious beliefs, he was also a gifted writer of journalism and radio
plays and now — at forty — was terminally ill with TB.

Deeny, whom Kennedy had met during his student days in Queen's, was
a doctor, and a rising star in the Department of Health (he was to become
chief medical adviser). A bluff Northerner of immense ability who did not
suffer fools gladly, he was closely associated with the drafting of all medical
legislation prepared in the department at that time, and was nicknamed 'jet'
for the expedition with which he would get things done.[11] Before Browne's
access to power, he had helped to overcome the Department of Finance's
unwillingness to approve the money needed for the Health Embarkation
and Typhus Eradication Scheme by taking extraordinary initiative. The
British government had warned Dublin that if emigrants were not deloused
before departure, the British authorities would do it to them on arrival.
Deeny organised a visit to the delousing centre at the Iveagh Baths in
Dublin, to which he brought the secretary of the Department of Finance,
J.J. McElligott. McElligott, faced with the sight of 150 naked men, shaven
of all body hair and painted with blue disinfectant, fainted and had to be
helped from the scene. Later he approved the necessary expenditure without
demur.[12] Deeny was more than an administrator; he was keenly interested in
the scientific aspects of disease control, especially tuberculosis, and was in

the process of doing pioneering work based on a field study in a particular Northern town.

Kennedy's other friend came from the other end of the island. He was Noel Hartnett, a brilliant young barrister, broadcaster and aspirant politician from south Kerry. Hartnett had joined Fianna Fáil, and had risen through the ranks to become a member of the party's National Executive. More than that, he was an extremely able political organiser, and was reputed to be one of the few people in the party who could enter the office of the party leader, Eamon de Valera, without first knocking on the door.[13] His work in defending people in criminal cases was legendary; on one occasion, he is said to have confronted one of his clients whom he had just saved from gaol with the injunction: 'You get off this time. Next time, it won't be the court you'll have to face . . . it will be me.' As a senior figure in Fianna Fáil, he was reputed to have greeted the news that the party had just received its first cheque for £500 from a wealthy businessman with the recommendation that it be sent back.When his advice was ignored, he remarked: 'We're a different kind of party now.'

At the time he first met Browne, he was still in Fianna Fáil. Later, in May 1946, he was to commit the unpardonable sin — in de Valera's eyes — of appearing as junior counsel at an inquest on Seán McCaughey, a Republican internee who had died on hunger strike. Angered by this, de Valera cut all ties with his erstwhile lieutenant. Hartnett's broadcasting role (he was a popular quizmaster on a programme sponsored by the Irish Tourist Authority, forerunner of Bord Fáilte) was terminated by the Minister for Posts and Telegraphs, P.J. Little, as soon as his name appeared on the media statement announcing the formation of the Clann, because he had 'taken part in very vehement and dangerous political controversy'.[14]

Hartnett's changing political fortunes did not affect his friendship with Harry Kennedy, and he was a frequent visitor to Newcastle, where Kennedy was then a patient. Increasingly, he found common ground in his discussions with Browne. The relationship forged here, initially at Paddy Kennedy's bedside, was to become one of the most important political friendships of Browne's life. It is impossible to overestimate the influence each had on the other, as it is to determine which of them, at any given time, was the leader, and which the led. Browne instinctively recognised Hartnett's enormous political gifts, even as he warmed to his wicked sense of humour and his iconoclastic tactics; and Hartnett recognised — may even have envied — the charisma he saw in Browne which guaranteed him, over and over again, the electoral success which, despite Hartnett's own talents, eluded him.

Virtually the entire August 1944 issue of the *Journal of the Medical Association of Éire* was devoted to TB. The formal inaugural meeting of the Post-Sanatoria League took place in the Mansion House on 27 September in the same year. The government, which had up to then 'been holding on, hoping that the problem would go away',[15] was galvanised into something approaching action. It published the Tuberculosis (Establishment of Sanatoria) Bill on 27 January 1945, and passed it on 5 February, enabling the minister to establish sanatoria wherever he felt they were needed. The subsidiary provisions of the Bill included the giving of power to the minister to use the Hospitals' Trust Fund for the erection of at least three sanatoria, which would subsequently be transferred to the appropriate local authorities.

At this point Harry Kennedy's other friend, James Deeny, made his appearance. Some time during 1945, Deeny got a letter from Kennedy asking him to come and see him in Newcastle. Noël Browne had put this idea into Kennedy's head.[16] Deeny took to cycling down to Wicklow on occasional weekends, and there had his first meeting with Browne, who, along with Kennedy, was 'very critical and indeed scornful' of the way Newcastle, and the service generally, was being run. Deeny observed that Browne's patients adored him, but noted his anger and sense of frustration. He was also struck by Browne's profound antipathy towards the Dublin medical consultants and surgeons, who would come down to Newcastle to perform thoracic surgery on TB patients, and then return to their lucrative practices, leaving the lower reaches of the medical profession to mop up.

The Public Health Bill, which was the manifestation of the government's response to these journalistic and ecclesiastical campaigns, was introduced in the Dáil on 15 November 1945, and contained an extraordinary series of provisions for the confinement of people suffering from infectious diseases. It proposed, among other things, that 'a person who knows that he is a probable source of infection with an infectious disease shall not expose himself in any street, public place, hotel or shop', and empowered chief medical officers, whenever they considered it necessary in the interests of public health, to order a sick person's detention 'in a specified hospital or public place until he gave a certificate that he was no longer a probable source of infection'.[17] It gave public authorities the right to inspect people against their will, and to compulsorily institutionalise alcoholics and drug addicts.

Fine Gael members of the Dáil erupted in protest. The Medical Association of Éire (later the Irish Medical Association) was incandescent: 'It is not a matter of the rights of the community against the individual for a short time, but the restriction of this individual for months or perhaps even years.'[18] Browne was also active in opposition to the Bill, although his opposition was not, at this time, in the public arena. Later he described it as the product of 'draconian and jack-boot methods' by the Department of Health, and of its 'neo-Fascist thinking'. It was, he said, his 'first political involvement to have played a small part in the rejection of the ugly and authoritarian 1947 [sic] Health Bill'.[19]

The Bill was undoubtedly severe, but so were the problems with which it was dealing. Although James Deeny had been closely involved with the preparation of the measure, this has been emphasised at the expense of the role of Dr Con Ward.[20] Ward, a Fianna Fáil TD, was parliamentary secretary to Seán MacEntee and increasingly had total responsibility for health, then still seen as a junior portfolio. He was appalled by the prevailing standards in public health care, and determined to improve matters by whatever means he thought were necessary. MacEntee, although considerably more conservative, tended to give him his head, recognising his dedication and energy. Ward was later hounded out of office, resigning on a technicality to do with his income tax returns, after having been made a particular target of the medical profession. In one sense, he was the Irish Medical Association's first scalp. In another, he was someone who, had he remained in politics, could have played the part that later fell to Noël Browne.

Browne was only one of many people in all walks of life who were worried and concerned about the 1945 Bill. Richard Ryan, a barrister, phoned McQuaid's secretary in considerable agitation to complain about the Bill's 'unusual and sweeping' powers, and about the absence of any guarantee that it would respect the rights of patients. McQuaid, however, after seeking the advice of a Canon O'Keeffe on the issue,[21] wrote privately to Dr Con Ward, warmly supporting the proposals and deriding the Fine Gael attacks, which he considered misguided. The manoeuvres surrounding this piece of legislation provide a fascinating illustration of the lengths to which this zealous and authoritarian prelate could go in terms of justifying the invasion of people's privacy and even infringement of their rights when he felt the issues were sufficiently grave. It was, in sharp contrast to the Mother and Child Scheme, an occasion on which the Church authorities, in the shape of Dr McQuaid, were prepared to sanction intervention by the State in medical care to a degree which evoked the hostility of the medical profession, at least some senior politicians, and many members of the public. Again in contrast to later events, Noël Browne here found himself opposing State intervention, while McQuaid favoured it.

Encouraged by this private reassurance, Ward told the Dáil that, in so far as ethical considerations were concerned, these 'might be left with safety to the ecclesiastical authorities'.[22] His Bill, however, was doomed, despite the support of Dr McQuaid, because of one possibly fatal flaw it contained, and because of the opposition of an even more important coalition than the prelate could assemble — one that included Dr Noël Browne. It also involved Browne, his patients, friends and associates in a public political campaign on a major health issue for the first time.

The major flaw in the Bill, apart from its cavalier attitude towards basic civil rights, lay in the fact that it was theoretically possible to designate tuberculosis sufferers under the Act (had it become one) and thus render tens of thousands of infected people liable to compulsory long-term hospitalisation, and worse. This was not stated anywhere in the Bill, which proposed to leave the list of notifiable diseases to be the subject of a future administrative decision by the minister. Slowly, but with an increasing sense of outrage, TB sufferers, their doctors and friends realised what might happen, and began to put pressure on Ward to state his intentions. The more Ward prevaricated, the angrier they got.

The government issued a White Paper on tuberculosis on 20 January 1946. This may have been intended partly to blunt the edge of the attacks on the Public Health Bill, but its primary genesis was the government's political embarrassment at the leaking of an assurance by Deeny, given in the course of a private meeting with Professor Dillon of the PSL and the Red Cross, to the effect that the government was committed to ending TB. When this report appeared in the newspapers, the government had to follow up with action, and the plan already prepared by Deeny and others within the department was effectively adopted as the White Paper.[23] It noted that the death rate per 100,000 from the disease was now 135 per year, less than half of what it had been forty years earlier but still very high by European standards; there were about 4,000 deaths nationally from TB as against 2,000 from all other infectious diseases.[24] The stage was being set for action, but the political climate was becoming increasingly volatile and the government was under pressure.

It failed to stem the tide of opposition to the Public Health Bill, and the campaign in the general press reached a climax in April–May 1946, with a series of apparently carefully co-ordinated letters to the newspapers from individuals and organisations. One of them was from Harry Kennedy, still a patient in Newcastle Sanatorium.

'What do the leaders of the Irish medical profession have to say to this,' wrote Kennedy, in words which may well have owed something to a bed-side chat with his medical adviser, 'or do they and their associates only become publicly articulate when a question comes up such as fixing a fee for diphtheria immunisation or a salary for army doctors? . . . The doctors' silence is matched by the silence of nine-tenths of the members of the Dáil . . . I wonder was this kind of self-government worth fighting for?'[25]

Two weeks later, there was another broadside — but this time from two members of the medical profession. Unlike many TB sufferers, who wrote letters to the newspapers but hid their anger and their desperation behind pseudonyms, the doctors were not afraid to sign their names. Praising the letter-writers from two sanatoria, they urged a different approach upon the minister — one based not upon incarceration and segregation but on the elimination of the underlying conditions in which TB grew: poverty, mental and physical strain, and medical and lay ignorance. 'Unless special care is taken in the interpretation of modern diagnostic procedures,' they added, 'the lives of the potentially healthy may be blighted by an un-balanced consideration of the needs of the potentially ill.'[26]

The letter was addressed to *The Irish Times* from a hotel in Galway, where Dr K.R. Stokes and Dr W.H. McPhail were on holiday. As it happened, they had more than a passing familiarity with the work, and the passionate convictions, of the assistant medical superintendent at Newcastle Sanatorium. Stokes was medical director of the Harefield County Sanatorium, where Noël Browne had worked before returning to Ireland; McPhail was not only the rehabilitation officer for the emergency medical services at the same hospital, but the genial Scot who had been asked to be best man at Noël Browne's wedding two years earlier but had gone absent without leave after demolishing the bottle of whiskey. (Later, he was a visitor to Noël and his family at the gate lodge at Newcastle, where he frightened the local wildlife by playing his bagpipes in the garden.)[27] Without implying a necessary cause and effect relationship, this offers at least circumstantial evi-dence of Browne's early awareness of the importance of the communications media in political matters, and his skill in harnessing them to his objectives.

Noël Browne, not content with challenging what he believed were the iniquities of the Public Health Bill, and working with the PSL, was already operating in the area of bricks and mortar. He had established a committee which was trying to build sanatoria with private funds he was hoping to collect.[28] Jack McDowell, a solicitor, who was a TB sufferer himself and instrumental in setting up the Post-Sanatoria League, had heard about Browne's initiative.

> He had a committee and, although uninvited, I went along to hear Browne speaking. Dr Harry Counihan was also keen on doing something about TB. We used to meet at Bewley's Cafe. Victor Bewley, Louie Bennett of the Irish [Women] Workers' Union, Ronnie Nesbitt — there were a lot of people anxious to help. Browne told the meeting what he thought should be done to eradicate TB — sanatoria and money were needed; £25,000 was needed. The meeting didn't appear to be shocked. We said, we'll try to collect it. We have no idea how to go about it and you go ahead with your sanatorium.[29]

Browne, whose public profile was becoming more pronounced, now took part, on 23 May 1946, in a deputation to Dáil Éireann to lobby TDs about the 1945 Public Health Bill, which had still not been passed by the Oireachtas and was the subject of continuing controversy. This deputation was effectively organised by Charles O'Connor of the Post-Sanatoria League, now a patient in Newcastle for the fourth time. It was arranged that the deputation from the

League, which he left his hospital bed to accompany, would meet a cross-party group of TDs which included Vivion de Valera, Dr Tom O'Higgins (to be Minister for Health in 1954–7), Jim Larkin junior and William Norton. The deputation included O'Connor's doctor, Noël Browne, and a number of former and current sanatorium patients and doctors.

After a preliminary meeting to rehearse their case, the deputation went to the Dáil.

> *When we arrived at Leinster House, I was able to show Dr Browne over it. He had never been in it before. The House was in session and debating some measure or other. From the Public Gallery I pointed out the Press Gallery, the Ceann Comhairle, the Clerk and the Assistant Clerk to the Dáil, the stenographers, the benches where the different Parties sat, the Taoiseach and members of his cabinet, the leading members of the Opposition, etc. He was so fascinated by the scene that we did not arrive at the meeting, which I, as the leader of the deputation, was to open, until after it had started at 5 p.m.*[30]

In later years Browne forgot this episode and did not refer to it in his autobiography, which indeed states that before his election to the Dáil he had never seen that body in operation.[31] The most sensible conclusion to be drawn from this is that, in 1946 at least, the thought of a political career was nowhere near his mind.

In the wider world of politics generally, opposition to the government was growing on a number of fronts, leading inexorably to the founding of the Clann na Poblachta political party at a meeting in Barry's Hotel in Dublin two months after Browne's visit to the Dáil, on 6 July 1946. Its birth had been prefaced by numerous signs and portents. The year before, Dr Patrick McCartan, an Independent, left-wing Republican candidate, had amassed some 200,000 votes in the presidential election against Fine Gael's Seán Mac Eoin (whom he actually outpolled in Dublin) and the victorious Seán T. O'Kelly; he was the only presidential candidate until Derek Nally and Rosemary Scallan in 1997 to secure a nomination from four county councils. The aftermath of World War II had left many working-class Fianna Fáil voters disillusioned by wages standstill orders and by the slow arrival of the promised rise in the standard of living. Fianna Fáil had been in power since 1932, and de Valera, now sixty-four, was still the master politician but beginning to show his age. A long and bitter strike by primary school teachers began in March 1946 and lasted until October. The establishment of a Lower Prices Council and a Women's Parliament added to the pressure.[32] The later resignation of Dr Con Ward, and the long-drawn-out Locke's Distillery controversy, both helped to undermine confidence in the government.

Clann's founding father, Seán MacBride, was a fascinating, intermittently charismatic character who had initially imagined himself a close associate of de Valera (as recently as 1945 he addressed the Fianna Fáil leader in personal letters as 'Dear Chief')[33] and whose Republican credentials were underwritten by his ancestry as the son of Major John MacBride and Maud Gonne. He had been chief of staff of the IRA, but had led part of that organisation, somewhat uncertainly, in the direction of constitutional politics, at first via a left-wing organisation called Saor Éire which attracted the keen attention of the police Special Branch and was condemned by the Catholic hierarchy. Part of his appeal for Republicans lay in his willingness to defend those accused of various crimes in both civil and military courts; he caused a sensation at the inquest on hunger striker Seán McCaughey with his question to the prison governor: 'Would you treat a dog like that?' As already noted, his junior counsel on that occasion was Noel Hartnett; the two men became so close that Hartnett was known, irreverently, as 'the shadow of the shadow of a gunman'.

The new party was a hybrid. MacBride himself identified at least five disparate elements which went into its composition: extra-parliamentary, Catholic intellectual, parliamentary, social reform, and Fenian.[34] Its core activists included a number of former IRA men who had decided to follow MacBride onto the path of constitutional politics, but were determined to retain control of the new organisation. Alongside them were young, often inexperienced but idealistic recruits, who saw in the Clann an opportunity to create a third force divorced from the rancorous politics of the civil war or — even more ambitiously — to fuse the twin currents of Republicanism and socialism into a source of unstoppable political energy. The Republicans themselves were divided. Some were conservative by inclination; others regarded themselves, at least in part, as the political inheritors of that tradition of Republican socialism which had briefly flowered in the mid-1930s in the 'Republican Congress'. Hartnett was one of the few founding members without that IRA tradition at his back, and both he and Peadar Cowan — a recruit from the Labour Party — had a measure of political experience that was to prove invaluable to Clann na Poblachta in its early years.

Many in the party were drawn from the ranks of disillusioned Fianna Fáil members; the party provided not only recruits like Hartnett but others like Aodh de Blacam, a journalist who created the famous 'Roddy the Rover' column in de Valera's *Irish Press* (terminated soon after he joined the Clann), who stood unsuccessfully for the party in Louth in 1948. But it also included others from a wide range of political backgrounds. National school teachers were especially well represented. The wilder shores of Republicanism contributed Ruairí Brugha, son of Cathal Brugha, who stood unsuccessfully as a Clann candidate in Waterford in the same year. Brugha had been interned by de Valera during the war, but went on in the 1970s to become a Fianna Fáil senator and TD, a loyal supporter of Jack Lynch, and a spokesman for Lynch's Northern Ireland policy in 1973–7. Populism contributed Stephen Coughlan, the Limerick ward boss who ended up as a Labour TD and a conservative thorn in the flesh of that party's 1969-generation socialists. Business and commerce contributed G.E. Russell, son of a prosperous Limerick family, who stood unsuccessfully for the Clann in three elections before being elected briefly as an Independent TD. One of the gentlest and most underestimated of Irish politicians, he ended up as a Fine Gael senator.

It was a party composed, the London *Observer* noted patronisingly after the 1948 election, of 'extreme chauvinists, or "incorrigible Celts", disgruntled IRA, a few ex-Communists, and some political adventurers. [MacBride's] success was probably due to the suffering of the working and middle classes now, as Irish prices steadily rise, and his anti-British line is always a good card to play in popular electioneering.'[35]

Their ranks did not, as yet, include Noël Browne, despite his friendship with Hartnett. His work in Newcastle, and his involvement in a number of voluntary associations, took up all his time. Also, his children were young, and family life had its attractions — and obligations. In so far as obligations were concerned, the chief focus outside his immediate family was his youngest sister, Ruth.

His oldest sister, Eileen, who had been a pivotal figure in the move to London and indeed had acted as surrogate mother to the entire family in the 1930s, had developed a severe case of TB. She was sent first to a sanatorium in Hazlemere, in Sussex, and then, in search of purer air, to an Italian sanatorium. By then her disease was too far advanced for any treatment, and she died in 1937. The responsibility for caring for the younger members of the family now devolved on Kitty, a highly intelligent, warm-hearted woman who had trained as a teacher in London, had gone briefly to America and returned to work in Middlesex schools during the war.

Kitty lived at Crawley in Sussex, where Ruth joined her after completing her long period of fosterage and education combined at the convent in Worthing. Ruth went to work in a clerical capacity at Lloyd's Bank, but Kitty's career pulled her again towards the United States, and both she and Noël felt that it would not be a good idea for Ruth to remain on in England on her own. A decision was taken that Ruth should come to live with Noël and Phyllis in Wicklow. Ruth is unsure whether the suggestion came from Noël, or whether Kitty had asked Noël and Phyllis if they would take over her para-maternal role. Either way, Ruth arrived at Newcastle, took a shorthand typing course at a Pitman college in Bray, and got work in a flour milling business in Dublin.[36]

Domestic life with Noël was companionable, rural and full of things to do. Most mornings he would bring his daughter Ruth out for a walk.[37]

There were picnics in Glendalough and visits to the beach, and shooting expeditions for rabbits with the family bull terrier, Butch, or a second dog, a dachshund. Noël tried to teach his sister how to shoot rabbits, but finally took the gun away from her, saying that she wasn't holding it properly. Ruth went on to live in Dublin and in January 1950 emigrated to the United States, where she first stayed with her aunt Martha, who had previously taken in Una.

Noël was now the sole member of his family in Ireland. His parents, Jody and Eileen were dead. Martha, who never married, lived in the south of England until her death in 1979. She retained strong Catholic convictions — convictions which brought her into sharp disagreement with Noël in the wake of the Mother and Child crisis. Una and now Ruth were in the United States. Kitty by now had returned to Britain but would join her sisters in the USA again later.

Noël's view of what had happened in Hollymount in 1929 carried over into his attitude towards some of his Cooney relations in America. He believed strongly that Una had been treated as a 'slave' by her aunt when she went to America that year. Ruth, however, is firmly of the opinion that this is inaccurate. Both she and Una, she says, had reason to be grateful for what was undoubtedly a genuine family welcome in a strange and sometimes intimidating country.[38] As the years went by, Noël kept up a warm and close relationship with his sisters, especially Ruth and Kitty. He corresponded with them in affectionate terms, and both visited him regularly in Ireland; on at least one occasion Kitty cared for the children when he and Phyllis were away on a continental holiday during his period as Minister for Health. Una did not visit Ireland again, but he met her later in the United States at an emotional meeting which affected them both deeply.

As Noël Browne's public involvement in health care issues was increasing, Fianna Fáil was already taking steps to lower the temperature. The departments of health and local government were divided, MacEntee remaining in local government, and health going to the avuncular and reassuring Dr James Ryan, who introduced the first estimates for his new department in February 1947. This was rapidly followed by two new pieces of legislation. One, the Health (Financial Provisions) Act 1947, although in principle a technical act, empowered the new minister to spend a substantial amount of money on the health services. The other, the Health Act of 1947, was to lay the foundations for Noël Browne's attempt to introduce a Mother and Child Health Scheme, although the difficulties he encountered could not have been easily foreseen at the time.

The genesis of the Bill was a memorandum from MacEntee to the Department of Finance in March 1946.[39] Finance opposed it, not just for the obvious reasons (it would cost money) but because it would amount to the 'socialisation of medicine' and would lead to the disappearance of private medical practice.[40] MacEntee, using his formidable powers of persuasion, secured government approval for the measure, but as soon as it reached the Dáil it ran into opposition, not least from Fine Gael, whose principal spokesman, Dr Tom O'Higgins, explained that most doctors in private practice made about three-quarters of their total income from treating children. The Catholic hierarchy had sent a note of its objections to the government, but these were — at this stage — not about the universality of the service proposed for mothers and children (similar provisions had been accepted without question in earlier legislation relating to the Dublin maternity hospitals) but about the supposed dangers to the morals of women and children embodied in the Bill's provisions for health education.

A communication after the passage of the Act, however, objected to its free, no-means-test aspect.[41] What had happened to engender this *esprit de l'escalier* is not clear, but Ruth Barrington's surmise is probably the best explanation available: the bishops had become exercised about the implications of the Health Bill passed by the Stormont parliament earlier in the same year, which had provided, among other things, for the takeover of hospitals, and which had raised the twin spectres of contraception and abortion.

James Dillon, then an Independent TD, had been so concerned about the 1947 Health Act that he launched a constitutional challenge to it in the courts. The fact that it was now sub judice gave de Valera an excuse to delay his reply — a holding one — to this episcopal broadside until 16 February 1948, only two days before he handed over power to John A. Costello in the wake of the general election.

The timing, and to some extent the outcome, of that election had already been foreshadowed by a number of key events in 1947. On 29 October three by-elections were held. MacBride was elected in one and another Clann candidate in a second. Fianna Fáil held the third seat, but a dissolution of the Dáil was now only a matter of time.

By now, Noël Browne was becoming more and more interested in politics. He struck up a relationship — which in hindsight appears quite extraordinary — with Oliver J. Flanagan, who had been elected to the Dáil for Laois-Offaly in 1943 under the unlikely banner of 'Monetary Reform'. Flanagan remained an Independent until 1950, when he joined Fine Gael, and was at the centre of a number of major controversies. In one of them, the Locke Tribunal, held to investigate matters associated with the takeover of a distillery in his constituency, published a report which effectively accused him of perjury; in the ensuing general election, his vote increased. More relevantly for the purposes of this narrative, he suffered from TB throughout 1947 and 1948, and was a long-term patient in St Michael's Hospital, Dún Laoghaire, where he was frequently visited by Noël Browne before he became Minister for Health. They became quite friendly on a personal basis although, apart from the question of TB, it is difficult to imagine what conversations they might have had.[42]

Noël Browne was clearly interested in joining Labour, and on different occasions gave two different versions of his early relationship with the party. According to his autobiography, Labour had said that his membership would 'not be welcome'.[43] In a 1978 interview, however, he said that he had decided against joining the party because it was too timorous, and because of its 'inverted snobbery' which made it hostile to adherents from the professions.[44] There was plenty of evidence of this hostility; Clann, Labour maintained, was 'a middle class lower petit bourgeois party of an opportunistic type . . . led by active ambitious personalities of the pro-fessional class'.[45]

Before any decision on his overt political commitment had been taken, Browne was also involved in setting up yet another organisation to provide professional muscle to back up the largely voluntary efforts of the PSL. This was an association of superintendents of sanatoria, who had formed an advisory group and wrote to Dr James Deeny in the Department of Health in the Custom House, asking for an appointment. Noël Browne, although not a superintendent (the actual superintendent at Newcastle, Dr Cullen, while a good doctor, tended to regard his position as something of a sinecure),[46] was a member of the delegation. Deeny, armed with the White Paper and with governmental approval for his plans, believed that he was on firm ground, and may even have assumed that his former acquaintance with Browne would facilitate a positive outcome to the meeting. He was quite unprepared for what was about to happen.

> *The group came in, with Noël Browne as Secretary; I outlined the scheme to them and made a general presentation on the subject and produced the plans of the sanatoria for their criticism and advice. The discussion proceeded pleasantly until Browne took over. He made a lot of scathing remarks and was downright rude and insolent. Now I had stuck my neck out on this thing, had taken it in hand, got it going and was producing results. So, I was not about to take calculat-ed rudeness from a young sanatorium assistant, no matter how able, whose expe-rience was extremely limited and whose remarks anyway were not helpful. Since he continued and no one could stop him, I terminated the meeting.*[47]

It is not hard to imagine the elements of the confrontation. Deeny, a decade or so older than Browne, and with the full weight of his department and his minister behind him, simply pulled rank. Although his account of the meeting some forty years later might be accused of benefiting from hind-sight, it can hardly be quarrelled with in broad terms. Indeed, the following day, Deeny was contacted by a no doubt somewhat abashed member of the group with a request for another appointment. Using the prerogative of power, he insisted that Browne be excluded from any further meetings. Almost immediately, Browne himself was on the phone, and came in to see Deeny personally to apologise for his remarks. In the course of their now friendly exchange, Browne asked if Deeny would have any objection to Browne's raising the matter of TB in public, and spoke about bringing political pressure to bear on the issue. Deeny sensibly said that he would not presume to advise Browne in this regard; he could well have been aware of Browne's increasingly close links with Hartnett and MacBride in the Clann.

As it happened, Deeny was shortly to publish, in December 1947, an epidemiological study he had done on the spread of TB in Lurgan over a twenty-five-year period. Its appearance, in the *Journal of the Medical Association of Éire*, was followed in January by a letter from Noël Browne attacking his findings. What prompted Browne's indignation more than anything else was Deeny's proposed remedy — the isolation of sufferers — and his downplaying of environmental factors involved in the spread of TB. Browne pulled no punches, but not all of them were above the belt.

> *I feel a little realism might have been introduced at this stage in Dr Deeny's paper by his letting us know what plans he has for the 700 families in Dublin City who have a consumptive living in the house and who have been recommended new houses owing to the unsuitability of their present residence. Is it suggested that these 700 families, for the sake of the consumptive amongst them, should be persuaded to enter a sort of Whipsnade Park, built on a hill somewhere away from the rest of humanity?*[48]

Looked at half a century later, the controversy appears to some extent a *dialogue de sourds*. Deeny was depicting, on the basis of empirical evidence, the spread of TB from house to house and within families in a small urban community. Implicit in his findings was the assumption that familial and social contact was a prime factor in the spread of the disease. Noël Browne, on the other hand, was arguing what was essentially a different case: that the incidence of the disease was strongly related to socio-economic conditions. In a sense, both were right — Browne about the social factors which exacerbated the disease, Deeny about the technical details of its transmission. Deeny defended his methodology; Browne stood by his version of the wider picture. In the end, the isolation policy derided by Browne was one which he put into effect with vigour after he became Minister for Health. It was certainly part of the solution.

By the time that Browne's reply to Deeny appeared, however, the Dáil had been dissolved, and its author was an election candidate. Deeny prepared a reply to Browne — and to another critic, Dr Galvin — but it was never published.

If the friendship between Kennedy and Deeny had introduced Deeny to Browne, but without establishing the basis for a positive relationship, Hartnett's friendship with Kennedy was part of the web which brought Browne inexorably into the political system. Kennedy had died in London on 6 December 1946, after being sent over from Newcastle for an operation which could not be performed in Dublin but which, in his case, came too late to save him. Hartnett had promised him before his death that he would do all in his power to ensure that Ireland got a comprehensive anti-TB service, and he urged his new party leader, Seán MacBride, to look the young Noël Browne over.

The opportunity arose almost immediately. Clann na Poblachta had commissioned the gifted young Irish film-maker Liam Ó Laoghaire to make a political film about the party and its policies, and Noël Browne, already enthusiastic, appeared in it. The film, *Our Country*, was extraordinary in many ways, not least because its appeal to the electorate was subliminal. The name of Clann na Poblachta was not mentioned (although few could have been unaware of the physiognomy of Seán MacBride, in particular), and it was shot in the style of a US newsreel. The film was being processed in London, and when MacBride and Hartnett decided to go over together in late 1947 to oversee matters, they invited Browne to accompany them. The journey, MacBride noted later, 'gave us a good opportunity to judge Dr Browne'.[49] He made a very favourable impression on MacBride, so much so that he was invited to the next meeting of the Clann's National Executive as a 'visitor' and quickly adopted as a Dáil candidate. He was elected to the Clann's National Executive shortly after the election, on 29 May 1948, along with Denis Ireland, whom MacBride was to nominate to the Seanad.

Even before his association with the Clann became public, Browne was now also appearing as a spokesman for another significant group, the Dublin Trade Union Council. Early in October 1947, that organisation's Tuberculosis Study Group had issued a statement protesting against the delay in mounting an effective campaign against the illness, and calling not only for better treatment facilities but for financial support for patients' families.[50] Browne spoke to a meeting of the Group in November, to which doctors, employers and the Red Cross also sent representatives. His proposal, basically, was to build a sanatorium in Co. Dublin at a cost of a quarter of a million pounds, to be collected by subscriptions from both workers and employers, to cater for the critical backlog — estimated at some 500 cases — of people who were waiting for admission to hospital but for whom no beds were then available. Browne's project was 'sympathetically received'[51] and a committee established to investigate methods of realising it.

The surge in voluntary agitation and fund-raising was rapidly overtaken by political events. Browne's association with Clann na Poblachta was now a matter of public record. In the 21 December 1947 issue of *The Clann*, the party's new newsletter, he wrote an article on what another Clann supporter, the journalist Maura Laverty, described as 'the crimes which the heartless Fianna Fáil mother has been committing against her sick children — crimes which would earn you and me, were we guilty of them, a just sentence of life imprisonment'.[52] The newsletter followed this up on 18 January 1948, as the election moved into its final stages, with a large photograph of Browne on its back page.

De Valera had dissolved the Dáil on 31 December 1947, reckoning that things could only get worse, and that an early election was his best chance of staving off defeat after sixteen years in power. The Clann political machine moved into top gear, energised by the considerable talents of Noel Hartnett, and Noël Browne was formally adopted as a party candidate for Dublin South-East. He did not make the choice himself,[53] but it is tempting to see Hartnett's hand in what was essentially a high-risk strategy. The constituency was a three-seater in which, since its original creation as Dublin Townships, seats had been held by MacEntee and John A. Costello, two of the biggest political heavyweights in the Dáil. It had also been the constituency in which MacBride won the by-election in 1947, with 28.4 per cent of the vote (beating Fianna Fáil's Tommy Mullins, who had 28.8 per cent, on transfers). By the time of the election in February 1948, the constituencies had been revised. MacBride migrated to Dublin South-West (where one of the Fianna Fáil candidates he defeated was the future Chief Justice and President of Ireland, Cearbhall Ó Dálaigh), and Browne took on the task of wresting the third seat from one of the two major parties which had traditionally held it on a turnabout basis.

Noël's fellow candidate for the Clann was Donal O'Donoghue, chairman of the party, who had been closely associated with MacBride for many years, including during the latter's military phase. In later years, Noël expressed his belief that he had been put in as a 'sweeper', or gatherer of votes which would ultimately secure O'Donoghue's election. If that was MacBride's strategy, it misfired badly; Noel Hartnett was in any case probably less in doubt about the eventual outcome than the over-optimistic O'Donoghue, who found on polling day that his and Noël Browne's expected roles had been sharply reversed.

It was a classic midwinter election, cold and wet. Ruth, although a stranger to the murky byways of Irish politics, accompanied Noël to some of his meetings, where she rubbed shoulders with Hartnett, MacBride and, on one memorable occasion, Maud Gonne herself.[54] Elsewhere, the insults and implications were flowing thick and fast. MacBride declared Clann na

Poblachta to be 'Irish Nationalists and Catholic and Christian'.[55] MacEntee responded by attacking MacBride's supposed links with communism.[56] Hartnett declared roundly that 'if at any time any member of this party proceeds to propagate the atheistic fallacies of Marxism he will be forced out of the party without further ado'.[57] *The Irish Times* published a table indicating that Clann na Poblachta had more doctors as candidates than all the other parties combined (they had nine).[58] Fianna Fáil published an advertisement proclaiming that its 'plan involves free medical treatment for mothers and children, to all persons suffering from infectious diseases, including tuberculosis'.[59] Almost swamped by all of this, there was a fresh outbreak of protest against literary censorship. Seán O'Faolain, who was writing continually to *The Irish Times* on the subject, managed to link the two topics by announcing, somewhat wearily, that he intended voting for the Clann, 'not that I have any belief that the Clann, or anyone else, will do much about it, [but] one must start somewhere'.[60]

In Dublin South-East, the David and Goliath scenario offered by the MacEntee-Browne contest was irresistible. Even more than that, the fact that tuberculosis was no respecter of social class divisions ensured that the loose, voluntary coalition which assembled behind Browne had unusually effective access to the media — far more so than would have been the case for other neophyte candidates. As soon as it became known that Browne had been invited to stand for the Clann in the constituency, as early as November 1947, Charles O'Connor called a meeting of members of the Post-Sanatoria League and other ex-patients to see if support for Browne could be organised.[61] The response was so enthusiastic that another meeting was called soon afterwards; PSL members agreed to canvass the constituency, go to Clann headquarters to address envelopes, and take up a collection for the party.

Other helpers included George Lawlor, his election agent, a Republican turned Marxist; Cáit Clancy, an Irish-speaking teacher from Co. Waterford, and P.A. ('Pa') Woods, a national school teacher who was the organising force behind the Clann in the constituency. Charles O'Connor's memoir gives a striking pen portrait of the campaign, which opened on 5 January 1948, and underlines the growing success of its efforts to use the media.

> *Dr Browne held meetings time after time, speaking from a coal lorry provided by Mick Dowling, a member of his election committee. I travelled with him in his small sports car to all his meetings night after night, stood listening to his speeches in the dank open air, made a mental note of them if a newspaper reporter was not present, wrote out the gist of them in my office the next morning, had them typed by a young, frail shorthand typist, who, like myself, suffered from pulmonary tuberculosis, and sent them to the Dublin newspapers.*[62]

A contemporary newspaper account gives a good flavour of Browne's approach.

> *The Irish people were dying under a government which had shown no real interest in their welfare, beyond a small group of industrialists and big business-men. It was a fact that in Dublin they had disease and conditions of slums and poverty which the governments of other civilised and Christian countries had shown were preventable and curable. This country was notorious throughout the world for its high death rate from gastroenteritis and tuberculosis.*[63]

He spoke in similar terms a week later at meetings in Rathmines and Sandymount.

One of his colleagues, Aodh de Blacam, who had left Fianna Fáil only weeks earlier, put his own gloss on what the Clann stood for. The party would, he said, go 'into the lost territory and win John Mitchel's people for John Mitchel's ideals'; it stood on the basis of papal encyclicals, and the social plan of the Bishop of Clonfert.[64] De Blacam was later to be closely associated with Browne as part of the 'Publicity Unit' which Browne formed in the Custom House. The reference to Bishop Dignan of Clonfert was prophetic, in a minor way. This bishop had earlier produced a plan for the social services, based loosely on the papal encyclicals, which had been brusquely rejected by Fianna Fáil; and Dr Dignan was later to be one of Noël Browne's few friends — probably the only one — in the upper echelons of the Catholic Church during the Mother and Child controversy. There is a certain piquancy in the fact that, in the middle of the election campaign, Clann na Poblachta criticised Fianna Fáil's rejection of Dignan's scheme, saying the party 'showed its contempt for the feeling of the nation by insulting the Catholic hierarchy'.[65]

De Blacam's combative (to put it mildly) approach to Northern policy echoed a strongly irredentist theme in at least some Clann speeches, and dealt with an area in which Browne's views at this stage appeared heterodox. He certainly evoked comment with one election speech at Ringsend, not reported in the daily press, in which he addressed the topic of Northern Ireland. According to his own version of this speech, Browne said that people were 'sick and tired of hearing about 1916 and 1922'.[66] In another version, Con Lehane, who was on the platform on that occasion, recalled

> *the embarrassing case of a public meeting in Ringsend . . . when Browne, in response to cries and heckles from the audience, told them that Mr de Valera had imposed the Civil War on the Irish people, a remark which made the other members of the Clann platform uneasy. Whatever their disagreements with Mr de Valera were, they never held him responsible for the civil war.*[67]

For this transgression, Browne was summoned to a lunch with MacBride, at which some of the intricacies of Irish history were explained to him. There is certainly evidence that — although he was not elected as a Republican, as he noted in his autobiography — his views on this topic were to develop dramatically during his period in government, under the influence, possibly, of both Hartnett and MacBride. Not only that, but his newfound enthusiasm for a Republican agenda was to survive into, and be nourished by, his later years in Fianna Fáil. The 1970s and 1980s were a long way off.

The election had still to be won, and Browne's helpers set to with a will. O'Connor's work went beyond noting down Browne's speeches. He knew Bertie Smyllie, who lived in the Dublin South-East constituency and who wrote a weekly column in *The Irish Times* under the pseudonym 'Nichevo', and privately sent him information about the candidate. His pump well primed, Smyllie uttered a magisterial endorsement of the idealistic young candidate. In a column during the campaign, he laid out Browne's medical and Trinity background and went on:

> I understand that Dr Browne has no interest in politics as such. He never stood on a political platform until a fortnight ago. But, apparently, his failure to get any satisfaction from the government in the matter of TB treatment has driven him into politics. A few years ago he married Miss Phyllis Harrison and they have two children. Dr Browne is honorary secretary of the Irish Tuberculosis Society, composed of medical men who are interested in TB. Indeed, I know of many bitter enemies of everything Clann na Poblachta stands for who would vote for him even if he went forward as the official agent of the Comintern.[68]

Although Smyllie had little time for the Clann's policies (he described its programme as a 'crazy pavement of economic fantasies'),[69] he was plainly intrigued, not just by Browne, but by the new party. At one stage, he ran photographs of a number of election candidates across the top of the front page of *The Irish Times*; Browne was included along with four other Clann candidates, compared with six for Fianna Fáil and five for Fine Gael.

Browne's meetings were crowded,[70] and the message rapidly got back to MacEntee: this upstart represented a threat which had to be taken seriously. The Fianna Fáil response, therefore, was carefully targeted, within the constituency and outside it.

Within the constituency, MacEntee could not be seen to be taking on Browne directly; to do so would be to give the challenger too much publicity. Additionally, he was no longer Minister for Health. The job was therefore delegated to MacEntee's running mate, Michael Yeats, the son of W.B. Yeats, who had been selected to fight for the seat held by Brendan Butler of Fianna Fáil since 1943. Yeats was armed with statistical material with which to refute, or at least to respond to, the damaging attacks coming from Browne. He used this material in speeches, and in letters to the national newspapers,[71] but these increasingly desperate responses served only to focus attention on Browne's campaign. Yeats's final throw, just before the election, was to detail the expenditure which had been committed to Browne's hospital in Newcastle, and to express, with a righteous indignation which would not have greatly impressed readers of The Irish Times, his 'regret that the sufferings of those unfortunate people who are afflicted with this terrible disease should be made the occasion for irresponsible election propaganda'.[72]

The Irish Times, its finger on the pulse (at least in Dublin South-East), had already seen the writing on the wall, and Smyllie editorialised: 'There were strong men before Agamemnon, and there will be statesmen after Mr de Valera.'[73] The crowds were more and more hostile to Fianna Fáil speakers, and by polling day on 4 February, the bitterness was running deep. Yeats and MacEntee did the normal politicians' tour of polling stations on that day, and met Browne along the way. MacEntee had a capacity, rare in Irish politics, for divorcing the personal from the political, and affably offered Browne his hand; Browne refused to take it.[74] MacEntee evidently did not take this calculated snub personally, and was to do his best for Browne in the 1954 election after his latter-day opponent had joined Fianna Fáil.

While MacEntee tried to fend off Browne in his own fiefdom of Dublin South-East, Jim Ryan, in the Custom House, was doing his best to neutralise the Post-Sanatoria League and its allies. The Department of Industry and Commerce suddenly rediscovered a letter sent by the Dublin Trade Union Council's Tuberculosis Study Group the previous October asking for the redevelopment of the old Foynes flying boat terminal — now a country club — as a sanatorium. On 3 January, the Department of Health wrote to the Council saying that a feasibility study was under way. And on 24 January, only eleven days before the election itself, the minister announced that he had made regulations under the 1947 Health Act permitting local authorities to make weekly payments to people who were being treated for TB.

This was an issue which was at least three years old. The PSL had been pressing for such allowances almost since its foundation, and had met Dr James Deeny to discuss it in July 1945. At that meeting, the chief medical adviser agreed that some kind of allowance would be necessary, but that the scale suggested by the PSL was exaggerated, so much so that it militated against any serious consideration of its case.[75] The way in which its previously rejected memorandum was resurrected modified the rapture with which the PSL greeted the announcement; it was, in effect, too little and too late. James Deeny, for his part, could hardly have foreseen what was in store for him.

The election was notable, not only for the bitterness it engendered, but for the high level of interest in the international media (engendered by the prospect of a defeat for de Valera) and for the high levels of anxiety evident on all sides. The British Minister (i.e. ambassador) in Dublin, Lord Rugby, reported gleefully to the Dominions Office in London that MacBride's talk of twenty-five or thirty seats had given rise to fear of the 'Red Menace', and that 'some diehards of the Kildare Street Club rushed to vote for de Valera's Fianna Fáil, abandoning even Fine Gael in their panic'.[76] The BBC ran radio reports on the election every day for a week. Radio Éireann, more experienced in restraining its enthusiasm, offered a prize of five pounds to anyone who might correctly forecast the result of the election.

De Valera's gamble nearly paid off. Clann na Poblachta, which had put up ninety-three candidates, won 13.2 per cent of the votes but only ten seats, and lost dozens of deposits. The magnitude of the Clann's increase (up eight seats from its pre-election position) disguised the effectiveness of de Valera's constituency revision; had the party won seats in proportion to its vote, it would have been returned to the Dáil with nineteen seats rather than ten. In Dublin South-East, John A. Costello was elected on the first count with 8,473 votes, more than 1,000 votes above the quota. MacEntee, with 7,371, had to wait until the fourth count to be elected. Browne, with 4,917, 200 more than the next highest candidate, James Douglas of Fine Gael, was elected on the fifth. O'Donoghue secured only 559 votes, a little more than 10 per cent of the first preferences won by Browne. Noel Hartnett himself was less lucky, polling 600 fewer votes in Dún Laoghaire than his Clann running mate, J.P. Brennan, who was elected, but who joined Labour after the collapse of the Clann and was defeated in the same constituency in 1951.

Following tortuous negotiations between all the parties opposed to Fianna Fáil, it was agreed that John A. Costello — rather than Richard Mulcahy, the Fine Gael leader — should become Taoiseach. The situation within the Clann was even more tense. There, the debate was between those who were prepared to join the government on agreed terms, led by MacBride, and those who felt that the Clann should maintain its political purity by supporting a minority administration, a group led by Con Lehane. The meeting of the National Executive of the Party which decided the issue began on 14 February 1948 and lasted into the small hours of the following morning; MacBride's position was adopted only by eighteen votes to sixteen.

MacBride chose the Department of External Affairs (now Foreign Affairs) for himself, and allocated the one additional cabinet post in his gift to Noël Browne, who was nominated to the Department of Health by Costello on 18 February. MacBride's choice of Health, and of Browne, startled some. There were undoubtedly personal factors influencing his choice of department. His sister and daughter both had TB.[77] Hartnett, his director of elections, had made TB a major plank in the Clann campaign, and he would have been struck by the way in which the electorate had pointedly preferred Browne to his lieutenant Donal O'Donoghue in Dublin South-East. His options were, it seemed, clear enough. Noel Hartnett himself was out of the reckoning, having failed to win a Dáil seat. There were, however, others whose claims would have to be considered, notably Con Lehane, a colourful Dublin solicitor who, like MacBride, had been involved in defending Republicans or embarrassing de Valera's government on Republican issues. The problem was that although some of the new Clann TDs had had military, or more properly paramilitary, experience, none of them, apart from Hartnett and Lehane, had any substantial political experience. Members of what Browne later referred to as the military wing of the Clann had been notoriously unsuccessful at the polls, and were to remain doggedly unelectable. They were still powerful in the councils of the Clann, however, and MacBride's choice of this political innocent for a cabinet post was made 'only in the teeth of fierce opposition from the older and more militantly Republican members of the party'.[78]

Dr Michael ffrench-O'Carroll, who was not a candidate in 1948 (he was a member of Dublin Corporation, and worked indefatigably in Browne's campaign team in Dublin South-East), believed that Hartnett had been influential in the choice of Browne as Minister for Health.[79] Another possible influence was Patrick McCartan, the medical doctor and elder statesman of the Republican movement, who apparently canvassed Browne's suitability strongly with MacBride.[80] Louie O'Brien, however, who was MacBride's secretary at the time and throughout his period in government, thought that the impetus had come from Joe McGrath, who had been involved in the setting up of the Irish Hospitals Sweepstakes.[81] According to her account: 'MacBride didn't realise Con Lehane thought he'd be the person who would get the second post. We were dumbstruck when Noël Browne was given Health. Joe McGrath gave [sic] MacBride £30 million from the Sweeps and MacBride had to promise Joe that this would be used only for the elimination of TB. This is why he put a doctor who himself had had TB in charge of it.'

Browne's youth, energy and plans were commented on nationally and internationally. *The Irish Times* devoted an entire front-page article to the subject, complete with photograph, celebrating Browne's achievement as 'a unique feature of Irish parliamentary history'.[82] Even the *Sunday Express* paid attention, not least in the light of the new minister's English public school background. 'At thirty-two, Beaumont-educated Dr Noël Browne, caretaker of the nation's health, is the youngest minister . . . He has plans for a nationwide anti–TB drive [and says] luxury hotels, set up by the previous government to attract foreign tourists, will be taken over if necessary.'[83]

Initially, according to MacBride's secretary, 'Seán thought Noël Browne was a saint — he could do no wrong.'[84]

CHAPTER THREE

'I'll Only Have One Crack at It'[1]

E lection to the Dáil meant substantial lifestyle changes for the young Noël Browne and his family. His children were just reaching the age at which they would remember their father when he disappeared frequently from view. He no longer worked a short walk away from the house, but left home early and arrived back late. Sometimes the only evidence they had of him was chocolate bars under their pillows when they woke up, leading to the suspicion that he worked in a chocolate factory. It took some time to arrange his departure from Newcastle; in fact, he remained technically employed there until October 1948. His place was then taken by Dr Harry Hitchcock, who had worked at Newcastle briefly under Browne, and whose sister, Grace, had been a girlfriend of Noël's before he met Phyllis. Hitchcock was now working in England, but Noël tracked him down and, in a telephone call, summoned him back to take over. 'With Noël,' the new locum recalled, 'you got a sense that he wanted it done yesterday.'[2]

It was felt that to continue living in the gate lodge at Newcastle would be inappropriate, so alternative housing had to be found for the new minister. Noël and Phyllis and the children moved to a rented house in Howth. It was only the first move of many; over the next half a century, the Brownes were to move house over and over again. Phyllis has counted twenty-nine moves, which is probably not an underestimate. They changed address five times during his three years as minister.[3]

Some of these moves were by choice. Noël would, typically, decide that it was time to go, or develop a dislike for changes in their immediate environment, and the family would up stakes again, with Phyllis, as ever, doing the organisation of it all. Others were from necessity. On at least two occasions in later years, the Brownes were forced to sell a house by bank managers. After Newcastle closed in 1963, a manager in the Bank of Ireland in Bray called them in and indicated that they would have to sell Roseville, a lovely old building to which they were probably more attached than any other home they ever owned. Much later, in the early 1970s, another bank manager forced them to sell the first cottage they owned in Baile na hAbhann in the Connemara Gaeltacht, on which they then owed the princely sum of £700. After 1974, their other base was the second cottage in Baile na hAbhann; bought not long after they had sold the first, it was a derelict ruin and has since been lovingly restored. It was to be many years before they found a small cottage to lease in Malahide; the owners, the Chadwick family, charged them a small rent, and eventually gave up collecting even that, saying it wasn't worth the trouble. When the cottage was sold with the adjoining big house, the new owners, the Noonans, continued the arrangement, and so Noël and Phyllis had, in effect, a grace and favour residence they could use whenever they were in Dublin.

In between was a hugely nomadic existence. It is impossible to trace all the houses in which they lived, but some of them can be identified from letters Noël wrote to the press, and from other sources. As well as the lodge in Newcastle, they include 'Inishmaan', Howth (1951); Galtrim Park, Bray (1955); St Brigid's, Enniskerry (1956); Roseville, Bray (1960); Ballyorney Cottage, Enniskerry (1961); Ellerslie Villas, Bray (1963); Belmont House, Bray (1968); Galtrim Road, Bray (1969); Killincarrig Road, Greystones (1971); Sidmonton Cottage, Bray (1974); Cloughmore and Malahide (various dates from 1973 onwards); and Bath Road, Balbriggan (1979). Some of the houses were rented; others were bought, often in a poor condition. Phyllis would work on them and improve them, and then they would sell up and move on.

> *Noël was so uninvolved with the housing aspect of our lives that he would ask, in the middle of a move, 'Which house should I come back to tonight?' His own ideal for a house would be remote, with no neighbours — but of course that was more expensive. And he hated walls.*[4]

The exceptional frequency of their moves suggests a pattern of delight followed by disillusion. Possibly the need that was expressed in so many moves was internal, rather than external, and could therefore not be satisfied by bricks and mortar. Each house move meant shedding part of the family's past; of the Browne papers now in Trinity College, Dublin, little survives that is earlier than 1970. The move to Howth meant, at least, that Noël was now closer to his work in the Dáil and the Custom House. But it did not mean that he was cosseted to the extent that a contemporary minister is. The Clann had inveighed against the indiscriminate use of State cars for personal purposes by ministers, and accordingly Noël Browne's open MG sports car[5] was still often pressed into service, often on windswept and bitterly cold journeys to succour units of the Clann's far-flung political organisation, while the American-built limousine dedicated to ministerial use remained warmly garaged at the Garda depot in the Phoenix Park.

The relationship between the new Minister for Health and his party leader was, if not close, certainly positive and comradely. There is a photo-graph[6] of Browne and MacBride together in the summer of 1949, taken on the occasion of the interview by Marje Cooney, Noël's cousin. Marje was quite taken by Noël's handsomeness, his somewhat rakish charm, and his newfound power.[7] The content of the interview, however, is not as revealing as the body language in the photograph. MacBride is speaking, expansively. Browne is leaning slightly forward, attentive to his words, with an open, trusting, even admiring expression. It is not the pose of an acolyte; but neither is it the attitude of a suspicious or inimical politician. In time that trust between the two would be shattered, but for the moment it seemed firm, and the basis on which MacBride had built into the new government's platform a determination to do something about health, and specifically about TB.

Quite coincidentally, one person who witnessed this mutual admiration was John Charles McQuaid, the Archbishop of Dublin. Shortly after becom-ing minister, MacBride had visited McQuaid at the Archbishop's Palace in Drumcondra to — in McQuaid's words — 'put himself at my disposal'.[8] Almost immediately, McQuaid made a return call on the minister at Iveagh House, but had to wait for some time as MacBride was in conference with the Italian Ambassador. When he was finally brought in, the very first thing that MacBride did — without even asking him to sit down or asking him about his call — was to say that he was sure McQuaid would like to meet the new Minister for Health. McQuaid said he would, and Browne was 'shown off as something MacBride was obviously pleased with'.[9]

The 1948 election had thrown up a new situation for the bishops — more particularly for those bishops like McQuaid and Bishop Michael J. Browne of Galway, who were among the most politically attuned members of the hierarchy. In McQuaid's case, a combination of intellectual brilliance and the fact that his see included the country's political and administrative capital ensured that his interest in politics was well-nigh obsessional.[10]

McQuaid's view of the new government was nuancé. There were parts of it he liked and parts of it which made him deeply unhappy. He was a confidant of the British Minister in Dublin, with whom he had frequent conversations on political matters. Not long after the change in government in early 1948, he had made his view of the new administration clear. As Lord Rugby reported to London: 'Although he was appointed to the arch-bishopric by the de Valera government [sic], he readily supported my view that the country as a whole had manifested a deep sense of relief with the passing of Mr de Valera and his government.' McQuaid heartily approved of Costello and the new Minister for Finance, Paddy McGilligan, but 'commented severely' on MacBride, whom he was 'evidently not prepared to trust . . . in view of his antecedents and upbringing'. The archbishop's views, Rugby added, were 'naturally . . . coloured by his detestation of Communism, and this came out particularly strongly in his poor opinion of Mr Norton'[11] (William Norton, Labour Party leader).

There was no reference to Browne in this conversation but, as later private comments by McQuaid displayed quite clearly, Browne's own 'antecedents and upbringing', especially his Trinity College education, inspired in the archbishop a profound and denominationally based distrust. The reference to MacBride is, however, of particular interest because there is now substantial evidence that the outward courtesies and formalities which each extended to the other masked deeply embedded suspicion (on the part of the archbishop) and hypocrisy (on the part of MacBride).

MacBride's hypocrisy is now, unfortunately for his reputation and due to the care with which McQuaid maintained his archives, a matter of public record. In 1948, shortly after his re-election to the Dáil and just before his appointment as a minister, he wrote by hand to McQuaid, from his home address in Clonskeagh, in terms which, even by the standards of the time, seem excessive. Although the letter was written privately, he described his filial submission as his 'first official act', and added:

> as a Catholic, a public representative and the leader of a party I shall always welcome any advice or views which Your Grace may be good enough to impart to me officially or informally . . . I beg Your Grace to pray that my colleagues and I may be given the wisdom and light to discharge our duties faithfully as Catholics and public representatives.[12]

Three years later, he was to express himself in equally obsequious terms. In between, however, he had, in his official capacity as Minister for External Affairs, put himself in a position to be asked by the Vatican about which Irish prelate should be given the cardinal's hat, and had advised against McQuaid.[13] This was known to Browne, and included by him in his bitter letter responding to MacBride's demand for his resignation; it was the only part of the correspondence which was not published, although an anonymous letter-writer, also in the know, thoughtfully took it upon himself to inform McQuaid about it.[14]

Fianna Fáil, out of office for the first time in sixteen years, did its best to exploit real or perceived weaknesses in the new administration, not least the lack of co-ordination between ministries and the frequent evidence that ministers were doing solo flights, with policy statements which had not been agreed in cabinet. Seán Lemass — who, in de Valera's absence on his anti-partition tour in America, had become the torturer-in-chief on the opposition benches — once famously remarked that all the public disagreements between cabinet ministers were an elaborate ploy designed to conceal the fact that secretly they actually agreed with each other.[15]

Noël Browne was, of course, a prime target. His youth and inexperience — his innocence, even, in relation to the murkier byways of Irish politics — combined with his passion and his occasionally headstrong tactics, attracted the attention in particular of his nemesis, Seán MacEntee. In contrast to Browne's predecessor, Jim Ryan, who on the whole offered constructive opposition — only bridling occasionally at suggestions by Browne that Fianna Fáil's legacy had been a wasteland of inaction — MacEntee isolated a number of areas where he felt that Browne was vulnerable, and sniped at Browne continuously on all of them throughout his first two years in office. One of them was Clann na Poblachta's attempt to seize the high moral ground by criticising the size of ministerial salaries — an area marked out specifically by Browne himself during the election campaign. Another was an accusation that Browne was discriminating against Protestants — nicely angled at Trinity's only graduate in the cabinet. The third was the charge that Browne was dishonouring Ireland's patriot dead by taking over part of the Rotunda Gardens which had been earmarked for the Garden of Remembrance, and using it for a temporary neonatal clinic. And the fourth was a major allegation of corruption in connection with land purchase for hospital use.

Part of the Clann's attraction for younger and more radical voters had undoubtedly been its campaign against jobbery and corruption in politics, and during the election it had made a political issue of the increases announced in ministerial salaries in 1947, when they rose from £1,700, at which they had been fixed in 1938, to £2,125,[16] or £48,528 in 2000 terms. During his by-election campaign that year Seán MacBride had declared that he would turn his TD's allowance of £624 over to the party if elected, and indeed seems to have done so (his substantial income from the Bar remained at his disposal, although his party activities would have reduced his availability to clients). This had, at the very least, conveyed the impression that if the Clann went into government, its cabinet members would forgo ministerial salaries, pass them over to the party, or possibly return them to the public purse.

No sooner had the Fianna Fáil deputies taken up their unaccustomed position on the opposition benches than they laid an ambush for Browne on this issue — presumably calculating that, as a neophyte minister, he presented a more vulnerable target than the more experienced, and elusive, MacBride. Browne's income had undoubtedly increased from the annual £500 or so which he received as assistant medical superintendent at Newcastle and which was now payable to his locum.[17] His new level of remuneration now became a political issue, and as soon as he introduced his first estimate as minister, MacEntee turned up the heat. He reminded the House that during the election campaign

> the present Minister for Health told the electorate that in his view, the present salary, the salary which he is now drawing, was at least £10 a week too high. He has not even suggested to the House that that economy of £520 per year should be made at his expense . . . a Minister, representing a Party which made its principal plea to the electorate the fact that a Minister's salary was £2,125, comes in here and unabashed, presents an Estimate to the House which contains a subheading providing that sum for him.[18]

MacEntee did not believe that ministers were overpaid, but challenged what he saw as a failure by Browne and MacBride to live up to their election rhetoric. Browne responded:

> I said that I would take whatever the salary was before. The fact of the matter is that I never actually made that promise in public, because, to me, it is a thing about which I would not like to talk, but, as it happens, I do not accept at the moment the full Ministerial salary, and we in the Inter-party government have adhered to that particular principle.[19]

Five days later, a Fianna Fáil backbencher asked the Minister for Finance whether any of the new ministers were refunding any part of their salary to the exchequer, and McGilligan replied in the negative. In the ensuing row, Browne clarified his position:

> Because this was not one of the matters agreed upon prior to the formation of the Inter-party government, I have continued to receive the allowance paid at the new rates, but I have continued to pay back to the Treasurer of Clann na Poblachta the difference between the old and the new rates. In so far as it is possible for me, I have kept my promise.[20]

In effect, therefore, he had forgone £425 of his ministerial income, and now had a combined income, free of income tax,[21] of £2,324, or just over £51,400 in 2000 terms, in common with his party leader, Seán MacBride. It was not clearly stated, but the implication is that the other members of that cabinet did not relinquish the increase.

The Dáil record, however, raises a number of questions about what was happening in Browne's personal life. He declares quite unambiguously in his autobiography firstly that he surrendered his entire ministerial salary, in accordance with Clann policy, and secondly that as a result of this he and Phyllis incurred substantial debts which they carried with them for many years until Dáil deputies were remunerated at a more reasonable level.

The first of these statements cannot be reconciled with what he told the Dáil in 1948. And, if what he told the Dáil was true, how was it possible for him to have incurred huge debts during his period as a minister and — even more inexplicably — failed to buy a house of any kind, given the fact that his income had more than doubled? We are left to guess at a number of things: the reasons for his frequent changes of address; the reasons for his indebtedness despite his substantial income (which indicate, at the very least, major problems in managing his finances); and the nature of the extra-ordinary stresses this whole period must have visited on his wife, though in her memoir, and in interviews carried out for this book, Phyllis made light of these.

The anti-Protestant charge was based on a decision by Browne to turn a Church of Ireland training college in the Phoenix Park, Coláiste Mobhí, into a sanatorium, and to relocate the college and its facilities to a hotel premises south of Dublin. Despite MacEntee's best attempts to stir it up into a controversy, this did not really catch fire, and the Protestant authorities, if they had complaints, kept them to themselves.

MacEntee evidently felt himself to be on firmer ground in relation to the Rotunda Gardens. 'Was there no other place to erect a temporary build-ing', he asked, 'except in the Rotunda Gardens on the site of the proposed memorial to honour those who died during the Black and Tan war? In the whole of the north city of Dublin no other site would satisfy the present Minister for Health except this site which had been dedicated to that holy purpose.'[22] MacEntee's ire was undoubtedly fuelled by the government's decision, three months after it came into office, to proceed with the erection of a cenotaph on Leinster Lawn to celebrate the founders of the Irish Free State and, by implication, to give greater priority to the memory of those who had come to an accommodation with the British than to the memory of those who had died fighting them.[23] The further implication is that Noël Browne's parentage would have made him suspect on the national issue.

Browne and his civil servants had seen MacEntee coming, and Browne was able to assure the house that not only had he consulted with the members of the old IRA who were particularly concerned with the Garden of Remembrance project, but 'it was very touching indeed to see the con-cern of these men to assist us in the provision of this hospital'.[24]

The land purchase controversy was potentially much more serious, as it involved Newcastle Sanatorium and land belonging to Patrick McCartan. What was at issue was the question of acquiring land on which to build a nurses' home, and negotiations had been in train for some time to acquire a site beside the sanatorium for this purpose. As Browne became minister, the negotiations were broken off and a dwelling house and farm situated a little further away, and owned by McCartan, were bought instead. 'When the owner of the purchased property happens to be a former neighbour of the Minister, a political colleague of his, and a nominee of the Taoiseach in the Seanad,' MacEntee remarked pointedly, 'we are entitled to have an explanation from the Minister.'[25] The explanation, when it came, was sound enough: if the field had been bought, a nurses' home would have had to be built on it, at a substantial additional cost, whereas the McCartan house was instantly convertible into a nurses' home, releasing twenty-six beds in the sanatorium. Although Newcastle had indeed paid a higher price for the property than the Valuation Office thought it was worth, the Hospitals' Trust Fund money used in the purchase had been based on the Valuation Office figure, and the balance had been provided by the sanatorium from its own resources.[26] Interestingly, in view of later events, one of MacEntee's charges was that Browne was a pushover for his medical colleagues: 'He seems in fact to be in a mood to surrender to them all along the line and then to brag about his generosity at the expense of the taxpayer and the public purse.'[27]

There was one other area in which Fianna Fáil perceived Browne to be vulnerable. This was Irish. Clann na Poblachta was hostile to the compulsory teaching of Irish (in the course of the 1948 election, one of its candidates had delighted Fianna Fáil by describing it as 'mental murder')[28] but had, no doubt wisely, refrained from importing this view into the new government's programme. This would have been met with fierce opposition, not only from Fianna Fáil but from Seán Mac Eoin and others in Fine Gael. Noël Browne knew virtually no Irish, and when a Fianna Fáil deputy attempted to embarrass him by putting down a question in Irish for him to answer in the Dáil, he had to have his answer transcribed phonetically so that he could read it. His questioner was so astonished that he did not volunteer a supplementary, which would have left the minister seriously at a loss for a reply. Browne compounded the felony by removing Irish as an essential qualification for the post of resident medical superintendent in Galway Central Hospital in November 1948.[29] On the other hand, he immediately sought to insulate himself from criticism by learning the language, and had regular lessons in his office with a native speaker from Connemara. This was never merely an insurance policy; when he later joined Fianna Fáil he took to wearing the Fáinne, and to the end of his life, he maintained his ability to speak the language and did so with evident affection.

Browne's tasks as minister, as he no doubt saw them himself, broke down into three areas. The first was to cope with the immediate expectations of those who had helped to put him into power, notably the Post-Sanatoria League. The second was dealing with the Department of Health and its personnel. The third, wider area was to implement a proactive health policy with the urgency he sensed was required. This policy was all of a piece, in which health care services and institutional services generally were to be integrated in a national structure which would respond to every medical need of the citizenry. It would be ambitious even today; in 1948, it was Promethean.

The rapidly increased expectations of the PSL could not be ignored; one of its most prominent advocates, after all, was now Minister for Health, and so a delegation approached him to ask him to build it a sanatorium.[30] There were, effectively, two committees tackling the TB issue: the PSL, and the one led by Dr Harry Counihan based on the discussions in Bewley's café. Browne's difficulty was that he was not really in a position to throw the weight of his department behind either, and indeed, now that he held the purse strings himself, he was not going to hand them over to anyone else. Accordingly, he prevailed upon his solicitor, Jack McDowell, who had been involved in both the committees, to create a de facto merger — not to build sanatoria, but to concentrate on the work of rehabilitating former TB sufferers. Initially, the group was hesitant. In McDowell's words:

> How were we going to set about rehabilitation? Most people felt that it wasn't really our baby — it was government's baby. They should be providing the money. We would do the work if they provided the money. We would build the rehabilitation centre even though we didn't know how to. It was indicated to Browne that this was how the committee felt. His reply to that was, 'I have no money that I can give you to set up' . . . It soon became very clear to us that, without his help, we could get nowhere unless we provided our own funds. One thing I was determined was not going to happen was I would not, if I could help it, go back to Browne and say we could do nothing.[31]

McDowell and his friends set to energetically, and the Rehabilitation Institute oak eventually grew from this acorn. Although Browne never gave them any money, none of them ever held this against him. In other areas, enmities began to sprout like weeds.

The Department of Health and its personnel attracted his suspicion on two grounds. He had already crossed swords in public with James Deeny about the latter's scientific publication on the spread of TB, and he had been, even if only behind the scenes, active in the campaign against the 1945 Public Health Bill, which he felt threatened to turn TB sufferers in particular into lepers and was the embodiment of draconian thinking among the departmental bureaucrats. The new minister was, therefore, determined to surround himself, in so far as possible, with people of his own choosing. First of all he took on Charles O'Connor of the PSL as his private secretary; O'Connor was succeeded by Dick Whyte, like O'Connor a post office employee (these were especially at risk from workplace-contracted TB as the conditions were very poor). A year later he was to be joined by Aodh de Blacam, who would play a vital role in the Mother and Child controversy.

Deeny and Browne themselves were not the only ones aware of the potential for problems caused by Browne's appointment to the Custom House. Two of the new ministers, Dr T.F. O'Higgins and James Dillon (Dillon had been at school with Deeny), telephoned the chief medical adviser to ask him if he would have any difficulty working with Browne. Deeny replied that he would work with Satan himself to end TB.[32] In fact Noël Browne's opponent, now his servant, made the first move, going to see the minister to welcome him on behalf of the professional staff in the department. Browne referred to the controversy he had touched off in the *Journal*; Deeny said that he had prepared a reply, but that it would now be impossible for him to publish it. However, he gave the minister a copy, and the two men parted on friendly terms, at least for the time being.

The tensions that would manifest themselves later between Browne and Deeny were not, however, the only operative ones. State medical policy was in its infancy; the department itself was only a year in existence. Medical care, moreover, was highly stratified. There was the dispensary doctor system, catering — very inadequately — for the poorest of the poor, and there was the hospital system, dominated by the consultants and, behind them, the voluntary bodies (for the most part Catholic religious orders) who built and owned the hospitals. The top tier, at least in Dublin, was composed of one person — the archbishop, Dr McQuaid, who controlled the appointment of consultants to the Catholic hospitals and, by virtue of this fact alone, wielded enormous power.

The doctors and the hospitals formed a powerful bloc (as demonstrated by the government's withdrawal of the 1945 Public Health Bill in the face of their criticisms), and their suspicion of the role of central government in the health service, in the light of what was happening in Britain, was intense. The function of the government, in their view, could be simply stated: to cater for those who could not afford private medical treatment, and to supplement (largely from the Hospitals' Trust Fund) the running deficits of the private hospitals in which they treated their fee-paying patients. Little of the 1947 Health Act had, as yet, been implemented, but their antennae had already been sensitised by the establishment of a separate Department of Health, a development described by Dr T.F. O'Higgins, then front-bench Fine Gael spokesman as 'expensive, extravagant and unwanted'.[33] They were as yet unaware of the new minister's views that private medical practice was unnecessary at best, and immoral at worst, and of his plans to make radical changes in the landscape of health policy.

There was, as it happened, yet another source of tension of which the public was unaware and which Browne was, at least initially, to turn to his advantage. This was the tension between the administrators in the Department of Health and the medical profession generally, but more particularly the medical consultants.[34] The doctors, all with university education and many with higher degrees, tended to look down on the civil servants, many of them Christian Brothers' boys, as mere functionaries. This attitude, of course, was spectacularly unfair to a whole generation of public servants, many of whom were intellectually brilliant but who lacked the access to university education conferred by social class, and who had come into the civil service through fiercely competitive public examinations. Nothing would have been said publicly, but disdain on one side, and class antipathy on the other, created a rich subtext for the political arguments that were to follow. In this way, a strange set of alliances was possible. Browne, with his soft Trinity accent, and his occasionally English mannerisms, who had worked shoulder to shoulder with colleagues in British hospitals as the National Health Service was being born, joined forces with the Christian Brothers' boys against the princes[35] of the medical profession and their clerical allies.

Key figures in all of this were the relatively new secretary of the department, Paddy Kennedy, and his second in command, Paddy Murray. Kennedy was a career civil servant with a background in revolutionary politics. Born in 1894, he was two decades older than his minister, and came from a Dublin middle-class family (his father, originally from Tipperary, owned a public house in Rathmines). He had left Belvedere in 1912 and went to UCD for a year, but needing a job he joined the imperial civil service and went to work in London, where he quickly fell in with other Irish exiles, met Michael Collins, and had the unusual distinction of inducting into the Gaelic League one Mr Willmore, later better known as Micheál MacLiammóir. He was transferred to Dublin Castle around 1918, and maintained his secret links with Collins.

After 1922, when he moved into the native civil service, he worked in Finance and Lands, and in 1937 he went to the Taoiseach's department as assistant secretary to Maurice Moynihan. During the war years, working in this department, because it was small — employing no more than about forty people — was a highly formative experience. Kennedy in particular built up a strong relationship with Moynihan and with Frank Gallagher, the head of de Valera's Government Information Bureau; the three men met regularly for dinner for many years. Like all civil servants, he kept his political views to himself, but few would have been surprised if his admiration for de Valera did not carry over into the ballot box. Michael Mulvihill, who came to the Department of Health later from the Department of Justice and worked as Browne's private secretary from Easter 1950 on, felt that Browne had by then come to distrust Kennedy unfairly because of his association with Fianna Fáil, and even suspected him of writing speeches for Jim Ryan during 1948 and 1951.[36] According to Deeny, when Browne came in, 'Kennedy faded into the background and let Murray take the blows.'[37]

Paddy Murray was generally thought to have been more of a Fine Gael man. Deeny felt that he was 'full of prejudices', which, in the light of Deeny's own strongly held opinions about most subjects, might be evidence of no more than disagreement; but he also described him as the hardest worker he had ever come across, although he was incapable of delegation and 'at one stage more than half the files of the Department were to be found in his room'.[38] Politics apart, civil servants shared with the minister a certain suspicion of the medical profession, born of the factors already mentioned, which was to make them his natural allies, and to some extent opponents, or at least critics, of the medical advisers within the department itself.

For the time being, all this was in the future. The medical profession had no reason to suspect Browne's intentions — indeed, in so far as he was passionately dedicated to the eradication of TB, they could assume that he was largely on their side. Change was in the air, especially for the crop of TDs who had entered the Dáil for the first time in opposition to Fianna Fáil. Browne, initially at least, tended to throw in his lot with the rank and file, preferring to eat in the general Dáil restaurant than in the cabinet dining room. In the restaurant, he often joined two of the new Fine Gael members, Michael O'Higgins (TD for Wicklow) and his brother Tom (Laois-Offaly), a barrister, who was to succeed Noël Browne as Minister for Health from 1954 to 1957; he eventually became Chief Justice and a judge of the European Court. Their father, Dr T.F. O'Higgins, was now Minister for Defence. The O'Higgins brothers used to chaff Browne about the honour he was conferring on their table, and found him modest and affable. Later, his appearances among the plebeians were to become more and more infrequent, and they assumed that he had been sucked into the maw of the civil service and effectively removed from circulation.[39]

Everything on the public record suggests that Browne threw himself into his new job and its responsibilities with considerable vigour. One thing which marked him out from other ministers was his close attention to the media; almost his first action was to establish a publicity and intelligence section, which was to oversee a remarkable public campaign involving all the media of communications: radio, film, newspapers and pamphlets. He was explicit about its aims and methods.

An experienced officer has been put in charge . . . I propose to make use of Press advertisements, booklets, leaflets, films, exhibitions and radio talks. In co-operation with the Minister for Education and the National Film Institute arrangements will be made for the showing of health films in schools and, in addition, it is hoped to purchase copies of health documentary films for distribution to the film renters for screening in cinemas throughout the country. I believe that the additional expenditure involved in such publicity will be money well spent and that the nation will reap rich dividends in the way of healthier citizens.[40]

Some of his Dáil audience on that occasion would have been well aware of the identity of the 'experienced officer' to whom Browne referred. He was none other than Frank Gallagher, a journalist and Fianna Fáil sympathiser of long standing, who had been editor of the *Irish Press* from its foundation in 1931 until 1934, when he resigned in a row with the board about its penny-pinching attitude to management. After a brief stint as deputy director of Radio Éireann, he took up the position at the Government Information Bureau, where he played a key role, not least during the war, in creating an interface between successive Fianna Fáil governments and the print and broadcast media.

He was, of course, an established civil servant, and could not be dismissed, but it was unthinkable that the new inter-party government would keep him on in such a sensitive role. It was probably due to his long-standing friendship with Maurice Moynihan and Paddy Kennedy that Gallagher was selected as media manager for Noël Browne. If Costello and his other cabinet colleagues had imagined that, by agreeing to this appointment, they were moving Gallagher off into a quiet backwater where he could do no harm, they could not have been more mistaken. Not that Gallagher ever rocked the political boat — he was too experienced a hand for that. He was seconded in 1949 to media work for the all-party Anti-Partition Campaign, but he had an able deputy in Aodh de Blacam, the former *Irish Press* journalist. Another helper from outside was Victor Browne, a commercial artist (and indeed also a former communist) who had migrated from London to Dublin and who was then the political cartoonist for the *Irish Press*. His bold line drawings embellished much of the publicity material produced by the Department of Health.[41]

Gallagher and de Blacam each wrote speeches for Browne as well as over-seeing the constant drive for publicity for both minister and department. A national competition for the best anti-TB slogan with a prize of £50 — over £1,000 in 2000 terms — excited the attention of no less a person than Brian O'Nolan, the senior civil servant who had been Seán MacEntee's private secretary when MacEntee was Minister for Health and Local

Government and who, in that capacity, occasionally signed the minister's letters to Archbishop McQuaid. O'Nolan, better known in his alter ego Myles na gCopaleen, the extraordinarily versatile humorist in *The Irish Times*, stuck his head out of his office one day as James Deeny was passing, to offer his own suggested entry: 'TB is Bad for You!'[42]

The publicity campaign involved, among many other things, the production of a range of films and audio-visual materials of remarkable range and quality. These would have included 'T. Bacillus & Co.', a puppet film made by Liam Ó Laoghaire, which dramatised ways of avoiding infection, and *Gnó Gach Éinne*, directed by Tony English for the National Film Institute, which illustrated problems of hygiene in a shop in Henry Street (presumably with the shopkeeper's co-operation). Gallagher's contacts in Radio Éireann undoubtedly helped as well; Browne not only spoke frequently on the radio, but used that medium to encourage Irish nurses working in Britain to return to work in Ireland's expanding health services.[43] The recollection of his homely, personalised broadcasts remained long after the scripts and tapes had been scrapped. He saw to it, too, that the radio was used for a series of health talks entitled *Conversations with a Doctor*, which were pioneering examples of public service broadcasting.[44] In all of this he was, of course, the beneficiary of the stranglehold which had been established over radio during the previous sixteen years of Fianna Fáil administration; and he was to use this access to the medium with dramatic effect at the height of the Mother and Child controversy.

All this expert media work had two main effects. Firstly, it helped enormously to make the population generally, and young people in particular, more aware of health problems and ways of tackling them. This in turn improved reporting of TB, and made early treatment more possible. Secondly, and inevitably, it made people more aware of Noël Browne. It may, as an unfortunate by-product, have encouraged the young minister in a hurry in an exaggerated belief that he could use public support and sympathy to solve some of the political difficulties he was to experience later in his tenure of office.

While his actions were indicative of a radical agenda in the area of disease control and treatment, some of his speeches were redolent of the social and cultural climate within which he operated and whose opinions he evidently shared, at least to some extent. In 1949, for instance, he delivered one speech in which he made no bones of his view that sex education for young people was unnecessary 'in view of the moral integrity and strong family life which results from the moral and religious teaching so readily and widely available in this country'.[45] In the same year, speaking at the opening of a hospital in Ballinasloe at which the Bishop of Clonfert, Dr Dignan, officiated, he praised the devotion of religious orders to the cause of healing, and observed that ideals based on Christian principles were 'the only effective barriers against the insidious infiltration of anti-Christian ideologies'. This phraseology is more de Blacam than Browne, but there is no reason to suppose that the minister disavowed the sentiments to any degree. It was, in fact, a government of quite outstanding piety. Seán MacBride, for all that he had been effectively excommunicated when a leader of Saor Éire, was particularly hurt by one suggestion — made by the reverend mother of a convent — that he prevented his children from going to Mass on Sunday. In his own defence, he adduced the fact that he had made his First Communion at a special mass in Rome celebrated by the Pope.[46]

One of Browne's early actions as minister, harking back to his own experience as a medical intern, was to organise a mobile medical emergency service available on a twenty-four-hour basis 'to act as an experienced back-up service for students such as I had been, so as to save the lives of infants who might otherwise die'.[47] The driven quality which characterised his period in office was born in part of his passionate conviction of the need for urgent action, particularly on TB. But it was also fuelled by a strong sense that he might not have long to live. When MacBride asked him to be Minister for Health, he discussed it with Phyllis before accepting; they had been told, on the basis of the best medical evidence then available, that he probably had about one or two years to live.[48] Although this was an improvement on the six months he had been given four years earlier, it was hardly over-optimistic. As he repeatedly told his close associate Dr Michael ffrench-O'Carroll, 'I'll only have one crack at it.' In fact he suffered a relapse from TB almost immediately after becoming Minister for Health, and he missed nine of fifty cabinet meetings in the calendar year 1948 (although three of these were in August, when he would presumably have been on holiday). His widow recalls that on a number of occasions in both 1948 and 1949 he was effectively running the department from his bed at home, as Paddy Kennedy brought papers out for him to sign.

His immediate predecessor in Health, Dr James Ryan, had in fact left him a substantial legacy. It included a Hospitals' Trust Fund of just over £10 million, invested in a bewildering array of securities ranging from Saorstát Éireann bonds to stock in Nigeria, Australia and New Zealand.[49] It also included plans, originating in the 1946 White Paper on tuberculosis, for three new TB sanatoria in Dublin, Cork and Galway, for which financial provision from the Sweeps money was already promised. There were an additional 135 proposals for new hospitals or the repair or improvement of existing hospitals, provisionally costed at £27 million for capital requirements alone (£619 million at 2000 prices).[50] He also inherited Dr James Deeny, who could justifiably claim authorship of many of these schemes.

When Noël Browne came to introduce the first estimate for his department — a supplementary estimate for £616,000 — on 6 July 1948,[51] he used the occasion to present an overview of what he had found and what he proposed to do.[52]

TB deaths were still increasing, he reminded the Dáil. Infant mortality was high, although immunisation had led to a dramatic decline in deaths from diphtheria; many county homes (which were not for the most part eligible for Hospitals' Trust money) were in an appalling condition; and medical research was an undernourished plant. He had already been out and about; one of his first visits was to St Brendan's Orphanage in Loughrea, Co. Galway, in an area in which he had spent much of his childhood. He had tea with his cousin, Biddy Kelly, and left her in no doubt about the proactive stance he intended to adopt in relation to the expenditure of tax-payers' money on public health institutions. 'I'm paying for them,' he told her bluntly. Even at that stage, there were concerns about his eagerness to get results. Other critics were less benign, accusing him of wasting his time in 'social visits'.

No objective observer could have assumed that the new minister's travels in any direction were purely social. An analysis of the key elements of his first estimate speech, however, discloses three core issues which were, separately and together, to bedevil his career in the Custom House and eventually to lead to his embattled resignation. One was the Hospitals' Trust Fund and the debts of the voluntary hospitals. The second was the 1947 Health Act which, despite his assertion that 'much has already been done to provide the services authorised by the Oireachtas', was still in some critical respects a blank slate, waiting to be written on, notably in relation to services for mothers and children. The third was in relation to the Health Services (Financial Provisions) Act 1947. This Act, notably its implicit decentralisation of health care, presented a powerful challenge, its dimensions as yet unrecognised, to the oligarchy of medical consultants centred on the main Dublin voluntary hospitals.

The combined deficits of the fifty-five voluntary hospitals which were getting Sweeps money had increased by more than 50 per cent between 1939 and 1946, were running in 1946 at £237,000, and were anticipated to rise to £340,000 — an increase of almost 50 per cent — when the 1947 figures were completed. In practical terms, meeting these bills would con-sume the entire revenue from the Hospitals' Trust Fund, without making any allowance for future increases. The Sweeps had been gearing up again after the war, but nobody could predict their future growth; their entire contribution to the health services, in terms of interest on the invested capital, had amounted to no more than £15 million since the establishment of the Sweepstakes in 1930.

'It will no longer be possible to pay annual deficits of unlimited magni-tude,' Dr Browne told the Dáil. 'In the meantime, everybody concerned with the management of institutions whose deficits are met from sweep-stakes moneys should realise that the utmost economy in expenditure is imperative.'

His definition of economy, where his own projected expenditures were concerned, was somewhat more elastic. It involved reducing the £27 million bill for hospital building to £15 million — almost £4 million of which would be for TB hospitals — and spreading it over seven years. In announc-ing this expenditure he actually presented it as a cutback, going so far as to apologise to the promoters of hospital projects which had not been selected for the 'grave disappointment' which he knew his decisions would entail. In fact it was a building programme of extraordinary magnitude. Even more significantly, he completely finessed the question of where the money was going to come from. The income from the Sweeps capital was running at about a third of a million pounds a year. If he were to rely on this source alone, it would take forty-five years — not seven — to finance his programme. But if he used the capital from the Sweeps, this would reduce the dividend income traditionally used to reimburse the voluntary hospitals' excess expenditure, at a time when this expenditure was increasing sharply.

Unless people believed that the Hospitals Sweepstakes were going to achieve previously undreamed-of levels of revenue, this was at best wishful thinking, at worst a refusal to look the financial facts of life in the eye. For the present, it was not commented on adversely either by hospital managers and consultants (although they would become more vociferous on this score when Browne revealed more of his hand in 1949), or indeed by Fianna Fáil. The consultants, presumably, thought that their industrial muscle would see their institutions through any rocky patch — one of the legacies Browne had inherited from Ryan was a promise to review their salaries — whereas Fianna Fáil, for its part, could hardly be seen to be opposing the building of hospitals because it was unclear where the money was coming from.

Common sense suggests that there were two factors which helped to paper over the financial cracks. The first was undoubtedly Browne's own sense of urgency and impatience. The second was the pact among the leaders of the various parties in government, which pre-dated the formation of the government itself, to agree to the utilisation of the Sweeps' capital fund. Although this treasure chest had already been opened up in theory by the 1946 White Paper, this was only for the three major sanatoria projected for the cities. The effect of the deal negotiated by MacBride was to give Browne a virtually free hand with the disposal of capital funds equivalent to about five years' departmental estimates. Browne was anything but experi-enced; on the other hand, he was likeable, energetic, and a doctor (even if his Trinity background made him always a little suspect in Costello's eyes).[53] Browne's electoral success, it should be added, would have suggested strongly to party leaders John A. Costello (with whom he shared a constituency), William Norton and Joseph Blowick, as well as to MacBride, that an anti-TB drive would be a key to electoral support at previously unimagined levels. MacBride had certainly discussed the matter privately with Joe McGrath, the founder of the Sweepstakes, and such a huge private benefactor to individual Irish politicians and parties that MacBride patently thought it prudent to secure his goodwill before taking such a radical step.[54] McGrath's nod of approval, and the pre-government agreement, were the keys which unlocked the treasure chest and left it standing, open, in the Custom House.

In relation to the implementation of the 1947 Health Act, Browne first of all indicated that some of the hierarchy's unpublished objections were about to be met. Specifically, the sections providing for compulsory medical inspection of children in certain circumstances, and giving health authorities power to compel school managers to provide certain facilities, were to be repealed or amended. One key section, however (Part III of the Act), was the one which gave health authorities power to provide health services for mothers and children. It had already evoked some rumblings from the medical profession, and from their political spokesmen in Fine Gael.

Browne, hedging his bets, told the Dáil: 'I have not yet made up my mind as to the exact method of providing the mother and child service and am awaiting the deliberations of the Council which I have recently established to advise me on matters relating to child health.' This Consultative Council on Child Health was one of the advisory bodies which Browne rapidly created in several important policy areas.[55]

The Health Services (Financial Provisions) Act of 1947 formed the third leg of the stool on which the new minister was now comfortably ensconced, the other two being his control over the Sweeps' capital and the cabinet decision on the Mother and Child Scheme. This financial legislation underpinned the 1947 Health Act by creating a new set of financial relationships between the Department of Health and local authorities. In embryo, it represented a radical decentralisation of health administration, and, as such — although this may not have been evident even to its original Fianna Fáil progenitors — a substantial potential threat to the network of consultants in the capital, and indirectly to their patron, Archbishop John Charles McQuaid.

In the complex medical politics of that era, to describe Dr McQuaid as the effective patron of Catholic private medicine is not an overstatement. He was chairman of both the Mater Hospital and St Vincent's Hospital. These two hospitals, run by the Sisters of Charity and the Sisters of Mercy respectively, had a near-monopoly of Catholic institutional medical care, apart from obstetrics, and were serviced by a battery of consultants in the Fitzwilliam and Merrion Square areas. These consultants in turn owed their

hospital appointments to Dr McQuaid, and their large incomes to the referral system of long standing in which patients had to be sent from all parts of
the country to Dublin for consultant care. What was true of patients was
equally true of samples. These had to be sent up in many cases by GPs to
the Dublin specialists for analysis, even of the most basic kind, work which
provided another lucrative source of income for the specialists, some of
whom ran mini-laboratories on their own premises.

The level of public medical services available outside Dublin and the
major conurbations generally was minimal. The 1947 financial legislation,
by establishing the framework for a system of medical care which would be
decentralised to the greatest possible extent, and which would provide a
wide range of specialist and diagnostic services on a county or regional
basis, was certainly patient-friendly, as its Fianna Fáil and Department of
Health authors evidently intended it to be. But it was also a demonstrable
threat to the incomes of the coterie of metropolitan specialists, and in the
hands of a radical like Noël Browne, especially as his attitude to private
medical practice became clearer and clearer, was positively incendiary.

For the time being, little or none of this was evident. Attention was
focused on Browne's onslaught on the major public health problems,
notably TB and cancer. His chief medical adviser, James Deeny, took a
benign view of Browne's action in announcing, immediately after his
appointment, 2,000 additional beds for TB patients which had in fact been
in the pipeline for quite some time but of which Browne was 'quite
unaware' when taking office. Politicians will be politicians, after all. In
another instance, Browne took the opposite tack, in self-defence; when he
answered questions in the Dáil about a major expansion destined for his
former hospital at Newcastle, he was able to deflect any criticism by pointing out cheerfully that the expenditure had been sanctioned by his Fianna
Fáil predecessor. He was less successful, as it happened, closer to home. Not
long after taking office, he made a determined attempt to have a clinic in
Ringsend, in his constituency, upgraded. Despite frequent prodding from
Browne himself and some of his staff, little had been done to achieve his
wishes by the time he left office.[56]

As Browne had come from a small sanatorium and its 'relatively closed'
world, Deeny gave him an extensive series of briefings on the national
medical scene, its problems, and the Department of Health's plans. A special
conference was even organised within the department at the end of July
1948, at which Deeny and the minister found themselves in agreement on
one crucial issue — that very little could be done for chronic fibroid cases
of TB in institutions, and that the scarce beds should be utilised for more
urgent cases.[57] All went swimmingly. 'The TB patients were delighted, since
he was very popular with them. The young people throughout the country

thought that he was wonderful, as indeed he was. He also had complete medical support at this time.'[58]

Within months, the honeymoon was ending, as suddenly as it had begun. The occasion was a student meeting in November 1948 at the Royal College of Surgeons in Ireland, for which James Deeny had written the minister's speech, a 'harmless and not controversial' address, praising some unknown medical heroes of Ireland.[59] Not for the first or the last time, the minister jettisoned his script and spoke from the heart. It was passionate, angry — and offensive. And it stirred up a controversy which was to buzz around his head like a swarm of hornets until he finally lost office two and a half years later.

In his address, the new Minister for Health made it clear that he was less interested in the glorious past of this or any other institution, and more interested in the future. In what was seen by senior members of the medical profession as an altogether unwarranted slur on their calling, he referred scornfully to the era of the 'barber-surgeons' as representing the past, contrasting this with his vision for the future. Doctors present at the meeting, particularly Leonard Abrahamson and W.R.F. (Bob) Collis, reacted strongly in defence of their profession. At a meeting in the department the next morning, James Deeny expressed his own objections, no doubt in characteristically blunt fashion. His reception by Browne, he noted later, was 'not cordial'. Whatever about Browne's future relationship with the doctors, his relationship with Deeny was now seriously at risk. He did not — to put it mildly — take kindly to contradiction.

In point of fact, although he was exaggerating, he was not entirely wide of the mark. As a president of the Irish Medical Organisation (the IMA changed its name in 1962) was to point out half a century later, most people who sought medical assistance up to 1900 had only one chance in two of benefiting from the ministrations of the profession, and many died from the hit-and-miss remedies that were common. It was not until the 1950s that controlled studies showed scientifically that medical intervention could be directly responsible for public health improvements.[60] In the College of Surgeons itself up to the early years of the twentieth century, the professors' genuine concern for the sick poor of Dublin was not complicated by the detailed knowledge of human physiology and chemistry that was to become available to later generations. One professor who died in the 1920s was apt to prescribe a crust of dry bread and a wineglass of champagne for sufferers from vomiting.[61]

But Browne's language was not calculated to assuage the fears of the doctors present, however much it might have appealed to his student audience (his postgraduate studies, it might be remembered, had ended only two years earlier). This was definably the point at which their admiration for his attack on TB and cancer began to shade into apprehension, and worse, about his overall plans for their profession.[62] Later, when the Irish Medical Association reacted by challenging Browne's claim in his speech that the profession had been adequately consulted about his proposed changes in health legislation, the stage was set for the battle that was to culminate in his forced resignation.

If this incident had not lost him the confidence of the medical profession (or of substantial, and powerful interests within it), the probability is that he was already in the process of losing it, or would have lost it in any case a few months later when he introduced his second major estimate for his department in the Dáil. A month before his speech in Surgeons, doctors had already published in their *Journal* their opposition to 'the provision of Free Medical Treatment to non-necessitous persons'.[63] In the same month as his address, they were protesting against another of his initiatives. Probably influenced by letters from individuals who felt that they had been treated poorly by dispensary doctors — the dispensary doctor system was, in truth, at the very bottom of every priority list, and the standard of care available must often have been severely trammelled by lack of resources — Browne took action. He put advertisements in the press, and went on radio, to announce that local authorities had been instructed to inform him within twenty-four hours of any complaints by patients against dispensary doctors.[64]

This impulsive response was, one can say with hindsight, tantamount to cutting the ground from beneath his own feet. It was not that the problem did not exist — some dispensary doctors of the era treated their patients as though they were members of a different species — or could not be solved. But Irish doctors were not, as yet, a fully homogeneous profession. Many of them were outside the ranks of their professional association. And of all of them, the dispensary doctors were the ones who might have become his allies in a strategic game which pitted general practitioners against the princely consultants. It is probably too much to say that by alienating them so dramatically at this stage Browne had sealed his own fate; but he had, at a stroke, greatly increased the magnitude of the task before him. Here too is the beginning of what appears to be a pattern — the satisfaction he found in identifying and denouncing enemies, even if this obstructed his journey towards a desired objective.

The political range-finding started in June, when Fianna Fáil deputies John McCann and Joe Briscoe put down questions about the Sweeps funds, and about how much of these had already been committed to the minister's hospital building programme. Browne first of all defended his decision to start eating into the capital with the argument that it was prudent because most of the holdings were in sterling, and sterling was depreciating.[65] MacBride, his party leader, had fought the election partly on a policy urging a break in the link with sterling and the repatriation of Irish assets held in Britain. Browne was now doing just that, and reinvesting them in the Irish health services. When McCann asked him, however, how it was proposed to finance the projected seven-year hospital building programme, Browne's answer could hardly have been designed to throw less light on the situation: 'By means of grants from the Hospitals' Trust Fund (which during the period will be supplemented by the income from further sweepstakes) as well as the contributions by the promoters of the various projects.'[66]

When he moved his second major estimate the following month, he was able to report substantial progress.[67] An additional 1,200 beds had been provided for TB patients, with a further 800 to come in the course of 1949. The 1948 infant mortality rate was the lowest ever recorded in Ireland, as was the overall death rate. Cancer deaths had decreased, as had deaths from diphtheria, whooping cough and measles. In many categories, the decline had been relatively slight; and Browne was careful not to claim too much credit, pointing out that Irish rates in all these areas were still distressingly high compared to those in other countries, and that much work remained to be done.

The small print of his speech, however, indicated the management style for which he was already becoming renowned in the Department of Health. In order to expedite building, the promoters of some smaller projects, whether voluntary organisations or local authorities, had been given authority to proceed without continually referring back to the department for approval, once agreement had been reached on costs. He envisaged stepping up the monthly expenditure on hospital building from £45,000 in January 1949 to £220,000 in January 1950 — by a factor of almost five — on sites or existing small facilities whose names have since then become part of public health history: Ardkeen in Waterford, the new Fever Hospital in Dublin (Cherry Orchard), Limerick Regional, Galway Regional, Portiuncula (Ballinasloe), Gurranebraher in Cork, the Children's Hospital in Crumlin in Dublin, and a new hospital at Manorhamilton in Leitrim. In conjunction with these plans, he produced, together with the Department of Local Government, a glossy brochure entitled *Ireland is Building*, designed specifically to attract Irish building workers back from Britain. The booklet contrasted Irish income tax rates favourably with those in Britain, gave details on wages, and was copiously illustrated with dramatic photographs of new housing schemes, hospitals and factories. 'Listen to special broadcasts to the Irish overseas', it added, 'every Sunday night at 11.0 p.m. Radio Éireann 531 m.'

It was when Browne came to deal with the Sweeps revenue, however, that the future suddenly turned cloudy, not least for the voluntary hospitals. It was clear that he was banking on an exponential growth in Sweeps revenue to help him pay his bills; but, in the meantime, the demands on those same funds from the existing voluntary hospitals were giving him 'cause for concern'. In 1948, he estimated, the deficits would have risen to £420,000, or a full two months' worth of his projected building programme, 'despite the substantial increases in maintenance charges levied by the hospitals in respect of patients sent in by local authorities', and despite an annual contribution of more than £100,000 from other public funds to the Dublin voluntary hospitals. 'I hope', he said, 'to be in a position to make recommendations to the voluntary hospitals concerned in the near future.'

Although it would be another year before Browne announced, with characteristic insouciance, that the amount of Sweepstakes funds which would be payable towards the deficits of the voluntary hospitals would be pegged at the 1948 level until 1952, the writing was on the wall, and the voluntary hospitals, and their associated consultants, knew it. Preparing himself for the onslaught he knew was gathering strength, Browne moved to close a gap in the hedge. In September 1949 he dispensed with the services of five members of the Hospitals Commission, for the most part venerable Fianna Fáil warhorses who had served on the Commission since its establishment in 1933, by simply refusing to renew their mandate when it expired. He replaced them with two other members — the minimum required under the legislation — ensuring that the Commission could not be used as a base from which an ambush could be mounted against his plans.[68]

The contemporary critique of Browne's early actions as Minister for Health has a familiar ring to it. As far as Fianna Fáil was concerned, all these plans were in the pipeline anyway. They would have matured, whoever was minister, as effortlessly as a car comes off an assembly line. Seán MacEntee, marking Browne vigorously, warned the public not to be dazzled by the efforts of the department's media people — the 'buglemen and fuglemen',[69] he called them — and said that people wanted to see concrete progress, not newspaper headlines.

Increasingly disgruntled administrators like Deeny shared this view. In addition, they jibbed at the minister's approach to obstacles, which they believed was to waltz around them. Deeny was opposed to the building of Cherry Orchard Hospital, and to the creation of St Luke's Cancer Hospital, on the grounds that existing facilities were adequate. In point of fact, as he admitted later in his own memoir, the decisions were subsequently justified by events. In the case of cancer care, there was a particular problem in that the logical development would have been to merge two existing Dublin institutions, one at Northbrook Road and the other at Hume Street, but institutional rivalries and vested interests prevented this. Later, Browne was to set up a Cancer Council under the chairmanship of G.E. ('Ted') Russell, who developed an enormous admiration for Browne and for his willingness to cut red tape to get the job done.[70]

Any assessment of Browne's early work in the Custom House must take his revisionist critics seriously, but, half a century on, it is difficult to see that they were right. Much of the criticism of the hospital building programme, for example, had its origins in the anger of those in the voluntary hospital sector at the filching (as they would have seen it) of the Hospitals' Trust Fund from them to build new hospitals, many of which would be under local authority rather than private ownership and control. This disappointment and anger was often hidden, especially in later years, behind the claim that the new hospitals were superfluous in any case; that streptomycin, which was becoming available after the war, was the miracle drug which put an end to TB, and the new sanatoria were so many expensive white elephants.

This argument was oversimplified and ahistorical. Oversimplified, because streptomycin, although remarkably powerful, was primarily of use in acute TB cases, notably those involving young children; it had much less to offer to older patients whose disease had become well established. Ahistorical, because streptomycin was all but unobtainable for many years; some Dublin doctors used to beg bootleg supplies from the US Embassy to treat sick children. And the cost was, for quite some time, extraordinarily high — £400 per patient was not uncommon.

The argument also discounts, to an unacceptable degree, the extent to which isolation, comfortable surroundings, hygiene, good food and rest served not only to strengthen individual sufferers' resistance to the disease, but to remove many potent sources of infection from the community. Browne himself was never under any illusion about the vital nature of the link between poverty and disease, particularly TB.

> Tuberculosis is not a problem which can be solved merely by the provision of beds and staff. Good housing conditions, adequate nutrition, appreciation of health hygiene and a more rational public attitude towards the disease are essential elements in the anti-tuberculosis campaign. Such measures as utilisation of mass radiography for early diagnosis, BCG vaccination, follow-up of contacts and a greater readiness on the part of sufferers to seek early treatment, will all play an important part, but the first essential is to provide institutional accommodation without a waiting period for persons who are found to need such accommodation.[71]

As far as the Hospitals' Trust Fund itself was concerned, it is hard to imagine that any Fianna Fáil administration would have agreed to the utilisation of the capital in the way that it was utilised by Browne. It would have foreseen the problems with the voluntary hospitals, at the very least, and balked at the prospect of the confrontation that would inevitably ensue. So for MacEntee and other political critics to suggest that they would have done as well as Browne — or even better — was disingenuous at best. Nor is it certain that they would have overcome the supplies problem which, even in 1948–9, caused frequent building bottlenecks. In Browne's case, his civil servants seem to have stolen a march on their colleagues by securing commitments from UK suppliers for building materials for the hospital building programme, to an extent that left many other government departments with building plans out in the cold.[72]

So much attention has been devoted to Browne's actions in connection with the TB campaign that the significance of some of his other initiatives has been, if anything, understated. Some of them were associated with the anti-TB drive; for instance, the national blood transfusion service, which was established in August 1948 primarily for the use of the thoracic surgeons who operated on TB sufferers, in time matured into a national resource of extraordinary value. Laboratory services were improved and decentralised (the first regional laboratory was provided in Galway in 1949). In 1949 a national BCG committee was set up, and the work of the mass radiography centre, which had been established under Fianna Fáil, was consolidated and greatly expanded. The effect of the BCG campaign was particularly marked: between 1948 and 1953 an 82 per cent decline in childhood deaths from TB was recorded in Dublin city.[73]

Decentralisation generally was a major theme of his administration. Outside Dublin, new facilities were provided in all the main provincial centres. Within Dublin, the stranglehold of the established interests was at least qualified by the development of St Kevin's as an acute hospital with a postgraduate medical school. Integration of services was the underlying theme. His celebrated, yellow-covered booklet on the Mother and Child Scheme (dealt with in more detail in chapter 5) contained an impressive diagram detailing 'How the New Service Will Work', showing a community health centre at the core of a series of relationships with schools, clinics, hospitals and laboratories.

With all this work to be done, public health took up virtually all Browne's energies in his first couple of years in office. But he also had to administer his department and share, as best he could, his family responsibilities with Phyllis.

In the detailed work of departmental administration, his less senior staff found him a courteous but firm superior, who expected as much as he was prepared to give. His office had a large map on the wall on which the progress in hospital building was marked with little flags; briefing sessions were frequent, and officials were expected to report progress on a regular basis. He was 'unusually frank' in his negotiations with the union representing many of the staff, the Local Government and Public Services Union.[74] In September 1948 the union objected to a ministerial circular which created a sex differential in bonus payments. When a delegation met the minister to discuss this grievance, he immediately abolished the differential. He was equally swift, although not so helpful, when another delegation from the same union came in to argue the case of the mental hospital officers, a category of workers with whom Browne might have been expected to have some sympathy. He told its members brusquely that they were wasting their time, as he was not impressed by their line of argument. On another occasion, he refused to consider the arguments of public health nurses for a 'special case' salary increase, although he accepted that this might be reviewed after the Mother and Child Scheme had been implemented.

If there was a fly in the ointment, it was in his attitude towards the fellow members of his profession, which was, at least in the opinion of Deeny and a number of other senior medical officials, that of a hanging judge. One senior medical adviser in the department was sidelined after conducting an inquiry into an allegation against a doctor which had come to the conclusion that the doctor was innocent of any wrongdoing. Deeny, though feeling more and more isolated, hung on grimly until the middle of 1950, when he was peremptorily moved to another area and his increasingly distant relationship with Browne came to an abrupt end. A number of commentators have suggested that this rupture was a major contributory factor in the development of the Mother and Child crisis, which followed almost immediately. The available evidence suggests, however, that even as experienced an administrator as Deeny would have been helpless in the face of the events that unfolded.

There was one other issue, however, which returned to haunt Browne in later years and which was at the core of the early conflict between the government and the Fianna Fáil opposition. This was the decision to declare Ireland a Republic and to leave the Commonwealth. The incident is interesting in itself in that Browne's version of events was challenged for many years, until later historical research proved him to be largely correct. But it is also interesting for the light it throws on Browne's attitude at this time to the question of partition and traditional Irish Republicanism.

There are two issues involved; the genesis of the decision to declare the Republic, and the related question of whether or not John A. Costello, at a subsequent cabinet meeting, offered his resignation for having intemperately declared his intention at a dinner in Canada. For some time after the decision was announced, journalists and others in Costello's confidence argued that his announcement in Canada had been preceded by a cabinet decision, and Browne's contention that no such decision had been made was discounted. More recent historical research, however, has supported the essential truth of Browne's account, notably in relation to the surprise with which Costello's announcement was greeted in Dublin, and the hurried attempts by MacBride to paper over the matter in Costello's continuing absence by introducing the necessary documentation to the cabinet.

The second question — Browne's allegation that Costello had been so embarrassed by the controversy that he had offered to resign at a subsequent cabinet meeting — is one on which it is less easy to come to a definite conclusion. Browne's opponents in later years maintained that no such cabinet meeting was held, but the public archives indicate that a meeting was held at Costello's house at a time which coincides with Browne's claim. However, the scanty civil service record of the meeting does not even indicate who was present apart from Costello himself, much less what was actually discussed. The best that can be said about the supposed resignation offer is that it is 'not proven'; it is certainly possible that an exasperated aside by the notoriously peppery Costello at the meeting may, in Browne's subsequent recollection, have assumed a greater importance.[75]

Of more interest, in retrospect, is the evidence that Browne's nationalism was, at this time, more than merely casual or incidental. The declaration of the Republic and the repeal of the External Relations Act, he says in his autobiography, had 'little significance' for him, and was 'a subject with which I was not deeply concerned'.[76]

A number of things should be remembered here. The first is that Clann na Poblachta was an unashamedly irredentist party; it had, prior to the election, adopted a policy which would have entitled Northern MPs to sit and speak in the Dáil, which caused the party some embarrassment when it entered government in 1948; and as late as 1950 MacBride himself was involved in a scuffle around the Tricolour during a march in Enniskillen in support for an anti-partition election candidate. Browne's recollection in 1986 of his attitude towards Republicanism may have been conditioned by his rejection of MacBride, for whom Republicanism came second only to religion, and it would certainly have been an inconvenient memory, given his increasing hostility towards Republicanism from the 1970s onwards. The contemporary evidence suggests that his attitudes were, at least at that time, closer to those of his party leader than he was later prepared to admit.

In August 1948 Clement Attlee was on a private holiday in Ireland, staying at a house in Mayo owned by one of his Downing Street advisers, Sir Anthony Bevir. Another Mayo summer resident was a British High Court Judge, Sir Charles Harman, whose family had maintained their home in Mayo for many years, and who was a friend of Bevir's. On 2 August (it has been possible to ascertain the date by reference to Judge Harman's game book), Harman was dining at the home of J.C. Garvey, a Westport solicitor, when Browne and MacBride arrived together unannounced. This seemingly casual meeting was apparently prompted by a belief on their part that Harman would be willing to arrange an introduction to Attlee for them. Judge Harman was very angry at this assumption that his private friendship could be exploited for political purposes and he left the house almost immediately.[77] Phyllis Browne, however, provides evidence that MacBride surmounted this obstacle. The Clann leader and Attlee subsequently turned up together — with, she thinks, Philip Noel-Baker — at a holiday cottage near Louisburgh which she and Noel were renting at the time. The visitors were unannounced, and had a lunch of eggs which she cooked over an open fire. They later all had dinner in a local hotel, but there is no record of what was discussed. Many years later, when Noël Browne was reminded of this by Nicholas Harman, Judge Harman's son, he clammed up. This suggests that the political matters discussed (possibly the question of Commonwealth membership) were of extreme sensitivity, to the extent that Browne did not want to elaborate on them decades later.

Less than a year later, on 12 April 1949, Browne was the person who reported to the Clann Standing Committee on the arrangements for the coming into force of the Republic of Ireland Act; at the same meeting, members unanimously passed a resolution congratulating Seán MacBride on his actions and noting: 'God speed your efforts to win back our occupied territory from the English aggressor.'[78]

Browne's own views on this topic, which he accepted in his autobiography had been conditioned at least in part by his education with the Christian Brothers in Ballinrobe, do not appear to have been much softened by his sojourn in England, and he found no difficulty in expressing them in forthright terms, inside and outside the Dáil. Part of this may have been in response to the needling from MacEntee already referred to, including the jibe that Browne did 'not like the idea of memorials being erected to those who died fighting the Black and Tans'.[79]

In between, Browne had been quite explicit about his own convictions. Early in 1949, when he was deputising for MacBride at question time in the Dáil (he generally took over the reins of External Affairs when his party leader was away on one of his many trips abroad), he was asked by another Clann TD to assure the House that the government would continue to deny 'the right of British troops to occupy part of our country by force'.

'I think', Browne responded robustly, 'there is no doubt that this fact must have been made sufficiently clear and cannot be over-emphasised — that we have in the past, in the present and will in the future continue to deny the right of British forces to occupy our six north-eastern counties.'[80]

It may be thought that Browne was here simply reading out the sort of background note for ministers which normally forms part of the equipment for answering parliamentary questions, and that the views to which he was giving support were MacBride's rather than his own. There is, however, abundant evidence on the record that this was not merely official Ireland speaking through Browne, but the expression of a personally held view. This in turn appears to have been conditioned by his early association with MacBride; as noted, his attitude during the 1948 election was somewhat more qualified. But it was a view which seemed, if anything, to grow in strength for as long as his relationship with MacBride remained positive. During the by-election campaign in the Cork South-West constituency in June 1949, when Browne was campaigning for the successful Labour candidate, W.J. Murphy (Clann did not field a candidate in the constituency), he referred scornfully to warnings by Gerry Boland of Fianna Fáil about Ireland's exit from the Commonwealth, and about the consequent deterioration in the relationship between Ireland and England. He likened Boland to Vidkun Quisling, who had maintained good relations with the German occupying forces in Norway during World War II. The deterioration in relations between Britain and Ireland, he said, was in fact 'due to the introduction in the English parliament of a Bill which has the effrontery and impertinence to presume to legislate for our people'.

> By the introduction of the Ireland Bill which the English people, through their parliament, have placed upon their Statute Book and have tried to continue in perpetuity the injustice of the unlawful occupation of our country by their armed forces. Good relations may be too expensively purchased . . . This isn't the first time Anglo-Irish relations have deteriorated and as long as the iniquity of Partition is maintained by Armed Forces of the British Crown it is likely that they may occasionally not be as amiable and friendly as Deputy Boland could wish.[81]

Even more dramatically, he told an audience at Cashel later in the year that

> Clann na Poblachta was committed to ensure that . . . for the thirty-two counties there was an established and independent Republic. They represented the younger generation and they were members of a constitutional organisation, but it would not be right for any body inside, or outside, the country to assume that because they were prepared to try to achieve their just rights by constitutional and democratic means . . . they were afraid of any other methods.[82]

This was in the course of a number of meetings which he addressed as part of an attempt to revive the flagging Clann constituency organisation around the country, and into which he threw himself with evident enthusiasm. Three days later he was to express himself in only slightly milder terms, when he told an audience at Tipperary that the country was faced with the task of the liberation of the Six Counties by a 'policy of resistance, using so-called constitutional methods which do not readily recommend themselves to young men'. 'The convictions about the evacuation of the Twenty-Six Counties', he added, 'are the same convictions which must inevitably bring about the evacuation of the six north-eastern counties. It is the earnest hope of the people that the same methods will not have to be used . . .'[83]

Browne even went North to speak at a meeting in Enniskillen on behalf of the anti-partition candidates in the ongoing election campaign in February 1950 — just a few weeks before his party leader was involved in the fracas there. He wanted, he said, to express his unmitigated opposition towards the continued occupation of this part of the country by the forces of the English government. Irishmen, by a majority of at least 80 per cent, demanded their country's unity and repudiated the right of Herbert Morrison's countrymen to any say whatever in the affairs of the Irish nation.[84] (Morrison was British home secretary.) Returning to the theme not long afterwards in Omagh, he appealed in particular to Northern Protestants to participate in a 'grand national renaissance', telling them that they 'would flourish in a State which guaranteed civil and religious liberty and that stood firmly by democratic equality for all'.[85]

Whether Noël Browne wrote these speeches himself, or whether they were drafted for him by the indefatigable de Blacam or by Hartnett, is to some extent beside the point. His action in going North to support the anti-partition candidates speaks for itself, and there is nothing in anything he said to suggest that these were the sentiments of an unwilling conscript to the irredentist cause. His suppression, in *Against the Tide*, of what was evidently a deeply felt political conviction at that time, is indicative of an unwillingness to acknowledge in public that he had ever, on any subject of significance, held any views other than those which he held in 1986, and for which, in effect, he wished to be remembered.

All this frenetic activity was taking place in the early part of 1950, and the pace was beginning to tell. In May he became quite ill. As he put it in a letter to Ruth, obviously written with the objective of minimising any alarm:

> what happened was that I went down to the west with a cold which considerably disimproved while I was down there. On my arrival back I felt rather terrible but because of one thing or another I didn't bother about my temperature until one evening I found then that it was pretty high. So I went to bed and had a most unpleasant time when I understand I had influenza and pneumonia. Out of this then there developed some fluid and, consequently, they are keeping me in bed until it is all completely gone. Fortunately it has become very much less and I understand I may be able to start thinking of getting up early in June.[86]

It was clearly more serious than he wanted to admit to his sister, but other evidence in the same letter suggests that he was at this stage thinking he might even be forced to radically change his lifestyle. Una had written to ask whether he would go out to the United States, and this was an option which he had considered 'from time to time'. The problem was that if he continued to work at his present rate, he told Ruth, he would face a complete breakdown in six to twelve months' time. The alternative was to lead a reasonably quiet life and 'Naturally . . . the chances of me leading a quiet life and being in politics are pretty remote.'

He was not, however, ruling anything out.

> *Naturally if I have to give up politics I would be anxious to consider going out to the States or to, possibly, New Zealand where they have a fairly civilised form of medical service, that is, if they think that I should give up politics and should get to a better climate. The position here, of course, is that by the time I have finished being Minister for Health I shall have so few friends in the medical profession that my chances of earning my living here will become more and more remote. As you know they are a pretty vicious bunch and are daily becoming more and more hostile.[87]*

There is a gap in this correspondence until 12 September of the same year, indicating the extent of his illness, or the degree to which he had again thrown himself into work, or both. When it resumed, he told Ruth that although he had been prevented from doing any hard work, he had been active in the local election campaign (which was disastrous for the Clann, as it picked up just thirty seats nationally, and only three in Dublin). He and Phyllis had been on a holiday to the south of France to escape the incessant rain that characterised that summer in Dublin, and found it uncomfortably hot; they were very glad to return. Kitty was making up her mind, finally, about emigration. She was to take up a position in early 1951 at the school run by the United Nations in New York, where she remained a valued member of staff until her final illness many years later.

When he wrote again in December 1950, the international political temperature had increased dangerously with the development of the Korean crisis. In an almost oblique reference to the unfolding Mother and Child controversy, he told Ruth that 'things have become complicated and don't look too well at all'. He plainly felt that there was a very real prospect of another world war — to the extent that he even contemplated sending his family away from a conflagration that might extend to Europe. Noting Kitty's plans for her departure to the US, he added sombrely:

> *Regrettable and all as it is even Phyllis and the two children may be the next ones who should consider doing something on similar lines because the international situation is certainly deteriorating very rapidly and I am afraid it does*

not appear as if we can be wholly unaffected by any repercussions. On the whole I think you are very lucky to be in America whatever they may think over there or whatever you may think yourself.[88]

The clouds gathering over Korea were real enough, but the conflict was contained. In the Department of Health, however, battle lines were already being drawn. He was engaged in a long-drawn-out battle with the Department of Finance about the projected cost of his Mother and Child Scheme, for which he had not yet received detailed financial sanction. In August 1950, he moved swiftly against James Deeny, a potential ally who had become an irritant. A new job was negotiated for him in charge of a national TB survey; it would take him out of the department and out from under Browne's feet. It was not the wisest decision Browne made, and it was an act of execution he did not even perform himself — Kennedy delivered the *coup de grâce*. Deeny and Browne would not meet again while Browne was minister.

In Government Buildings in Merrion Street, too, the political climate was becoming daily more unsettled and even stormy, with little prospect of improvement.

CHAPTER FOUR

'Yer Not Going to Let the Doctors Walk on Ye, Noël?'[1]

F or half a century, from the age of confessionalism to the age of post-denominationalism, the story of Noël Browne and the Mother and Child Scheme has exercised its unique grip on the public and political imagination of Ireland. For thirty years after it happened, it was the stuff of legend. Then, in 1986, the publication of *Against the Tide* set down a fascinating account of what had happened, with its greedy doctors, its scheming bishops, its vacillating politicians, and its Byronic hero. It had all the ingredients of a postmodern fairy tale, especially as it didn't have a happy ending.

But the story of the Mother and Child Scheme is not just, as Noël Browne told it, a story of one man against the world. It is a tale of shifting loyalties, of mistaken decisions, of powerful friendships and equally powerful enmities. It is a story, too, of opportunities missed, of amateurishness in government, and of the headlong rush into near-extinction of the political party which propelled Noël Browne and Seán MacBride into the cabinet. It has been dealt with, over the years, in a number of different studies,[2] and has been referred to in countless books and newspaper articles. The only treatment centred on Noël Browne's role in the affair, however, is that supplied by Browne himself. It is a version which has been accepted for so long in the public mind that it seems almost to be tempting fate to revisit it; but no biography of Noël Browne can shirk the challenge it poses.

There are so many actors in the drama, and so many twists and turns to the story, that it is necessary to divide it into a number of phases. Like all divisions of complex material, this risks oversimplification, but it helps to clarify the issues involved and to give a sense of how the rate at which the controversy developed accelerated so uncontrollably, particularly towards the end.

The first phase pre-dates Noël Browne and the formation of the inter-party government. It dates from 1945 until shortly after the change of government in February 1948. The second phase is relatively low-key, and involves the preliminary work on the scheme and early interaction between the Department of Health and the doctors. It dates from June 1948, when Browne brought his first proposals to cabinet, to early October 1950, when he had had his first meeting with the bishops. The third phase is one of confusion, of people talking and arguing at cross purposes, or not arguing at all when they should have been. This lasts from October 1950 until early in 1951. The fourth phase, the climax to the whole affair, will be dealt with separately in the following chapter. It begins in January 1951 with the circulation of an anonymous document in Dublin urging support for Browne's scheme and containing harsh criticism of the medical profession. It includes tense meetings between Browne and MacBride, the resignations of Noël Browne and Noel Hartnett — in Browne's case from the Standing Committee of Clann na Poblachta, and in Hartnett's case from the party as a whole — decisive interventions by the bishops, and the fall of the government.

Phase I

The beginning of the story pre-dates Noël Browne by several years, and is well documented. It had its origins in a committee chaired by Dr James Deeny, who had been appointed to the department as chief medical adviser as the war ended, and who felt an urgent need to shake up a system of public health which had by and large fallen into abeyance during the preceding years, and to devise a health service which met post-war expectations. Deeny's committee produced, in 1945, a blueprint for a national health service. It was never published, but the ideas it contained were accepted by the Minister for Local Government and Public Health, Seán MacEntee, and his parliamentary secretary, Dr Con Ward. These ideas became, in turn, the foundation for the White Paper on the health services, which was accepted by the government in 1947.

This White Paper, 'the most radical document ever written on the reform of the health services',[3] outlined a complete health service which was to begin with free medical care for TB sufferers. This provision was introduced in 1946. It was then planned to proceed via services for mothers and children (the 1947 Health Act) to free hospital and specialist services for everyone. The intermediate aim was the one which fell to be implemented by Noël Browne, and forms the main subject matter of this and the next chapter. The failure to implement it meant that this objective, and the ultimate objective of the White Paper — a free medical service for all — were both inherited by the 1951–4 Fianna Fáil administration, which achieved them, in a limited way, in the 1953 Health Act.

The 1947 Health Act had something in common with the controversial 1945 Public Health Bill which never passed through the Dáil, in that it embodied substantial provisions for the extension of compulsory school inspections and the education of mothers in child welfare. It also included, critically, provision for a free medical service for all mothers and children in the State without a means test.

Many of the clauses in the 1947 Act, notably those dealing with the Mother and Child Scheme, were the creation of Dr Deeny. Although he could not and did not claim authorship — this was a political function — he was not slow to publicise it. At a meeting of the Infant Aid Society in Dublin in mid-1947, for example, he praised the Bill (it was not yet an Act) as one which would 'provide a free medical service for women before, during and after childbirth, and for every child from birth up to the age of sixteen'. The basis of the scheme would be prevention; and there would be free inspection of children during pre-school days.[4] Political approval, and impetus, came from Dr Con Ward.

Deeny's philosophy was to break the cycle of disadvantage which affected the poorer sections of the population. Any health scheme, he believed, should be universal so as to reduce the taint of pauperism. And he felt that the experience of the war — when people had grown used to an unprecedented set of regulations controlling many aspects of their lives — was a context in which measures of compulsion to control infectious diseases could also be introduced into the health services, for the best possible motives. He was particularly concerned at the dreadfully high levels of infant mortality. Later, he suggested privately that the mistake they had made with the Bill as it was originally passed was to overload it — they should, he said, have remembered the precept of Occam's razor.[5]

The Catholic hierarchy initially objected to the compulsion provisions of the Act. In a later private letter to de Valera the bishops objected also to the provisions of the Mother and Child Scheme, on the grounds that it 'was directly and entirely contrary to Catholic social teaching, the rights of the family, the rights of the Church in education, and the rights of the medical profession, and of voluntary institutions'.[6] They were especially worried about provisions for the health of mothers, including their education in respect of motherhood. They were also unhappy about changes in the compulsory inspection of children in schools. Although compulsory inspection of schools had been on the statute book since 1919, the 1947 legislation extended this to include all schools, especially secondary schools. This was the main source of the bishops' concern with this aspect of the new scheme: they were anxious about the inspection of girls at an impressionable age.

Deeny, as it happened, had been largely behind the provisions dealing with schools which the bishops found objectionable. Together with a doctor from Dublin Corporation, he had carried out a survey of health conditions in a number of Dublin national schools — including one in Killiney, close to

Dr McQuaid's house. Deeny gave the completed report to Dr Con Ward, who sent it on unaltered to McQuaid, suggesting that he should do something about it and offering to send Deeny to discuss it with him. McQuaid refused, on the grounds that he wouldn't speak to junior civil servants. Deeny, who had a number of examples of improvement schemes for health in schools which had been enthusiastically adopted by Catholic dioceses in the United States, wanted to take the matter further but then, in his own words, the new minister, Noël Browne, 'butted in and spoiled everything'.[7]

The bishops' letter might have led to negotiations with de Valera and the bishops, but this possibility was pre-empted by James Dillon's constitutional challenge to the Act. Probably grateful for the breathing space, de Valera did not deal with the matter in any way prior to the 1948 election.

Phase II

The new government, therefore, faced two pieces of unfinished business in connection with the Act. One of them related to the elements of compulsion for school inspections, and the education of mothers. The second related to the provisions of the Mother and Child Scheme, and the bishops' objections noted above.

Plainly, sorting out the problems of the 1947 Health Act was regarded initially with as much urgency as organising the assault on tuberculosis, and the situation was tackled by Browne and his officials almost as soon as he assumed office. They acted in the knowledge that not only the bishops but the doctors — who had described the Act as the first step in the socialisation of medicine — were deeply unhappy about some of its proposals, and they knew that this unhappiness would have to be persuasively addressed. But both Browne and the government as a whole made one potentially fatal error in underestimating the opposition of the doctors, or in assuming that it was opposition only to a particular aspect of a particular scheme. The doctors' opposition was fundamental, in that it was based on a belief that the full implementation of the 1947 Act was not only objectionable in itself, but was the thin end of a wedge that would hold the door open for the introduction of a national health service on the British model. They were determined — not least because they knew they wielded more political power — not to be bullied or bribed as they believed their British counterparts had been; and they had more powerful allies.

Addressing the concerns of the doctors and the bishops meant that the 1947 Health Act would have to be amended. The first important political question therefore was: what amendments would be brought in, and how far would they go? Noël Browne, in his autobiography (written without access to cabinet papers which became available only after the passage of the

National Archives Act in 1986), says that on becoming minister he was 'determined to *extend* the no-means-test principle of the 1947 Act to the health care of mothers and their children' and that 'the amending Bill presented by me to the Cabinet in June 1948 *kept* the no-means-test principle' (emphasis added).[8]

This version of events, however, presents a number of problems. In the first place, the 1947 Act already embodied a no-means-test principle for the health care of mothers and children, so no extension of its provisions on this score was necessary. Browne's statement that the amending Bill presented by him to the cabinet 'kept the no-means-test principle' of the 1947 Act is therefore, given the ordinary meaning of words, in conflict with his other statement that this principle was extended by him in what he was now presenting to cabinet.

Secondly, the heads of legislation presented by him to cabinet, far from being an extension of what had been enacted in 1947, were potentially a dilution of it, in that they introduced for the first time the possibility of charging for some mother and child services. In other words, although it repeated the principle of the 1947 Act, as Noël Browne notes, it also opened the door to a radical modification of it.

But there is a more serious difficulty, which is underscored not only by the cabinet papers on the issue but even by Browne's own speech in the Dáil on the occasion of his resignation three years later. Speaking on 12 April 1951, he made the situation completely explicit, and much clearer than the version in his autobiography.

> Under the 1947 Act passed by the then government authority was given to introduce a free scheme for which there would be no means test, and the only way in which it would be possible to introduce a scheme by which local authorities could collect fees and impose a means test would be by the amendment of the 1947 Act. I put that proposal before the government in 1948 and pointed out to them that if they wanted a scheme which would not be free to all and which would have a means test they must amend that Act. The section containing that suggestion headed my draft to the Government. They directed me as a Government decision to exclude from my proposed draft Bill the section which would have enabled them now to charge for this scheme if they so wished.[9]

The cabinet documentation itself is of further help in elucidating the circumstances surrounding this decision, and the reasons for it. The memorandum to the government from Noël Browne, dated 9 June 1948, proposed a number of amendments to the Act which would meet some of the bishops' objections, particularly in relation to compulsory medical inspection and requiring schools to make inspection facilities available. Significantly, it also included the following passage:[10]

> *Head 3 of the Scheme is designed to enable the Minister to make regulations providing for the payment of a charge to health authorities or to other persons for services rendered under Part III (Mother and Child Service) of the Act. It was proposed at the time the 1947 Health Act was enacted that this service would be made available free of charge to all sections of the community and accordingly no provision was made for the making of payments by persons availing of the service or the fixing of charges by health authorities. In the event of a decision to restrict the free service to certain categories, a provision on the lines indicated at Head 3* will empower the Minister to provide for payment by other classes availing of the service. *On the other hand the new provision will not prevent the Minister from providing a free service should such be considered necessary in the future. The Irish Medical Association has intimated that it objects to the principle of providing free medical services to non-necessitous persons and* while the Minister for Health does not propose at this stage to commit himself to the acceptance or rejection of the point of view of the Association *the amendment of the Act in the manner proposed will lessen the opposition of the medical profession to it.*

The document helps to clarify an otherwise obscure section in Noël Browne's autobiography in which he describes the response of the cabinet on 25 June to his memorandum. He records the leader of the Labour Party, William Norton, booming across the cabinet table at him: 'Yer not going to let the doctors walk on ye, Noël?' But this raises a critical question: why, if Brown had submitted a free-for-all scheme, would Norton accuse him of letting the doctors 'walk on him'?

The answer is that Browne's proposal was not for a free-for-all scheme (although it did not exclude this possibility), but for a scheme which explicitly included the possibility of charges. Browne's political problem in 1951, and in later years, was that it would have been difficult for him to admit to this without seriously undermining his subsequent stance (although, as we have seen, he made a glancing reference to it in his own resignation speech). A clue to what happened, and to his thinking at the time, is contained in an unpublished passage prepared for his autobiography.
Browne wrote:

> *I warned that I thought it inconceivable the Irish Medical Association would not contest the free provisions of the Fianna Fáil Mother and Child Act* [sic]. *Misjudging my warning, Norton wrongly assumed that as a doctor I was tending to side with the medical profession and proceeded to harangue my Cabinet colleagues into ignoring me. Norton was quite wrong since it was I out of all*

of them who was determined to oppose the Medical Association in their attempts to damage the scheme. My temporising move was a tactical one in what I knew must become an intricate and complex struggle against the powerful medical pressure group. Under pressure it was Norton who was to capitulate before the opposition of these same members of the medical profession, whom he had safely in Cabinet chosen to anathemise [sic].[11]

The reference to a 'temporising move' seems to indicate the memorandum proposing a scheme embodying charges (the fragment of text is incomplete). But if Browne's submission of this memorandum was a calculated gamble, in which he proffered to the cabinet a scheme in which he did not believe, in the hope that it would be rejected, it was an extraordinary risk to take. T.F. O'Higgins, as Browne well knew, had retained an officership in the Irish Medical Association; along with Costello, James Dillon and Richard Mulcahy, he was a stern critic of empire building by the Department of Health. It is highly unlikely that any of these ministers would have objected to a Department of Health proposal suggesting that doctors might be allowed to charge for certain services. Equally, if Browne's memorandum had been accepted in the form in which he had presented it to government, it would have been difficult — to put it mildly — for him subsequently to reject the doctors' arguments out of hand.

There is an alternative version of what happened, necessarily speculative, but which fits in with more of the known facts. This is that Browne accepted the advice of his departmental officials to the effect that the doctors had to be placated, or at least quietened down by the introduction of a scheme in which they *might* be paid. The possibility that Browne had in mind at this time the prospect of agreeing to at least some level of charge for the service is given added weight by a memorandum from Deeny to the assistant secretary of the department, Paddy Murray, which, although dated a year later, records that the minister was persuaded at this stage to separate the new service as far as possible from any association with the dispensary system, and felt that people would attach more value to a service to which they contributed.[12] This in turn had financial implications, in that if the scheme was to be operated by general practitioners rather than by dispensary doctors the costs would be measurably higher. These financial considerations were to feature prominently in the final phase of the controversy.

If we accept, therefore, that Noël Browne brought his memorandum to cabinet in good faith, and was even prepared to defend the necessity of the passage on charges because it would offset anticipated medical opposition, we have to examine the wider political context and the internal dynamics of the cabinet to assess what happened next.

The wider context had both a national and an international dimension. Nationally, the cabinet — still insensitive to the dangers from an aroused medical profession — would have assumed that Fianna Fáil was the only opposition it had to worry about, and that Fianna Fáil would never oppose what was essentially its own scheme. Indeed, only ten days earlier, in his reply to Noël Browne's first estimate speech, Dr James Ryan had wondered why Browne had made no announcement on progress in framing regulations for a mother and child scheme under the 1947 Act. And he had added:

> The [argument] put up by the medical profession . . . that . . . the private practitioner in the small town was in danger of losing any practice he might have in maternity and treatment of children . . . [was] a question requiring a great deal of consideration, but even a difficult problem of that kind should not prevent the scheme from being brought into operation . . . It should be possible to do something for the private practitioner by giving him some share of the extra work.[13]

Ryan was unaware of the fact that the delay was largely the product of Department of Finance anxiety about the cost of the new scheme. His speech, however, reads almost as if he had had access to a leaked copy of Browne's memorandum to cabinet. His approach was certainly eirenic and offered, at least by implication, reasonable co-operation from Fianna Fáil in getting a workable scheme off the ground, even if it meant modifying the free nature of the scheme envisaged in 1947. It was also a lightly coded warning about the potentially disruptive and dangerous consequences of medical objections, and an explicit suggestion that the original scheme might have to be amended to head off such potentially fatal opposition. Neither Browne nor anyone in the government, however, understood this warning, or heeded it if they did. On the contrary, they assumed not only that the original scheme was fireproofed because it had been passed by a Fianna Fáil government, but that Fianna Fáil would oppose them root and branch if they tried to amend it. This is underlined by Browne's unpublished assertion that cabinet support for a no-means-test scheme 'was caused by their fear of the political row which the Fianna Fáil opposition could reasonably create were the Coalition to abolish the "free principle" of the 1947 Act'.[14]

The international context also undoubtedly played a part. Dr Paddy Fanning, who did not particularly like Browne[15] but who was closely involved in drafting departmental responses to IMA criticism of the Mother and Child Scheme in 1950, remarked once that what was going on contemporaneously in Britain was one influence; that it was impossible to do nothing, with the changes that were taking place there.[16] This was a reference to the efforts by the post-war British Labour government to bring in a comprehensive health service, and to the battle between the medical profession and Nye Bevan, Attlee's Minister of Health in that government, over the funding of this service.

If there was not to be a means test, there was really no feasible alternative to a universal scheme funded out of general taxation. Some of Browne's opponents, notably within the medical profession, advocated a scheme based on social insurance. An insurance-based scheme would have presented major difficulties in Ireland at this time, because such a low proportion of the population was in insurable employment, and many were farmers on smallholdings.

There was also one politically significant difference between the NHS plans and the approach being developed by Browne, in that the British government secured the ultimate acceptance of the scheme by doctors because it involved them to a considerable degree on the committees which managed it; Browne's initiative, while it involved power-sharing between his department and local authorities, did not offer any such incentives. And there was an important subtext, which never emerged into the public manifestations of the controversy, but of which both Browne and his medical opponents were keenly aware: the implication that doctors who participated in public health schemes might have to face greater exposure to the income tax authorities. Browne admired Bevan's way of dealing with this problem — by fixing doctors' remuneration from the State at a level which would make this less painful for them — and had similar plans for his own scheme.

Although the British NHS proposals had received substantial parliamentary approval in a Commons vote in May 1946, the British Medical Association, representative of wealthier suburban doctors rather than general practitioners, had mounted a major rearguard action and involved Bevan in a long-drawn-out battle. In a speech to the House of Commons on 9 February 1948, only four months before Browne brought his proposals to cabinet, he described the BMA committee as 'a small body of politically poisoned people' and 'a squalid political conspiracy'.[17] Both Norton and Browne would have been watching these developments closely. Browne specifically alludes to Bevan's conflict with the doctors in his autobiography, and in an unpublished fragment refers to Bevan's book, *In Place of Fear*.[18] Browne, however, did not have a large political party and movement behind him, as Bevan did; it would take another three years, and loss of office, before he was free to turn on his tormentors in the same way. But if there was an uncanny parallelism, at certain points, between the political trajectories of the two men, their temperaments were markedly different. Bevan was certainly difficult to work with politically, but his impetuousness did not preclude a willingness to accept party discipline for other, shared objectives, and he seems to have been better liked personally, even by his political opponents within the British Labour Party.

This also has a relevance to the internal dynamics of the cabinet. Conscious of what was happening in Britain, Browne noted in the unpublished section of his autobiography dealing with this issue: 'It would be particularly difficult for Mr Norton, as leader of the Labour Party, to abolish the "free" element of the health scheme.'[19] Indeed it would have been, if that had been his intention. But the documentary evidence points, instead, to the fact that it was Browne, rather than Norton, who first proposed an amendment which would have made it possible to charge for the Mother and Child Scheme, and Norton who queried it. Norton's line about letting the doctors walk on him was evidently quoted by Browne to highlight the Labour leader's later change of tack on the same issue; but the way in which Browne experienced and interpreted this remark helps to provide a clue to his subsequent behaviour. In this, as in some other areas, his autobiography reveals more about its author than he would, perhaps, have wanted us to know.

The situation was now replete with ironies, some of them more readily discernible at the distance of half a century than they were to the participants at the time. If the above analysis is correct, the position was now roughly as follows: the scheme proposed by Browne to cabinet had been rejected, at Norton's behest, in favour of the original no–means–test alternative. This was of course with Browne's pleased agreement. He records Costello asking at the meeting: 'Which do you prefer, doctor?' which again underlines the implication that it was not just the cabinet but Browne who had to choose between the free option and the option which included a possible means test.

Browne was now in a politically embarrassing position. His memorandum to government included the possibility of a means test, if only for tactical reasons. But he was now being politically upstaged by William Norton on that very issue. To rule out the possibility of a means test, he had to abandon his own proposal, as he did. He then went off to draft his scheme in the quite justified belief that he had the full support of the cabinet, but unaware, as they all were, of the perils in store.

The one awkward bit of evidence that does not quite fit into this scenario is Browne's statement in his autobiography that he warned the cabinet about the difficulty of implementing a no–means–test scheme. In his book, this assertion precedes his account of the 25 June cabinet meeting. It makes more sense, however, if his warning was issued at the meeting itself, after his memorandum had been ambushed by Norton, rather than earlier. The somewhat erratic chronology of *Against the Tide* makes this hypothesis quite believable.

There are two other pieces of evidence which, although circumstantial in character, further support the hypothesis. One is Browne's reported distrust of departmental secretary Paddy Kennedy. If Browne thought that he had been ill-advised in bringing the original Department of Health scheme to cabinet, and had been seriously wrong-footed by the fact that Norton had been able to take the high moral ground on this issue, he would have been slow to forgive the person who, in his view, had helped to get him into the mess.

The second is Browne's attitude to Norton. The portrait of him in *Against the Tide* is one of the most vituperative pieces of writing in any non-fictional work published in Ireland in recent years, and is not excused by the fact that its object was dead when it appeared. The tone of the piece, as it happens, rebounds on its author. With the possible exception of readers who think that Noël Browne's judgments are infallible, the effect of this splenetic piece of prose has been, if anything, to evoke sympathy for Norton. It is undeniably true that Norton, and the rest of the cabinet, reneged[20] in 1951 on their commitment of three years earlier, on the basis of which Browne had drawn up his scheme. But they did so, rightly or wrongly, in the belief that even a watered-down scheme would be better than no scheme at all — a view which Browne conspicuously did not at that time share.

Browne's sense of betrayal would have been enhanced by his memory of Norton's jocose questioning of his radical credentials in 1948. He would never forgive Norton for having depicted him in cabinet as cautious and fearful. The more experienced, older politician had identified unerringly the one weak spot in his armour, and had put him unexpectedly, and embarrassingly, on the defensive on an issue which was critical to his understanding of his own mission. In 1951 the same William Norton led the retreat from Moscow, his flank dangerously exposed.

Browne now had an unambiguous cabinet decision behind him, in that it had been decided there should be no means test. His proposals for amending the Bill in its other aspects — the education of mothers, for instance — had been accepted. Its progress, however, was overtaken dramatically by the controversy about the draft regulations for the Mother and Child Scheme although they did not form part of the Bill itself. As events unrolled, the regulations were to assume a much greater importance than the Bill. The absence of a means test was not only to excite hostility in the medical profession and its ally, the Catholic hierarchy, but to become an integral part of a complicated power play within Clann na Poblachta itself. It was a controversy which was to expose weaknesses and misjudgments on the part of virtually everyone concerned.

For the time being, however, work went ahead on the new Bill and the associated regulations (drafted in part by Deeny). What is significant at this stage is that it went ahead without any consultation with the medical profession — indeed, on foot of a rejection by Browne of the doctors' request for consultation. Dr P.J. Delaney, secretary of the Irish Medical Association, wrote on 29 April 1948 looking specifically for an amendment of the 1947 Act to require the minister to consult with the medical profession before making regulations for the schemes it created. Receiving no reply, he wrote again on 13 August 1948 repeating his request. Paddy Kennedy now wrote back to disclose that the government was in the process of drafting amendments which would repeal sections dealing with schools inspections, and would protect parents' rights. In so far as the draft regulations for the Mother and Child Scheme were concerned, however, he was uncompromising:

> In view of the fact that the more important regulations proposed to be made under the Health Act 1947 will be submitted to the National Health Council or other consultative councils set up under section 98 of the Act the Minister is of the opinion that the amendment of section 5 (1) of the Act to provide for consultation with the medical profession prior to the making of regulations is unnecessary. The objections of the Medical Association to the provision free of charge of a Mother and Child Health Service have been fully considered and the Government has decided against making any change in that respect in the Health Act, 1947. As regards the proposals outlined in the White Paper on the Health Services, I am to state that as the future development of these services is being reconsidered no useful purpose would be served at present by the reception of a deputation from the Association to discuss the White Paper proposals.[21]

In the debate on Browne's resignation two and a half years later, John A. Costello was to say that he had not even seen this letter until shortly before the crisis. The doctors were enraged, so much so that they immediately sent a copy to Dr McQuaid; but they do not seem to have alerted either Costello or O'Higgins, who might have been expected to be sympathetic. The draft regulations, at the end of the day, were not submitted to any council, and when they were finally submitted to the doctors, it was only on Browne's explicit condition that the absence of a means test was non-negotiable. Certainly the doctors dragged their feet, as will be seen later. But Browne, too, was at this stage playing for time. Equally significantly, it appears that he had already assumed that it would be impossible to obtain the doctors' agreement, and it is probably true to say that his scheme was effectively doomed from this point on.

As it happened, he was not without some potential support among doctors, even later than this point. The *Irish Times* medical correspondent noted almost a year later that 'the country has long needed a man of Dr Browne's capabilities and discernment, and one would be genuinely sorry if he should fall heir to the indiscretions of his predecessor'.[22] This particular anonymous doctor did not, however, reflect the opinions of the upper reaches of his profession. The same issue of the newspaper reported the blunt statement of IMA president Dr Patrick Moran that although a free mother and child scheme had distinct popular appeal, it would 'pauperise the people and prostitute the profession'. What happened next was a testament to obduracy on the part of the doctors and their clerical allies, but also to the fact that this obduracy collided, head-on, with a minister who was temperamentally opposed to consensus and motivated not only by ideology but by personal feelings of extraordinary depth and power. 'The emotions', as Lenin once wrote, 'are unskilled workers.'[23]

The outline of the scheme was not completed for another year. This was not due to any dilatoriness on the part of Browne or his officials, but because of anxieties within the Department of Finance about the likely cost of the scheme. The secretary of Finance, J.J. McElligott, believed — on moral and philosophical grounds, he stressed, rather than on financial grounds — that pride in one's ability to pay for medical services should be encouraged: 'That very proper pride will surely be steadily diminished if the farmers' sons and daughters can get this medical benefit without any transfer of cash.'[24] At the same time, there were others in the department who accepted, certainly at this early stage, that although a very heavy increase in State expenditure would be involved in the new scheme, 'we gave our sanction to the health campaign with our eyes wide open to the possible financial implications'.[25]

In the interim, the ground was being prepared. The mechanism chosen for this was a Consultative Council on Child Health, set up by Browne on 13 May 1948, under the chairmanship of M.W. Doran, an engineer who was also chairman of the Hospitals Commission. This Council dealt only with the maternity services provided in the three Dublin maternity hospitals, but its work had obvious implications for the development of a national scheme. Browne had inherited Doran from the previous administration, but evidently got on well with him, and retained him in his position when he purged the Commission in 1949. The other members included a number of prominent doctors, including Dr Bob Collis (who was, as it happened, also a Clann supporter), Dr Seamus Dundon, Dr T.M. Kavanagh of Temple Street and Dr Alex Spain of Holles Street, as well as senior officials from a range of government departments and Dublin Corporation. James Deeny was not a member, not for any hidden reason, but because as the senior medical adviser in the department he would in due course have to comment on the Council's findings.[26] Its terms of reference were to advise the minister on the measures which it deemed likely to be most effective for the improvement of the health of children generally, or of any particular class or classes of children, and especially for the reduction of infant mortality. In making its recommendations the Council was required to have regard to any arrangements which might have been made by the State or local authorities for the promotion of the same ends, and to the respective statutory functions of the Department of Health and other state departments and local authorities.[27]

When the Council reported in 1949, Noël Browne accepted its recommendations in principle. This did not advance a solution of the problem, however, because the Council's recommendations were confined to the situation in the three major Dublin hospitals, where it advised that the scheme should be restricted to the first six weeks of an infant's life, instead of the year originally envisaged by the department.[28] The Council envisaged that after the age of six weeks a record regarding each child would be passed to the Corporation, whose responsibility it would then be (under the projected national Mother and Child Scheme) to make available medical care.

The work of this Council, although it was remarkably expeditious in its meetings and in dealing with its terms of reference, might have delayed to some extent progress on the national scheme. As already noted, the primary factor was Department of Finance hesitation, but planning might also have suffered from the minister's own ill health — a recurrence of TB — in his first eighteen months in office. Between 29 November 1948 and 4 February 1949 he was able to attend only three of the fifteen cabinet meetings held; he was hospitalised for almost a month and had a reduced workload for some four or five weeks' convalescence.

In relation to the Mother and Child proposals, Browne told the Dáil:

I completely agree with the project but have no intention of being panicked into bringing into operation a scheme which might not be capable of giving me the results which I require, that is, the protection of the mother in the period of maternity and of the child in its childhood and early adolescence to the age of 15 or 16. There are a number of different interests which need to be consulted.[29]

The first thing to do, however, was to prepare the Bill itself. This was submitted in draft form to the government, with a memorandum, on 10 October 1949. By and large the memorandum indicated that the Bill was doing no more than putting flesh on the bones of the government decision of the previous June. There was only one section which had an implication for the Mother and Child Scheme. This was section 4, which empowered the minister to transfer, by regulations, medical assistance functions from a public assistance authority to a local authority; this power was required to facilitate the administration of the Mother and Child Service. In his memorandum, the minister noted: 'It is likely that that Service will use the services of dispensary medical officers appointed primarily for medical assistance work, and it is considered necessary, to ensure more effective administration, that the one local authority in the area should be responsible for both the Mother and Child Service and the dispensary service.'[30] Although it looked like no more than administrative housekeeping, this provision had an important implication in that it assumed that ordinary general practitioners would not be involved in operating the scheme. This added to the growing opposition among those members of the Irish Medical Association who were general practitioners, and had their own powerful committee within the IMA structure.

The government approved the text of the Bill at an ordinary meeting on 4 November 1949; Browne was present. There is no indication that the question of regulations arose at that meeting, or at any meeting until very much later. Nor — importantly from Browne's point of view — was there any conditionality; a more experienced government might well have insisted that the draft regulations, with their inevitable cost implications, would have to be brought back to cabinet for further approval. A number of keen episcopal noses were, however, sniffing the wind. Just after the government decision, Bishop Browne of Galway wrote to Archbishop McQuaid to say that the Bishop of Limerick had been in touch with him to express his concern that the government's proposals were going ahead.[31] It was to be almost a year before the hierarchy got around to clarifying its position.

Almost immediately, Seán MacBride, answering for an ill Noël Browne, told the Dáil that 'draft proposals' had been prepared for mother and child health service schemes, and that he hoped 'at a very early date' to publish them and initiate consultations with the interested parties.[32] One of the most interested parties was the Department of Finance, which was raising objections to the level of payment envisaged for dispensary doctors as part of his proposals. In February 1950, in the middle of this argument, Browne wrote to Costello to accept a further delay: 'In view of the essential nature of our mother-and-child proposals it is with some misgivings that I reconcile myself to a postponment of any of its provisions.'[33] In an attempt to buy goodwill from Finance, Kennedy even managed to shave £10,000 off the Department of Health's projected 1951 estimate in other areas. By the end of May, Browne was confident enough to tell the third Ard-Fheis of Clann na Poblachta (in a report he was unable to deliver personally because of illness) that

> *possibly my most formidable task for the future is the implementation of the draft scheme for a comprehensive mother and child scheme, which has been drawn up in my department . . . this scheme will mark probably the greatest single step forward towards the ensuring of my objective, of ensuring that there shall be equality of opportunity in matters of health, particularly in the susceptible age groups.*[34]

Although little was happening that was visible to the public during this stage of the development of the Mother and Child Scheme, it would be a mistake to assume that the public was unaware of it. This is because of the activities of the Clann organisation, which had identified the scheme as a major political asset — perhaps its only remaining one — and publicised it energetically at meetings and in newsletters up and down the country.[35] This ensured that the proposal developed a life of its own, independently of what was happening (or not happening) in cabinet, and of the protracted wrangles between Health and Finance about the cost of the scheme.

The Clann needed an issue like this. As early as February 1948 Lord Rugby was reporting to London, after a conversation with MacBride, that 'The new party as a party is a blank cartridge. Already party members in the country are complaining about being sold out and are resigning.'[36] In March the American Ambassador, George Garrett, told his superiors in the State Department that the Clann was 'a dead duck'. Four months later R.M. Beaudry of the American Embassy was being even more scathing: 'Clann na Poblachta may be a dead issue. Organisational work continues throughout the country, but the party is broke and several people whose judgement I respect say that the party which fought the last election is no more.' Garrett added his sixpennyworth in the same dispatch. The party, he pointed out, had attempted to purchase a Georgian house as its headquarters for £5,000, but the sale had fallen through; it owed the printers £400 for the election and the printers were now dunning MacBride personally for the money. MacBride's sole remaining utility, Beaudry suggested, was that he might sponsor some sort of minimum wage legislation 'to prevent large sections of the working population from adopting socialism in some more or less extreme form'.[37]

By the end of 1948, these experienced observers discerned a new sense of fluidity in Irish politics which might even at this stage break the traditional party mould. George Garrett reported on a lengthy conversation he had had with Hugh Smith of *The New York Times*, who was propounding the thesis that a political merger might be effected between the groups headed by Costello, McGilligan, Dillon, MacBride and Cecil Lavery, the Attorney-General. This group, he thought, would be expected to follow a centrist policy, with the remnants of Fianna Fáil on the right and Labour on the left. 'Smith', he added, 'has gone so far as to put the question of such a possibility to Noël Browne, who replied that it was "a bit early" to make any statements along that line. It is, however, interesting that Browne did not deny the suggestion or consider it outside the realm of possibility.'[38]

MacBride, sensitive to the problem, attempted to counter it subsequently by publishing a newsletter for party members, which appeared on an intermittent basis until the end of 1950. Its first issue, dated October 1949, observed chattily: 'The very fact that members of our Organisation criticise us shows how closely they follow national affairs . . . Now and again we hear the complaint that our party is inactive . . . We are at times charged with being just a piece of the Fine Gael machine.'[39]

The difficulties enumerated so light-heartedly here were in fact only the tip of an iceberg. The party, as Browne points out in his autobiography, was basically itself an unsteady coalition between younger radicals and old IRA men. What the former had in common was inexperience; what the latter shared was unelectability. Moves by Browne and Hartnett to alter the balance of this internal coalition were rudely rebuffed; on more than one occasion, they unsuccessfully tried to get Michael ffrench-O'Carroll, an energetic young Dublin doctor who was elected to the Corporation in the Clann interest, co-opted onto the party's National Executive to provide them with moral and political support.

MacBride himself was by this stage a wasting asset. He was out of the country frequently, and for all the plaudits he received for making External Affairs a high-profile ministry —possibly for the first time in the history of the State — this meant that he left his backyard dangerously untended. Nor did staying at home always solve MacBride's difficulties; sometimes it made them worse, as he participated in government decisions which stank in the nostrils of his own supporters. By the middle of 1950, a combination of problems must have persuaded him that he had better attend to national rather than international matters, and try to heal some of the festering sores that were developing in his absence.

By then, however, he was running out of political capital in both cabinet and party. Lord Glenavy, the former secretary of the Department of Industry and Commerce who had resigned from that position in 1932 on reaching the peerage and who was undoubtedly a Fine Gael supporter, expressed himself tartly to Lord Rugby in June 1950:

> Lord Glenavy said that Mr MacBride became more of a problem every day. Feeling against him was hardening very much inside the Government. He realised himself now that he was not making a success of his European activities, and his colleagues were entirely clear that he was being a failure in that field. They had been delighted that he should stamp about in the European field since that kept him out of the internal field and kept him busy. Unfortunately, his failure to make an impression overseas was now diverting him back into the internal field in which they had no desire to see him active.[40]

Rugby added that there had even been a contretemps caused by McGilligan's desire to retire as Minister for Finance because of ill health. MacBride, hearing of this, had demanded the succession, and had threatened to withdraw his party from the government unless he got it. An alarmed

John A. Costello had dealt with the problem in the only possible way — by prevailing upon McGilligan not to resign.

The draft Mother and Child Scheme was sent to the Irish Medical Association, and to members of the cabinet,[41] on 10 June 1950. A fortnight later, the first meeting was held between officials of the department and IMA representatives. An additional 1,500 copies of the draft scheme were sent to the IMA for its members, and the first deputation from the Association met Browne in October.

This chronology assumes considerable significance in the light of what happened later, particularly in so far as the government was concerned. At the height of the controversy in the following March, the Taoiseach was told by his civil servants that they could find no record of any proposals for the Mother and Child Service being submitted to the government. James Ryan, as Fianna Fáil Minister for Health, told the Dáil in June 1953 that Mr Costello had received a copy of the scheme only on 7 November 1950.[42] The copy of the scheme in William Norton's papers, however, is date-stamped in June. These facts are not irreconcilable, as long as it is assumed that Noël Browne sent the scheme only to a certain number of cabinet ministers on a personal basis, or that he sent it to all of them without making it the subject of a specific request for cabinet approval. If he had not made such a request, it would be open to civil servants to finesse the fact that the document had actually been received in June, not least to enable the Taoiseach to deny any official knowledge of it.

Noël Browne could also have adopted such a course of action — notifying his cabinet colleagues without seeking specific approval — quite deliberately. After Michael D. Higgins became a cabinet minister in 1993, he had a lengthy conversation with Browne in which the older man told Higgins that he had observed, during his time in cabinet, how ministers' proposals could continually be delayed or obstructed simply because other ministers or their departments kept coming back with requests for additional information. If Browne had observed this happening in 1948–50, as he undoubtedly had, this would have been an additional incentive for him to keep documentation away from cabinet unless he had no alternative but to produce it. In the event, the fact that Finance did not (until the very last minute) raise any serious objections, and that he had a unanimous cabinet decision in favour of the principle of the scheme, it is more than likely that this is what happened.

Regardless of the motivation involved, the difficulty of the situation was compounded by the unwillingness of either Costello or MacBride to bring the matter up at cabinet level, even after 7 November 1950, on which date Costello was apparently enlightened about the document. It was not formally raised at cabinet until 6 April 1951, by which time the die had long been cast.

Costello defended this at the time of Browne's resignation by arguing that he had been trying to secure a compromise outside the cabinet — had, indeed, defended Browne's scheme to the doctors as late as 27 November 1950, as part of an attempt to negotiate on his minister's behalf.[43] There were complications involved. Browne was not a member of Costello's party, and Costello for this reason would normally have dealt with MacBride rather than directly with him. Communication between MacBride and Browne was fitful and becoming increasingly strained. However, it is hard to avoid the conclusion that an earlier recourse to cabinet on the whole issue, had Costello or MacBride been willing to adopt this course of action, while it might not have defused the crisis, might have made it possible to engineer a less dramatic resolution of it.

The delay created a vacuum, which was filled by Browne (and Hartnett), who made almost all the critical moves thereafter until early in March 1951, as cabinet colleagues and opponents alike took their eyes off the ball.

This was the general context in which, in July 1950, Noël Browne spoke to the Dáil about the projected Mother and Child Scheme; when he told deputies that a 'tentative scheme has now been prepared, and it will soon be considered by the Irish Medical Association',[44] his information was already a month out of date. It is also important to point out that Browne's own health, or more precisely ill health, was an equally significant part of the context within which the political problems associated with the Mother and Child Scheme were unfolding.

He was ill in December 1949 and January 1950, when Seán MacBride took questions for him in the Dáil. Certainly he was unable to deliver his speech to the Clann Ard-Fheis in May 1950. The absence of any press cuttings of speeches or public statements by him during this period in the GIS series in the National Archives suggests strongly that it was illness that kept him away. Whatever the reason, or reasons, it is remarkable that he attended only eleven of the fifty-one cabinet meetings held between 14 March and 26 September 1950, and had an unbroken run of non-attendances from 14 April to 25 July, although he was on hand to answer questions in the Dáil on 4 June and deliver his estimate speech on 11 June.

It was far from coincidental that he was talking about resignation at this time, not only to his immediate family but to political colleagues. In 1986 he told a researcher that he had indeed offered his resignation to MacBride, or at least asked MacBride to 'move him from Health' and that this was still not publicly known.[45] It would certainly have been possible for MacBride to move Browne, at his own request, to a less demanding ministry on the grounds of ill health; and it would have made it easier to solve the impending Mother and Child controversy without the government losing face. It was an option MacBride must have later regretted not taking but, for the time being, he plainly still regarded Noël Browne as an asset rather than a liability.

It is also striking, and possibly very relevant, that Browne appeared to be, at quite a late stage in these proceedings, under a serious misapprehension about the way in which cabinet government actually worked. On 23 August 1950, at a time when he was attending cabinet meetings only intermittently, one of his civil servants phoned the Department of the Taoiseach to enquire what the quorum was for a cabinet meeting, and whether decisions were taken by majority vote. This was explicitly in reference to a meeting on 15 August, which had been attended by the Taoiseach and only three other ministers — O'Higgins, MacBride and Daniel Morrissey (Minister for Industry and Commerce) — along with the Attorney-General. Browne was told tersely, through his intermediary, Mr Whooley, that there was no such thing as a quorum for a cabinet meeting, and that decisions were taken on the basis of collective responsibility, rather than by majority vote.[46]

The problem about these elements in the equation — the muttering about resignation and the apparent unfamiliarity with cabinet methodology — is that this was a critical period for the Mother and Child Scheme and for the necessary work of securing public and political acceptance for the regulations and the ideas they embodied. The outline of the scheme was completed in June, right in the middle of this period of Browne's prolonged absence from cabinet.

The question of resignation, on health or other grounds, is central to the story, because it brings into sharp focus Browne's view of coalition, and a tension within Clann na Poblachta which had been obscured by the decision to go into government, but never entirely forgotten, about the role of a minority party in any such arrangement. According to Browne, he and MacBride had initially agreed that participation in government would be purely tactical, to be terminated when it suited the Clann best, but that the party leader had subsequently changed his mind. 'MacBride and I had agreed to pull out when we had demonstrated our competence as administrators . . . I had even offered before the Mother and Child Scheme to resign and be replaced by someone like McQuillan in Lands . . . MacBride had gone over to the lawyers in Fine Gael. He disagreed with me that the issue was a good one to break with Fine Gael.'[47]

Whether MacBride had 'agreed to pull out' in any sense that would be accepted by MacBride himself is arguable; but he had certainly had enormous difficulty in persuading the Clann to join the government in the first place. At the end of the negotiations, the party had been committed to supporting a government whose programme included only two specifically Clann proposals: one relating to reafforestation, the other to the TB campaign. Both objectives had been in large measure achieved, or at least satisfactorily inaugurated, by the end of 1950. What was the party to do now?

Browne's view, which he maintained consistently, was that any minority party should get out when the job had been done. This was a point of view which had a certain crude logic to it, but it ignored the dynamics of cabinet government and raised a larger question: what party would voluntarily enter coalition with a smaller grouping which had declared in advance that it would withdraw its support from government, not because a promise had been broken, but because a promise had been fulfilled? It could well be argued that Clann na Poblachta had used its bargaining position poorly as the government was being formed in 1948; but this reflects on the Clann itself, rather than on the other parties.

The situation now was that MacBride, for all his absences abroad, was patently in it for the long haul and would not go voluntarily. Equally, Noël Browne felt that the Clann was in grave danger of losing its political soul. Each of the contemporary issues therefore has to be seen not just as an issue in itself, but as an element in the internal political struggle which had erupted again within the Clann. Noël Browne, with his close associate Noel Hartnett, was now indisputably operating a double strategy. One strand had as its objective the creation of a free-for-all Mother and Child Scheme; the other had the implicit, and increasingly the explicit, aim of forcing the Clann out of government in order to preserve its ideological purity. Noël Browne's autobiography, which has been hugely influential in determining the general public (and to some extent academic) reading of these events, emphasises the former at the expense of almost completely obscuring the latter. In retrospect, it can more clearly be seen not only that his motives were mixed, but that these objectives were incompatible and that, sooner or later, one of them would have to take precedence over the other. For the time being, however, the internal contradictions were disregarded, and Noël Browne pushed determinedly ahead.

Phase III

He had two obstacles: the doctors and the bishops. The doctors had received his outline of the Mother and Child Scheme in the summer, but it was not until early October that they asked him to meet a deputation. This deputation, on 24 October, asked him if it would be all right to delay the IMA decision until the end of the following month, and he agreed. This request was evidently tactical.

The bishops, in what now looks suspiciously like a pincer movement, wrote formally to Costello on 10 October to express their opposition to the Mother and Child Scheme (and incidentally to other aspects of the Bill which Browne was not unwilling to change). The following day Browne met three bishops — McQuaid, Browne and James Staunton, Bishop of Ferns and secretary to the hierarchy, at Drumcondra. The letter was read over to him and a discussion took place, at the end of which Browne apparently believed that he had satisfied the bishops, but Dr McQuaid, at least, believed that he remained intransigent.

Browne's own account of this meeting is to some extent ambiguous, in that he maintains simultaneously that he had made concessions which, in his view, satisfied the bishops, but that he left the meeting also convinced 'the bishops would support the wealthy consultants'.[48] The most favourable construction to put on this apparent conflict is that Browne considered the sections of his Bill dealing with education in motherhood and the compulsory element in its provisions to be those most important to the bishops. He would not have been alone at this time in believing that bishops were concerned with matters of reproductive morality almost to the exclusion of all other considerations. He was prepared to compromise on these — even to drop them completely, if needs be — and could credibly have assumed that this effectively disposed of the bishops' complaints. He appears to have discounted the bishops' attitude to the means test issue at this stage as one in which they were acting in a subordinate role to the doctors, and thought that they would abandon this once the doctors had been satisfied (or faced down).

A number of other factors suggest that Noël Browne should be given the benefit of the doubt on this issue. Bishops tended to adopt an Olympian attitude in dealing with politicians and indeed with everyone else as well. Their utterances were frequently Delphic; they could quite easily express disapproval in general terms, leaving anxious (or, in Browne's case, combative) politicians in the dark as to precisely what kind of proposal might meet with their approval. The confusion was compounded when he discussed the matter at a meeting he had with Costello the next day. Still believing that he had satisfied the bishops, he was completely at cross purposes with Costello, who appears to have assumed that Browne's assurances covered the entire spectrum of episcopal objections, including the means test issue.

He now went into the next phase of the controversy believing that his main opponents were the doctors. He was at one in this with his advisers in the Department of Health, principally Kennedy and Murray, but he also had one key ally who was to play a critical role in what ensued, both inside the party and outside it. This was the man who had discovered Noël Browne and whose organisational genius had secured political power for MacBride: Noel Hartnett.

For a number of years, Hartnett's home was the gate lodge at Roebuck House, MacBride's handsome residence in Clonskeagh. Politically, he was as Republican as his party leader; he came from a south Kerry family which had been burned out of Kenmare by Free State forces during the Civil War (Hartnett *père* was an old IRB man). His sympathies were with Browne and the younger element in the party, but for the early part of the inter-party government's period in office, his loyalties were undoubtedly also with MacBride. He accompanied the party leader on a propaganda trip to the United States, making a speech in Boston — in the company of other gifted speech-makers such as John F. Kennedy, Mayor Curley and Archbishop Cushing — which, according to MacBride, matched anything the Americans could offer.

This continuing loyalty was despite MacBride's decision not to give Hartnett one of the two Senate seats in his gift. One went to Patrick McCartan; the other — the one Hartnett had half-expected — went to Denis Ireland, a Northern Protestant nationalist. MacBride, admitting that Hartnett had been disappointed by this decision, defended his action many years later on the grounds that it would have smacked of the type of patronage he had attacked during the general election campaign.[49] Such appointments to the Seanad are, of course, whoever their beneficiaries may be, patronage in its purest form, and it was at the very least ungenerous of MacBride to fail to reward his national director of elections in this way. One way or another, disappointment matured into disillusion and, eventually, into opposition.

The only government appointment forthcoming for Hartnett was a directorship of the Irish News Agency, which was eventually set up early in 1950. Conor Cruise O'Brien, who was seconded from his civil service job in MacBride's department to act as managing director of this enterprise, recounts that Hartnett, though 'still formally a member of MacBride's party . . . was in fact at this stage MacBride's deadly enemy'.[50] Hartnett displayed this enmity by proposing a resolution which ran directly counter to MacBride's declared wishes. MacBride had defended the agency in the Dáil against criticisms by Irish journalists by agreeing that it should not engage in the dissemination of 'hot', i.e. current, news in a way which would threaten their livelihood. The other members of the board, unaware of the deterioration of the relationship between Hartnett and his party leader, supported Hartnett's proposal to allow the Agency to disregard this commitment, innocently assuming that he was advancing it with MacBride's tacit approval. MacBride shrank from the proffered confrontation, and left the Agency to O'Brien and Hartnett to run as they wished.

While it undoubtedly suited MacBride in later years to portray Hartnett's actions as motivated solely by personal pique, nobody who knew the man would have believed that his motivation could have been so jejune. He was frustrated, certainly, but he also had a deep loyalty to the Clann and a profound belief, which Browne shared, that it had the potential for radically altering the shape of Irish politics. His role in the unfolding drama is one which has never been fully explored, and was referred to only fleetingly by the person who had good reason to know it best — Noël Browne.

In his autobiography, Browne maintains a certain distance from both Hartnett and the Hartnett–MacBride split. 'I did all in my power to remain detached from their quarrel,' he wrote. And he concluded that Hartnett's decision to resign from the party in February 1951 was an 'essentially self-indulgent, petulant gesture'.[51] Although Browne and Hartnett stayed close for long after 1951, their relationship surviving even the tempestuous period surrounding the formation of the National Progressive Democrats in 1958, a sense of distance seems to have ensued thereafter. Hartnett had a long and painful illness before his death in 1961 and, although nobody in his family spoke publicly about it, friends of theirs noticed a sense of hurt because Noël Browne effectively cut all ties with his former comrade-in-arms, not even visiting him during his final illness. This process continued long after Hartnett's death. In 1986 he brusquely rejected the suggestion by an interviewer that Hartnett had been his political mentor; he was, he said, 'nobody's puppet'. Hartnett, he suggested, had simply been a close colleague of MacBride's who had been discarded by the party leader when he had no further use for him.[52]

As Browne noted in an unpublished fragment of his autobiography, however, 'the role of Hartnett, both in the formation and in the final collapse of the Party, has been under-estimated, as it has also been in the collapse of the first Coalition Government'.[53] A proper understanding of this role involves a closer examination of the relationship between Browne and Hartnett, not only because of the unacknowledged role that Hartnett played in the latter stages of the Mother and Child controversy, but in the light of a number of critically important friendships which Hartnett enjoyed and which were, in turn, harnessed to Noël Browne's chariot.

A month after his meeting with the bishops, the tempo of events quickened. This was on 9 November 1950, when two pivotal events occurred. The first was that Costello gave Browne, for the first time, a copy of the letter from the bishops. The second was that MacBride invited Browne to dinner that evening to discuss their political differences, which had become increasingly apparent in the preceding few months, and in which Hartnett featured prominently.

In his autobiography, Noël Browne maintains that he assumed Costello was giving him the bishops' letter solely as a matter of record, and that, as it pre-dated (by one day) his meeting with the three bishops in Drumcondra, it had been superseded by that discussion and by the understanding he believed had been reached. He did, however, have Kennedy prepare a lengthy memorandum in response to the points made in the letter, and gave it to Costello as the basis for a reply by the Taoiseach. The tone of this memorandum[54] reinforces the view of both Browne and his department that issues other than the means test represented 'the fundamental objection of the Hierarchy to the scheme',[55] and that the concessions he was prepared to make adequately met this objection.

Costello did not send this memorandum on to the bishops for some time thereafter. Browne, on the other hand, assumed that it had been sent. In his speech on Browne's resignation in the Dáil several months later, Costello maintained stoutly that he had, on a number of occasions, informed Browne that his memorandum had not been forwarded to the bishops, because negotiations were ongoing, but he did not specify when he first informed Browne of this. Additionally Browne, in so far as he thought that there might be any substance in the bishops' objections on the question of the means test, was operating on the basis of assurances from a theologian that these objections were based on Catholic social — rather than moral — teaching, and were therefore of a lesser order of significance than the other objections they had raised. At the beginning of November, therefore, Browne had at least some grounds for assuming that his difficulties with the scheme, serious though they were, were not insuperable at least as far as the bishops were concerned.

This was the context in which MacBride now invited Browne to dinner at the Russell Hotel. He had decided to approach Browne, he wrote in a contemporary note, 'before Hartnett got to him'.[56] Although MacBride was unaware of it, he was too late.

There are two versions of what transpired at this dinner. The best-known is Noël Browne's version, published in his autobiography in 1986; the second is MacBride's version, apparently written down that same evening as a memorandum to himself, and sent by him afterwards, in a slightly altered version, to Donal O'Donoghue, chairman of the Clann.[57] The versions have some elements in common, but differ on details. No matter which version one believes, it was an extraordinary meeting between two cabinet colleagues, and one, moreover, in which Noel Hartnett's role featured prominently.

In Browne's version,[58] he said that he warned MacBride of the danger of a split between them over the Mother and Child Scheme; warned that he would publicise any interference by the Church, should it occur; and predicted that MacBride, and the Clann, would pay a price for all of this. MacBride's version is, it must be said, more persuasive, because it is contemporary and because of the factual detail it contains, little of which Browne specifically denied and some of which he confirmed.[59] In this, he claims that he warned Browne of 'intrigues' involving Hartnett, but says Browne riposted that unless MacBride followed his and Hartnett's advice, he would be finished; that Browne threatened to resign; and that he claimed he wished to return to private medical practice anyway.

In MacBride's version, Browne told him calmly that the Clann would soon be wrecked completely, when he resigned.

> *He said . . . that for over a year he had set himself deliberately to pick a row with me. That he had done so on every occasion we met privately and that, having failed in that way, he had decided to do it openly at meetings so as to force an issue with me. If he didn't succeed he could resign and force an issue that way. That he would have done this before now but he wanted to get his Mother and Child Scheme through first, or resign on that issue. That if this did not provide him with an issue upon which to bring down the government he could find another. Now that I knew the truth I should ask him for his resignation and appoint a new Minister for Health.*[60]

There were two other significant aspects of Browne's remarks, as reported by MacBride. One was in relation to Hartnett. If Browne was not speaking on behalf of Hartnett, as this account suggests, he was giving every impression of doing so. Time and again he volunteered Hartnett's name, urging on MacBride the importance of friendship with him, and the value of his advice. The other was in relation to an earlier occasion when Browne had offered to resign when ill (this was presumably during the previous summer) and had been dissuaded by MacBride, who urged him to take more rest.

The conflict of evidence is ultimately not capable of any definitive resolution, but a couple of points might be made. In Browne's favour, it is highly unlikely that he would ever have expressed a wish to go back to 'private' practice. He always detested the fee-for-service aspect of private medical practice, and went to inordinate lengths later to remain a salaried doctor in the public service rather than going into private practice. Browne also denied that anything he said was an announcement of a leadership coup against MacBride. But this does not occur in MacBride's account — it is an interpretation of it by Browne. It is beyond doubt that Browne was critical of MacBride's leadership at the meeting; but this was as part of a general critique whose main burden was that the Clann was finished anyway, in which case the question of who might or might not be its leader was largely academic.

MacBride, on the other hand, was a lawyer. His training would have encouraged him to minimise evidence unfavourable to himself, and maximise evidence wounding to his opponent; but it seems unlikely that he fabricated any part of the conversation either in his contemporary note or in his subsequently published recollection based on this.[61]

One major conflict of evidence relates to the Mother and Child Scheme and the role of the bishops, which Browne insists was crucial to the meeting and which MacBride maintains had little to do with it. If Browne believed that he had actually satisfied the bishops' objections, and that the letter Costello had given him earlier that day had merely been an aide-mémoire, it is hard to see that this topic would have been a centrepiece at the meeting.

It is possible to understand both versions of the meeting if one comes to the conclusion that Browne, while not actually threatening explicitly to wreck the Clann and bring down the government, left MacBride under no illusion that this was a distinct possibility. Browne had in any case made statements of this kind, according to hearsay, to other members of the Clann's National Executive in previous months, notably Michael A. Kelly.[62] And Browne, in January 1951 at a meeting whose minutes he did not subsequently dispute, was to admit at least that he had been intent on picking a row with MacBride for quite some time. Regardless of Browne's actual words on 9 November, the outcome of the meeting was to put MacBride on tenterhooks. Within days, he was circulating his memorandum of their conversation to cabinet colleagues and beginning to work out a strategy for confronting Browne within the Clann. Costello was now directly aware of exactly what was going on within the party. His apparent unwillingness either to confront Browne personally or to urge MacBride to do so created further space in which the controversy could expand.

The evidence is circumstantial and to some extent contested, but it is hard to avoid the conclusion that, by now, Browne's objective of reinvesting Clann na Poblachta with its original political morality was assuming an ever higher priority on his personal agenda. Noel Hartnett, always close to Browne, now became if anything even closer, providing him not only with invaluable moral support but with a set of skills, particularly in drafting documents, which were to become increasingly evident as events gathered pace. Hartnett's friend Brian Walsh, a Fianna Fáil lawyer who was to become a most respected judge of the High Court and later the Supreme Court, was also closely involved as draftsman and adviser during the final stages of the crisis.[63] So was the theologian already mentioned, a friend of both Walsh and Hartnett, whose role will be discussed later.

Between Browne's November meeting with MacBride and the end of the year, the various protagonists were manoeuvring for position. The bishops sat back, content in their belief that although their objections had not yet been met, Catholic loyalty would eventually prevail. Costello in all probability assumed that MacBride was dealing with the problem of Browne. MacBride was in the difficult position of looking for allies in his struggle with Browne in a political party — the Clann — which was totally wedded emotionally and ideologically to Browne's scheme. The doctors were taking an initiative of their own, distributing a questionnaire to their members to which Browne quite reasonably took exception, as it was plainly designed to elicit a hostile response.

There is some evidence, unbelievable as it may seem, that Browne was even considering calling on the hierarchy to express positive support for his scheme. This evidence — which tends to underline his contention that he believed he had effectively satisfied the bishops' objections, at least up to November — comes from the papers of the late Aodh de Blacam.

De Blacam combined a deeply Catholic sensibility with a radical social conscience and a perfervid anti-communism (in which he resembled at least to some extent his party leader Seán MacBride), and his papers contain a letter drafted for Browne to send to McQuaid on the Mother and Child Scheme.[64] The draft is undated, but internal evidence makes it clear that it was written on 25 November 1950, some six weeks after Browne met the bishops.

The letter took as its starting point an article in that day's *Irish Times* in which the paper's anonymous medical correspondent assailed Browne's Health Bill as 'State medicine' deriving, through British example, from a Russian origin. 'The Custom House', the article concluded, 'looks to the Kremlin.' De Blacam's draft reply, speaking in Browne's persona, observes:

> *I am obliged to take a serious view of this attack on our policy in regard to health services — and cannot dismiss it as a mere journalistic squib — because I have cause to suspect that it is designed deliberately to prejudice Catholic opinion against the Mother and Child provisions which are due to come into force early in the new year . . . The essence of the impending Mother and Child provisions is that the State will ensure to all mothers and children in the State, and not to downright necessitous cases alone, free pre-natal and post-natal care of the best standard available. Payment to physicians will be made on a capitation basis. I think it can be safely affirmed that the need for such benefits is not confined to the poor. Most wage-earners, while not ranking as 'necessitous', find the expense of due maternity care a heavy burden . . . All who think with me (and this means the whole of the legislators who enacted the Irish law) are persuaded that State care of mothers and children on this basis is in no way Communistic. Rather, indeed, we hold that such measures are a safeguard against Communism, since they give the lie to propagandists who represent the Communistic countries as more careful of the people than free countries like our own. In my judgement, the success of the present effort to defeat our Irish measures for the care of mother and child would be an indirect but most effective victory for Communistic agitation.*
>
> *Your Grace will appreciate, I am sure, the sincerity of our desire to establish and maintain a truly Christian social order. For this reason, I appeal for a definition of the proper function of the State in regard to health services. I look to your Grace to vindicate our principles and policy in this regard, thereby checking at the outset a propaganda which is calculated to taint the good name of Christian administrators, to impugn their motives, and to frustrate their endeavours. When your Grace has had time to consider these submissions, I would like to call in person for a fuller discussion of the matter.*

The reason for quoting this document at such length hardly needs elaboration. It was written by a close associate of Browne. Although it was evidently never sent — a copy of it would certainly have been in McQuaid's archives had this been the case, together with McQuaid's reply — it is all but inconceivable that it would not have been discussed between de Blacam, Browne and possibly Hartnett. If it was, the obvious conclusion is that it was, for Browne, a bridge too far at this stage, although, as we will see, it mirrors in some respects the position he would adopt in relation to both Archbishop McQuaid and Bishop Staunton several months later.

As the temperature rose, Costello felt that he ought to provide some leadership, and, with O'Higgins, attempted to mediate between Browne and the doctors at a meeting on 27 November 1950, just before the date on which the doctors had intimated they would respond formally to Browne's scheme (they later postponed a decision yet again, secure in the knowledge that the bishops were in the front line on the issue). The 27 November meeting was critical for two reasons. One was because, although Costello and his colleagues actually supported Browne in their discussions with the doctors, the strength of the medical opposition led the Taoiseach to re-examine the whole question afterwards, and effectively marked the beginning of a change of heart on his part and on that of his other cabinet colleagues. The second was that Browne at first suspiciously misread the nature of Costello's intervention and assumed that it was an attempt to undermine him and his negotiating position. He was later disabused of this notion, and apologised to Costello for entertaining it; but the seeds of distrust were already germinating rapidly.

Early in December, when no reply had been received from the IMA, Browne pressed the Association again, only to be told that it had sent its views, instead, to the hierarchy. By Christmas, the IMA was telling the minister that it was preparing an alternative scheme of its own, but refused his request to expedite its consideration of this matter. As the Association temporised, Browne was running out of time, and out of patience. The endgame was about to begin.

CHAPTER FIVE

Endgame

B y the beginning of 1951, Browne's opponents were marshalling their forces, but there was, at this stage, little appreciation within the Clann as a whole of the crisis that was developing in its upper echelons. The December 1950–January 1951 issue of the Clann *Bulletin* dealt with the Mother and Child Scheme in some detail, stating firmly that the scheme should be non-contributory and without a means test. MacBride, however, increasingly concerned by the possible fallout from his deteriorating relationship with Browne and Hartnett, and conscious of the fact that his survival in government depended on a resolution of the problem, was the first to move. He called a meeting with Donal O'Donoghue and Noël Browne on 4 January to try to bring matters to a head.[1] At that meeting, Browne completely denied having threatened to resign at the Russell Hotel dinner with MacBride, but admitted saying that he was systematically trying to pick a row with him, at first privately and subsequently in the open. The heated meeting — Browne frequently accused MacBride of lying — ended after three hours with Browne charging that any split in the Clann would be MacBride's responsibility, but agreeing to reconsider the situation and, in the meantime, to co-operate with his party leader.

Matters then accelerated rapidly. At a meeting of the Clann National Executive two days later Browne gave a lengthy account of the Mother and Child Scheme which would, he hoped, become law within the next few weeks. This was the point at which it appeared, even if only briefly, that Browne and Hartnett's anti-coalition strategy might actually work. MacBride was clearly only barely in control of the situation. The meeting congratulated Browne on the scheme, and the following motion was proposed by Noel Hartnett and seconded by Con Lehane:

> That the Ard-Chomhairle instructs the Coiste Seasmhach to consider the advisability of withdrawing at an early date our Ministers from the Coalition Government, and that they report the result of their deliberations to a meeting of the Ard-Chomhairle to be convened not later than February 14th.

Lehane, it should be remembered, was not only the person whose ambitions had been frustrated by Browne's appointment to cabinet three years earlier, but chairman of the Clann parliamentary party. This was an unambiguous challenge to MacBride's authority. It provoked a lengthy discussion, at the end of which Noel Hartnett, presumably because he accepted that he would fail to get a majority, withdrew his motion rather than put it to a vote.[2] It was nonetheless a shot across MacBride's bows which he could not afford to ignore.

In his autobiography, Browne makes much of the role played by Lehane and the older men and of their apparent stranglehold over MacBride. He seems to have ignored the fact that at least some of these people — the 'gunmen' as he used to term them dismissively — were as suspicious of MacBride as he was himself, and were only marginally less hostile to the idea of coalition than the many Republicans who had vanished from the party immediately after the formation of the government in 1948.

Some of these, also, would have had roots in the socialist republicanism of the 1930s, and were therefore more likely allies of Browne in any confrontation with MacBride over the Mother and Child Scheme than he might have been prepared to accept. By underestimating the differences of opinion between them and MacBride, and by regarding them as relics of a bygone era to be despised and even insulted, Browne was yet again cutting himself off from a potentially important source of political support.

Archbishop McQuaid, as it happened, was already planning his own counter-strategy in close collaboration with Costello. They had a telephone conversation on 14 January in which, McQuaid noted the following day, Costello had made no secret of his dissatisfaction with Browne, not least because he foresaw that Browne might resign, carrying away the support of the Clann, and that this would mean the fall of the government. On 16 January, at the hierarchy's standing committee meeting, McQuaid recommended that his fellow bishops should allow the government as much time as possible, because, as he put it, 'I do not consider it advisable to give Dr B. and the Clann the chance of going to the country on the basis that the Bishops destroyed the Mother and Child Scheme for *poor* women and children.' Plainly savouring the prospect of victory, he added: 'I have already broken Dr B's scheme to socialise the cancer services: and my success so far, I say so far, gives excellent grounds for hoping that we can break the free-for-all Mother and Child Scheme.'[3]

McQuaid was unaware that, at least for MacBride, the fact that this was a 'Clann scheme' was now rapidly becoming secondary to the need to ensure his own and the government's survival, and that Noël Browne's objectives were not confined to introducing socialised medicine, but had for some time also encompassed a more urgent, and rather more feasible, project: the political burial of the Clann and its leader. Nor could he have been aware that giving Browne more time (advice which Costello evidently took) actually played into Browne's hands.

This was the context in which Browne made his next move. It was by any standards a major intervention in the controversy, and its significance is heightened by the fact that Browne makes no mention whatsoever of it in his autobiography, despite its very serious implications for his (and MacBride's) membership of the cabinet.

This was the circulation in January 1951 of an anonymous cyclostyled document to many households in Dublin, particularly in the newly built Corporation housing estates in the inner suburbs. Entitled *Is It Needed?*, it began with a quotation from the 1916 Proclamation about cherishing all the children of the nation equally, and argued that 'the poor and their children are the ones who get hurt under voluntarily organised private enterprise'. It fulminated against the medical profession in terms which immediately hinted at its inspiration, describing some of them as 'scum'.

> *Fitzwilliam Square would like us to retain the mentality epitomised in the supercilious condescension of the 'big house charity to the dirty peasant retainers' — we'll have no part of it . . . One of the reasons why doctors are objecting is that for the first time they will begin to pay income tax. It's hard luck! But isn't it about time we started to find out what they are actually 'making', especially the ones in the 'Squares' and the 'Crescents'? . . . We all agree that the doctor must get a fair wage and we will give it to him but he will get a fair wage, not the profit of a black marketeer.*[4]

Among the major factors influencing Irish doctors in their fear of 'State medicine' were contemporaneous developments in Britain, of which Irish doctors would have been only too aware; they had seen Bevan defeat their colleagues across the Irish Sea, and were apprehensive about the possibility of the same fate befalling them. The doctors may also have been apprehensive about the changing role of the Department of Finance. Originally opposed to initiatives suggested by Dr Con Ward because they would have involved the creeping introduction of what it saw as socialised medicine, Finance had now become even more anxious — not about the Mother and Child Scheme itself but about the cost implications of a fee-for-service method of payment, which it saw as allowing doctors to write their own cheques on the State's coffers; the department was angling for a more manageable (from its point of view) capitation grant approach. The doctors were, however, conscious of the fact that, in tandem with the bishops, they were in a much stronger position than their British counterparts. Interestingly, however, many young Irish doctors, stifled by the low income levels and lack of opportunities for advancement at home, were to emigrate to Britain precisely during this period, often permanently, in search of a more meaningful and financially rewarding career under Bevan's despised scheme.

News of the pamphlet did not take long to spread into the upper reaches of government, and the Minister for Defence, Dr T.F. O'Higgins, was incensed, describing it as 'a foul sheet of lunatic libel . . . written by an unknown scribe and circulated by an invisible agency'.[5] What particularly upset him, it appears, was an 'insinuation' by Noël Browne to John A. Costello that this document might even have been circulated as part of a 'black propaganda' exercise by the IMA itself, in which O'Higgins was an office-holder, and Costello's apparent willingness to consider this as a possible explanation.[6] Costello never spoke publicly about this document, and there is only hearsay evidence to support this version of events, but the speed with which the IMA moved to exonerate itself at O'Higgins's behest — and, in the process, to establish as far as possible the origins of the document — speaks volumes for the organisation's sensitivity on this issue.

The resources of the Irish Medical Association were applied to this task. A considerable amount of espionage was carried out by both sides. At least one highly placed member of the IMA was giving information privately to Browne about the Association's views and plans; likewise, there was a mole in the Department of Health, who was supplying the IMA with information. Neither has ever been identified.[7]

The Association's secretary, P.J. Delaney, hired a private detective for £100 to ascertain the source of the document. The first evidence, however, came at an IMA council meeting when Dr Jack Sheehan said that he was actually a member of Clann na Poblachta, and had in this capacity been present at a meeting in Dún Laoghaire where Hartnett had distributed copies of the document with instructions that they were to be burned afterwards. Meanwhile, the detective had followed up leads pointing to Hartnett and to Browne.

One IMA member, Dr Nuala Sheehan, reported that she had been having coffee in Robert Roberts' café in Grafton Street when she had heard two men discussing the document, saying that now T.C.J. O'Connell, a surgeon prominent in the IMA campaign against the scheme, had a copy of the document, 'the cat was out of the bag'. The detective brought her down to the Four Courts, where she picked out Hartnett and 'a solicitor from Co. Offaly' as the men she had seen. Pursuing his enquiries further in the Custom House itself, the detective came across a girl in the copy room who had been fined for losing stencils, and was aggrieved at this. She led them to a porter who, 'with some encouragement', brought the detective to the bins where the missing stencils were found.[8] James Deeny was to claim later that even his desk had been ransacked by an anonymous hand.[9]

The hunt was over — but if the document had originated in the Department of Health, did this mean the minister was the author? The best information available on the issue comes in the record of a speech MacBride made a couple of months later at a meeting of the Clann National Executive, in which he referred for the first time to the anonymous document and to a discussion he had with Browne about it shortly after the IMA had challenged the minister directly to say whether or not he was the author. At that point, according to MacBride, Browne

> did not want to stand over the document. He felt that on the one hand it would make the position with the Mother and Child Scheme more difficult and he was not prepared to take credit for the document because of its intemperate language. I felt that it would be unwise for him to deny knowledge of the document as it might be traced back to him. It was agreed that he would disassociate himself from the circulation of the document.[10]

In the event, Browne did precisely that, deploring the way in which the document had been circulated, but being careful not to deny the central charge that he had been its author. Few people doubted that he was. John Whyte, author of the seminal *Church and State in Modern Ireland*, believed that this had been the case, as did Ruth Barrington, whose study of the origins and development of the health services in Ireland is the authoritative work in this field. A contemporary observer in the American Embassy — although probably misled about MacBride's role — noted: 'The Embassy has learned on reliable authority that the anonymous document was in fact distributed with the full, prior knowledge of Dr Browne, and presumably, of Mr Seán MacBride, and that he read it to several members of the Clann, as well as to some doctors with whom he is friendly, several days before its distribution.'[11]

An irony in all of this was that T.C.J. O'Connell, a son of the former Labour Party leader T.J. O'Connell, TD, regarded Browne in at least some sense as a friend, and had actually campaigned for him in Dublin South-East in 1948. Throughout the controversy he remained on first name terms with Browne, who, he said, showed little understanding of general practice, and failed to realise that it was medically wrong to have different doctors looking after different members of the family. The main fear of the profession, he believed, was that the doctors would become 'State employees'. Nonetheless, at one point he went privately with Dr Bob Collis to see Browne in an attempt to broker a deal, without success. Thirty years later, he was still expressing the belief that — the Mother and Child Scheme notwithstanding — Browne was the best Minister for Health the country had ever had.[12]

But was Browne the author of the document to which O'Higgins, O'Connell and the IMA en masse had taken such exception? The more likely possibility is that, although Browne evidently committed the resources of his department to its production, Noel Hartnett also had a major role in drafting it. Its style is forensic, as it poses questions, one after another, and then answers them with a mixture of cogent argument and pithy abuse. It is designed explicitly to appeal to a working-class and lower-middle-class electorate, in the hope that this would build a groundswell of popular and electoral support for the scheme which would outflank the cabinet and perhaps even the doctors. In the event, it was a serious miscalculation on both counts.

It was not only a miscalculation; it introduced into the government a serious breach of faith which involved not only Browne but MacBride. If Browne, in the full knowledge of the origins of the document, allowed or encouraged Costello to believe that others were responsible for it, it was an economy with the truth which boded ill for his role in this or indeed any future government. Costello, once he had been apprised of the outcome of the IMA investigation, would have expected MacBride to deal with Browne — but MacBride, on his own admission, was conniving with Browne to sidestep the issue of knowledge and authorship. There was now a deviousness and dissimulation at the heart of government which spelt out its death sentence as unmistakably as anything that happened in the following weeks. And Browne's decision to avoid this episode completely, in his own version of what was and what was not important about the Mother and Child Scheme, inevitably raises questions about his reliability as an authority on some of the other issues involved.

It is significant that the circulation of the document was followed almost immediately by a row between Browne and MacBride about financial matters. On 5 February Browne reacted sharply to a request that he reduce the estimates for his department on the understanding that he would be allowed to bring in a supplementary estimate later to make up any deficiency, particularly in the Mother and Child Scheme. Browne claimed to see this relatively unexceptional cooking of the government books as an attempt to use a procedural device to undermine funding for the scheme, and threatened to resign. The context clearly indicates that this was an early occasion on which Browne perceived an issue which might be used to bring down MacBride, but withdrew when he — and presumably his supporters — realised that the arcane details of the government's accounting system could hardly be expected to generate much public enthusiasm for an election.

Three days later, he did resign — but from the Clann's standing committee, not from the cabinet. On the same day, Noel Hartnett resigned from all his positions in the party and from the party itself. Neither Browne nor Hartnett mentioned the Mother and Child Scheme in the context of the rationale for their resignations.

Hartnett's resignation was ostensibly on the general grounds that Clann na Poblachta had virtually abandoned its fundamental political or social philosophy, and on the particular grounds of his objection to the appointment of a government supporter to a sub-post office, in Baltinglass, Co. Wicklow, an unsavoury piece of patronage which he and Browne had failed to get MacBride to oppose.[13] He did not, however, release his own resignation letter to the press until 15 April, after Browne's resignation as minister, when it was plainly designed to add to the momentum created by this cataclysmic event.

Browne's resignation from the standing committee was prompted, according to his letter, by the machinations over the estimate for his department, and was accompanied by a blistering attack on MacBride for 'unwarranted attacks . . . from . . . a man whom I had believed was both my loyal colleague and my friend'.[14] An article in *The Irish Times* shortly afterwards claimed that the resignations (including Browne's from the standing committee) were evidence of a split in the party. MacBride tried unsuccessfully to stem the flow of rumours, with a forthright speech in Cavan and a private letter to *Irish Times* editor Bertie Smyllie, in which he stated baldly: 'There was an attempt at a Palace revolution — led by our friend N.H. It failed. He resigned. His resignation was unanimously accepted.'[15] He tried equally fruitlessly to get Browne to write to *The Irish Times* to deny any split.[16]

The timing and apparent co-ordination of the two resignations puts quite a different gloss on the dismissive assessment of Hartnett's decision in Noël Browne's autobiography as petulant and ill-judged.[17] Indeed the two men became, if anything, even closer in the hectic days and weeks that followed. By the end of February the fallout from Noel Hartnett's resignation was still being felt, at least in Clonskeagh, where MacBride and Hartnett were writing to each other from opposite ends of the avenue of Roebuck House and, occasionally, meeting late at night to trade insults. One such meeting was characterised, in Hartnett's view, by MacBride's 'hysterical frenzy'; or, if you accepted MacBride's version, by Hartnett's propensity for 'uttering denunciations and threats of libel actions'.[18] By early March, according to diplomatic observers, 'there was, inside the Cabinet, considerable controversy over Dr Browne's future in the Government'.[19]

The first letter from the IMA giving its preliminary views on Browne's scheme was received in the Department of Health on 3 February, some eight months after the draft scheme had been sent out. Browne was clearly being paid back in kind for his earlier refusal to consult the Association, but the stakes were now higher. Further delays were either negotiated or engineered by the IMA, culminating in a letter telling the minister that no decision would be taken before its central council meeting on 8 March.

These delaying tactics were intimately related to actions by the bishops. These actions, as has been well documented by James Deeny and Ruth Barrington, were to some extent supported by the public polemics of a doctor, James McPolin, who had developed an interest in theology and who was at this time expounding his ideas in a series of articles in various publi-cations, including the 1947 issue of the IMA journal in which James Deeny had publicised his findings on tuberculosis. McPolin, originally from Belfast, was, at best, an odd character. He had, in Deeny's opinion, been guilty of such dereliction of duty in his work as the Limerick County Medical Officer for Health that he would, in the ordinary course of events, have merited dismissal. The fact that he kept his position, even after having incurred the enmity of such a powerful opponent as Deeny, speaks of support or protection, explicit or implicit, at a higher level. McPolin publicly claimed in 1951, at the height of the crisis, that he had received a letter from the Department of Health threatening him with dismissal because he had 'written an article for a local newspaper'.[20] This could not have been at Deeny's instigation, as he had left the department the previous year. Browne's forced resignation shortly afterwards saved McPolin at the last minute.

McPolin's views, ultra-orthodox though they were, might not in them-selves have been significant if they had not had fertile ground in which to grow. The context was related partly to the nature of Church–State relations at the time, and partly to a set of assumptions shared by all senior politicians, including Noël Browne, about the need to defer to ecclesiastical authority in certain areas. The basic difference between politicians — and the spectrum was not very wide — was not about whether deference was due, but how much.

The Catholic Church had, in a sense, had a relatively easy ride with the Free State government of William Cosgrave. Even here, however, there had been a ruffling of feathers over the 1930 Vocational Education Act. De Valera, when he came to power in 1932, had provided some evidence that personal piety was not necessarily a guarantee of subservience; his outmanoeuvring of critical members of the hierarchy on some contentious clauses of his 1937 Constitution (although he ceded to their views readily enough in others) was an indication that he could not be relied on in all circumstances. Some sources close to the hierarchy had indeed been expecting a major confrontation between Church and State at some stage; but they expected it in education, not in health.[21]

The hierarchy itself was, much more than it is today, fundamentally a collection of independent republics, some of them far more powerful than others. Many of the bishops, particularly those with small rural dioceses, were little more than glorified parish priests. They were pastors of varying degrees of competence, with little or no interest in national affairs; few of their names have come down to us for reasons good or bad. There was, too, a strong principle of territoriality. Clerical protocol dictated that bishops did not interfere in each other's dioceses; there was even a detailed set of rules — for the most part increasingly ignored, except by sticklers for detail like

McQuaid — governing the extent to which any cleric could cross diocesan boundaries with impunity. In these circumstances, the hierarchy itself was very loosely organised, and for years lacked anything remotely resembling an efficient secretariat. When Dr William Conway became Archbishop of Armagh in 1963, for instance, he was unable to find in the archives of the archdiocese any copy of the controversial letter sent by the bishops to de Valera in October 1947 about the Health Act of that year.[22]

A loosely organised and mostly uninterested hierarchy was, in turn, easily persuadable by its most articulate and forceful members. Browne described them as 'the political bishops',[23] and to a large extent he was correct. But how correct was he in assuming that the Archbishop of Dublin, Dr McQuaid, was effectively his chief opponent?

The historian John Whyte, who interviewed many of the key figures in this controversy for his influential if cautious book on Church–State relations, came privately to the conclusion that Bishop Browne of Galway had at least as significant a role as McQuaid.[24] He was the author of the hierarchy's first letter. He would also, in his former capacity as a Maynooth professor, have tutored a number of other members of the hierarchy, particularly those from small rural dioceses — in contrast to McQuaid, whose pre-episcopal history was confined to Blackrock College. In his autobiography, Noël Browne characterises his namesake as a bon vivant, even a gourmand, and something of a buffoon; but this may have been seriously to underestimate this particular opponent. 'Browne's strong convictions', Whyte noted later, 'came out well in my interview with him. He is completely Bourbon on the issue; is serenely convinced that the hierarchy did quite the right thing. (Which of course made him all the easier to interview, because he didn't think he had anything to be ashamed of.)'[25] He was also more prominent than any other bishop, in the post-resignation controversy, in defending the hierarchy's stance.

What then of McQuaid? Unlike Browne of Galway, he kept his head well down in public, except in so far as he gave permission to Costello to publish details of their exchanges as part of Costello's defence of his position in the Dáil. His recently released archives, however, which were not available to Whyte when he wrote his work, and which McQuaid does not even appear to have referred back to prior to his interview with Whyte in 1969, give a unique insight not only into the organisational role he played in the crisis, but into his own motivation for the stance he took.

His organisational skills were an important part of the total response. At the level of the hierarchy itself, he made sure at every juncture that procedures were followed, that documents were transmitted in time for proper consideration, and that the troops were marshalled effectively. On a personal level, he used his close relationship with Costello to the full, sometimes meeting him or talking with him on the telephone several times in the same day, and recording these discussions with a clarity which gives them powerful force as a contemporary record, often in contrast to the more poorly organised recollections of his principal opponent more than three decades later. This is not to say that McQuaid's version of events is not also, in its own way, self-serving; but the fact that it is a record written within hours — sometimes within minutes — of the events it describes gives it an immediacy and a credibility which is hard to discount.

At this stage the bishops were still — not least in line with the advice they had been given by McQuaid at their January meeting — holding their fire. Paddy Kennedy was anxious. He had warned Browne to be very careful in his dealings with the hierarchy, and with McQuaid in particular. A very devout and convinced Catholic himself, he nevertheless totally disagreed with the stance being taken by the bishops. At one stage he went on his own initiative to St Patrick's College, Maynooth, where he discussed the matter with someone — never identified — who supported his belief that what the department was doing was consonant with Catholic morality.[26]

Browne may have been misled by this apparent inactivity on the part of the bishops; unknown to him, McQuaid and Costello met to discuss the issue some seven times between the hierarchy's two standing committee meetings on 16 January and 3 April.[27] The archbishop was now aware from these conversations not only that Costello and his Fine Gael, Labour and Clann na Talmhan colleagues had abandoned Browne, but that MacBride had done so as well. On 3 March *The Irish Times* asked pointedly why MacBride had withdrawn his support from the Minister for Health. A week later, they reported that Browne was now isolated, in no small part due to his own stubbornness, but 'if he goes, something clean, something pure, something rare will go too'.[28]

Events were now to develop at a speed which gave the bishops no option but to move swiftly to defend their territory. At the beginning of March, Browne finally decided that he had had enough, and launched a final blitzkrieg, a multi-pronged offensive which was a desperate, but to some extent calculated, last throw. It will be remembered that 8 March was the day on which the IMA had told him it would be coming to a final decision on his scheme, and this was clearly a significant factor in his timing. He issued a statement on 5 March saying that he had broken off negotiations with the Association as agreement was plainly impossible of achievement.[29] He had simultaneously prepared an attractive pamphlet outlining many details of the proposed Mother and Child Scheme (much of which had not received the approval of the Department of Finance for the potential expenditure involved), and distributed it widely on 6 March, including sending a copy to every member of the Catholic hierarchy. His department had prepared a major series of newspaper advertisements extolling the virtues of the scheme, which appeared as the pamphlet was reaching people through the post. Finally, in an attempt to outflank the IMA opposition — only some 800 of the total 1,900 IMA members had expressed active opposition to the scheme in the Association's internal poll, and about 700 more doctors were not members of the IMA — he had written individually to every medical practitioner in the country inviting them to signify their assent in principle to the scheme, subject to final agreement on methods of payment.[30]

McQuaid, alerted to what he now believed was a serious misunderstanding of the position by Browne — or a challenge to his authority, which was of course even worse — replied immediately to the minister with an icy clarity 'lest our position go by default'.[31] He underlined his contention that he had not agreed to the scheme at their meeting the previous October, and proceeded to 'reiterate each and every objection made by me on that occasion'.

The day on which Browne was given McQuaid's riposte — 8 March — was as significant in its own way as was 9 November 1950. MacBride had arranged for a peace conference to take place involving himself, Browne and William Norton, just before he left for Paris and the United States.[32]

Norton — prompted by both Costello and MacBride — was most active in attempting to engineer a compromise. His final best suggestion was that the scheme would apply only to those families with an income of under £1,000 a year, or just over £20,000 in 2000 terms. This offer was never seriously entertained by Browne. Louie O'Brien, Seán MacBride's long-time personal secretary, maintained steadfastly that Browne had accepted this compromise at a late night meeting with MacBride in Iveagh House which she had attended, and that Browne had stormed back into MacBride's office the following morning to renege on the commitment.[33]

Her recollection on this point is questionable, however, not least because MacBride, lawyer that he was, would not have hesitated to advance this at the time and subsequently in his critique of Browne, had it actually happened. And any temptation that Browne might have felt to accept a compromise at any time would have brought him up against a most unambiguous threat from his closest associate, Noel Hartnett. Ten days after the fateful meeting in the Russell Hotel the previous November, at which Browne had failed to convince his party leader of Hartnett's indispensability, Hartnett told MacBride he had warned Browne that if he compromised in any way on the Mother and Child Scheme he would 'denounce him publicly'.[34] The only evidence we have for this is a memorandum of the conversation by Seán MacBride, written in the heat of the controversy and within hours of it taking place. In spite of the fact that it is the evidence of a hostile witness, there is no particular reason to suppose it was fabricated. Coming from Hartnett, it was not a warning that Browne could have safely ignored.

Browne was handed Dr McQuaid's letter at lunchtime on 8 March by his private secretary.[35] He immediately decided not to go to the planned meeting with Norton and went instead, with the letter in his pocket, to the Radio Éireann studios, where he broadcast in passionate and fluent English and Irish about the benefits of his scheme. The following day the newspapers were full of the dramatic advertisements extolling its virtues.

In MacBride's absence Browne continued his offensive, aimed at both the doctors and the bishops. The Department of Finance, however, alarmed by the wealth of uncosted detail in the booklet, wrote immediately to Kennedy conveying the minister's protests at 'publication of the details without obtaining his prior approval' and noting that 'such publicity is all the more objectionable as the scheme now announced differs substantially from those previously sent to this Department'.[36] On 14 March this was followed up by a terse note directly from McGilligan to Browne, expressing Finance's concern at the fact that the scheme he had announced on 8 March, and which McGilligan had now fully assessed, would be 'much more costly in the earlier years than was previously estimated'.[37]

On the same day, after getting this note, Browne went directly to Costello to try to persuade him to convene a special cabinet meeting for that evening in order to commit an additional £30,000 to the Mother and Child Scheme. This was the figure which Kennedy had been trying to persuade Finance would be the only additional cost if private practitioners were brought into the scheme, as Browne now agreed, in order to undermine the opposition of the medical profession. He told the Taoiseach:

> If I get the £30,000 I will have the doctors killed on Sunday . . . it will be finished for all time . . . the private medical practitioners are meeting on Sunday and I believe that if I get the £30,000 the controversy will be at an end. The doctors will be killed and beaten but if I do not get the money now there will be trouble from the doctors.[38]

There were, however, a number of problems about Browne's tactics in this regard, prescinding entirely from the extraordinary violence of his language. One was that his figure was a hopeless underestimate. The Finance estimate for the additional cost of the measures included in his booklet was £530,000; challenged to justify the lower estimate, one of the department's assistant secretaries, John Darby, had telephoned Finance on 8 March to increase the estimate of the additional money needed to £309,000.[39] It was a long way from £530,000, but it was much closer to the Finance figure than it was to the utterly unrealistic £30,000 which Browne was still using in his appeal to Costello a week later.

Regardless of the money, there were other difficulties. Browne had, as early as 1948, alienated the potentially vital constituency of dispensary doctors by inviting aggrieved patients of theirs to complain directly to him. He had been increasingly open about his desire to see a gradual socialisation of the medical profession, for instance saying in tones of withering sarcasm to a meeting of the Dublin Rotary Club that he had never known patients whose treatment was free to feel that 'their physical or moral welfare was in any way impaired by being denied the privilege of the money transaction with their doctor'.[40] On 5 April 1951 James Dillon, who had by that stage abandoned a brief attempt at mediation which is dealt with later in this section, went so far as to remind Costello of a statement he remembered Browne making to the effect that he was 'determined to have State medicine'.[41]

This fear was common to all Browne's medical opponents. He had also put himself in a cleft stick, attacking what he implied was the venality of the medical profession, and simultaneously (by asking Costello for an emergency allocation of money for the scheme) identifying it as the factor which would enable him to solve his political problems. By continually raising the spectre (as the doctors saw it) of a wholly State medical service — an issue which was really quite distinct from those involved in the Mother and Child Scheme — he was upping the ante for himself, and exciting alarm and despondency in equal proportions in the other medical constituency whose goodwill was essential, the private practitioners.

These can easily be seen, at least in retrospect, as major tactical errors, especially if one assumes that he still had realistic hopes of a settlement at this stage and was not simply using the controversy to undermine MacBride. In later years, there was a certain ambiguity about his own interpretation of these tactics. Although he generally maintained that he had never intended to bring down the government on the issue, he told an interviewer in 1986 that he felt the row was 'an excellent issue on which to go to the country; he spent a year making it one'.[42] The logic of this position is clear: if the government was not prepared to go to the country on the issue, he now had no alternative other than resignation and the precipitation of a crisis, however much he might subsequently have shied away from this analysis of his options. In so far as anyone's motives can be assessed at this remove in time from the events concerned, the most likely explanation seems to be that at this point, and possibly even for some time beforehand, the second strand of his approach — the destruction of the government in order to restore the vision and the idealism of Clann na Poblachta — was the issue dominating his strategy.

Costello, who refused his request for the additional funds, told him bluntly on the same occasion that the bishops had not been satisfied, and that no scheme which failed to get their approval would get through the cabinet. In later years, Browne maintained that this was the first occasion on which this had been made clear to him. MacBride, on the other hand, argued that Browne had known this since January, or early February at the latest. Costello, in his Dáil speech on Browne's resignation, told the House he had informed Browne orally on several occasions that his draft reply to the hierarchy had still not been sent. If one accepts Browne's surprise as genuine — and this is difficult enough — it could only have been on the basis of an altogether unrealistic assessment of the value of the advice he was getting from other clerical quarters, an obsession with the opposition of the medical profession which blotted out all other considerations, or some combination of both.

Be that as it may, he now attempted to strengthen his position by dividing the hierarchy, or at least securing some measure of episcopal approval for the scheme. In this he was assisted, with the best of intentions, by his cabinet colleague James Dillon, the Minister for Agriculture, who was still at this stage an Independent, and had somewhat heterodox views on the application of Catholic moral teaching to certain social issues.

Dillon's legal challenge to the 1947 Health Act had queried the constitutionality of some of its sections, particularly those dealing with compulsory inspection of children and the education of mothers. On the question of the Mother and Child Scheme, however, he was at least partly, and temporarily, on Browne's side. As part of his campaign on the 1947 Act, he had even written to Pope Pius XII to ask if it was contrary to the natural law to have a mother and child health scheme without a contribution from the insured person. He received a formal acknowledgment of his letter, and was invited to call to the papal nunciature, where a priest informed him that the Holy See did not like giving rulings on general issues, as this was contrary to its practice, and asked if he could state a particular case. In the event, he never took it any further.

Remembering the events of 1951 some fifteen years later,[43] Dillon said that he thought the bishops had been badly handled. He had evidently discussed the case with the archbishops of Westminster and Liverpool. Based on what they had told him he would, he said, have suggested to the Irish bishops that they should contact their British counterparts, 'whose house-keepers were looked after under a non-contributory scheme, and ask them how they squared their consciences with it'. He thought better of offering this advice in public, or to his colleague in the Department of Health. He did, however, contact Archbishop Walsh of Tuam and ask him whether he would see Browne 'and get him to be reasonable'. Walsh replied: 'Ask him to call on me, and I'll be delighted to talk over the whole thing with him, quietly and off the record. Then I can have a word with McQuaid and Browne, and see if we can't settle it.'[44] But Browne rushed off to see Walsh on 17 March[45] without having made an appointment, and when he got to Tuam the bishop was away; the meeting never took place, and indeed, to judge from a subsequent letter from Walsh to McQuaid at the end of the crisis, it is doubtful whether it would have been helpful.[46]

There was, however, an additional clerical complication which contributed to a misunderstanding on Noël Browne's part about the nature of opposition to his scheme by the hierarchy as a whole. This was his relationship with the Bishop of Clonfert, John Dignan, the author of a scheme for social insurance which was extremely progressive in character, whom Browne had met on a number of occasions, and in whose diocese he had opened a sanatorium. Finding Walsh away, Browne diverted to Loughrea, where he found Dignan at home and had a private conversation with him. This clearly convinced him, at the very least, of Dignan's support for his scheme, and he came back to Dublin 'cock-a-hoop'.[47]

The problem, as James Dillon knew but Browne did not, was that Dignan was possibly the least influential advocate he could have had on the bench of bishops. In Dillon's assessment, his appointment to the episcopate in 1924 had been an act of revenge by a Vatican Curial official, Mgr Luzio, who had visited the country during the Civil War and had been snubbed by the Irish bishops. Dignan, Dillon thought, had the capacity to be 'a thorn in the flesh of others' and was 'a wild, irresponsible kind of person who was delighted to embroil Browne with Bishops Browne and McQuaid, but didn't help him to get out of the impasse'.[48] The truth is probably slightly less picturesque. Dignan certainly embarrassed his fellow bishops by making statements of a pro-Republican kind, even at his episcopal ordination, but this did not necessarily mean that he supported the IRA or even that Luzio had been primarily responsible for his appointment. There was certainly concern in Rome about the bishops' generally hostile attitude towards Republicans, but this was due more to anxiety about the pastoral consequences of wholesale excommunication than to any deep sympathy with the Republican cause, especially armed Republicanism; and Mgr John Hagan, the Rector of the Irish College in Rome, who shared this view, would have had more of a say in Dignan's appointment than Luzio.[49]

Noël Browne went into battle, therefore, under serious misapprehensions about both the strength of his allies and the determination of his opponents. But he was also, in the course of the controversy, to give hostages to fortune in the shape of undertakings to Archbishop McQuaid and Bishop Staunton, which seriously qualify the interpretation he subsequently put on his resignation and which were not fully revealed until the opening of the McQuaid archives many years later.

On Wednesday, 21 March, he attempted to issue, through the Government Information Bureau, a statement describing the Mother and Child Scheme as a 'Government' scheme. Forewarned by the Bureau, Costello ordered the issuing of the statement to be halted. When asked by an angry Browne why he had done this, he said: 'Because I am the Taoiseach.'[50] He told Browne directly that no scheme would be implemented in any shape or form until the bishops' objections had been met; at around the same time, clearly exasperated, he was telling McQuaid that even if the bishops agreed, he would not stand over any scheme which had not been agreed by the doctors.

The following afternoon a suddenly — and from the bishops' point of view unexpectedly — contrite Noël Browne came to see McQuaid at his own request. Only one version of the meeting is extant — that recorded by McQuaid himself.[51]

> Dr B. began by 'abject apology' for troubling me on such a day. Described his notes and impressions concerning our interview in October. I told him exactly how he had behaved. He was very surprised and apologised, saying he had been very nervous. But he was convinced that all points had been most happily cleared and T(aoiseach) after his interview gave him same impression. The letter was delivered to Taoiseach in November. He was amazed to find that Taoiseach had never sent onto Hierarchy his answer. To all this I made no comment. Dr B. asked me to believe he wanted to be only a good Catholic and to accept fully Church's teaching. I accepted that attitude. Dr B. asked me if scheme was in my opinion contrary to Catholic teaching.

McQuaid explained his objections to the scheme — the critical one, in this context, being that the free-for-all scheme was 'an unjust tax' because such a tax could not be regarded as reasonably necessary in view of the common good.

> Dr B then said: well, that is the end. It will be very serious for the Government and the people and me. I shall leave the Cabinet and political life. (I interjected 'it need not be.' He answered: 'but it is. I had thought I could make it different.'). It is a life I was forbidden to take up, for I was given only a few years to live, and I have a wife and two children.

McQuaid agreed to a request from the minister that the bishops should re-examine the scheme as a matter of urgency, and Browne, as he left, 'thanked me effusively. Again apologised for all in which he had been faulty.'

McQuaid's account, despite its overtones, rings true. It is especially convincing if we accept that Browne's view of his role as a believing Catholic was as he stated it — that in a conflict between what he believed necessary as a politician and an authoritative and unambiguous ruling by the leaders of his Church, he would have to accept the latter, whatever the personal consequences for himself. This assumption is given added force by an interview he had, again at his own request, with Bishop Staunton of Ferns eight days later. This interview is — unlike the McQuaid one — mentioned by Browne in his autobiography, but is there described as 'uneventful'. In a strict sense, this is true, but Staunton's account of it, as he later reported to McQuaid, adds considerably more depth. Browne first of all repeated his excuse that he had been under a misapprehension about the bishops' attitude from 11 October 1950 to 8 March 1951, and then told Staunton that

> *as far as he was to blame he regretted very much the situation that had arisen, that he was fully prepared to accept the decision of the bishops as to whether the scheme or part of it were contrary to Faith and morals, that if they decided that the scheme was opposed to faith and morals he would, as a Catholic, not proceed with it, however painful it would be to him as a man to drop it, that he would resign his position as Minister of Health as he had not been able to implement his promises.[52]*

Browne's considered reply was now delivered to the hierarchy with a request for an authoritative ruling. While he waited for this, he had to contend with the first phase of MacBride's counter-attack within the Clann, which was launched at a meeting of the party's National Executive on the evening of 31 March, the day after his meeting with Staunton. Browne attended the meeting briefly and then left, suspecting that a hanging jury had been assembled. The meeting went on to discuss the matter in his absence and eventually — it went on into the small hours of 1 April — passed two resolutions. The first reiterated the executive's support for Browne's scheme, but expressed its 'fear that the successful implementation of this service may be jeopardised by the manner in which the whole problem is being handled by Dr Browne'; the second expressed its 'grave concern and disapproval' at Browne's attitude and conduct, and called on him to show greater loyalty and co-operation.[53]

Browne, although increasingly isolated, was not entirely without friends. At one point during the crisis MacBride met Jack McQuillan in Leinster House and indicated that he wanted to talk to him. 'You're a good friend of Noël Browne's,' he said. 'He'll listen to you. He's not well. He needs a holiday — a cruise on a ship, perhaps, maybe even for three months.' McQuillan replied: 'It's you who needs the cruise.' It was the last time MacBride and McQuillan ever spoke to each other.[54] Kennedy, although he would have had some differences on policy matters with Browne, also had a poor opinion of MacBride.

The bishops considered Browne's response at their general meeting in Maynooth on 4 April, and the following day McQuaid personally delivered his letter containing the hierarchy's judgment to Costello at 5 p.m., remaining to discuss it with him for an hour and a half.[55] McQuaid expressed concern to Costello about the apparent stiffening of attitude on the part of the Clann evidenced by the resolution passed at that party's executive meeting; Costello assured him that MacBride had agreed to this simply to protect his back politically. The Taoiseach also gave McQuaid significant new information which indicated that not only MacBride but Norton were in political difficulties on the issue: 'Dr B. had succeeded in working up the Labour people through Mr Noel Hartnett and Dr Sheehy Skeffington (both Trinity College men) and the Women Workers through Miss Louie Bennett (Protestant).'[56] There had been, Costello informed McQuaid, an incipient rebellion in the Labour Party ranks, which he had quelled only by addressing an inter-party meeting of deputies, 'at which he had to deal firmly with misconceptions of several Labour people, including Mr Sean Dunne TD'. McQuaid added in his memorandum on the matter: 'A meeting of the Labour Party had experienced a similar attempt at propaganda and vote in favour of Scheme, following presumably on activities of Trades Union Congress some days ago when they called on their 200,000 members to support Dr B.'s scheme. Mr Davin, TD, in the Chair had successfully countered the vote in favour of the Scheme.'[57]

Costello, now in possession of the definitive response of the hierarchy to Browne's considered defence of his position, showed it to him at a meeting on the same evening attended by both Norton and Brendan Corish, Labour TD and parliamentary secretary for Local Government and Defence. Browne, after reading the letter, declared to William Norton: 'It is all right. The Bishops have not condemned the Scheme on grounds of morals.' Costello reported this to McQuaid the following day with the addendum that 'Mr Corish, TD, Parliamentary Secretary, who was present, remarked: "If I had not heard the remark, I could not have believed it to be possible."'[58]

This final document from the bishops was, as John Whyte has cogently pointed out, poor in its argumentation and tendentious, and raised new issues to which Browne had not had an opportunity to reply. The critical factor now, however, was not the logic of the situation but the power equation and the quantity of political blood that had been spilt. Costello and the remainder of the cabinet had effectively abandoned Browne even before the bishops finally spoke; the cabinet meeting of 6 April did no more than cross the 't's and dot the 'i's.

Meanwhile Costello had been given vital ammunition by McQuaid with which to counter Browne's continuing assertion that the bishops' objections could be disregarded because they were based on social rather than on moral teaching. Catholic social teaching, McQuaid informed Costello calmly (and Costello dutifully reported to the cabinet), was simply Catholic moral teaching on social matters. What happened around the cabinet meeting on that day is not contested by anyone: Noël Browne asked each of his colleagues for their verdict, and then — when the unanimous verdict had gone against him — said that he needed time to consider his position. This is the traditional formula invoked by any office-holder contemplating resignation, and the members of the cabinet plainly had no difficulty in acceding to his request, if only because they were reasonably sure of the probable outcome.

But even as the government announced that it had decided not to proceed with Dr Browne's scheme but instead to draft a new one in accordance with the guidelines issued by the hierarchy, the train again began to look as if it were about to come off the rails. Immediately after the cabinet meeting Browne, in his capacity as a member of the Clann's National Executive, but without informing MacBride in advance, called a special meeting of the executive for 8 April, as he was entitled to do. There was a surge of popular and trade union support for him, and after a meeting he had with a Trades Union Congress delegation on the morning of that day, he announced publicly that he was deferring a decision.

Forty members of the Clann executive were present that evening for what was effectively a showdown between Browne and his party leader, which lasted into the early hours of the following morning. Here, however, he was outmanoeuvred, or at least outgunned. The meeting opened with a lengthy and emotional speech from Browne, in which he distinguished between his loyalty as a Catholic and his political convictions. 'As a good Catholic I accept without question the ruling of the Hierarchy on that matter, [the Scheme's conflict with Catholic social teaching] and the question of a means test scheme I leave to my successor [it might be noted that he had not yet resigned] to introduce if he so feels.'[59]

He also, however, drew attention to the new development — the fact that he had that day received a deputation from the TUC, as a result of which he was now reconsidering his position. He made it clear that up to that moment, he had been 'placing my resignation in the hands of Seán . . . and the Taoiseach'. Now backing away from his implied intention to resign, he was attempting to revisit the question Hartnett had raised at the executive meeting three months earlier. For him, the question now facing the Ard-Chomhairle was 'to decide whether they go on in the Inter-Party government or not'.

This formulation of the political question was rejected by MacBride, who told the Clann executive that Browne had telephoned him the previous day to tell him that he intended to resign, and questioned his sudden vacillation. He then put his own leadership on the line by reformulating the choice before them even more tellingly: 'If you want to ensure that Dr Browne is left in the Government, you should remove me from leadership of the Party.'

Browne replied to MacBride, but in an increasingly incoherent fashion. MacBride responded again to Browne, going into minutiae to an extent

which added nothing to his case. Then the Ard-Chomhairle voted on a resolution, proposed by Dermot Corcoran and seconded by Jack McQuillan, in
which the body reaffirmed its 'complete loyalty' to Seán MacBride as party
leader, and acknowledged his right and the right of the executive 'to take
any action . . . required to maintain party discipline and loyalty to the
leader'. Another resolution, urging MacBride to reopen negotiations with
the hierarchy, was defeated.

Jack McQuillan was, and remained for many years, a staunch friend of
Noël Browne's. Why then did he second a resolution which had the effect
of tying Browne hand and foot to the decisions of MacBride and the Clann
Executive? This resolution, passed unanimously at a meeting at which
Browne had been present, was thrown in his face by Con Lehane during
the debate on his resignation later in the Dáil, and was proof enough of
McQuillan's miscalculation and of his own tactical disarray. McQuillan's
interpretation of it, in his resignation statement some time later, indicated
his belief that the resolution allowed Browne to buy a certain amount of
time. But time was a commodity which had been totally exhausted.

Browne's action in meeting the TUC and endorsing its suggested compromise — that women should each contribute ten shillings to secure their
entitlements under the scheme — was too little and too late. Compromises
are generally negotiable in politics or anywhere else, provided that the
wounds are not too deep. By now, however, there were hospital cases everywhere and the government was on life support. The compromise was not
seriously considered by anyone — not even, it would appear, by Browne
himself, since he did not make much play of it in his autobiography.

If everyone had not already lost patience with him, his public statement that
he was reconsidering his position in light of the TUC's suggestions was the
final straw, both for the peppery Costello and for MacBride, who now realised
that if he did not act immediately Browne would not be the only casualty.

There was a further cabinet meeting on 10 April. It is unclear whether
Browne attended; he was still technically a member of the cabinet and the
minutes merely note that 'all ministers' were present. On the same day,
MacBride wrote formally requesting his resignation; the letter was delivered
by hand to Browne, on the steps of the Custom House, by MacBride's
private secretary, Brendan Dillon.

Browne submitted his resignation later on the same day, but with effect
from the following morning, 11 April. He spent much of the intervening
time, in what can only be described as an act of historical vandalism,
destroying files in the Custom House. It was an action perhaps understandable given his state of high emotion, but none the less inexcusable. He was
not alone: 'bone weary, I sat down for the last time at my ministerial desk.
Opposite me sat a dishevelled and as always unkempt Noel Hartnett.'[60]

When a Clann member, Kevin White (later chairman of Amnesty International in Ireland), called to Noël Browne's house at this time without notice he found Browne, Hartnett and Brian Walsh assembling letters for publication in the newspapers;[61] they were to appear in all the national media, with astonishing effect, on the morning of 12 April.

Aftermath I: Noël Browne

Three different assessments of what happened require to be made. The first is of Noël Browne's own motivation and, in particular, of his apparently contradictory attitude towards the bishops — dismissive and supine by turns. The second is of the actions and motivations of the bishops, especially Dr McQuaid. The third is of the tactics and objectives of the medical profession.

Browne's religious sentiments are as difficult to assess as many other aspects of his mercurial personality. Although he was the product of a Catholic education, and a Jesuit one at that, he had not grown to manhood under the shadow of episcopacy. His undergraduate education in Trinity was, by definition, culturally light years away from the clerically supervised, almost cloistered existence of his contemporaries in the National University colleges.

Few attempts were made, while Noël Browne was alive, to persuade him to offer an explanation of this apparent volte-face in the face of the final ultimatum from the bishops — one, moreover, which he could reconcile with his uncompromising anticlericalism from the 1960s onwards. There is the possibility that Browne was playing for time; that he was calculating that, from a political point of view, it would be better for him to resign in the face of the bishops than to resign in the face of the doctors; and that the interviews with both McQuaid and Staunton were effectively part of an elaborate exit strategy which he would later exploit to his own advantage. This possibility is hinted at in an explanation he gave on RTÉ's 7 Days programme in 1971, when he said that he had accepted the hierarchy's judgment 'because he wanted to remain in politics and continue his work for social progress'.[62]

To accept this hypothesis, however, involves accepting also that Browne was capable of quite extraordinary levels of hypocrisy and mendacity. Some of his most bitter critics, not least those who suffered under the tongue-lashings he was wont to administer in later years, would be quite prepared to believe this about him. But it is not consistent with his other, private statement to a meeting of the Clann at the height of the same crisis: 'As a Catholic I feel I have one duty. I have accepted that duty . . . I loathe political life and want to get out of it.'[63] And is it a credible analysis of the Noël Browne of 1951, of the man who said, in his public resignation letter to the

Clann, 'I cherish deeply my own Faith and have always been loyal to it'?[64]

It would be wrong to attribute to the Noël Browne of the late 1940s and early 1950s the anticlericalism typical of the 1960s and later years. He said in his autobiography that he had abandoned the practice of religion while a young doctor in Britain during the war, and at around the same time told an interviewer in *Hot Press* that he was an atheist who no longer believed in God.[65] As late as 1984, however, he had told the readers of *The Irish Times* that he had for some time been a 'happily confirmed lapsed Catholic'.[66] This self-description is in itself interesting, in that by implication it avoided the two other definitions which former members of the Catholic Church often apply to themselves: agnostic and atheist. His opposition to the institutional Church did not preclude an interior life, nor was the existence of such an interior life necessarily inconsistent with his desire that there should be no religious service at his funeral.

There is evidence, moreover, that between his service in Britain and his later years Browne's attitude towards Catholicism, on a personal level, veered between scepticism and commitment in a way which appears to have been to some extent independent of the political battles he was then waging with the hierarchy. When Ruth came back from London to live with Noël and Phyllis at Newcastle after the end of the war, she and Noël went to mass together.[67] Dr Charles Lysaght, who was in charge of the Department of Health's sanatorium building programme, worked closely with Browne. He accompanied the minister privately to Mass on holy days of obligation during the working week, both walking to a church near the Custom House, and observed his evident deep level of commitment.[68] A number of years later, when his children were teenagers, Noël Browne bowed to an instruction from his local parish priest in Bray, Co. Wicklow to remove his younger daughter, Susan, from the (Protestant) Kingstown Grammar School and send her to a convent school. The priest, Fr Breen, issued this injunction on the basis of the promise he assumed had been made about the Catholic upbringing of the children when Noël and Phyllis were married — unaware of the fact that the promise had never been made. Noël, nonetheless, complied.[69] He was even prepared, as will be seen later, to threaten a public legal action against someone who questioned his religious commitment several years after the conclusion of the Mother and Child debacle.

One of the most telling accounts of his own religious feelings, however, was not offered until 1968, when, in a long series of interviews with the then political correspondent of *The Irish Times*, Michael McInerney, he spoke warmly of the unnamed theologian whom he had consulted during the Mother and Child controversy. Describing him as a 'courageous priest', Browne observed:

The extent to which I hold on to my religious beliefs today I owe to the great integrity of this man and to the consolation given to me by him at that time. I felt then, and I still do, that a Church which a man of his intellectual calibre found tolerable, and indeed acceptable, must have some real merit.[70]

Even later, when I had a conversation with Noël Browne in Leinster House in the early 1970s, I found his by then legendary anticlericalism thrown into sharp relief by the extraordinary feeling with which he spoke of the religiously driven altruism of the members of some religious orders, particularly those who had devoted their lives, without the slightest expectation of human gratitude or even an observably human response, to the welfare of those suffering from unutterably profound levels of mental disability. In a sense, this is all of a piece with what we know of Noël Browne's personality. Whatever his faults, cynicism could not be numbered among them. He was much given to strong, even passionate commitments, and it is not unlikely that even religion — or some sort of faith, to use a less institutionally conditioned word — would have featured among these commitments, even if only intermittently and perhaps confusedly. *Tempora mutantur, nos et mutamur in illis.*

The identity of the theologian, and the nature of his relationship with Browne and with others involved in this controversy, is, even today, of considerable interest. He was Mgr P.F. (Frank, to his friends) Cremin, then Professor of Theology at Maynooth, and a member of a remarkably gifted family.[71] A brother, Con Cremin, worked in the Department of External Affairs, including a stint as ambassador in Berlin during the war, and later became secretary of the department itself, where he wielded enormous influence.

Cremin had achieved his doctorate and his Maynooth appointment at an extraordinarily young age. He was born in October 1910, was therefore only five years older than Browne, and had received ecclesiastical preferment as rapidly as Noël Browne had received political office. He also had close links with some of the other major players. He was friendly with Brian Walsh, lawyer and Fianna Fáil member. Walsh was a Francophile, and taught French to students in Maynooth on a part-time basis; later his brief at the college extended also to civil law. Cremin had also, coincidentally, shared a bench in the national school in Kenmare, Co. Kerry with the young Noel Hartnett, whose father was a pharmacist in the town.

Hartnett's family moved to Dublin after the Civil War when his father's business was burned out, but Noel was then sent back to Killarney to school in St Brendan's, where he met the young Frank Cremin again. The two schoolboys, though now a year apart in school because of Noel's enforced transfer to Dublin, renewed their friendship, and concluded a mutual assistance pact: Cremin helped Hartnett in maths, which was his weakest subject;

Hartnett helped Cremin in poetry. Some seventy years later, Cremin could still recall the mark Hartnett got in the Junior Certificate in mathematics: it was 127 out of 600, the pass mark being 120.[72] Partly as a result of the coaching from Cremin, Hartnett got a one-third scholarship at St Brendan's on the results of his Certificate examination; Cremin got a half-scholarship the following year.

The initial contact with Browne was, however, through Walsh. Walsh had got to know Browne through Hartnett, whom he had worked with in the Law Library. One day in Maynooth Walsh asked Cremin what he thought about the Mother and Child Scheme, and when he heard his — typically forthright — views on the topic, suggested that he come and talk to Noël Browne about it. This led to the first of many meetings, most of which were held in Walsh's house in Drumcondra; the utmost secrecy had to be observed, and on occasion Cremin would be dropped back to Maynooth at 5 a.m. in Noël Browne's State car.

Cremin's view, which finds an echo in *Against the Tide*, was simplicity itself: if a free scheme was wrong for Catholics on this side of the border, how could it be acceptable for their co-religionists on the other side? This issue, which Cremin courageously and rightly raised, was one to which the bishops, not least Dr McQuaid, were not insensitive, and it is their role that must now be addressed.

Aftermath II: the bishops

In relation to the bishops, there are now no serious scholars who will maintain that the nature and extent of their intervention can be justified by any norms — even those prevailing in 1951 — unless one is prepared to accept a concept long condemned by the Catholic Church itself, that of situational ethics. Broadly speaking, this is the argument that circumstances condition morality, and is anathema to a Church which prefers to deal in moral absolutes, whatever their particular application. In the case of the Mother and Child Scheme, the hierarchy was unwilling to make an issue of, much less condemn, the British government's introduction of the free National Health Service in Northern Ireland. This was, as Mgr Cremin saw (with the logic and clarity which led him to defend his Church's position on other, equally controversial issues such as birth control), logically indefensible and morally questionable. But, as he remarked philosophically many years later, when logic faces power in the ring, it is basically no contest.

The archives of the Archbishop of Dublin, Dr McQuaid, reveal not only his motivation but a level of either self-delusion or breathtaking arrogance (depending on one's point of view) which severely undermines the thesis that he and his brother bishops were doing no more than expressing, albeit in strong terms, a legitimate pastoral concern on the issues involved. His motivation is most clearly found in a lengthy letter he wrote to Mgr Ettore Felici, the Nuncio, within days of Browne's resignation. In this he makes plain that he has been looking at the whole situation in a much wider context — that of the spread of left-wing forces in Europe generally, and more particularly in Italy.

> The effect of the Hierarchy's judgement on the Scheme has been decisive. The Government, with admirable loyalty and open courage, has accepted that judgement and rejected Dr Browne's scheme. The whole country has equally accepted. The Leftist elements in the Labour groups and Women's Associations, linked with these Groups, have repeated the calumnies of the Irish Times . . . The attack from Labour is directed from Communist elements in Europe and in the Irish Workers' League . . . When I broadcast on the issue of the Italian elections, I took occasion to give the warning that the attack on the Church in Ireland would come under the guise of patriotism and social reform. The present issue is a perfect example of the technique used in our country. The Leftists are urging that the Church has blocked social progress, has failed to help the poor, has wished to impose a means test.[73]

McQuaid's concern with the left and its growing influence is also seen clearly in a number of other key documents. In March, in his report to the hierarchy on the ongoing crisis, he urged the bishops to reject the scheme, arguing that if they did so, 'we shall have saved the country from advancing a long way towards socialistic welfare. In particular, we shall have checked the efforts of Leftist and Labour elements, which are approaching the point of publicly ordering the Church to stay out of social life and confine herself to what they think is the Church's proper sphere.'[74] A month later, forwarding his own draft of the bishops' final response to Bishop Staunton of Ferns, he noted that he had 'kept a careful eye on the Trade Unions especially the TUC and the Clann politicians . . . I have equally considered, in the draft, the very probable criticisms of leftist Labour, in particular, that the bishops should confine themselves to their own sphere of morals.'[75]

In other words, just as Dr Browne was drafting his demonology, with the help of his friends and supporters, Dr McQuaid was engaged in a parallel activity in Drumcondra. Even this, however — which is to some extent explicable in terms of the Cold War ideology of any senior prelates who had contact with their European colleagues — pales into insignificance behind McQuaid's explicit, but resolutely private, rationale for rejecting the argument that for the government to bow to the bishops in this instance would be a blow to any hope of national reunification because of the effect it would have on Protestant and unionist opinion north of the border.

McQuaid's attitude to partition was more complex than is generally supposed. His biographer, for example, assumes that McQuaid was fundamentally irredentist, and at one in this with his political alter ego, Eamon de Valera.[76] A close reading of McQuaid's proposals in relation to Articles 2 and 3 of the 1937 Constitution, however, strongly suggests that his nationalism was considerably more moderate than that of de Valera. Lord Rugby found him to be 'an Irish nationalist with a broad-minded outlook'.[77] The British Minister went on to give details of McQuaid's 'broad-mindedness' which, even today, have a post-nationalist tinge to them. McQuaid fulminated in particular against what he described as the 'complete racket' of anti-partitionism. 'Many people active on both sides of the Border', he told Rugby sternly, 'would be horrified if their efforts led to the ending of partition.' Although he had nothing to say in defence of Orangemen, they could not be forced to go anywhere they didn't want to go, and partition was basically 'a godsend to politicians, particularly to extremists and Communists'.

As the Mother and Child crisis concluded, McQuaid was dealing with the argument that Home Rule was Rome Rule in terms whose implications would have astonished even Rugby, and offered hostages to the unionists, had either been aware of them. Writing again to Felici in the context of the Fianna Fáil replacement for Browne's scheme, he referred to the 'more subtle approach of the Leftists', which was to argue that the decision of the bishops was damaging to the cause of national unity, and that it would now be impossible to remove partition. He was brutally frank about his own view of the consequences:

> *The outcry in the Protestant North, following the unjust presentation of the Bishop's* [sic] *judgement by the Irish Times, is indeed typical. But what many fail to see is that the* Protestants now see clearly under what conditions of Catholic morality they would have to be governed in the Republic. *The political enticements held out to them are now judged by them to be only snares to trap them in a Republic dominated by the Catholic Church. Thus, the arguments of the liberal Catholics, who seem to put national unity before the interests of the Faith, have been discredited in the eyes of Northern Protestants. (Emphasis added.)*

It is difficult to interpret this in any way other than as an acceptance that the unionist assessment of the fate awaiting them in a united Ireland was indeed correct (although McQuaid would never have put it quite in these terms). In effect, what the archbishop was saying was that where the Church had the power, the Church made the rules. As has been noted, it is a stance which not only contrasted strangely with the Church's silence on health policy in Northern Ireland, but identified a considerably more hardline and politically tendentious position than that advanced publicly by McQuaid and other bishops in defence of their right merely to make their views known on matters of pastoral concern.

There is some evidence[78] that McQuaid himself was taken aback by public reaction to the bishops' intervention and the government's acceptance of their condemnation of Browne's scheme, to the extent that he played quite a different role in the negotiations between the government and the bishops over Dr Ryan's subsequent Health Act. In the first flush of victory, however, he was not to know that his assessment that 'the whole country has equally accepted' the situation was not only over-optimistic, but dangerously so. Although it was far from clear at the time, the victory that he and Bishop Browne had engineered had a pyrrhic element to it, not least in that it fatally weakened his own voice in later years.

Many years after the controversy Dr James Kavanagh, who had been prominent in defending the bishops at the time, reviewed Noël Browne's autobiography in a Church publication. 'On reflection,' he wrote, 'I think that to have *condemned* the Bill [*sic*] was a tactical error. Though at the time I felt there were reasonable objections which should be considered, I was surprised when the hierarchy actually *gravely disapproved* of the Bill and this precipitated the fall of the Government.'[79] Another bishop, Dr Donal Herlihy of Ferns, put it more bluntly: 'We allowed ourselves to be used by the doctors, but it won't happen again.'[80]

Aftermath III: the doctors

The next question to be dealt with is the nature, extent, motivation and justification (if any) of medical opposition to Browne's scheme. It is certainly the case, as has already been argued, that a number of senior medical consultants, for the most part living and working in Dublin, would have had their incomes affected by one or another aspect of Browne's policies. The Mother and Child Scheme, as it happened, would have made little or no difference to them. They stood to be much more seriously affected by the decentralisation of specialised medical services planned by Noël Browne and by the diversion (as they would have described it) of the Hospitals' Trust Fund to public medicine in general and specifically to the sanatorium programme. The Mother and Child Scheme also worried the consultants, not particularly because of any immediate effect it might have had on their own income, but because of its potential for splitting the profession, and their fear that it was merely the prelude to a full-blown system of State medicine, which would undoubtedly have an effect on their income stream in the longer term. One of McQuaid's medical correspondents, Dr Brendan Roantree from Dún Laoghaire, wrote to express his considerable apprehension that the dispensary doctors would vote against the IMA on the issue.[81] The dilemma, as he saw it, was that if Browne's scheme excluded the private practitioners, they would suffer 'grave material loss and the right to our livelihoods'. If Browne succeeded in inveigling the dispensary doctors into participating in the scheme, however, this raised an equally fearsome prospect — that of 'State medicine'.

Roantree's letter pre-dated the resolution of the controversy, but one of his colleagues, Dr John Shanley of Merrion Square, writing on the day of Browne's resignation, was even more explicit.

> *Opposition was not activated by mere monetary considerations, though no doubt the doctors too will be misrepresented by designing individuals. As a matter of fact doctors would be much better off financially in most cases under the proposed scheme: dispensary medical officers would have their salaries (and pensions) increased by almost 100 per cent (vide the ex-Minister's 'White paper'), the capitation rate offered to private practitioners was generous, and in particular the staffs of the voluntary hospitals would be paid for the enormous amount of voluntary work which they gladly do at present for nothing and with no material return (except for the vague and in many cases quite un-remunerative status they hold as hospital consultants).*[82]

Shanley, praising the archbishop for his denunciation of 'this insidious effort to enslave medical practice', identified the real enemy — Lenin, who, he wrote, had declared that 'the socialisation of any State should first begin with the control of the medical profession, because peoples are most naturally influenced through their emotions and what evokes more powerful emotions than sickness, birth and death!'

Most versions of the events of 1951 concentrate either on the relationship between Noël Browne and the doctors, or on that between Noël Browne and the bishops. In so far as they criticise Browne, they tend to put the blame on his inexperience. But almost all the members of the cabinet were inexperienced in the wielding of power; only Paddy McGilligan, Richard Mulcahy and Costello himself (as Attorney-General 1926–32) had cabinet experience, and that was sixteen years earlier. The inter-party government itself was a new creation, made up as they went along.

Partly under the influence of Browne's compelling narrative, and partly because it necessarily involves making the distasteful choice between MacBride and Browne as witnesses, few have seriously explored the possibility that the critical endgame was in fact the one played out between these two men, with the future of Clann na Poblachta, rather than the Mother and Child Scheme, as the stake. In this scenario, the Mother and Child Scheme can be seen finally as the instrument of Browne's policy, rather than its primary objective.

This is not to say that Browne wanted to supplant MacBride as leader; there is no evidence that he did, or that he ever said he did. But a renewed and revivified Clann, with Noel Hartnett restored to its ranks, would have presented a different prospect entirely, even if it was, by this stage, only a mirage. Nor does it mean that Browne did not believe passionately in the value of his scheme — of course he did. But both his objectives — the implementation of his scheme and the challenge to MacBride's betrayal (as he saw it) of the vision of the Clann — had a strong emotional content that prevented him from seeing the extent to which they were incompatible. In the end, the fact that he adopted an all-or-nothing scenario, which in any contemporary view of the circumstances virtually guaranteed that he would get nothing, strongly suggests that the scheme itself was now becoming, like Browne himself, a sacrifice on the altar of some higher God.

At the end of the day, Noël Browne became and remained a hero to many, especially the poor of Dublin. Unaware of the infighting and power plays which had characterised the controversy almost from the beginning, they responded intuitively to the way in which he had empathised with them in their plight. His defeat did not improve their situation, and, indeed, postponed sorely needed improvements in health care for a number of years; but they carried on, as they had done for so long, as best they could, choosing to interpret his defeat as a kind of moral victory.

But the history of the affair shows more than Browne's passion and his concern for the poor and underprivileged; it also demonstrates his extraordinary knack for turning friends into enemies, and for alienating important constituencies. Whatever inner demon drove him forward also held him back; the undeniable achievements of the early years in office were succeeded by a situation in which, paradoxically, he enhanced his public reputation on the basis of a political disaster, and was left with hardly a political friend in the world. Hartnett stayed with him. So did Jack McQuillan, Michael ffrench-O'Carroll and a few others. But he would never exercise government power again on behalf of those whose social and economic interests he had championed, which is a bitter enough epitaph for someone who said he wanted to change the world. An editorial in the *Manchester Guardian* just after his resignation observed of Browne: 'He can command much sympathy in the country, but no politician of ordinary prudence after reading his reply to Mr MacBride will ever be willing to have him for a colleague.'[83] To the extent that this was true, we have to look at Noël Browne not only as a victim — the role in which he has most commonly been cast since 1951 — but as a principal actor in the drama which enfolded him. Someone once remarked of George Orwell — in an entirely different context — that he was a 'refugee from the camp of success'. In his years in the political wilderness that followed, Browne might have had occasion to reflect on his own fate in similar terms.

For the time being, however, public indignation about his fate was widespread, and the dissolution of the Dáil was plainly only a matter of time. Nor were some of those who had worked with him unmoved. When Noël Browne left the Custom House for the last time, some of his civil servants did not attempt to conceal their tears.[84]

CHAPTER SIX

The Fianna Fáil
Mother and Child Scheme

W hen John A. Costello returned to his office on 12 April 1951 after replying to Noël Browne's resignation speech in the Dáil — a dogged defence of his position, delivered with some indignation and considerable forensic skill, which had taken him five hours to prepare — he was told that one of his senior advisers, the economist Paddy Lynch, wished to see him.

Lynch had been in the 'bull-pen', the section of the Dáil chamber reserved for civil servants, during Costello's speech, when he was approached by an usher with the information that there was an urgent personal telephone call for the Taoiseach. Pointing out that he could hardly interrupt Costello, then on his feet, he asked who was on the line; it was, he was told, Dr McQuaid.

Lynch left the chamber to take the call, explained to the archbishop that he could not speak to the Taoiseach at that moment, but offered to give him a message as soon as he had finished. The archbishop was cross — very cross. He told Lynch that he had just received a 'remarkable request'. The Irish News Agency had asked him to write, immediately, an article of 1,000 words giving the bishops' point of view on the Mother and Child controversy. McQuaid knew well that the Agency had been set up by MacBride, and that Noel Hartnett was on the board of directors. And he wanted representations made to the Taoiseach about it, as soon as possible. When Lynch delivered this message, Costello put his head in his hands, exclaiming: 'Dear God! This is the end.'[1]

He had good reason to be weary, and depressed. It was, in a sense, the unkindest cut of all to be asked at this juncture to accept responsibility for the Irish News Agency, a MacBride initiative with which he had never been happy. It was certainly an unwelcome addition to a growing pile of misfortunes. MacBride and the remains of Clann na Poblachta were still onside, but the future of his government was now in grave jeopardy, and effectively depended on the votes of Noël Browne and a handful of others who could choose a moment, or an issue, on which to bring it down whenever it suited them.

The contrast with what was happening in Britain is instructive. Nye Bevan, who had planned to resign on 9 April and make a personal statement on 11 April on the question of NHS charges, actually resigned eleven days after Browne's resignation, on 22 April. His statement in the House of Commons the following day, according to the historian of the British Labour movement Kenneth Morgan, was 'a political disaster, the worst of his career'.[2]

The debate on Browne's resignation, by comparison, did Browne little or no harm. It took place over two days, on 12 and 17 April, and in an atmosphere of high drama. It was tough, toe-to-toe stuff, but also complicated and difficult to disentangle. Few people would have read all the densely packed columns in the newspapers, or understood the context in which charge and counter-charge were being made. More, on the other hand, would have read at least a large part of the voluminous correspondence which Browne released to the newspapers on the night of 11 April and which was published the following morning; reading other people's letters, after all, is far more fun than reading Dáil debates. Browne, by doing this, had not only lifted the curtain on a corner of Irish political life that had been concealed from view for decades, but seized the initiative. Not many people would have read every word of the correspondence; even if they did, few of them would have been aware of much of the context within which they had to be assessed. Browne's letters, however, had high visibility. They were carefully crafted to put each of his decisions in the best possible light, to gloss over any inconvenient facts, and to portray his opponents, clerical and political, as intransigent and obscurantist. Few people who knew Browne well believed that he had written them all himself; the inference was that both Hartnett and Walsh had been intimately involved in the composition of at least the early ones.

He was immediately buoyed up by two significant factors. One was a groundswell of public opinion, noted by American diplomats in Dublin, generally more sagacious and wide-ranging in their comments on Irish political and social affairs than their British counterparts, who tended to be obsessed with the issue of partition. Already, at the end of 1950, they had noted that Browne's BCG vaccination programme was 'ahead of Britain'.[3] The day after the publication of the Mother and Child correspondence in the papers, they reported 'considerable sympathy for the position of Dr Browne who is looked on as somewhat of a martyr', describing him as someone who was 'unfortunately . . . politically naive, but who has a reputation for integrity, which has captured the imagination of many people'.[4]

The second critical factor was undoubtedly the support of *The Irish Times*, which, although it enjoyed only a small circulation (then not much more than 30,000 copies a day, mostly in Dublin) and tended still to be characterised as pro-British, had a disproportionate influence in that its readers included disaffected Catholic intellectuals and others who regarded their own country as sadly in need of liberal reforms. On the day it published the correspondence, the paper printed an editorial — written, Dr McQuaid told the Nuncio, by a 'traitorous Catholic'[5] — entitled 'Contra Mundum', which excoriated government and the Catholic Church alike. 'The most serious revelation', it commented, in a phrase which has been reprinted thousands of times in the intervening half-century and which helped to define the parameters of analysis for as long, 'is that the Roman Catholic Church would appear to be the effective Government of this country.'[6]

From then until the debate on Noël Browne's resignation concluded in the Dáil on 17 April (and indeed for some time afterwards), *The Irish Times* published a considerable volume of letters on the controversy, most of them favouring Browne. Its columnists also addressed the issue. 'Nichevo' (R.M. Smyllie's personal pseudonym) told his readers: 'I am afraid he will go under, because there is no place for idealists in Irish — or any other — politics.'[7] The anonymous author of the 'Report to Housewives' used her column to suggest that 'one solution to the problems of the moment might well be the return of the witch-doctor — who at least, if he could not cure his patient, poisoned him off with very great dispatch and little expense to the community in general'.[8] This somewhat liberal interpretation of the column's brief provoked one of Dublin's senior obstetricians, Dr W.F. O'Dwyer, Master of the Coombe maternity hospital, into the counter-accusation that the columnist's style bore a close resemblance to that of the famous anonymous document which had been circulated in the Corporation housing estates, and into a bitter attack on Browne's 'almost oriental munificence in the development of State medical institutions'.[9] The anonymous columnist replied with scarcely veiled satisfaction the following day to deny the charge, but underpinned her right as a woman to comment on the issue with a telling quotation from Kipling: 'The toad beneath the harrow knows/Exactly where each tooth-point goes'.[10]

The *Irish Times* political columnist Aknefton (a composite of the Dublin actress Sheila Greene and her partner, the WUI official Chris Ferguson) was more circumspect: 'Noël Browne resigns and escapes with clean hands. In doing so, however, he makes it utterly impossible for the very powerful forces on which he could depend to rally behind him.'[11] This at the least indicated some chagrin at how Browne's departure left the forces then gathering in the TUC to support the scheme suddenly bereft of a leader around whom they could rally.

Noël Browne's maternal grandparents, Patrick A. Cooney (1837–1906) and Catherine Moran Cooney (1844–1913) (photo courtesy Marje Cooney).

Noël with one of his grandchildren (photo courtesy Ruth Wick Browne).

Making scones on an open fire in Connemara (photo courtesy Ruth Wick Browne).

Noël and Michael D. Higgins in Galway, 1987 (photo: The Irish Times*).*

At home in Connemara (photo: Joe Shaughnessy).

In old age (photo: Bobbie Hanvey).

With Michael D. Higgins, making a television documentary for RTÉ (photo: The Irish Times*).*

One of Noël's less well-known accomplishments was as an accordion player (photo: Bobbie Hanvey).

Noël Browne, in probably his last public appearance before his death, speaks to the children at Carrabane NS, Co. Galway, with their teacher, Colum McGuinness (photo courtesy Clem Walsh).

The *Irish Press* reported the resignation with evident glee at the government's discomfiture, but without saying anything which would have alienated the hierarchy or Catholic opinion generally. This was perhaps to be expected. What was altogether less predictable was the attitude of the *Irish Independent*. Although its news reports were unmistakably, but delicately, written in such a way as to imply support for the embattled Costello, they did not carry as much impact as the *Irish Times* coverage, not least because the *Times* reports were frequently on its front page, while the *Independent* front page was still, in 1951, reserved for advertisements. The *Independent* maintained editorial silence throughout the controversy. The same was true of its feature coverage, which did not miss a beat; on the day the correspondence was published, it contented itself with regaling its loyal readers with the thirty-fourth in a fifty-part series of articles on 'The Lives of the Popes'.[12]

Why would this paper, which was to be praised by Dr McQuaid three years later on the occasion of its half-centenary for its 'policy of distinctive loyalty towards the Church',[13] withhold active and vocal support from the bishops on this occasion? At this remove in time from the events concerned, no definitive answer can be given; but it should be remembered that Noël Browne had maintained friendly relationships with many members of the Chance family, who were major shareholders in the paper. When Arthur Chance, Neville's oldest half-brother, suffered his fatal stroke, his daughter Jilly turned first to Noël for help, and Noël was the doctor who attended him and organised his admittance to hospital. Others in the family, too, recall his long-standing warmth towards them and the members of the extended family, often at similar times of crisis.[14] They would hardly expect their paper to come out and support him simply because of this relationship — possibly they did not even want to. But they could at least see to it that he was not publicly traduced in their pages. The *Sunday Independent*, as it happened, took a slightly bolder editorial line, publishing pro-Browne letters more prominently than its daily sister paper.[15]

The Dáil debate, when it came, was notable for a number of things. Fifty years later, Costello's speech reads, in particular, as an effective refutation of many of the charges made against him by Browne. The accusation that he had bowed to the will of the bishops he plainly did not consider derogatory. He did not reply to Browne's charge that on an unspecified date, but at any rate before 14 March, he had challenged Costello and other ministers to 'consider this matter not as individuals but as a Cabinet and that if they so wished reverse their decision of 1948 to exclude a means test'.[16] It is arguable, as I have already suggested, that Costello should have taken this course of action much earlier in his own interests and in the interests of his government, but it was a charge against which he could not defend himself without disclosing his private discussions with McQuaid.

Browne's speech is of interest for its identification of the bishops' objection as the one which carried weight with the government to the exclusion of all others. This is particularly noteworthy in light of the fact that the bishops vanished from his demonology almost immediately thereafter, and did not figure in any of his pungent speeches during the subsequent general election campaign. He was strong, too, in his criticism of Costello's decision to endorse the bishops' condemnation of the scheme because it was not in conformity with Catholic social teaching, although his indignation looked odd beside his almost immediate acknowledgment that, as a Catholic, he accepted their decision 'without hesitation'.[17] In the popular memory, this admission on his part was to prove less durable than the accusation which preceded it.

When Browne completed his speech and sat down, there was applause from the Fianna Fáil benches. It was the only sound to be heard from that side of the House until the end of the debate, when Mr de Valera remarked: 'We have heard enough.' One Fianna Fáil deputy was briefly unable to restrain himself, and interjected a remark, but was quickly hauled back by one of his colleagues with the telling phrase: 'Let it be between them now and let us keep out. Our scalps are fairly safe while they are at each other.'[18]

And they were at each other. Peadar Cowan, who had been expelled from Clann na Poblachta on a different issue in 1948, was scathing in his attack on his former party and its leader, and bolder in his attacks on the bishops than anyone, including Browne. Con Lehane, who had, only months earlier, been expressing criticism of MacBride in the inner councils of the Clann, now rowed in behind his leader; newspaper speculation was that he was likely to take Browne's place at the cabinet table. Most unexpected of all, at least to those who were unaware of the friendship which had been cemented in the TB ward of St Michael's Hospital during 1947, was the contribution of Oliver J. Flanagan, who described Browne, with classic hyperbole, as 'the best Minister for Health this country had [and] the best Minister for Health in any Government in Europe'. MacBride, he announced, had 'killed the goose that laid the golden egg . . . [Dr Browne] was too powerful; he was too popular; he was achieving results.'[19] Browne himself, almost as if to distance himself from the maverick Independent, was to describe this intervention as 'surprising'.[20]

In Dublin, there was an extraordinary rallying of public support for Browne, particularly among women. Louie Bennett of the Irish Women Workers' Union, Mary Kettle and Mrs W.R. O'Hegarty were among a group who signed a telegram to Costello urging him to meet a deputation, and on 12 April a huge meeting was arranged for College Green to protest at the changes the government proposed to introduce in the scheme. This meeting, which was attended by some 2,000 people, was organised to a large extent by Peggy Rushton, a rising star in the burgeoning advertising industry who was later to achieve fame as the public relations executive in London who persuaded Harold Wilson to wear a particular brand of rain-coat. Professor Mary Macken of UCD, who had impeccable feminist credentials stretching back over many years, was in the chair. Dr Michael ffrench-O'Carroll told the meeting that 'as a Catholic, he would like to state that he accepted without question the rule of the bishops, but he deplored that the attitude of the Hierarchy should have been used for political purposes, and withheld from the nation and Dr Browne, and that the whole nation should be humbugged and misled'.[21] The trade unionist Donal Nevin, who was also involved in organising the meeting, was told by one irate woman that he shouldn't even be on the platform because he was a man.[22]

Outside Dublin, support for Browne was more muted, but nonetheless discernible. On the other hand, opposition was even more vocal. The Dublin correspondent of the *Connaught Sentinel* told his readers that the government had been excessively lenient, tolerant and considerate in its treatment of Browne, and 'The general view appears to be that it would be good for the world if there were a Catholic hierarchy in every country and in a position to expound the moral law with the same effect.'[23] The *Drogheda Argus* reserved most of its ire for *The Irish Times*, the 'mouthpiece of the Protestant community'.[24] The editor of the *Sligo Champion* (with admirable economy, the editorial was repeated word for word in the Donegal *People's Press*) remarked acidly: 'Dr Browne, having cut his own throat, is asking who stabbed him in the back.'[25] The *Dundalk Democrat* accused him, by inference, of 'bishop-baiting'[26] and praised de Valera's restraint.

On the other hand, at least some provincial papers were not cowed. The Waterford *Standard* described the means test as a 'degrading anachronism' and Browne as someone who had 'won himself an honoured place in both Irish and medical history'.[27] The *Leinster Express's* Dublin correspondent, who ranked the cabinet crisis behind the current vegetable shortage, said that it was doubtful 'if in the history of democratic government, a Minister has ever relinquished office for reasons less connected with selfish interests'.[28] The Drogheda *Independent*, taking the opposite view from the *Argus*, said that his gesture aroused 'public admiration',[29] and the Monaghan *Argus* endorsed a Fianna Fáil deputy's description of Seán MacBride as 'Pontius Pilate'.[30]

Reaction in Northern Ireland was as had been expected (or feared, depending on one's point of view) by many of the participants. *The Irish Times* reported speeches by the Unionist MPs W.B. Topping (13 April), Edmund Warnock (19 April) and the Prime Minister, Basil Brooke (20 April), in which they all drew what they considered to be the obvious lessons from the affair; later, the Unionist Party was to publish the correspondence as a pamphlet, to warn its followers about the fate that would befall them in a united Ireland.

The newpaper correspondence columns continued to reverberate with the controversy. There was a notable contribution from Dr James Kavanagh, who had written privately to McQuaid in mid-1950 with a sharply critical analysis of the scheme, and who was later to become an auxiliary bishop of Dublin known for his links with the trade union movement. In a lengthy letter published in all the papers, he backed the bishops' action implicitly by arguing that 'zeal and sincerity without wisdom can be dangerous', and that 'social services are not financed by a transfer of the income of the rich to the poor. Rather do the lower income groups pay for it through indirect taxation.'[31] This statement might be regarded as an accurate description of the way social services actually operated in 1951; but the facts could also be turned the other way, and used to justify an argument in favour of an extension of income tax on the wealthier sections of the community. This was not, however, Dr Kavanagh's intention. He warned, instead, that the vagueness of detail in the scheme made it a serious danger to 'the rights of the nation'. The rights which were so endangered were carefully not specified. The *Church of Ireland Gazette* made the politically literate point that 'some of the doctors who rejoiced over the defeat of Dr Browne's proposals were Protestants. On the other hand, a majority of those who lament the defeat of the Bill belong to the Roman Catholic Church.'[32] And an evidently well-read Mr Ernest P. Hare of Enniskillen quoted the Rev. Walter McDonald, whose tenure as a professor in Maynooth many years earlier had been rudely interrupted by the bishops for his outspokenness: 'The greatest danger to religion is likely to accrue from any serious attempt on the part of the clergy to deprive the laity of their political rights, under the pretence that such rights counted as nothing when weighed against danger to faith and morals.'[33]

Politically, the temperature was increasing uncontrollably. Costello, instead of inviting MacBride to nominate a member of the cabinet to replace Browne (his reasons for not doing so hardly need elucidation), took over as Minister for Health himself. He was not in a mood to be trifled with; one of his first actions was an attempt to discipline the two senior civil servants — Paddy Kennedy and Paddy Murray — who had been most closely involved with Browne, evidently believing that they had failed to protect the government in the course of the controversy. He made a veiled reference to this after the general election when — now consigned to the opposition benches in the Dáil — he spoke on the new Fianna Fáil government's first health estimate. 'I did notice', he said guardedly, 'that there was, in the course of the day-to-day administration of this department, being done, by administrative action, something which was, slowly, no doubt, but surely, leading to socialised medicine.'[34] When Costello became Minister he sent for Dr J.D. McCormack, a senior medical adviser in the Department, who was a friend of his from Portmarnock Golf Club, and asked him to give him a briefing on the workings of the Department. McCormack, as he later recounted it to another senior medical adviser in the Department, Dr Charles Lysaght, confirmed that there was a prejudice against the medical profession among the lay administrators. This confirmed Costello's unease about the manner in which Browne had been advised and, according to McCormack, he spoke of taking some action against those who had advised him, but was dissuaded from this. The outcome was that Costello decided that doctors should deal with doctors, and set up a medical committee to negotiate with the medical profession, on which the Department was represented by McCormack and Lysaght. This committee did not outlast the fall of the government, when the non-medical civil servants re-asserted their control.[35]

Had Costello but known it, his successor, Eamon de Valera, would have to engage in extraordinarily protracted three-way negotiations with the doctors and the bishops to get the next Health Act agreed. And he was faced almost immediately — and, luckily for him, privately — with an anomaly about the means test for medical services which was brought to his attention by penny-pinching civil servants eager to capitalise on Browne's fall. A Department of Health official minuted him as early as 16 April about the existing Maternity and Child Welfare Schemes, reminding him that

> under the existing M. & C. Schemes there is no means test for women insofar as clinics and general instruction is concerned but there is a means test for the provision of medical care. There is no means test for children under five except in regard to the provision of food. The M. & C. Schemes are very little developed outside the county boroughs. Are these schemes to be continued without a means test?[36]

Already, he added, some of the doctors in the Royal Victoria Eye and Ear Hospital had objected to the treatment of non-necessitous persons under the School Medical Service. Was this scheme also, he asked, to be continued without a means test?

Costello ducked. Three days later, the official noted on the file: 'Discussed with Taoiseach. Schemes which are in operation now should be continued on their existing basis.' Nor was this the end of the pressure. The Dublin assistant city manager spoke to a senior departmental official about the neonatal scheme financed by the Corporation in the three Dublin maternity hospitals (the limited 'Mother and Child Scheme' which had been discussed by the Consultative Council on Child Health), and said that 'in view of recent developments, he and the city manager felt that the scheme will have to be amended to include a means test. He said they were worried about the expenditure at present being incurred and they proposed to ask for an interview with the Taoiseach to discuss the matter.'[37]

The interview does not appear to have taken place. By now, the inter-party government was on a highly greased slipway leading to a general election, and the chocks had been knocked away. Dr Michael ffrench-O'Carroll, who had been one of the Clann's few successes in the 1950 local elections in Dublin, resigned from the party; his letter supporting Noël Browne was published in *The Irish Times* on the very day that Browne's resignation was announced. Jack McQuillan TD joined Browne by resigning from the Clann on 13 April. The party organisation itself was more deeply divided than ever before. Dublin South-East branches went completely over to Browne; the Galway organisation decamped in high dudgeon; Cork split. Everywhere in the country, the Mother and Child Scheme and its fate were at the centre of hot debate in Clann branches and constituency organisations.

The Dáil was dissolved on 5 May, after the government was threatened with defeat — not on the Mother and Child Scheme but on the price of milk. There was, however, no real doubt about what was happening behind the scenes. *The Irish Times* opined:

> The fundamental cause of the dissolution, beyond any doubt, is the affair of Dr Browne . . . Cowan, McQuillan and Browne are the vital men in the Dáil since then, who were determined to unseat the government at the first opportunity, because they said that Mr MacBride had unconstitutionally asked for the resignation of his colleague and was aiming at dictatorship. The Government's strongest point was its weakest link, and Mr MacBride became that link.[38]

The allegation that MacBride had acted unconstitutionally in asking for Browne's resignation was little more than a debating point. Technically it was correct; MacBride did not have the power to demand the resignation of any member of the cabinet. But Costello did, and made it abundantly clear that he had allowed MacBride to approach Browne directly out of courtesy to his role as party leader; and that if MacBride had not done so, or if Browne had refused, he would have stepped into the breach himself. It was, however, the sort of point likely to appeal to potential dissenters in the ranks of the Clann itself.

The campaign was notable for a number of factors. As noted, there was a remarkable surge of public support for Browne, above all among women. They helped to organise a meeting for him in the Mansion House on 8 May, from which more than 100 people had to be turned away because there simply wasn't enough room in the hall. The Mansion House meeting was not only designed to focus support; it was connected to the fact that a strong anti-Browne campaign had been fomented by his opponents. Hilda Tweedy of the Irish Housewives Association, which was backing Browne, recalled later how their speeches at the College Green meeting 'were drowned by the crowd singing "Faith of our Fathers"!'[39] Related to this was a strong, if indirect, anti-Browne campaign by senior members of the medical profession. Browne himself, and his fellow rebels, meanwhile took pains to distance themselves from any criticism of the Catholic Church.

MacBride, the party leader, was angrily heckled at meetings around the country.[40] In his own constituency of Dublin South-West, his campaign was almost completely eclipsed by that of Dr Michael ffrench-O'Carroll, who was now running as an Independent in support of Noël Browne. South-West was not even ffrench-O'Carroll's home base; he had moved there because his own home was in Dublin South-East, Browne's electoral base. His Dáil campaign was a thing of rags and patches; he attached a little trailer to his car and, with the help of a small but devoted band of supporters, criss-crossed the constituency. Everywhere he went he met huge sympathy for Browne on working-class doorsteps; when the votes were counted, he had two votes for every one of MacBride's, and his former party leader only just scraped back into the Dáil.[41] The Clann as a whole went from bad to worse, being reduced from ten to two deputies.

The role of women in Browne's personal election campaign can hardly be underestimated; indeed, it was a major factor in all his electoral successes from 1948 until his last election in 1982. In 1951, however, it was specifically focused on his defeated Mother and Child Scheme. A 'Mother and Child Scheme Committee' was set up, operating originally from an address in Berkeley Road. During the campaign, it moved into 13 Clyde Road. This was not only conveniently in Browne's constituency; it was the home of Dr Betty O'Shea, who had earlier argued, in the letters column of The Irish Times, that working-class women in labour were being denied the benefit of anaesthetic assistance on cost grounds. This in turn provoked a furious rejoinder from the most senior obstetricians in Dublin — Drs O'Donel Browne and J.K. Feeny of the Rotunda, Arthur Barry of Holles Street and W.F. O'Dwyer of the Coombe — rejecting her charges.[42] She returned to the attack during the election campaign,[43] this time more specifically on the means test issue, and as part of the Mother and Child Scheme Committee. By this time the doctors had evidently decided that to reply again would only give her further unwelcome publicity. The case she made has to be marked not proven; although it is quite probable that the abuses she alleged did take place, such practices were probably not policy in the strict sense of the word, and many individual doctors would have been horrified at the suggestion.

The tactics adopted by Browne and his companions during the election were, it can be seen in retrospect, clearly designed to avoid a potentially costly direct confrontation with the bishops.[44] Browne himself continually alleged that the real reason for the fall of the government was a secret deal between Costello and the IMA (he was not to know that such a deal was two governments into the future). He told a constituency meeting in one of a number of similar speeches:

> *The Oireachtas . . . has now been repudiated and* sacrificed solely because of the representations of a handful of doctors and not, I reassert, as they have tried to represent, because of the opposition of the Hierarchy. *Mr Costello has decided that in future our country shall no longer be ruled by the ordinary methods of democratic government, but by bodies such as the medical pressure group.*

He added spice to his message by suggesting that politicians' pay should be determined by the Federation of Rural Workers, and accusing General Seán Mac Eoin, who had earlier capitulated to Dr McQuaid on the issue of legal adoption, of behaving like 'a perambulating saint'.[45]

A few days later, he returned to his theme, telling a meeting in Milltown in Dublin that

> *the opposition that destroyed the scheme was the opposition centred in the specialists in Fitzwilliam and Merrion Squares, and there was no other opposition . . . In the opposition raised to my scheme by their Lordships the Hierarchy, there was no reference made whatsoever to the desirability of including a means test in the scheme, and the necessity that a means test should be included . . . I will not, under any circumstances, vote for any amendment of the Health Act which will authorise any Minister to bring into life . . . this means test, the pauper law, the red ticket and all the rest of it.*[46]

Opposition to Browne was muted during the election campaign. The most direct assault on him came from Bishop Michael Browne of Galway, who charged that the establishment of his scheme 'would soon eliminate the free medical practitioner and create a socialised medical service'.[47] Fine Gael and Clann speakers had obvious reasons for not wanting to bring up the matter, although Paddy McGilligan, the outgoing Minister for Finance, said that he was 'quite proud of what had happened'.[48] Costello, challenged about Browne by a heckler at an election meeting in Tullamore, retorted briefly that he had not intended to say anything about Dr Browne, but that it was 'a case of family responsibility, and the individual responsibility of the father of the family, where he can, to look after himself. That was why the scheme was condemned by the Hierarchy.'[49]

Dr Browne's Clann opponent in Dublin South-East, Dr Patrick McCartan, was in an invidious position. He had been canvassed briefly during the crisis to act as an intermediary between Browne and McQuaid, whom he knew, but had found himself favouring Browne.[50] He had stayed with Clann na Poblachta, and now found himself fighting a battle he almost certainly knew he could not win. His published criticisms of Browne were mild indeed; they were chiefly directed at Browne's 'lack of courtesy' in publishing the correspondence without the permission of his correspondents, and at the fact that 'though young, he should have known that they would be used in the Six Counties to justify occupation'.[51]

Fianna Fáil's silence was equally tactical. MacEntee attacked Costello on the Mother and Child Scheme, not Browne. In Dublin South-East, as the *Irish Times* constituency profile pointed out, Fianna Fáil was

> *not quite sure what to make of public enthusiasm for Dr Browne, but . . . hopes to benefit from his intervention . . . Any votes he takes, it feels sure, will be at the expense of Fine Gael and Labour, [Labour decided, no doubt wisely, against running any candidate in South-East] so that the better he polls the more chance there is of Fianna Fáil's second candidate, Mr Michael Yeats, sliding into the last seat . . . Therefore, Mr MacEntee felt it expedient not to alienate Dr Browne's supporters. On the other hand, he did not want to get mixed up in the Browne controversy himself: that might lead to awkward questions. Silence, he concluded, was the safest policy.*[52]

The only quizzical note came from Aknefton in *The Irish Times*, who noted that 'even Dr Browne seems singularly obscure. He claims to stand by his former policy: yet, at the same time, he makes it quite clear that he has accepted the ruling of the hierarchy and that his scheme is now "past history"'.[53] Aknefton's qualified support obviously — given its anonymous authors' links with the organised left — reflected opinion within the upper reaches of the Labour and trade union movements. Some felt that Browne's use of the TUC delegation at the height of the crisis had been manipulative.[54] He had spurned Norton's attempts at mediation, and indeed had been critical of Norton in cabinet.

Bertie Smyllie made it clear that, as far as he was concerned, one candidate above all others deserved support. Calling — with modified rapture — on voters to give the inter-party government another chance, he endorsed Browne in terms which, as far as can be ascertained, have never been used in respect of any individual candidate by the editor of any national paper, before or since, in the final run-up to an election: 'We hope the courageous and idealistic Dr Browne will head the poll in South East Dublin.'[55]

The election outcome was, effectively, a hung Dáil. Fine Gael actually increased its share of the vote by 6 per cent and its seats by nine; Fianna Fáil, on the other hand, gained only one seat, and was still five seats short of an overall majority. Labour and National Labour (the party had reunited in 1950) lost three seats. The critical factor was the vote for the Independents; including the ex-Clann candidates Browne, McQuillan, ffrench-O'Carroll and Cowan, they had amassed almost 10 per cent of the national vote and fourteen seats. In Dublin South-East, Browne achieved an astonishing result, going from 4,917 first preferences in 1948 to 8,473 (although the figures are not strictly comparable because the constituency boundaries had been redrawn). He had narrowed the gap between himself and the constituency poll-topper, Costello, from 3,500 votes to 750, and beat MacEntee (who had beaten him by almost 2,500 votes in 1948) by 140 votes. In a contest between these three giants, the second Fianna Fáil candidate was simply not at the races; and the hapless Dr McCartan, despite the fact that he had polled exceptionally well in Dublin in the 1945 presidential election, managed only a paltry 569 votes.

What drove the physically frail Browne to such a dramatic outcome was an electorally powerful combination of compassion and anger. 'Anger', it has been observed, 'enlivens if it has room to move, and kills if it hasn't.'[56] The anger which impelled Browne to his first election victory had been an anger at dreadful — and remediable — social conditions. It was now part of a coalition of angers, whose objects included his former colleagues in Clann na Poblachta, the doctors, the bishops, and anyone else who had acted to frustrate his designs. In time, this coalition was to change shape, with some elements dropped and others added. It would also descend, at times, into what the psychiatrist Heinz Kohut described as narcissistic rage, 'a need for revenge, for righting a wrong, for undoing a hurt by any means'.[57] For now, however, it was still primarily the anger which revives and invigorates, the anger linked to a willingness to take risks, a public emotion evoking respect and loyalty from an electorate which shared that particular anger but was afraid or unable to express it, and was profoundly glad that it was able to vote for a candidate who could.

Elsewhere, the election of Michael ffrench-O'Carroll in Dublin South-West, a predominantly working-class constituency, and of Jack McQuillan in the rural Roscommon constituency, prompted Aknefton into an unwonted burst of enthusiasm for the wide social spread of the constituencies which had supported these radical candidates: 'The Irish people are in revolt against all that is worn out and faded in Irish politics.'[58]

The *Irish Times* editor was in no doubt about what would happen now. Browne, ffrench-O'Carroll and Cowan, he guaranteed his readers, 'assuredly will not vote in favour of de Valera'.[59] Browne himself was less sure. Interviewed in Irish at the home of his friend John Conneely in Cois Farraige, he made it clear that he had still to make up his mind.[60] In fact his options were quite limited. Joining Fine Gael was out of the question. Rejoining the Clann was an even more ludicrous prospect. Membership of Labour was hardly an option. Labour TD James Everett had apparently vetoed his membership application to the ITGWU, made after the election, and he had instead joined the British-based Amalgamated Transport and General Workers' Union. And he could hardly join Fianna Fáil so soon after proclaiming his independence.

Politics, however, does not allow people to postpone hard decisions indefinitely, and he had to make up his mind quickly: for whom would he vote when the Dáil came to elect a new Taoiseach? He was assisted, in this hurried process, by his friend Brian Walsh, who arranged a secret meeting between Browne and de Valera's deputy, Seán Lemass, which took place in a parked car in Harcourt Street. Lemass, who insisted that there would be 'no deal' with the newly independent deputy, nonetheless promised that, in so far as Fianna Fáil could, 'we'll try to give you a good health service'.[61] This, in effect, was the beginning of a relationship which was characterised, on Lemass's side, by some affection and, on Browne's side, by respect. Long after Lemass died, I wrote to Browne to ask if he had any particular memories of the former Taoiseach; he replied that he had not, but that he had always had a regard for him, and felt that he might have achieved much more but for the fact that 'the Spaniard', as he put it, had made life difficult for him.[62]

Browne's view of the role of the Independent in such a crunch situation was clear-sighted: whatever you did, you were wrong.[63] But if his former partners in government were not courting him, they were certainly courting others. At the same time as Browne was meeting Lemass in Harcourt Street, senior Fine Gael politicians were meeting Dr Michael ffrench-O'Carroll to persuade him to come over to their side; Peadar Cowan was to allege that they had even offered him a ministry. What actually happened, however, was that at a meeting with Norton and Costello in Costello's house in Leeson Park, Norton did his best to persuade ffrench-O'Carroll of the merits of a social insurance scheme which would, if they were returned to government, take the place of Browne's Mother and Child Scheme. Ffrench-O'Carroll, however, was impervious to such blandishments, not least because he felt that the rate of contributions required to make such a scheme viable would be so high that they would be a penal imposition on the poor; if they were reduced to a merely token level, they would cost more to collect than the revenue they would generate.

There were, as might have been expected, intense discussions between Browne, ffrench-O'Carroll and other deputies about what would happen when the Dáil met for the first time. Browne, for his part, was anxious that he should not be isolated, and should determine policy: 'I want people who will go with me all the way,' was how he put it.[64] The deputies whom the election had put in such a pivotal position now noticed that this was a very strong aspect of his personality, which was to cause problems later on. He was not a man for consensus. More problematic still, although he could participate with others in arriving at a conclusion about a course of action to be adopted, he was quite capable of publicly adopting a different position shortly afterwards, and regarded it as impertinent or irrelevant if this incon- sistency was subsequently pointed out to him. These characteristics, hidden from the public at large, were over the years not only to frustrate many of his own political ambitions, but to cut him off or alienate him from all but a small number of close personal political associates.

When Noël Browne spoke on the nominees for Taoiseach, he said that he was not completely opposed to the concept of inter-party government, but that it could only work for a limited time where there were fundamental differences between the parties, and that although he would vote for de Valera, and continue to vote for the Fianna Fáil party, he would do so only for 'so long as that Party conscientiously pursues the objectives laid down in their 17-point programme'.[65] He was closely followed by ffrench-O'Carroll, who made it plain that, although he was supporting Fianna Fáil, his support would depend 'purely on the manner in which they deal with the practical issues with which the Irish people in the recent general election have so clearly indicated they are most concerned'.[66] Oliver Flanagan, weaned by now from his extravagant enthusiasms of two months earlier, described Browne's as a 'feeble speech',[67] but the most pungent attack on the former minister came from James Dillon, who took particular exception to Browne's statement that the controversy which had led to the fall of the inter-party government was now, as far as he was concerned, an incident which had passed. Describing himself as 'vacillating between sympathy and something closely approximating to hatred for evil', Dillon went on:

> Not all the eloquence of every deputy can catch up with the mighty army of lies which is marching behind that standard at the moment all over the world to prove that in Ireland it is true what Salisbury, what Balfour, what Carson said — that Home Rule was Rome Rule. That is the brief for every slanderer, for every libel merchant of this country all over the world and, what is worse, for those who differ from us most fundamentally in the ideological sphere that is their brief to prove that to be free men you must destroy the Church. I know he never meant that. I know that ideologically he and I think the same. I know that if my Catholicism were compared to his the comparison would, in all probability, be to my disadvantage, but he must forgive me if it makes me sick with horror that his inexperience, his lack of wisdom, his incapacity to understand the consequences of the things he said and did, should bring upon us the irremediable disaster of his published allegations.[68]

Not even Dillon's oratory could, by this stage, alter decisions that had already been taken. De Valera was elected Taoiseach by one vote, garnering the support of the Independents Browne, ffrench-O'Carroll, Cowan, Patrick Cogan and Seán Flynn. The one TD who refused to join the trend was McQuillan, who voted for Costello and against de Valera on the grounds that the electorate had refused to give Fianna Fáil a mandate and that, if they were returned, the country would be 'back to a dictatorship system once again, because the leopard cannot change its spots'.[69]

Some of Noël Browne's spots were not for changing, either — at least, not yet. On one of the first days on which de Valera, now Taoiseach, answered opposition questions in the Dáil, Browne flagged his own Republicanism by asking de Valera — in Irish — whether he proposed to take any action on the vexed question of allowing Northern elected representatives access to Dáil Éireann. This was an issue which had been Clann na Poblachta policy since 1946. De Valera played for time, suggesting that Browne raise the matter in the forthcoming debate on the Taoiseach's estimate.[70] Browne's decision not to raise it again was in itself a pointer to the fact that he and Eamon de Valera had a relationship that was already moving onto a different plane.

The euphoria of his election triumph was succeeded by a series of events which operated like a noose tightening around his political future. His first year as an Independent exposed his powerlessness as issue succeeded issue, and his rhetoric returned to haunt him. Almost immediately, he was faced with the new government's Social Welfare Bill, introduced by James Ryan. He spoke and voted in favour of the second stage of the Bill, although this put him in a particularly anomalous position, because — unlike Norton's Social Welfare Bill, for which Browne had actually voted on the very day of his resignation — it actually contained a means test. He now told the Dáil, inexplicably, that he had voted for Norton's Bill (which had fallen with the government) 'although I disagreed with it', and that he was voting for the current Bill as someone who was 'a confirmed believer in what has been described as the Welfare State'. He went on to defend Ryan's decision to bring in a bill with a means test on the grounds that it would be very difficult to bring in a bill without one in the absence of full employment.[71]

His supporters must by then have started to wonder what was happening to him, but worse was to come. Browne and the other Independents were now faced with an equally embarrassing problem: the 1952 Budget, introduced by MacEntee, the Minister for Finance, on 2 April, the earliest date on which a budget had been introduced in the history of the State. This was driven both by MacEntee's deep fiscal conservatism and by near-panic in the Department of Finance about the balance of payments.[72] It raised income tax by a shilling in the pound, and imposed price increases on bread and butter, tea and sugar, drink and petrol. In the case of basic food commodities, these increases were the result of removing a framework of subsidies which had been in existence for some time. The Budget, according to J.J. Lee, 'probably contributed significantly to both the reality and the atmosphere of depression', but it is likely the government had calculated that the Independents 'might swallow unpalatable medicine at this early stage, due to their reluctance to go to the country so soon again, that they would not stomach later'.[73]

In the case of Browne and his Independent allies, it was a canny calculation. Browne acknowledged in his autobiography that he had spoken in favour of the Budget, but added: 'As I had during the Coalition government, I chose to ignore those policies disagreeable to me in order to concentrate on the issue of the health services.'[74] As it happens, he went even further than supporting the government with his voice. Although his speech was critical of the Budget on some points, he encouraged MacEntee and de Valera to justify it on the grounds that 'these serious and hard impositions which strike at everybody, from the youngest infant up to the oldest amongst us, are imposed in order to maintain our independence and our national sovereignty'.[75] Not only that, but he voted for each and every one of the Budget resolutions on 2 April 1952, an action which prompted his future party leader, Brendan Corish, later to exclaim with grim satisfaction from the Opposition benches: 'He is in the net.'[76] He followed this up with votes for the Finance Bill's various provisions in May, although he was absent from the House for a number of divisions on one day.

The debate on the estimates for the Department of Health followed, in which Costello, still acting as Fine Gael spokesman on health, indirectly accused Browne of having attempted to 'resurrect or implant in the minds of certain sections of the people of Dublin something very much akin to class hatred'.[77] No legislation is involved in an estimate debate, which deals only with matters of administration, but Browne evidently felt the need to make a stand now on the one issue with which he had been so publicly identified. He warned the minister that 'I propose to vote against any legislation that will introduce a means test.'[78] He did not have to wait long for an opportunity, and when it came, he had to swallow his words, after tortuously and obviously unhappily attempting to rationalise his abandonment of the principle on which he had brought down the previous government. This was when Dr James Ryan introduced the 1952 Health Bill, which was eventually to become the 1953 Health Act but which was effectively not implemented until after the next change of government in 1954. The Bill had a long and difficult passage through the Oireachtas and through the various interest groups outside it, as will be seen.

The voting record of the Dáil after the change of government shows clearly the extent to which Fianna Fáil could rely on his support. He was rarely absent, and does not seem to have voted against the government on any occasion, unlike ffrench-O'Carroll, who voted against the government at least once — on 29 October 1952, on a question dealing with the interest charges on loans under the Small Dwellings Acquisition Act, finding himself in the opposite lobby to Browne on this occasion. Both deputies voted with the government for the suspension of Brendan Corish after a Dáil row in March 1953.

This consistency reflected to some degree a new stability in his private life. Although his marriage to Phyllis was an extraordinary source of strength and joy to both partners for a period of over fifty years, they had failed to put down roots, moving from one rented house to another in a way which consumed resources and must have been, on occasion, unsettling emotionally as well. They now built a house in Enniskerry — St Brigid's — which was the first they had ever owned. Later they were to move to a house which particularly appealed to them in Bray. Roseville, on the Dublin Road but set back from the traffic, was a rambling old house of great charm which had previously been a home for deprived city children. It had not been lived in for some years, and had what optimistic estate agents would describe cheerfully as 'potential', but Phyllis Browne's domestic skills turned it over time into an attractive home.[79]

Browne's view of the Fianna Fáil cabinet during this period can only be inferred, but one strong like, and one strong dislike, are both evident. Seán Lemass, Minister for Industry and Commerce, frequently came in for praise. Lemass, Browne felt, had 'done more to establish the prestige of our people and of our industries in the time in which he has been in office' than almost anyone else.[80] He was, on the other hand, regularly critical of Lemass's colleague, the Minister for Posts and Telegraphs, Erskine Childers.[81] Part of this undoubtedly went back to 1950, when Childers, in the course of a speech on Browne's Health estimate, had attempted to ridicule the British National Health Service with an anecdote about a man who had rung up a doctor in the middle of the night to pay a house call because his child would not go to sleep, believing that this was his entitlement under socialist legislation.[82]

The moment of truth for Noël Browne, which came during the long debates on the 1952 Health Bill, is of considerable interest. The Bill introduced a free scheme — but only for mothers and infants up to six weeks of age, as contrasted with Browne's far more ambitious scheme, which would have included children up to the age of sixteen. After six weeks, a means test would be implemented to determine who would continue to have free treatment, and who would not. The issues of reproductive morality had long been disposed of, and Noël Browne readily supported Ryan on these; birth control and abortion were, he said, against the natural law and 'objectionable'.[83] But the core of the Bill, politically speaking, was the means test issue.

The discussion on the Bill, which went on until the summer of 1953, was punctuated by long wrangles, especially between Browne and McGilligan about the financing of Browne's projected Mother and Child Scheme, in which James Ryan helpfully weighed in on Browne's side, armed with Department of Finance documents. Although Browne criticised some of the Bill's provisions, he did not vote against them, with one exception, which is discussed below. There were, in fact, comparatively few Dáil divisions on this particular piece of legislation; although the debates dragged on, the official reports give a strong impression that politicians on all sides of the House were weary of the altercations, and fearful of the consequences of another explosion. Browne voted in favour of the Bill's second stage on 26 February 1953. He told the Dáil on 15 April that he was supporting the Bill because it contained a 'tiny moiety' of the principle for which he had resigned.[84] On 23 April he voted for the money resolution associated with the Bill, and he voted for the fifth and final stage on 30 July. In between, he supported the government in a confidence vote on 2 July which it won by seventy-three votes to seventy-one. There were no votes specifically on section 26 of the Bill, which incorporated the means test. He voted with the government against Labour amendments on 24 and 25 June, neither of which was related to the means test issue.

It is worth noting that, in most of the divisions on this Bill, Fianna Fáil was joined in the lobbies by the Labour deputies, so that Browne was effectively voting with his former colleagues in favour of measures not dissimilar to those he had refused to accept while in government with them. His only vote against any section of the Bill was on 15 July, when he called a division on the one amendment he had put down himself, designed to delete a section giving the managements of county homes the right to require inmates to work, should they consider it necessary. This vote was unusual in that there was absolutely no prospect of a government defeat on the issue; Browne was supported in the lobbies only by Labour, Fine Gael abstained, and Fianna Fáil voted against. If the ironies of the situation were not lost on the participants, they did not choose to make political mileage out of them.

Browne's position, as he explained it on a number of occasions, was that he was constrained to do what he did because a majority in the Dáil were in favour of the measure — that he was, one might say, swimming with the tide, rather than against it. This was an attempt to recreate the rationale of his position as minister in the previous government, when he had argued that in introducing his free scheme he was doing no more than giving legislative form to the will of the Dáil as it had been expressed in 1947.

The problem about this position, however, is that his opposition to a means test should logically have impelled him to vote against Ryan's Bill at the second stage, the first occasion on which the Dáil expressed a concrete opinion on the measure. If the Bill passed second stage, he could then vote for the remaining stages, with some measure of consistency, on the technical grounds that this measure also had now received the support of a majority in the Dáil. But he chose not to do this, and voted for the second stage of the Bill on the grounds that it had — despite enshrining a number of means tests — also, in some vestigial fashion, protected the principle of free access to medical services for all mothers and children.

The intellectual tightrope he was walking may have provided him with some personal rationale for his actions, but it did not impress anyone else. The politics of the situation were unmistakable. If his opposition to all means tests in 1951 had been on a matter of principle, why was he not opposing them now? If it was not a principle now, what had all the fuss been about then? More to the point, if it had not really been a principle then, his actions in 1952 and 1953 added considerable weight to the argument that his principal objective, during the 1951 crisis, had been the political destruction of MacBride or, at the very least, the withdrawal of Clann na Poblachta from the government.

Browne's one vote against the government, on a comparatively minor issue, may have been a gesture, but it was little more than that. Fine Gael hung his May 1951 statement of refusal to vote for a means test around his neck, but to no avail. He was now to accept it in certain circumstances, he said, 'as a temporary measure in view of the fact that it appears to be the wishes of the majority of the House . . . I think that is the one bright part of this Bill — that the principle has been maintained, possibly slightly vitiated, but I do not think in effect vitiated.'[85] The concept of a principle which was simultaneously 'slightly' vitiated but not 'in effect' vitiated was not one which appealed to his critics. During the debate on the fifth and final stage of the Bill, Browne congratulated Ryan handsomely for having incorporated in the Bill 'the seed' of the idea of equal opportunity in the health services. Jim Larkin, speaking from the Labour benches immediately after Browne, commented wryly: 'If the seed is there it is buried very, very deep.'[86]

Many years later, in 1983, the government released through the State Paper Office (later the National Archives) a whole series of documents from the 1951–4 government, which provoked Browne into a bitter attack on the legislation for which he had voted as an Independent deputy, and on the party which had introduced it.[87] This attack, which was amplified in his autobiography, described the accommodation which de Valera and Ryan had come to with the bishops as a capitulation 'and an infinitely more shameful betrayal of the principle of representative democracy and the desperate health needs of our sick poor'. De Valera, he charged,

> by repudiating his own Act of Parliament [the 1947 Health Act] at the behest of the Roman Catholic bishops, in the minds of the Northern Protestants, established the Catholic nature of our State. Right to the present time, on the issues of divorce, contraception, non-denominational educational services, and now abortion, none of our lesser leaders has dared to interfere with the undemocratic precedent set by de Valera.[88]

There is a problem about this. It implies, unmistakably, that Browne would not have accepted de Valera and Ryan's compromise had he been aware that it was acceptable to the bishops. To put it in other words, the acceptability of the scheme, in so far as he was concerned, depended, not on its content, but on whether it had been agreed with the bishops or not. Even half a century later, it is difficult to detect any logic to this position, all the more so because it was widely known — and mentioned by several speakers in the Dáil — that de Valera had had a run-in with the hierarchy during the drafting of the Bill. Browne himself, given his own experience, could hardly have doubted that negotiations of some kind would have been in progress. The gimlet eye which he turned on de Valera's 1953 compromise in 1983 was not accompanied by any compelling explanation as to why he would have acted or voted differently had he been aware of all the circumstances.

The context, however, is relevant. In 1983 Fianna Fáil had just been behaving in a particularly supine and opportunistic way on the question of the constitutional amendment on abortion, and Browne was anxious to apply the tar-brush retrospectively. Moreover, in 1983, and in 1986, he could not have been aware of the content of the McQuaid archives, which throws considerably more light on these negotiations than that provided by the State papers or, indeed, by John Whyte's admirable earlier study of Church–State relations.

These archives, while confirming the general tenor of the negotiations between the government and the hierarchy, make it clear that some members of the hierarchy had serious reservations about the compromise. It is equally clear that the medical profession were positively incandescent, not just at the Bill, but at the fact that the bishops had agreed to it. And they suggest that McQuaid, in particular, was by this stage — perhaps because of his experiences in 1951 — playing a different part, one which prioritised agreement over confrontation. It was certainly significant that the contretemps involving a sharply critical letter which the bishops sent to the papers, but which was withdrawn after de Valera went personally to meet Cardinal D'Alton on the matter in April 1953, took place while McQuaid was away in Australia.

McQuaid wrote a memorandum for his own files on meetings he had had with senior members of the IMA about the Bill in the latter part of 1952.[89] In these meetings the doctors were describing the Bill as 'essentially evil' and 'intrinsically bad'. McQuaid, however, had two objectives. The first was to persuade the doctors that the Bill, though defective, had by agreement been so far amended as to permit the hierarchy to abstain from public approval or disapproval. The second was to avoid giving the doctors the slightest impression that they would get any support from the bishops for 'corporate resistance to the Health Bill when it becomes law'.

The extent to which he succeeded is evident in a wry comment many years later by T.C.J. O'Connell, who in 1952–3 was leading the IMA crusade against Ryan's bill, as he had against Browne's scheme. Initially, Archbishop McQuaid supported the doctors, but then — to their astonishment — backed off after the bishops had negotiated a compromise with the government which the doctors found profoundly unacceptable. At one meeting after this sudden reversal, according to O'Connell, McQuaid asked the doctors tersely if they were going to fight the Act 'by taking to the mountains with guns'! The effect of the compromise between de Valera and the hierarchy, O'Connell said, was like losing one's best troops.[90]

McQuaid certainly had his problems. On one hand, he was quarrelling with Ryan about the £1 a year which mothers would have to pay to qualify for the scheme; on the other, he was having to cope with the fears of Bishop Lucey of Cork that 'Socialism little by little is as bad as Socialism in one sweep.'[91] Three years later, the wounds still not entirely healed, he was to write to a Vatican Curial official to explain that, although the Bill, now an Act, had never received the approval of the bishops, 'the crookedness of the measure was made sufficiently straight to avoid further condemnation'. Both Ryan and Lemass, he added disdainfully, had shown themselves to be mentally incapable of grasping the principles involved; the latter, as Minister for Industry and Commerce, had been 'chiefly responsible for the very noteworthy socialisation of our country'; and the Act itself would come to be seen as 'one of the unfortunate measures of Mr de Valera's government that have tended to emphasise the trend towards excessive State intervention and, I would add, a latent anti-clericalism that fears the influence of the Church and will always seek to eliminate that influence from public life'.[92] Because it suited his book to do so, he regarded Ryan and Lemass's opposition as symptomatic of feeble-mindedness. The truth of the matter, which his subsequent sentence hints strongly at, was that there was at the time an internal division in the government, with Ryan and Lemass taking a hard-line position, and de Valera — whose role in the negotiations had been affected by his absence in Utrecht for an eye operation — determined that a compromise was achievable, as indeed it was.

Unaware of the detail of these negotiations, and even more so of the deep disapproval of the scheme still seeping through the hierarchy and the rampant frustrations of the medical profession, Browne continued to experience the problems of supporting Fianna Fáil from the outside. He knew that the party would claim the credit for anything positive, and that he and his companions would get the blame for anything negative. His experience in Clann na Poblachta notwithstanding, he had developed a fairly well worked out view on the importance of political parties as such: loners could only do so much. In this he differed — and it would have been one of the few differences ever between them — with his wife. It was an organisational rather than a political difference; at many points during his sojourns in one or other of the political wildernesses he inhabited, Noël would remind himself out loud of the importance of group action; Phyllis, more conscious of the compromises that had to be made within party structures, and perhaps of the intense demands made by party organisations on their more high-profile members, preferred it when he was an Independent.[93]

After about a year in this invidious position, Browne apparently decided to swallow his pride and attempted to join the Labour Party. Norton, unsurprisingly, 'refused him membership'.[94] He then took the initial steps towards launching a new political party. It would be left, but anti-communist. To this end, he called a meeting in the home of the Keatings. Seán Keating, the painter, had done a powerful portrait of him in 1951. May Keating was an activist who had been closely involved in the Mother and Child Committee and other support groups in the same year. She was fond of Noël; she once gave him a present of one of the original copies of the 1916 Proclamation, which now hangs over the fireplace in the home of Noël's daughter Ruth. The Keatings' son, Justin, the future Labour Party cabinet minister, was at this stage a teenager involved in a small communist-front-type organisation.

At least two of the participants at this meeting have recollections of it, but at this remove in time they are necessarily indistinct. One remembers it as an attempt — of which there would have been many at this time — to rally the forces of the left.[95] Another remembers it chiefly for two things. One was a warning by Noël Browne that the danger from communism was not to be found in front-type organisations like the Irish Workers' League, but in individuals like Dr John de Courcy Ireland and others. The second was an acute sense of puzzlement. The reason for which the meeting had been convened was never made clear, and indeed he left the meeting no wiser than before about Browne's plans or general ideas.[96]

It now seems evident that this meeting was part of an initiative by Browne aimed at creating a political vehicle which would rally people who thought like him around the flag of a new party, or at least testing the temperature of the water. It was an ill-kept secret. Even after the election, there had been rumours that a new formation was on the cards, but they died out. By the autumn of 1952, no doubt in part because of the hostile reaction to the Budget of that year, the rumours were revived and became more widespread. They were given a substantial impetus by the death of Alfie Byrne, son of the popular Lord Mayor of Dublin of the same name, who had been an Independent Dáil deputy for the Dublin North-West constituency since 1948.

'Dr Browne', the usually well-informed correspondent of the Commonwealth periodical *The Round Table* told his readers, 'is trying to form a new party, but it is difficult to see in what respect, apart from his views on specific issues, any programme he could formulate would be materially different from that of the Labour Party.'[97] Apart from Browne himself, the new party would have included Noel Hartnett (who had been elected spectacularly to the Seanad as an Independent in the 1951 general election, no doubt as an expression of the same sentiments that had contributed to Noël Browne's Dáil success in the same election); Brian Walsh, the Fianna Fáil-inclined barrister who had helped Hartnett and Browne during the Mother and Child imbroglio; and Dr Michael ffrench-O'Carroll, the ex-Clann, Independent TD for Dublin South-West.[98] The *Irish Times* columnist Aknefton — whose links with the trade union movement have already been noted — was of a similar view, stressing the theory that a political party had to be an expression of the economic interests of a class, or a large stratum, in society, and questioning whether Browne could pretend to represent any such group not already covered by a political party.

Browne, of course, was in a difficult situation. Labour had shown itself unresponsive to his overtures. On the other hand, Labour-inspired commentators were patronising his moves to set up a new party on the grounds that anything he could do, Labour could do better. The impending by-election in Dublin North-West brought matters to a head. A high-profile candidate for a new political party would have been guaranteed publicity and, perhaps, even a seat. Browne, according to rumour, had just such a person in mind: Ernest Wood, a prominent member of the Senior Bar with radical views, and one of the best-known orators in a legal system which was not short of them.[99] He also lived in Enniskerry, close to Browne.

Browne had until then kept his plans for the new party under wraps, but his cover was blown on the morning of 9 September 1952, when Wood revealed all in a letter to the editor of *The Irish Times*. The new party, he said, had already been formed; he had agreed, after a personal request from Browne and Hartnett, to contest the forthcoming election in Dublin North-West; and he had been unanimously selected as the candidate at a meeting of the party on 29 July. He had, he said, been moved to admiration by Browne's loyalty to his election pledges and by his resistance to Church interference in the affairs of a democratically elected government.

However, he added, 'I have now been informed by Dr Browne that I am not acceptable to him as a candidate.' Brian Walsh, he informed the newspaper's readers, had been of the same opinion as Browne because Wood was 'too strong a personality to be controlled'. He continued, in terms which blighted the hopes of the new party as surely as frost in spring:

> *In view of his failure to put in black and white his ultimate aims, I have been prompted to criticise him, and am unable to render that unquestioning loyalty*

which Dr Browne requires of his party . . . I am also, however, moved by fear of secret policies. I am also moved by recent manifestations in Irish politics of the tendency to mask dictatorship behind a lip-service to democratic forms. Must Irish ideas (and idols) always be born like the Morning Glory, which shrivels and withers before the noonday sun?[100]

Wood's biting words prefigured the controversies which were to dog Noël Browne's footsteps into, and out of, the four other political parties he either joined or helped to found between this and the end of his political career. The barrister was not the first, or the last, of Noël Browne's actual or potential allies who found themselves suddenly dispensable at short notice when they questioned his judgment. Even some of those who stayed loyal to him throughout his twists and turns wondered at his capacity for biting the hands that nourished him, sometimes right up to the elbow.

At the same time, even those who served with him but later turned against him bore witness to the charismatic aspect of his personality. Charisma itself is a somewhat ambiguous concept. Theologically, it signifies the gift of grace, the intuitive recognition by laypeople that a saint has intimate contact with God. Its Roman equivalent, *facilitas*, signifies a hero's innate ability to lead a project to success because of the access he has to the divine. Some psychologists, on the other hand, regard it as a personality disorder in which charismatic leaders and those who follow them are bound together by psychological needs at least as much as by any shared objectives. A more balanced analysis suggests that the charismatic is 'exceptionally responsive to the other's emotional nuances if they support his or her fantasy, but not if the other asserts difference or autonomy'.[101] Whichever model may be adopted — and no single model can do justice to the complexities of any human personality — there is little doubt that Noël Browne possessed, or exercised, charisma, and that, paradoxically, this was not always to his advantage.

As things turned out, Fine Gael's Seán Mac Eoin made it clear that they would not oppose the candidature of Alfie Byrne's son in the by-election, and Thomas Byrne was elected to take his father's seat, with more than 60 per cent of the first preference vote. He held the seat until 1961. It is doubtful whether even Wood would have made much of an impression against such unstoppable populism.

The failure to make a showing in the by-election threw Browne's supporters — they were known as 'Éire ar Aghaidh' — into some disarray. Many of them had been operating in the firm belief that he and Hartnett could and would formally launch a new political party to the left of Labour. At the end of September 1953, he told them bluntly that in his opinion the time was not ripe for the emergence of another political party, and that he had to decide between the cowardly choice of leaving politics or joining either Fianna Fáil or Labour. The Labour Party, he said, had consistently opposed progressive legislation since 1945, and therefore he was forced to join Fianna Fáil.[102]

It would be wrong, however, to assume that this decision was one entirely forced on Browne by circumstance. That would be to ignore a number of key factors: his continuing conviction that membership of a party was, all other things being equal, the best way of getting policy implemented; his admiration for Seán Lemass, who he felt had dealt fairly with him over the thorny question of the health services; and his Ballinrobe-engendered Republicanism, which had been battle-hardened by his British public school experiences and enhanced, rather than dimmed, during his membership of Clann na Poblachta. In a later interview, he specifically instanced his admiration for Lemass, who he had hoped would revive the 'old glory and radicalism' of Fianna Fáil after de Valera's departure.

There was also a personal factor. Joan Ryan, the wife of Senator Eoin Ryan, was a sister of Florence Hartnett, Noel Hartnett's wife. Eoin, son of James Ryan, then Minister for Health, was a rising star in Fianna Fáil. Although a career in law and business meant that his politics were eventually confined to the Seanad, he was to become — and to some extent still is — a trusted elder statesman of the party. In the early 1950s, he was one of a group of younger people — C.J. Haughey and Brian Lenihan among them — who were moving into key positions in the organisation as the old guard began to look like bowing out. There was another strand to the relationship: Ryan owned a yacht in Dún Laoghaire, and Noël often went out with him, before he owned a boat of his own.

The Health Bill had been effectively disposed of in the summer of 1953. Browne and his allies moved quickly after Wood's letter in *The Irish Times*. On 28 October, de Valera told a meeting of the Fianna Fáil parliamentary party that 'Deputies Dr Noël Browne, Dr Michael ffrench-O'Carroll and Patrick Cogan had expressed their desire to become members of the party and proposed that they be accepted as members'.[103] Dan Breen seconded the motion, and, after a discussion, it was adopted unanimously. It may or may not have been significant that Seán MacEntee was not present; he would in any case have been unlikely to oppose the proposal by de Valera, not least because it hugely strengthened Fianna Fáil's position in the Dáil. The three who joined operated as a group. At the time, Browne had some anxiety that the others might not follow him in.[104] Peadar Cowan did not join. Described once by Lemass as being 'as clever as a pet fox', he was to some extent unstable, organised a private volunteer force with the express intention of invading Northern Ireland (most of its adherents seem to have been planted by the security forces or by groups loyal to Archbishop McQuaid) and was eventually the subject of bankruptcy proceedings.

Jack McQuillan — despite his strong reservations about de Valera — also had discussions with Fianna Fáil at around this time. He was offered a position as parliamentary secretary with responsibility for undeveloped western areas, in which he would have had an extraordinary impact.[105] Negotiations foundered, however, on the question of whether he would be automatically adopted as a Fianna Fáil candidate in the next general election in his Roscommon constituency. The Fianna Fáil view was that he would have to win his spurs within the organisation in the normal way and indeed, given that the Fianna Fáil deputy in the area, Gerry Boland, was by then already sixty-eight years old, this should not have been too difficult. In the event, McQuillan decided to stay where he was, and the new job was given to Jack Lynch.

Before the parliamentary party meeting, de Valera had had a private meeting with Browne. The only criticism he expressed, and on which they agreed to disagree, was of Browne's decision to publish the correspondence between the parties at the time of the Mother and Child row.[106] Fresh from a very similar series of private encounters with the bishops himself, de Valera certainly had reason to be sensitive about such matters.

Both Browne and ffrench-O'Carroll went into the party with colours flying. Browne, in a statement, declared that 'the pledges which I gave to the electorate in my constituency have now been fulfilled, and . . . any contribution I am capable of making in the future for the common good can best be made as a member of Fianna Fáil'. Ffrench-O'Carroll was even more explicit, claiming that the passage of Fianna Fáil's Health Act 'confirms the fact that the health crisis of the inter-party government need never have taken place and justifies my aim in standing as an Independent deputy'. He was joining Fianna Fáil, he said, because he believed the country was returning to a two-party political system and that Fianna Fáil was truly representative of the people; and that it was the duty of the young people to see that the ideals which de Valera stood for would be carried through to the next generation.[107] Ffrench-O'Carroll was defeated in Dublin South-West in 1954 and subsequently became a Fianna Fáil senator.

Newspaper comment was cautiously welcoming of these developments. *The Irish Times*, whose editorial admiration for Browne was to wane after Smyllie's death in September 1954, observed:

> *Some time ago we commented on Fianna Fáil's lack of young blood: these independent defections will supply a most necessary transfusion. Dr Browne's energy, and the freshness of his ideas, may well be the leaven necessary to leaven the Fianna Fáil lump, and it will be a thousand pities if the lump is content to absorb him and his companions without consenting to be leavened. These are men whose outlook is settled on 1953, rather than 1923, and for that reason*

alone the Government will do well to accept them as people with a real contri-bution to make, and not as mere ciphers in the division lobby.[108]

The diplomats observing these events from the calmer atmosphere of the US Embassy were more circumspect and, as it later proved, more accurate.

Dr Browne was elected as an Independent, and some of his followers had hoped to establish a new progressive labor party with him as its leader. Those plans will have to be changed. Whether Dr Browne as a member of de Valera's Fianna Fáil party will have the same appeal as Dr Browne the Independent, who had been 'disgracefully' treated by Fine Gael and was the champion of the masses, remains to be seen. The same is true of Dr ffrench-O'Carroll.[109]

The British Embassy, equally quizzical, noted that there was 'some question how easily they and the old guard will shake down together'.[110]

Some of Noël Browne's long-time supporters were deeply disturbed by his move into Fianna Fáil. Edward Thornley (brother of David Thornley) noticed what he described as a 'massive defection' of supporters at this time. Thornley is undeniably an unfriendly witness; but his evidence, however discounted, gives a flavour of the fierce passions Browne aroused, among both his opponents and his supporters (and perhaps especially among those who crossed from the latter camp into the former).

Whatever about his erstwhile supporters, Fianna Fáil at large welcomed Noël Browne like a prodigal son. In the aftermath of the 1952 Budget, his accession, and that of ffrench-O'Carroll, helped to refurbish the party's radical credentials (Cogan was useful for another reason, as he had until then been an Independent farmer TD from Co. Wicklow). Hartnett, now an Independent in the Seanad, also announced in October his intention of rejoining Fianna Fáil. Browne, however, was the one who threw himself most wholeheartedly into his new party's activities. The Fianna Fáil archives show that his attendance at parliamentary party meetings was exemplary, although there was not much time left for him to make an impact at this level as the next election was little more than six months away. After his first meeting of the parliamentary party, Browne was leaving in the company of Senator Michael Yeats, who apologised for the interminable length of the proceedings. 'Not at all,' he replied, enthusiastically. 'I was delighted to be able to listen to all these criticisms of Government policy. You know, I am used to a party in which, should there be the slightest criticism, then some-one proposes a vote of confidence in the leader.'[111]

By January 1954, he was declaring himself proud to be a member of Fianna Fáil, and privileged to work with 'the men who were returned to the Dáil to break the subservient tradition of the Cumann na nGael party of allegiance to an outside king'.[112] He gave early notice that he would not be a 'cipher': at the parliamentary party meeting on 27 January he moved a resolution declaring that 'in present circumstances a policy of financial austerity is no longer justified', and calling on the party to adopt 'progressive policies' with which to mount an electoral fightback. This stung de Valera into a strong defence of his position, in which he was backed up by Frank Aiken, the Minister for External Affairs and one of his most trusty lieutenants. MacEntee, possibly fortuitously, was absent. Browne, finding discretion to be the better part of valour, eventually withdrew his resolution.[113]

After losing a number of by-elections in late 1953 and early 1954, de Valera, his position rapidly becoming untenable, called an election for May 1954. Browne was now on the Fianna Fáil ticket in Dublin South-East with Seán MacEntee. The contrast with the two previous elections could not have been more marked. Even in *The Irish Times*, Browne received scant enough coverage. His speeches were confined almost exclusively to the cost of living issue, on which he continually challenged Fine Gael to justify its claim that it could bring down the prices of essential foodstuffs. Unwisely, given the nature of the constituency and Fianna Fáil's unpopularity, he made John A. Costello the object of most of his attacks.

The election was notable for MacEntee's attitude to Browne. His own position was considerably less secure than it might have been, given the memory of his 1952 Budget and his uncompromising — if occasionally misguided — defence of the public finances. He behaved exceptionally generously towards Browne in the circumstances, operating a primitive form of vote-splitting, and urging Browne to go out and get every vote he could for himself. He also allowed Browne — and this would have been almost unheard of in Fianna Fáil election campaigns — to distribute personalised election literature, as long as his own name was included. Eddie McManus, the tough Belfast man who was MacEntee's right hand in the constituency, was aghast at such unselfishness towards somebody who, he feared, might threaten MacEntee's seat.[114]

One of Browne's pieces of literature featured artwork (by Harry Kernoff, RHA, it is rumoured) depicting all the Dublin hospitals with whose establishment or refurbishment Browne had been associated as Minister for Health. Circulation of this document soon attracted the attention of an ever-vigilant Seán MacBride, who immediately sent a copy to Archbishop McQuaid's secretary with a letter whose combination of spitefulness and obsequiousness was by now truly remarkable. Drawing McQuaid's attention to Browne's claim to have inaugurated the new Children's Hospital in Crumlin, he went on:

> *This hospital is in my constituency and many attempts have and are being made to suggest that Dr Browne is responsible for the erection of this hospital.*

My recollection is that the project for this hospital was initiated by His Grace long before Dr Browne was ever heard of. Can you confirm my recollection on this point? If my recollection on this point is correct should something not be done to let it be known that it was not Dr Browne who was responsible and that it was His Grace? I hope that you are keeping well and are not too over-worked. Please say a prayer for me.

Dr McQuaid's secretary's reply was circumspect, to say the least: 'When the Hospital opens — and this should be within a reasonable time — it will be possible to make the position clear. Meantime, I thought it more advisable not to worry the Archbishop with the enclosure.'[115]

On the face of it, putting Browne on the ticket with MacEntee was a justifiable risk. It was a swing constituency — the third seat could go either way — and Browne's high profile was a distinct advantage. Not least because of the chances that MacEntee took, it very nearly came off. On the first count, MacEntee and Browne split almost equally between them the 43 per cent of the vote which Fianna Fáil garnered; Browne was some 400 votes behind MacEntee's 5,971, with more than twice the first preference votes of John O'Donovan, the second Fine Gael candidate. But Fine Gael was on the rampage, not least in the wake of MacEntee's Budget and his decision not to accept a civil service arbitration agreement. Between Ernest Blythe in the 1920s and Richie Ryan in the 1970s, there can hardly have been a more unpopular Minister for Finance than MacEntee was in 1951–4. Costello added 2,000 votes to his 1951 total, and dragged in O'Donovan on his coat-tails. The Labour candidate, Vincent McDowell, had a critical 1,455 first preferences. When eliminated, he transferred only 327 votes to Browne as against 1,236 to O'Donovan, which, with Costello's massive surplus, guaranteed O'Donovan's election. Even more significantly, MacEntee won the third and last seat, without reaching the quota; at this stage, he was only 108 votes ahead of Browne.[116] After the count was finished, MacEntee paid a handsome, and by all accounts genuinely felt, tribute to his running mate. He had never, he said, had a more loyal or a more unselfish team-mate.[117] Browne replied in similar vein. Behind the rhetoric, however, the hard men in the party organisation — particularly McManus — were privately vowing that this would never be allowed to happen again.

For the time being, Browne's star was well established in the Fianna Fáil firmament. In common with another defeated candidate, C.J. Haughey — who had just failed to edge out Harry Colley, George Colley's father, for the second Fianna Fáil seat in Dublin North-East — he was elected at the head of the poll to the party's National Executive at the 1954 Ard-Fheis, an extraordinary achievement for a first-time delegate. Other delegates were evidently impressed by his fighting speech in defence of James Ryan's

Health Act, in the course of which — changing tack, it would appear — he now blamed Labour, rather than Fine Gael, for 'sabotaging' the 1947 Health Act legislation and putting it 'irretrievably into oblivion', because that party had held the casting vote in the inter-party government. The principle of the Fianna Fáil Act, he averred in a phrase of which he was fond, was that nobody should have his pocket searched to see if he could afford to have his life saved.[118]

In the ensuing three years, as he was no longer a member of the Oireachtas, his major contribution was to be made through the National Executive. De Valera in fact offered him a nomination to the Seanad, but he turned it down, on the grounds that that he would not take an Oireachtas position that he had not won by election.[119]

His success at the Ard-Fheis saw him appointed to the party's finance subcommittee at the first meeting of the National Executive on 25 October.[120] The following month, he was appointed to a subcommittee of the executive on the restoration of Irish, chaired by de Valera; other members included Eoin Ryan and Brian Lenihan. His concern with policy matters soon became evident. At the executive meeting on 14 February 1955 he raised the question of the party's overall policy profile, in response to which de Valera agreed to ask the policy committee of the party to provide the executive with a précis of the draft statement of policy as soon as possible. The minutes do not record whether such a statement was ever delivered, but even if it was, it was not debated.

By the executive meeting of September 1955 Browne was turning his attention to education, a topic in which he had not shown much interest heretofore but which was, under one heading or another, to exercise his attention from then until the end of his political life. On 12 September he put down a notice of motion on the topic, and when someone queried the support for it, he got eight executive members to agree with him (he needed only five). At the following meeting, on 26 September, he moved his resolution, urging acceptance of the 'principle of equal opportunity in education for all sections of the community'. De Valera, whose highly attuned political antennae detected danger in this radicalism, had the motion amended so that the uncompromising statement of principle was modified to an acknowledgment of 'the desirability of aiming at' equal opportunity. Nonetheless, a committee was set up to examine the practical application of this principle with particular reference to the school leaving age, the size of classes, the recruitment of teachers, and the improvement of opportunities for higher education. The other members of the committee, along with Browne, were Eoin Ryan, Brian Lenihan, Stephen Ennis, Sean Moylan (a former Minister for Education), Dr Michael ffrench-O'Carroll, Jack McCann and Michael Yeats.

Browne's recollection (and that of Michael Yeats) is that the committee did excellent work. Its findings were discussed over a number of meetings of the executive where it got a broadly favourable reception, but Browne later argued that it was all effectively neutralised by de Valera, whose legendary caution — even, as he then was, in opposition — led him to insist that its recommendations (which do not survive) could be implemented only when resources permitted.[121] Yeats, who did most of the committee's drafting work, thought that Browne was better at criticising than at translating this criticism into practical proposals, and that he 'never understood that politics is the art of the possible'.[122] Despite Browne's apprehensions, the recommendations were publicly endorsed by the 1956 Ard-Fheis, although it was many years before they filtered through successive cabinets and into the educational system itself.

Browne was not neglecting constituency matters, although he offended one cumann by declining to join it.[123] In November 1954, for example, he proposed at the Dublin South-East Comhairle Ceanntar (constituency council) that the traditional political activity of checking the voters' register by calling to houses in the constituency should be carried out by 'people who should have an answer to questions that may be put to them, such as what we intended doing on emigration, prices, social services etc.'. He also suggested the creation of a wide network of information bureaux which could deal with constituents' practical problems.

The problem about this policy is that it risked raising expectations that could not be met by any voluntary organisation, even one as well rooted as Fianna Fáil. Sean Moore, a Dublin Gas Company worker already becoming active in the Fianna Fáil organisation in the constituency, noted as much when he told the same meeting that 'This idea was tried out in the Ringsend area but it proved too much for the Cumann as the number of people looking for assistance and advice on all sorts of problems was overwhelming.'[124]

Noël Browne, however, had one advantage that few TDs or aspirants had: his wife, Phyllis, who supplied the domestic support which was absolutely essential. Noël's household skills improved over time, to include cooking as well as DIY, and in later years he delighted in building fireplaces out of cut stone in many of the various houses through which they moved, even scouring scrapyards for old doors and windows which would be painstakingly refurbished.[125] In these early years, though, he was a man who left most of these trivial matters to others — in practice, to Phyllis. Phyllis accepted this burden with total selflessness, and a dedication to his personal and political welfare that was extraordinary even by the standards of the times. She not only typed his constituency correspondence, but helped out in more practical ways. On one occasion, Noël sent an impoverished constituent up to his own house with a request that Phyllis — an accomplished seamstress — should make a First Communion dress for the constituent's child. She took it in her stride. On another occasion, she similarly obliged another constituent by making her a wedding dress.[126]

Noël Browne, of course, had a following that was political as well as personal. The South-East constituency had some seventeen cumainn, but one of the most critical of them, from his point of view, was the Kevin Barry Cumann. This was set up specially by the party for students from University College, Dublin and Trinity; at this time, overt political activity was banned in both colleges. Although the branch had no specific geographical location (all normal branches covered particular polling areas), it was assigned to the South-East constituency. When Browne joined, the Kevin Barry Cumann was in poor shape. Its secretary, the future solicitor Micheál B. Ó Cléirigh, wrote to the party's national organiser, Seán Lemass, in February 1955 that 'we can only show fifteen diehards for every meeting', and urged him to get every cumann throughout the country to furnish him with a list of university students in Dublin who came from their area. 'It is the same idea', he added helpfully, 'as the Catholic Girls Protection Society — when they are going to England their names are sent to a priest who sets the machinery in motion to look after them when they arrive in England.'[127]

Browne's arrival, however, led to an influx of new members into the cumann. One of them was the Trinity student David Thornley, who had been a supporter of Noël Browne's since 1951, when he had campaigned for him as a schoolboy. Although born and educated in England, he had come to Ireland with his mother, a formidable woman, after his parents' marriage had broken up. Academically brilliant, David took first class honours in his undergraduate degree in history, and did a doctorate on Isaac Butt. According to his widow, Thornley was fascinated by people who — like his father — were English, but who had come to Ireland and made it here. Noël Browne, although not English, had the English public school cachet.[128] His early attitude towards Browne was, by all accounts, only just this side of idolatry; he may even have seen in the older man something of a charismatic father figure to replace the one he had lost. Their later relationship, however, was to undergo many vicissitudes, ruptures and reconciliations, and it finally ended in tears, as Thornley's own expansive but vulnerable personality clashed fatally with Browne's unforgiving temperament.

There was one occasion on which even Thornley's loyalty was shaken at this early stage. Taking constituency clinics for Browne in Ringsend, he was begged by an elderly woman to get Browne to come to the clinic in person so that she could explain her difficulties to him. When he mentioned this particular request to Browne for the second or third time, Browne asked: 'Does she want to touch the hem of my garment?' The irony, if irony there was, escaped the younger man completely; it was an exchange he never forgot.[129]

His decision to follow Browne into Fianna Fáil now, however, was a critical one, because he had a following. An undated list of members and visitors to cumann meetings in the Fianna Fáil archives includes, among others, Michael Davern, the future Fianna Fáil TD and junior minister, Proinsias Mac Aonghusa, Loughlin O'Kennedy, later closely associated with the pro-Biafran movement in Ireland, and Brendan Scott, who was to stay with Browne in many of his future political peregrinations, and was a beacon to many on the left.[130]

Lemass did all that he could to encourage the newcomer, forwarding him letters from time to time on issues out of which he felt Browne might be able to make political capital. There is an almost fatherly tone in the correspondence — Lemass was sixteen years older than Browne — as for instance, when Lemass forwarded a cutting from the Donegal *People's Press*. The cutting was an attack on radicalism in Irish politics and Lemass noted that although the newspaper concerned 'is as you possibly know a strong Fine Gael organ and probably not read by anyone except dyed-in-the-wool Fine Gael supporters . . you may, however, feel like singeing their whiskers'.[131]

Browne's political activity was necessarily curtailed to some extent by the fact that he was no longer a member of the Oireachtas. He had rejoined the staff of Newcastle Sanatorium in his former position of assistant medical superintendent in June 1951, and was to remain in this position until October 1963. His modest salary there was supplemented only by his ministerial pension of £300 per year (approximately £6,050 in 2000 terms).

Noël Browne's exile from the Oireachtas did, however, give him time for other things, not least for sailing. He joined the Irish Cruising Club in 1956,[132] along with Dr Peter Mitchell, and remained a member until 1963. Both men had earlier been together on a lengthy cruise to the west coast of Scotland in a thirty-two-foot cruiser-racer called *Minx of Malham*, designed by the famous Laurent Giles and owned by Paul Campbell (ICC Commodore 1954–8). Noël was on the cruise for the first week, which was notable for a long, hard run north from Dún Laoghaire, in the course of which they averaged 5.5 knots for a trip of 203 sea miles. The wind rose to force 7, and at one point the yacht had to heave to in 'howling blackness' in the Sound of Jura. Campbell's log of the cruise, from which this description is taken, records Noël and Peter turning out at 4.30 in the morning to put full sail on the boat; it also notes Noël's lack of appetite.

Ashore, matters were hardly less lively. Browne's political activism was noteworthy. In 1956, for example, the official records for the Fianna Fáil National Executive showed that he had missed only one meeting out of twenty-six.[133] C.J. Haughey, who had been elected with him, attended twenty-four. His impetuousness and radicalism, however, eventually began to ruffle feathers, inside and outside the party. At the 1956 Ard–Fheis, he was again elected to the Committee of Fifteen (the National Executive), but he was now closer to the bottom than to the top of the list. Seán MacEntee had come to the conclusion, apparently with some regret, that Browne would never find his true home in Fianna Fáil.[134] And one delegate, Frank Clarke from Greystones, took advantage of a general debate on policy to launch an outspoken attack on Browne, asking whether the executive could rein him in and prevent him writing letters to the papers. Browne, he charged, had singled out the Catholic bishops as the targets for 'his bitterness, his spite, and his venom'. No other denominations were attacked, and this was the socialist party line — the line adopted anywhere and everywhere the Church was persecuted.[135] He went on to link Browne's name with 'that other famous socialist and doctor — Dr Hewlett Johnson, the Dean of Canterbury'.

Johnson, of course, was famously known as the 'Red Dean' for his radical pronouncements on political matters. Browne, however, was far from flattered by the comparison. Indeed, he was angry and upset, and instructed his solicitor to write to Clarke on the grounds that what he had said was 'clearly actionable [and] a gross unjustified and unwarranted slander deliberately calculated to injure Dr Browne'. The letter — presumably written by Noël Browne's old friend Jack McDowell — continued:

> As you are aware Dr Browne is a member of the National Executive of the Fianna Fáil party and was in fact standing for re-election to that body when your speech was delivered. Apart altogether from considerations concerning the Fianna Fáil party and Dr Browne's political life we feel we scarcely need to impress on you the seriousness of your accusations made against a practising Catholic and which were given the widest publicity in the newspapers.[136]

Clarke replied in January 1957 to say that he did not say, or mean to imply, that Browne was a communist, and gave permission for the letter to be published. Wiser counsels prevailed within the party, however, and the final decision made was that 'in the interests of unity in the party and to avoid the loss of Mr Clarke's services to the party' Browne agreed not to publish Clarke's letter 'unless the absence of a public reply is made grounds for an attack on Noël Browne or Fianna Fáil, or he is advised by the Party leadership to publish it'.[137]

Nor was this the only straw in the wind. An aggrieved Fianna Fáil voter from Leinster Square, Rathmines, wrote to Mount Street to express her conviction that Fianna Fáil, although the party best equipped to solve the country's economic ills, was 'suspect . . . as long as [it] harbours Noël

Browne'. She would not vote for the party in the next election if he remained in it, she said, adding that 'were Dr Browne a non-Catholic I could excuse his attitude but I cannot tolerate a renegade'.[138]

Worse was to come. In the Dublin South-East organisation, Eddie McManus was moving against Browne. MacEntee did not have to act directly; McManus was running the operation in his interests and in no one else's. When the time came, the blow was delivered with clinical accuracy. The constituency agreed to nominate two candidates but — instead of Browne — elevated Sean Moore to the second spot on the Fianna Fáil ticket. Browne must have been stunned at this turn of events, and issued what diplomatic observers termed 'a characteristically long and bitter' statement to the press, in which he suggested that there had been 'clerical' objections to his candidature.[139] He had one hope left: the choice of candidates had to be ratified by the party's National Executive, of which he was of course a member, and on which he had — or thought he had — a fair sprinkling of supporters. It was entirely possible, although not certain, that the executive would add his name to the list, leaving the three Fianna Fáil candidates to fight it out on the hustings between themselves.

The critical National Executive meeting took place on 15 February 1957. Eoin Ryan proposed that Noël Browne's name be added to the list of candidates; the proposal was seconded by Matt Feehan, a former army officer who was a party stalwart and who played a major role in the launch of the *Sunday Press*. There was an intense discussion of about an hour and a half, during which Gerry Boland intervened to say that he had crossed swords with his share of bishops in the past, but accused Browne of 'bishop-baiting', which was, he said, a different matter altogether.[140] Browne was by no means without supporters in a contest which pitted Fianna Fáil's old guard against its younger, more impatient members with an intensity that this particular forum had never before experienced. Then MacEntee stood up and delivered the *coup de grâce*: if Browne was added to the ticket, he said, he would withdraw.[141] De Valera, whose support for MacEntee in this confrontation was evident, if silent, moved towards closure. Browne's support started to melt away; Feehan passed a note to Ryan saying that he was going to withdraw, and did so. Dan Breen, who had long admired Noël Browne's feistiness and shared his hot-headedness and political radicalism, stepped into the breach, but it was not long before it became clear that it was a lost cause. He too withdrew. De Valera then enquired whether the proposal still had a seconder. C.J. Haughey offered, but nobody had any stomach for further conflict, and the discussion petered out.

MacEntee and Browne together had to await the final outcome of the meeting, sitting side by side on chairs outside the room. When he returned home afterwards, MacEntee confided to his wife and daughter: 'Actually, I rather liked him.'[142] MacEntee's comment, in a sense, summed up the dilemma for Fianna Fáil of its association with Browne. He could be extraordinarily personable. The rank and file, who had little to do with him on a day-to-day basis, were greatly taken by him, and the relationship was to some extent mutual; one of his long-time supporters surmised many years later that Noël might have been happiest in Fianna Fáil, in the sense that it was a large, potentially radical movement which could provide huge political backing for new ideas.[143] Those who worked more closely with him, however, found that consistency and accountability — two key forms of political currency within large organisations — were not concepts which held much attraction for him. Fianna Fáil's Michael Yeats, by no means a severe critic, suggested that 'as he grew older, for Noël Browne the only political views worth considering were his own'.[144] Lemass, who as director of elections had the unenviable task of seeing his former protégé afterwards in the hope of minimising the damage that might ensue from these events, told a party colleague later that he had found Browne 'bitter . . and full of venom . . incapable of listening to reason, and filled with hatred'.[145]

By now, and not least for these reasons, Browne's future in Fianna Fáil was bleak. The next meeting of the National Executive, on 11 March 1957, under the agenda item 'correspondence' heard a letter from Noël C. Browne notifying it of his resignation from the organisation. The resignation was accepted.[146] The mythology is that Browne was expelled — a mythology which owes its existence largely to a statement to this effect in his autobiography.[147] But the mechanism was, at the end of the day, secondary to the message: a connection which had lasted over three years, and in the course of which Browne had not only recognised but in some sense helped to reawaken the early social radicalism of Fianna Fáil, had ended in mutual recrimination, hostility and disillusion. Noël Browne was on his own again.

CHAPTER SEVEN

The Night of the Big Wind

T he March 1957 election saw the second inter-party government in severe difficulties. The end of the Korean War had precipitated a recession; unemployment and emigration were increasing dramatically; and the outbreak of the 1956–62 IRA border campaign had politically destabilised the government, which was being supported from the outside by MacBride's now minuscule Clann na Poblachta. Fianna Fáil's vote improved by 6 per cent and it won exactly half the seats in the Dáil. Four Sinn Féin candidates elected on a wave of public sympathy for young IRA men killed on the border refused to take their seats, so de Valera had a comfortable overall majority. MacBride lost his seat.

In so far as the Dublin South-East constituency was concerned, the figures suggest that had Browne and MacEntee stood together, they might well have secured two seats for the party. By now, however, this was an entirely academic question. Costello's first preference vote slumped by more than 4,000, consigning his running mate, John O'Donovan, to oblivion. Browne's vote, although up by only 500, was just ahead of MacEntee's, and more than twice that of Sean Moore, who had replaced him on the Fianna Fáil ticket. It was in fact a small transfer from Costello which put him over the quota and into the Dáil again.

Browne's election campaign was supported by a large and heterogeneous group of adherents. Chief among them was David Thornley who, having followed Browne into Fianna Fáil, now followed him out again. An unexpected campaign worker turned up in the shape of Brendan Behan, whose play *The Quare Fella* had been produced, first in Dublin in 1954, and in London in 1956, to considerable acclaim. 'He gave me his fullest support,' Browne told an associate later, 'A very sweet man . . . extraordinary language.'[1]

Behan's canvassing technique, as described to the historian Owen Dudley Edwards, then a student involved in the campaign, was probably unique: 'I'm going to go to the fucking wealthiest and snobbiest districts. I'm going to knock on the doors and tell them I'm Brendan fucking Behan, and tell them not to vote for that fucker Browne, and that, if they do, I'll come back and knock their fucking door in. That's the way to get the vote, isn't it?'[2]

Noel Hartnett was Browne's election agent. Seeing the two of them together — Browne ascetic and remote, Hartnett small and dark — led Edwards to christen them 'the saint and the goblin'. Although he was intermittently — and seriously — ill, Hartnett was still at this time 'a total bundle of mischief, intensely refreshing, with a notable wink — and preposterous beliefs in socialism'.[3]

Some of the new group of people coalescing around Browne noticed — with affection, it must be said — a number of his idiosyncrasies. Some of his phrases had distinct overtones of his education in pre-war Britain; many of the women who helped in his campaign might have been surprised to hear the candidate refer to them as 'dear old things', or even, when he could not remember a name, as 'Mrs Doings'.[4] More problematic, however, was his hearing loss. This disability, which he attributed to poor treatment he was given for measles in his youth, could have quite a serious effect on his social and even political relationships. He told very few people about it, so that many of those dealing with him were unaware of it, and conversations sometimes went seriously awry. There is, a friend noted, 'a profound arrogance on the part of people with unimpaired hearing — an assumption that everyone has heard everything. The sweet smile with which Noël greeted certain things was simply non-comprehension. Because of this, important meetings with Noël Browne really had to be on a tête-à-tête basis; threesomes were particularly risky.'[5]

Even at that stage there were unsuccessful attempts to found a political party, involving election helpers like Matt Merrigan, prominent in the Amalgamated Transport and General Workers' Union (Noël Browne's union), and Máirtín Ó Cadhain, the writer and TCD lecturer in Irish who had been interned during the war for his Republican sympathies and who, indeed, had been the subject of a cabinet row in the 1948–51 government when MacBride and Browne sought to have him appointed to an advisory body on the Irish language. Ó Cadhain lived up to his reputation by later denouncing everyone involved. Another Irish language writer and propagandist involved in the campaign was Rex MacGall.

De Valera's overall majority did not lessen diplomatic interest in Browne, who was, the British thought, 'a man of great, though limited enthusiasms, who is more prepared to speak his mind than many people in this country, and who showed this in his first speech over the election of the new Taoiseach'.[6]

The British enthusiasm for Browne was premature, and based on a misreading of his speech. When de Valera was nominated, Browne spoke briefly, declaring that he would support legislation which he believed to be progressive and oppose it when he believed to the contrary. He then announced his intention of abstaining on the nomination of de Valera 'because I feel that my vote could be misunderstood'.[7] Immediately after he had finished, Seán Lemass, who had evidently feared that Browne would vote against de Valera, walked across to him and shook his hand.[8] Not for the first time, the British had been mistaken in using de Valera as a litmus test for Irish politicians.

Browne was now, once again, in the difficult situation of being an Independent deputy who basically wanted to be in a party. Both Fianna Fáil and Fine Gael were excluded, although for different reasons. Clann na Poblachta had been reduced to a cipher. Labour, in the person of William Norton, had set its face against him. If nobody would have him, perhaps the best thing to do would be to revisit the option that had tempted him briefly in 1953, and start a party of his own.

David Thornley, as one of the prime movers in all of this, had already been thinking organisationally, and had founded an organisation called the 1913 Club, basically to act as a combined left-wing think-tank — a kind of Irish equivalent of the Fabian Society — and a support group for Browne. It included many erstwhile members of Fianna Fáil's Kevin Barry Cumann. Thornley was president; Owen Dudley Edwards, who was secretary, eagerly enlisted likely young acolytes, including me, then in my first year at UCD. Many in the group were strongly influenced by left-wing members of the British Labour Party, such as Nye Bevan. Browne himself regularly read *Tribune*, that tendency's house organ. Other adherents included people like Aidan Clarke, the historian, then a member of the Irish Workers' League, who was friendly with Thornley (although Thornley was hostile to communism); Petria Hughes, another TCD student, who married David Thornley; and Gery Lawless, the Republican agitator who later brought a successful case against the Irish government in the European Court of Human Rights.

The choice of 1913 — the year of the lockout by the Dublin employers of Jim Larkin's Transport and General Workers' Union — was for very specific reasons. Thornley argued for it on the grounds that this was the last year in which socialism and nationalism had combined their forces in Irish politics. Nationalism, however, was to become one of the irritants in the organisation, as Browne was at this stage, at least to many of his followers, growing suddenly and increasingly sceptical of patriotic rhetoric. His irredentism of 1949 and 1950 in the Clann, honed by his years in Fianna Fáil, had not survived his rejection by the latter party and, indeed, seemed to have gone rapidly into reverse. His rejection by Fianna Fáil, however, is unlikely to have been the only factor. The recrudescence of political violence in 1956 was undoubtedly another; Browne spoke with some feeling to associates of the 'delusions' under which he believed the young men going North with rifles were operating.[9] A third factor was the fall of the 1954–7 government, which had been caused largely by MacBride's anxiety about the cabinet's hardline attitude towards Republicans. Browne's deep-rooted hostility to his former party leader had by now also led him to reject MacBride's vocal anti-partitionism and, by implication, the actions of the IRA, who he believed drew encouragement and some measure of political legitimacy from loose statements by former cabinet ministers. David Thornley was of a similar view, although later he was to become deeply nationalist in many of his attitudes.

The 1913 Club fulfilled its role as a broad church. Speakers were invited from all political parties and none, and even though speakers from the larger parties knew that they were being in some sense set up, they came along cheerfully, gave their best, and stood their round. This would have been particularly true of the Fianna Fáil speakers, the young Turks of the party, among them Charles Haughey, Brian Lenihan and Erskine Childers (a slightly more unlikely candidate for young Turk status). The Club was also a forum for left-wing and liberal thinkers like Peadar O'Donnell and Owen Sheehy Skeffington. James Dillon agreed to come along to speak on behalf of Fine Gael, but his own party hierarchy heard about it and stopped him; Dillon was furious. The Club used to hold meetings in the basement of 33 Kildare Street, where occasionally someone would read a paper. Petria Hughes read one on education, helped with her presentation by Noël Browne, who was increasingly interested in the subject.[10]

Towards the end of 1957, however, the 1913 Club began to run out of steam. There were internal wrangles, leading to accusations that Thornley was involved in trying to create a personality cult. Owen Dudley Edwards fell into disfavour, and would have been arraigned before the other party officers if he had not made a pre-emptive strike by sending in his resignation. The meeting which had been convened to try him then had, instead, a lengthy discussion on the knotty problem of whether to accept his resignation, or reject it and then expel him.

The Club was, nonetheless, a key mover in the steps that were being taken to found a new party. The more experienced political observers knew that something was in the wind. As the American Embassy reported to Washington:

> *A reliable source who was associated closely in politics with Noël Browne in the past is of the opinion that Dr Browne will soon reveal his socialist leanings in the coming Dáil debates. The source believes that Browne will try to beguile some of the Independents — he is reported to have great personal charm —*

> *and create a nucleus for a new party. It was suggested by the source that Mr John Murphy, recently elected Independent representing the Unemployed Workers, would most likely be first approached by Dr Browne.*[11]

Jack Murphy, as he was known, was not the best of building blocks for a new political alignment. He was an unemployed building worker who had been interned as a Republican during the war, and was leader of an Unemployed Protest Committee set up in Dublin in 1957. The Committee organised a number of public meetings, which were lively affairs, and their protests evoked considerable attention and — on occasion — quite un-provoked physical attacks from the Gardaí. He was then put up as a candidate in the Dublin South-Central constituency for the 1957 election, largely because its Labour TD, Jim Larkin junior, had decided to retire from repre-sentative politics and devote himself full-time to the Workers' Union of Ireland. In that election, Fianna Fáil won a second seat in the constituency, displacing the Fine Gael TD Tom Finlay. The battle for the last seat was between the Labour candidate Roddy Connolly, James Connolly's son, and Murphy, who won by more than 1,000 votes. Despite his quite unexpected success, Murphy was in an invidious position, expected to mount further protests at a time when he had no political leverage. He went briefly on hunger strike, but quickly found out that he lacked both the experience and the organisation to make a mark in the Dáil. His supporters were a hetero-geneous lot, and included a wide spectrum of left-wing activists, including members of one or another tiny communist or communist-front-type organisation, who optimistically saw his election as the inauguration of a new era in Irish politics.

There was a general sense of ferment in the non-Labour left, not least because of Browne and Murphy's success. There was a small magazine called *The Plough*, which, although edited by a Labour activist named Maisie McConnell, was definitely not a Labour paper and acted as a forum for a number of left-wing people, including Browne himself. What happened next seems to have been a barely concealed struggle for leadership of this growing but inchoate group, and was noteworthy chiefly for a speech by Noël Browne in which he rounded on communists and fellow-travellers with considerable ferocity.

In his autobiography,[12] Browne dates the speech to 1958, and describes it as a counter-attack by him aimed at preventing the appointment of Justin Keating as editor of *The Plough*. The speech, however, was in fact made in 1957, which alters the context significantly; if it had been made in 1958, it would have been after the formation of the National Progressive Democratic Party. Justin Keating had never been interested in becoming, or being considered as, editor of *The Plough*,[13] but his mother, May Keating, was an indefatigable political activist who kept open house for a variety of radicals and dissidents of every possible hue. What seems to have happened is that Browne, becoming suddenly alarmed at the thought that these meetings might give birth to a movement, or even a party, which might escape from his direction and control, decided on a pre-emptive strike.

Ostensibly an attack on emigration, his speech[14] modulated into a dark warning about its effects, particularly on people who believed in social progress. Such people, he feared, might lose heart or — worse — 'find themselves being used as dupes by Communists or fellow-travellers'. Quoting Nye Bevan, who described communism as 'the death-watch beetle in the body politic', he advised his audience to be wary of the 'cunning fellow-traveller in his spurious sympathy for the democratic idea' and to be 'quite firm in closing the door against Communist interlopers'. A contented, satisfied and prosperous people, he believed, made poor material for the totalitarian ideas which were the essential hallmarks of the communist society. Immediately afterwards, Browne broke with May Keating.[15]

In the last two months of 1957 and early in 1958, newspaper reports indicated that Browne's supporters were growing more confident. Owen Sheehy Skeffington was closely involved; he held weekly discussion meetings on politics in his home which were — unusually, it must be said — attended by people from every social class. Another participant was Michael McInerney, a former member of the Communist Party of Northern Ireland, where he had been a trade union organiser, who was now the political correspondent of *The Irish Times*. This was no small help to the nascent political organisation around Browne; for many years thereafter, Browne enjoyed McInerney's total support and loyalty. On occasion the journalist, who had inherited Smyllie's admiration for Browne but not his scepticism, even wrote political speeches for him. It was a relationship which foundered sadly towards the end of Browne's period in the Labour Party, when he became convinced — quite wrongly — that McInerney, then a member of the party in Browne's constituency, was intriguing against him in favour of Ruairí Quinn. When McInerney, still devoted to the author of the Mother and Child Scheme, arranged a special presentation ceremony for him many years later, Browne did not turn up.

Another key figure in the circle of people around Noël Browne at this time was Laurence Roche. Roche was a charismatic figure who had left school at eighteen, spent eight years at sea, briefly attended a seminary, and then went to Trinity as a mature student in 1956 to study forestry, in which he later became an internationally renowned expert. He was a passionate debater who 'preached socialism and berated nationalism as the opium of the Irish people',[16] and in 1958 invited Noël Browne to be one of the speakers at his inaugural as auditor of the college's Historical Society.

Browne was immediately impressed by Roche, who was twelve years his junior, and involved him in discussions about the best way forward. Roche was the person who suggested the name for the new party, and the decision to launch it was effectively taken at a small meeting in his rooms in Trinity.[17] The co-founders, with Roche and Browne, were indubitably Noel Hartnett and Jack McQuillan.

Noël Browne's affinity for students went beyond Trinity's walls. He was also at the epicentre of a memorable inaugural at UCD's Literary and Historical Society in 1958, where the iconoclastic Owen Dudley Edwards had been elected auditor. Edwards had chosen the teaching of Irish history as his subject, and delivered a robust critique of the way in which much Irish history teaching had been somehow permeated by nationalism. Noël Browne was one of the speakers to his address and, now firmly in his post-nationalist phase, warmly endorsed Edwards' thesis. Something of the context of the occasion can be gathered from the facts that the president of UCD, Dr Michael Tierney, refused to take the chair, and a number of highly placed clerics, including William Conway, coadjutor bishop to Cardinal D'Alton in Armagh, and Bishop Lucey of Cork, declined to participate.

The only cleric who could be persuaded to enter this lion's den was the Rev. Michael O'Connor, C.S.Sp., who with characteristic courage and brio gave an excellent account of himself. Somewhat to the surprise of his audience, he declined to fulfil the role expected of him by attacking Browne; this was taken up by another speaker, Lord Pakenham, who spoke for ideological purity with the invisible cloak of Eamon de Valera around his shoulders. He apologised to Browne at the dinner after the debate, a function which was also memorable but for a different, and more private, reason. Edwards had written to a wide range of earlier L & H luminaries asking them to contribute to the cost of such a dinner, and indeed to attend themselves. Seán MacBride contributed and accepted the invitation, only to change his mind dramatically when he heard that Noël Browne was to be an honoured guest. There was a delicious irony in the fact that Browne was supping — even if only partly — at MacBride's expense.

The National Progressive Democratic Party (the word 'National' was sometimes unaccountably missing from its election literature) was launched at meetings in Dublin and Roscommon on 16 May 1958. It was originally destined to be called simply the 'Progressive Democrats', which would have seriously changed the future face of Irish politics, but the irreducible nationalism among Browne's supporters secured the addition of the word 'National' to the title. Only a cynic would suspect (but cynics are sometimes right) that the coverage given to the launch was not based entirely on objective news values.[18] The report filled a large part of the front page of The Irish Times, and contained virtually the full text of the new party's policy statement.

This statement was notable for a number of things, many of them clearly the result of a strong input from Noël Browne's co-founder of the party, Jack McQuillan, TD. It was not, even by the standards of the times, a particularly socialist document. Nationalisation was not advanced; the banks were not mentioned. It did, however, plainly envisage the State taking a major role in economic development, a policy area in which McQuillan was probably to the left of Browne, and on which he may have considerably influenced him.

Jack McQuillan, who had been elected for the Clann in 1948 but had resigned from the party at the height of the Mother and Child controversy, was a politician of enormous integrity and courage. He fought and won a seat in Roscommon in successive elections against extraordinary odds, not least the total hostility of one of his county's two newspapers (the one circulating in his area of the constituency), which refused to publish his name in any context whatsoever. Renowned as a footballer (which didn't harm his political career), he served with distinction in the Defence Forces, where he developed a propensity for upsetting his senior officers. Ideologically, he was a genuine rural radical, with a profound and politically literate commitment to economic and social development. More importantly, in this context, he was a close friend of Noël Browne's, probably the best friend Browne ever had in politics and certainly the most constant, remaining a confidant right up to Browne's death in 1997. He died in March 1998.

McQuillan's ideas could be seen in the new party manifesto's denunciation of sums wasted on the army — 'a museum piece in the present epoch of atomic terror', and its commitment to the rapid development of fisheries, forestry and land reclamation. The old hostility to MacBride can be seen in its criticism of 'a chain of extravagant and burnished embassies in the capital cities of the world in a vain attempt to obtain prestige by pretentious display abroad'. More unexpected, however, was its forthright condemnation of Irish language policy adopted by all major parties since the foundation of the State, declaring that it was

> nothing short of political insanity to try to force our youth to learn a language which gave them no advantage in the land where 750,000 of them were destined to live and work. Yet the language revival was said to be the primary objective of national policy — a viewpoint which is the measure of our opponents' smugness and lack of realism.

This bold statement was noted by the British Embassy as 'a matter for some surprise'. Browne, it told London, was 'one of the few persons in public life who has for some time not disguised his socialist sympathies . . . J. McQuillan is an exuberant but not very responsible independent.'[19] The editor of The Irish Times, W.A. ('Alec') Newman, less enthusiastic than his political correspondent, was in Olympian mode. Dr Browne and his associates, he suggested, were ahead of their time, and should have waited another three years or so, by which time, he thought, other progressive forces in the Dáil would have emerged in their true colours.[20] Browne retaliated vigorously. He and Jack McQuillan, he argued, had been waiting for ten years already, and could not share the editor's 'cold detachment when dealing with public life in Ireland'. His riposte marks a distinct change in his rhetoric. As Minister for Health, although he had plainly been influenced by Nye Bevan's socialism, his campaign for better health services had most frequently been embellished by appeals to Christian values, and fuelled by an unmistakable compassion for those suffering from the poverty endemic in 1950s Ireland. Now, Christian values were pushed to one side, although never entirely abandoned; and compassion was shot through with streaks of ideology and the incipient language of class politics.

> Leader-writers, like all our political leaders, seem to have all the time in the world to wait before conceding any real urgency about even beginning to set about our social and economic problems. But then, how many of them must subsist on 26s. a week? Or, of their children between the ages of 14 and 17, how many — illiterate — peddle newspapers on street corners, or push messenger bikes from morning to night in all weathers? It is easy to sleep on another man's wounds.[21]

The new party, no doubt wisely, eschewed a confrontation with Fianna Fáil in the South Galway by-election in May. Neither this nor Browne's speech of the previous November prevented Fianna Fáil's M.J. Kennedy, a parliamentary secretary in the government, from evoking the 'red scare' in traditional terms — naming no one, but providing more than enough hints that the real object of his attack was Browne and the new party. *The Irish Times* swung into a defence of Browne, quoting his 1957 anti-communist speech with approval, and suggesting that Kennedy's 'trumpeting of false fears can only indicate a real fear, however unjustified, of the new party'.[22]

The launching pad for the National Progressive Democrats, as it turned out, was none other than Jack Murphy, who was becoming increasingly disillusioned with politics. He wrote privately to Archbishop McQuaid complaining that he did not know what to do next. McQuaid, not least because he believed that Murphy was being leaned on by communists and left-wingers of various persuasions, responded to his private entreaties for help for his working-class constituents by encouraging him to resign, and was instrumental in finding him alternative employment.[23] Murphy's resignation on 12 May 1958 was a bitter blow to many of his supporters. He later emigrated.

The resulting by-election provided a much better opportunity for the new party's first test of strength. Polling day was set for 25 June, and the party — hardly more than a group at this stage — chose Noel Hartnett as its candidate. This bald statement, however, does not do justice to the controversy which enveloped the selection process and which was to lead, in a very short time, to a dramatic parting of the ways between Browne and the till now devoted David Thornley.

The processes of candidate selection were somewhat akin to those which operated to choose the leader of the British Conservative Party up to the 1960s; candidates just emerged. Browne wanted Laurence Roche to stand, but Roche declined. Browne then suggested Hartnett, who himself was initially not enthusiastic, preferring to support Roche. There was an added difficulty in that the local activists were not keen on Hartnett. Browne, however, felt that he was a stronger option than Thornley. Party members who objected to his decision, or felt it had been mistaken, were given short shrift. One of them was Petria Hughes, who observed that Browne was not someone who took easily to criticism or contradiction.

> I remember going in to meet him in his office in the basement of Leinster House, just after Noel Hartnett had been selected as candidate in the [Dublin South-Central] bye-election. He asked me what I thought of his candidate. I liked Noel Hartnett personally, but thought he was certainly not a good candidate. I told Noël: 'If you walked out into Kildare Street and asked the first person you met to be a candidate, he'd be a better candidate than Noel.' Noël said nothing, just put his head down at a slight angle on his hand. I learned later that this was his way when he was in disagreement with anyone: he wouldn't look them full in the face, so that they would not see the anger in his face.

'Ironically in this case,' as one commentator has noted, 'it was Browne who was cast in the role of the authoritarian in an internal party democracy row.'[24] But it was even more complicated than that. David Thornley believed that his long dedication to Browne, and the very hard work that this had undoubtedly involved, entitled him to serious consideration as a candidate. He would probably have been prepared to defer to Roche; but what was difficult for him to swallow was the fact that even with Roche out of contention, he would not be chosen. He was, as Browne remarks with uncharacteristic mildness in his autobiography, 'annoyed' by this development.[25] On the face of it, however, it was not an unfair decision. Despite Thornley's long commitment to the cause, it is hard to see that the electors of Dublin South-Central would have warmed to him. His accent was irredeemably English and in 1958, long before the advent of television, this was a noticeable handicap. He was to secure election easily in 1969 in the equally working-class Cabra area, but that was after a decade of Irish television, during a large portion of which he had established a reputation as an incisive and intelligent current affairs interviewer and commentator. For the time being, he banked his fires; but they were to burst into life again almost as soon as the by-election was over.

The NPD campaign emphasis in the by-election was clear: Hartnett's own track record and politics were secondary to the fact that he was being supported by Browne. In a list of nine points for canvassers, Hartnett's record came eighth.[26] In first place was the injunction to

> *tell [the voters] that he is Dr Browne's candidate. They will know who Browne is, but it is essential to point out that he is not the candidate. Tell them that Browne is the workers' man, that he has fought for them in the Dáil for the past ten years, that he is responsible for the free health service, that he is the ONE man in the Dáil who constantly fights the poor man's cause.*

The campaign focused strongly on working-class issues. Perhaps the NPD's greatest success was to evoke a last-minute change of heart on Seán MacEntee's part, when he reversed a previous decision to restrict supplies of the anti-polio vaccine. Initially, the campaign headquarters were in Holles Street but they later moved to more commodious premises in Camden Street, where the young Proinsias Mac Aonghusa, NPD 'Director of Publicity', cranked out speeches on his typewriter at breakneck speed. He was quick to recognise that newspapers did not have the resources to cover every possible campaign meeting, and cannily exploited their willingness to rely on press releases. Both Browne and Hartnett would occasionally wake up to the news that they had made yet another important policy statement at a meeting which neither of them could remember taking place.

This thoroughly modern aspect of media management was all of a piece with Browne's belief in the importance of press coverage generally. At one stage, he privately upbraided *The Irish Times*, arguing that it was giving inordinate coverage to the first-time Labour candidate, Frank Cluskey. Casting his net even wider, he wrote to Kingsley Martin, editor of the *New Statesman*, with a letter for publication. Martin, possibly recognising that readership of the magazine would not be widespread among the electors of Dublin South-Central, did not print the letter, but wrote a paragraph in its Diary instead, praising the NPDs for their 'moderate, secular, radical programme'. The Irish government, Martin observed in phrases emblematic of British left-wing attitudes towards Ireland, 'is not tyrannous, but, like Salazar's, it fosters faith at the price of ignorance and censorship, and in practice is nearly as indifferent to the abysmal poverty of the peasants.'[27]

The peasants of Dublin South-Central, as it happened, were to be further confused by the late entry into the campaign of no less a personage than Seán MacBride. In what was to be his last electoral outing, MacBride, who had lost his Dáil seat in 1957, was making a desperate attempt to re-enter national politics. Myles na gCopaleen, in *The Irish Times*, was not impressed. He consulted Dinneen's well-known Irish dictionary for a definition of 'Clann' and found that it was derived from the Latin *planta*. Consulting his Latin dictionary in turn, he came up with the following: 'any vegetable production that serves to propagate the species. A sprout, shoot, twig, sprig, sucker.' He went on to wonder whether it was also related to the Greek verb *planao* — 'to cause to wander, to lead astray; to lead into error; to deceive.'[28]

Impervious to such barbs, MacBride deluged the constituency with his death's-head posters, but did not deign to campaign in person.[29] There was a devastatingly low turnout — only 34.2 per cent — and MacBride, despite his physical absence from the hustings, came third on the first count, only 60 votes behind the Fine Gael candidate, and more than 300 ahead of Hartnett, who was eliminated immediately and lost his deposit. Pat Cummins, the Fianna Fáil candidate, a solid trade unionist, was elected on the fourth count without actually reaching the quota.

It was, in a sense, an astonishing result. There were 11,500 non-Fianna Fáil first preference votes, compared to Cummins's 6,000, but the transfers went all over the place. Only just over a quarter of Hartnett's votes transferred to MacBride and, on the last count, Cummins was effectively elected less than 1,000 votes ahead of MacBride on the basis of transfers from the Fine Gael candidate.

As far as Browne, Hartnett and the NPDs were concerned, it was a dreadful disappointment. Failure went to the new party's head. Almost immediately, a meeting called to decide on a central structure for the organisation ended in rancorous disagreement. Even the arrangements for the meeting provoked argument, as Noël Browne 'excluded some applicants because they were Communists, although they had supported his campaign in 1957'.[30] Nor did Browne himself deny this aspect of his organisational plans. He had kept known communists clear of the new party, he said later, on pragmatic rather than ideological grounds because he had seen 'the Department of Justice file on the Communist Party' and was afraid of a smear which would damage the NPDs at a time when he wanted to publicise socialism.[31]

This tactic was observed at first hand by Edward Thornley, who says that David described it as 'The Purge'. Much later, defending his brother against Noël Browne's deeply wounding portrait of him in *Against the Tide*, he gave this description of the preliminaries for a meeting of Browne's supporters.

I was present on one occasion when Dr Browne telephoned David at our house and asked him to read out the names. I heard Dr Browne's repeated 'Out . . . Out'. The number of supporters dwindled as a result at successive meetings. I had asked David what was the fault of these unfortunate non-persons in the Dr Browne microcosm of a Socialist state: were they IRA, Communist or fascist? David explained to me they were nothing of the sort: they were merely people for whom Dr Browne had an aversion. On more than one occasion, he would go over a list of adherents with Browne before calling a meeting, to have certain names summarily removed from the list. This was on the grounds that they did not always agree with the course of action that was being proposed.[32]

Noël Browne, he maintained, never engaged in political discussion at these meetings, and 'the more fluent and intelligent contributions seemed to elicit an expression of tight-lipped hostility from him'.

If Browne, and his allies, thought that excluding communists would guarantee a trouble-free birth for the new party, he was soon disillusioned. The foundation meeting, organised in Moran's Hotel on 3 July 1958, and chaired by Noel Hartnett, rapidly developed into a major row about the formation of the party's National Executive.

In one corner, Browne argued that the party was too young 'to have the luxury of democratic elections'. He added: 'I will certainly not agree to having an election here today. The executive will be chosen by deputy Jack McQuillan and myself.' McQuillan agreed: 'Why should we be hamstrung by some group elected here?' he asked. 'We know where we are going.'[33]

In the other were a furious David Thornley and others, including members of the 1913 Club, who were substantially outnumbered. Both the format and conduct of the meeting had plainly been affected not just by Browne's self-protective approach to the issuing of notices, but by a fear which McQuillan and Hartnett shared of the potential influence of fringe groups without any clear left ideology. Even before the first meeting of the new party two months earlier, Hartnett had predicted gloomily that 'there will be someone trying to commit us to the artificial insemination of ducks'.[34]

In the course of a three-hour meeting, Browne and McQuillan rejected a compromise solution whereby half of the executive would be chosen by McQuillan and himself, and the other half elected. Matters were brought to a head by a vote of confidence in the leadership, proposed by Noel Hartnett, after which Thornley and about fifteen others stormed out. By his action, Thornley said, Browne had forfeited his right to call himself a leader of democratic socialism. He added: 'You have also forfeited the right to call yourself my leader.'[35] Another participant, Owen Dudley Edwards, christened the occasion 'The Night of the Big Wind'. The next day, the 1913 Club issued a lengthy statement severing its connection with the NPD party on the grounds that the meeting had been rigged by being confined to 'supporters carefully vetted by Dr Browne', and declaring that it could not 'help to foster the cult of a new "chief" who is always right on fundamentals'.[36]

The political correspondent of *The Irish Times* engaged in a damage limitation exercise on behalf of Browne, suggesting that it was a meeting of election workers rather than a party meeting as such, since none of Jack McQuillan's supporters had come from Roscommon, and indeed that no actual members of the party had ever been enrolled.[37] The whole affair then became the subject of a venomous correspondence between mostly anonymous members of the two groups in the *Evening Mail* (there was a tacit agreement between them not to wash their dirty linen in the pages of *The Irish Times*).

Thornley's supporters argued that the 1913 Club members were 'clinging to democracy when their leaders throw it aside'.[38] Browne and McQuillan, they alleged, were now supported only by 'the School Children's Protection Association, the Export of Horses for Slaughter Group, and . . . a number of political discontents who hope that Dr Browne will table questions concerning their pet grievances in the Dáil'.[39]

Browne's supporters countered that Thornley had 'never had a democratic election (or indeed any other kind of election) from his members, although the [1913] club has been in existence for nearly three times as long as the party where the chairman campaigned for such election'.[40]

Thornley's departure from the scene was not the only evidence of discontent. *The Plough*, which had in a sense been a stamping ground for Browne before the establishment of the new party, criticised both Browne and McQuillan for not going to Jack Murphy's aid when he was plainly out of his depth in the Dáil, and gave the NPDs a very lukewarm welcome.

> *The Party has failed to make its policy clear except on such inessential points as the cost of our embassies and the Presidential establishment, the possibility of doing without an army and some rather muddled criticism of the Government's policy on the language . . . Does it aim at the Welfare State? Advocate . . . planning for full employment? Increase in . . . benefits? If so it should have been the substance of their first Manifesto.*[41]

Undeterred by the two cheers from their left, Browne and McQuillan pursued a highly ambitious agenda in the Dáil. Browne's own political concerns were no longer limited to health and social welfare. He had already, in 1951–4, spoken on a number of new topics, from restrictive trade practices and western development to aviation. In 1957–61, however, he focused closely on what he plainly considered to be the key issues. Economics did not figure largely (when they did, it was often as an adjunct to condemnations of emigration), but other questions, which did, were to be closely associated with his political campaigns from then until the end of his parliamentary career.

One of them continued to be health. Here, apart from any measure involving a means test, which led to interminable and mostly unproductive wrangles, Browne's speeches were thoughtful, constructive and progressive. The new Minister for Health was Seán MacEntee, who had been demoted from Finance by de Valera, partly at Lemass's insistence, because of a perception that he had been responsible for the 1954 election defeat. He brought in amending health legislation in 1957 to introduce further charges in an attempt to save some £180,000, and was predictably opposed by Browne for reneging further on the 'magnificent' 1947 Health Act.[42] 'Deputy Dr Browne,' MacEntee commented eirenically, 'I think like myself, tends to exaggerate his point of view.'[43]

In so far as mental hospitals were concerned, Browne was beginning to articulate a concern, in particular, about the plight of involuntary patients, such as old people who had been so confined not because they were mentally ill but simply because they had become too much trouble for their relatives. It is a measure of the slowness with which progress was recorded in this area that it was not until 1999, and Brian Cowen's Mental Health Bill, that the question of providing a proper review system for involuntary patients was seriously and adequately addressed.[44]

In this, as in a number of other areas, Noël Browne was plainly ahead of his time, and garnered little or no support from his fellow parliamentarians for initiatives which today seem commonplace or even out of date. He doggedly pursued the Minister for Education, Jack Lynch, on the question of corporal punishment in schools, arguing that the recalcitrant child was not a bad child, but merely a child who was emotionally disturbed or had some emotional dysfunction in the background.[45] He succeeded in forcing Lynch into an indirect admission that the use of the strap was not explicitly prohibited, and accused him of thereby extending the circumstances in which adults could beat — 'flagellate', as he put it — small children.[46] The silence from other deputies on this issue was redolent of the social culture of the day. Nor did he get any support when he asked the Minister for Education whether he would do anything about a situation in which a child had been forcibly removed to an industrial school from his father's care, against the declared wishes of the father and the child, for not attending school or Mass. The minister replied blandly that he had no function in the matter, as it was solely the concern of the court of jurisdiction.[47]

Browne was again on his own on the issue of capital punishment.[48] He had discovered, in the 1957–8 estimates of the Department of Justice, a sum of £40 earmarked for 'executions' or, as Browne chose to redefine it, 'hangman's expenses'. It was now generally accepted, he argued, that 'the murderer . . . is psychopathic. He is a sick man, mentally deranged. What he needs is hospital treatment. Killing is no solution of the problem.' His protests evoked little more than coarse jocularity which is, even at a remove of more than four decades, quite disturbing. The Minister for Justice, Oscar Traynor, and other deputies affected to believe that what Browne was objecting to was the designation of the subhead, rather than its purpose. One deputy went so far as to suggest that his objections might be met by transferring it to the vote for the Department of Industry and Commerce, where it could be allocated to the ESB for the purchase of an electric chair.

He was among the first to raise in the Dáil the question of the then current Fethard-on-Sea boycott. This was an extraordinary situation in which the children of a mixed marriage had been removed from the jurisdiction by their Protestant mother, as a direct result of which Protestant shopkeepers in the small Co. Wexford town were being boycotted by their Catholic neighbours. De Valera, in response to a Dáil question from Browne, while expressing his belief that the boycott was 'ill-conceived, ill-considered and futile', also appealed to anyone who had influence with the absent mother 'to respect her troth and promise and to return with her children to her husband and home'. Even this was not enough for Brendan Corish (in whose constituency this had occurred), who implied that there was, in fact, no boycott, and asked de Valera 'to ensure that certain people will not conspire in this part of the country to kidnap Catholic children'.[49] The seeds of a future antipathy between Corish and Browne were already being sown.

Even without the knowledge that they were going to be confined to the role for sixteen years, Fine Gael and Labour were settling into the business of being a rather lacklustre opposition, uninspired and uninspiring. In these circumstances, Browne and McQuillan became the *francs tireurs* of the opposition benches, hugely active at question time, and raising issues calculated to embarrass both sides of the House. Between 1958 and 1961, the NPDs originated no fewer than seven of the nine motions discussed in Private Members' Time in the Dáil. Browne and McQuillan managed to do this quite simply because they out-thought and outplanned Labour and Fine Gael. Woken finally from their slumbers, these two parties engineered a change in the Dáil standing orders in 1962 which defined a 'party' as an organisation having at least seven TDs, and confining Private Members' Time to motions advocated by such parties. The gang of two was equally active at question time. In the two years 1961 and 1962 alone they asked almost 1,400 parliamentary questions, 17 per cent of the total.[50]

These issues, it has to be said, were sometimes removed from the bread-and-butter issues of the day. They included a number which had figured prominently in the menu set out by the National Progressive Democrats at their inauguration, the costs of the presidential establishment and the Irish revival policy among them.

Browne raised the language issue early on in a Dáil question to de Valera, arguing that the existing policy was a 'mixture of blackmail, coercion and bribery' which had resulted in widespread disrespect for Irish throughout the country.[51] He then discovered a procedural device whereby, by putting down a resolution urging the referral back of the estimates for the Department of Education, he could return to the topic. It was, he said, a sad truth, but there was no doubt that the next generation simply would not understand the contention of their elders that the retention of the language was an inseparable part of nationality. But it could not be imposed, because 'all our experience shows that you cannot dictate to the next generation'. James Dillon, nettled, charged that Browne, when a minister, had 'as bigoted a mind on the subject of the Irish language as I ever met' and that he 'used to be dashing up and down in a red car to the Gaeltacht'. When he then asked Browne to specify the generation to which he belonged, Browne replied succinctly: 'The in-between.'[52]

Two years later, after Lemass had succeeded de Valera as Taoiseach, Browne and McQuillan put down a formal motion[53] calling on the Dáil to express its belief that the government should carry out a referendum to ascertain whether a majority of the people would favour the replacement of compulsory by voluntary methods. Although the motion was defeated by sixty-four votes to eleven, it split the Dáil parties in a highly unusual fashion. Browne and McQuillan were supported only by members of the Labour Party and one Independent, W.A.W. Sheldon.[54] The sixty-four deputies opposing them, along with a serried phalanx of Fianna Fáil members, included at least one Labour Party deputy, Dan Desmond, and the Fine Gael deputies Richard Mulcahy and Richie Ryan. Some five years later, and in the wake of a vigorous and controversial campaign by the Language Freedom Movement, Dillon, as leader of Fine Gael, was to adopt a policy of non-compulsion in relation to Irish — a policy which provided one of the few differences between Fianna Fáil and Fine Gael in the 1965 general election campaign.

One of the issues on which Browne and McQuillan apparently felt strongly, but which did not find its way into the NPD manifesto, was the abolition of the Seanad. Hartnett had been a member of it; Browne himself was to secure election to it in 1973; but in November–December 1957 it was, for the two deputies concerned, yet another example of a waste of public money that could be more productively employed. In proposing the abolition of the Seanad 'as at present constituted',[55] Browne and McQuillan had plenty of ammunition, not least the publicly recorded opinions of the Taoiseach, Eamon de Valera, who had proposed its total abolition in 1928 and had actually abolished it briefly in 1934.

Browne initially expressed the view that the Seanad might be maintained in existence as an advisory body; by the end, he had come to the conclusion that it should be abolished completely. It was, he said, 'an over-elaborate, complicated, useless, futile and pretentious body . . . an expensive pet to maintain'. Fine Gael demurred; it was prepared to consider alternative methods of election to that body, it said, but not its abolition. In the end, Browne and McQuillan withdrew their motion in return for an under-taking from de Valera to appoint a commission to examine the whole question of the Seanad and its future usefulness. It was, in a way, an unexpected concession — but despite later probings by both deputies, no report was ever published by the group set up by de Valera, and the controversy rapidly fizzled out.

There were, however, two other issues in which Browne and McQuillan figured prominently. One of them was the attempt to change the electoral system from proportional representation to the first-past-the-post system operating in Britain. The other, which was entirely Browne's initiative, was the relationship between the Taoiseach and the Irish Press group of newspapers.

Fianna Fáil's proposal to change the electoral system united all the other parties and Independents in opposition. Browne's arguments[56] were related partly to the border campaign then in progress — was de Valera going to create a situation in which the young men who had accepted his invitation to put their point of view before the country were going to be driven back into the arms of the activists? His other major point was that it would enshrine civil war politics as an ineradicable aspect of the Irish parliamentary system. He effectively ridiculed the argument expressed by the Fianna Fáil TD Lionel Booth that PR led to the emergence of extreme parties.

> *Deputy Booth an extremist? The Fianna Fáil Party an extreme party? It may have been an extreme party once. In its great days, it was a radical and progressive party, the party of the ordinary people, and in those days it did great things for Ireland, but it could hardly be said to be an extremist party today.*[57]

Nor was he afraid to let his anti-communism out for a walk, if he felt that circumstances required it. At one point, he labelled the government's philosophy as democratic centralist — a codeword for communist — and when the government chief whip, Michael Carty, was defending the straight vote on the grounds that it was a simple system, Browne riposted: 'There is a simpler one in Moscow.'[58] This did not necessarily take from another of his interventions in which — and it is one of the earliest statements of this kind attributed to him — he declared himself roundly in favour of 'progressive Socialist policy'.[59]

The matter of de Valera and the *Irish Press* was equally meaty, and an issue which Browne and McQuillan had to themselves. They put down the following motion:

> *That as the Taoiseach, in continuing to hold the post of controlling director of the Irish Press Ltd, while acting as Taoiseach, holds a position which could reasonably be regarded as interfering or being incompatible with the full and proper discharge by him of the duties of his office and further as he has not considered it necessary to indicate the position to the House, Dáil Éireann is of the opinion that he has rendered a serious disservice to the principle of integrity in Parliamentary government and derogated from the dignity and respect due to his rank and office as Taoiseach.*[60]

Forty years later, such an evident potential for conflict of interest on the part of a Taoiseach would have led to the establishment of a judicial tribunal, or worse. But the *Irish Press* was, for de Valera, more than just a newspaper. It was a national institution whose creation he had dreamed of in the early 1920s, but which had not come to fruition until 1931. The paper had played a key role in the critical general election of 1932, and indeed in all subsequent general elections, as well as providing the Fianna Fáil faithful around the country with a combined talisman and information system, especially when the party was in opposition. It was no mere party mouthpiece; Fianna Fáil deputies frequently complained, in the privacy of the party meeting rooms, that it had failed to pay sufficient attention to their speeches. It played a critical role in the intra-party debate about the modernisation of the economy between Lemass and the old guard in the 1950s.[61] And it was the product of a gifted generation of journalists and writers that had included Aodh de Blacam and many others such as Benedict Kiely and, later, Sean J. White. Above all, however, it was de Valera's personal pride and joy. On one occasion, he even surmised that given an inescapable choice between politics and newspaper proprietorship, he would have chosen the latter.

Browne, who had been given a present of two shares in the company, constructed an exegesis of the saga of de Valera and his ownership of the *Irish Press* which touched two very sensitive spots. The first was the way in which de Valera had extended his and his family's control over the enterprise by acquiring shares cheaply from the thousands of small investors who had been induced to buy them decades earlier. De Valera's only defence to this charge was that he had derived no remuneration either as a director or from his shareholdings — a defence which sat uneasily beside the undisputed fact that his shareholding, in what was then a reasonably profitable enterprise, was itself worth a very large amount of money.

An equally sensitive point related to Northern Ireland. The highly successful *Sunday Press*, which had been established in 1949, had a habit of running lengthy, dramatically presented articles about Republican derring-do in the War of Independence on its feature pages, while its news pages detailed the plight of those members of the modern IRA caught up in the recurring violence on the border. One of de Valera's biographers suggests that this leitmotif of the *Sunday Press* actually contributed psychologically to the decision to launch a fresh border campaign in 1956,[62] but whether it did or not, Browne's point was certainly awkward and unpleasant for de Valera at the very end of his long Dáil career. Eventually, the Taoiseach, by now aged seventy-six and to all intents and purposes blind, left the hard work of the defence brief to his colleague Seán MacEntee, but the damage had by then already been done. Fianna Fáil won the vote easily — there was never any doubt about it — but de Valera was overheard to say to Mulcahy, the Fine Gael leader, as they went up the Dáil steps to the division lobbies, 'I never thought you would do this to me.'[63] Behind this remark, it is thought, lay an unwritten — perhaps even unspoken — pact between de Valera and Mulcahy, in which two areas of major potential embarrassment to their parties were left rigorously undiscussed: in the case of Fianna Fáil, the *Irish Press*; and, in the case of Fine Gael, the Hospitals Sweeps operation.

It is probably fanciful to suggest, as Browne does in his autobiography, that this was the event which finally prompted de Valera to think of resigning. But it certainly added to the problems which the government was then experiencing, and which led to de Valera winning the presidency in the summer of 1959 only very narrowly, and to the defeat of the constitutional amendment aimed at changing the electoral system, the subject of a referendum on the same day.

It was a good summer for Browne in more ways than one. His combined income of salary from Newcastle, Dáil allowance and ministerial pension was enough to allow him to contemplate the purchase of a boat. Sailing was — with music and reading — one of Noël Browne's passions. In Dublin or in Connemara, where he later owned a small open wooden sailing boat, he found that getting onto the water was deeply satisfying. Often, if he wasn't helming or if conditions didn't demand much in the way of strenuous activity, he would be found up in the bow of the boat, in a private world of his own.[64] In the early 1950s, he had owned an old wooden boat called *The Bat*, which he bought in west Cork and sailed up to Dún Laoghaire. After he lost office, this had to be sold.[65] At some point in 1958 he was able to replace it, and therefore acquired, not just any boat, but one of the most historic boats in Dublin Bay — the Dublin Bay Seventeen-Footer *Rita*.

Rita's sail number was '1' because she was the very first boat of this famous class to arrive in Howth in April 1898 after the original five sailed down from the builders, Hilditch of Carrickfergus. Her former owner, since 1945, had been Alan Montgomery, later the editor of *The Irish Times*. It may well be that one of the reasons Browne acquired *Rita* at this stage was because Paul Campbell had put his cruiser-racer *Minx of Malham*, on which Browne regularly sailed, up for sale. Noël Browne owned *Rita* only for the full 1959 season, according to the class records; like the other boats in her class, she was fun to sail, but very wet.

For all the vicissitudes of his political life, however, his personal life remained a warm haven to which he could return, and contribute, much more frequently than had been the case when he was a minister. Susan recalls how Noël taught them how to sail, to make gardens, rear chickens and other animals.

> *We could make fires in the open and camp out. Cheaper by the chip, at crack of dawn in the Dublin markets, we bought fruit to make jam and cider — sometimes champagne, sometimes vinegar. With a free afternoon we might climb to the top of Kippure to see the view. The unexpected was the norm. A swim under a waterfall at Glenmacnass, tea at a turf fire, a read, exhausted home to sleep. When we could afford it, they encouraged us to appreciate good food and wine. His favourite tipple is green Chartreuse.*[66]

There was one dark note in all of this: Noël Browne disliked Christmas, and on occasion refused to mark it in any special way, preferring to go out sailing on his own rather than involve himself in traditional festivities. His family, without ever knowing precisely why, accepted this, assuming that it had something to do with his childhood experiences.

On the political front, very little now remained before the 1961 election and, with Seán Lemass's election as successor to de Valera in the summer of 1959, all political parties were gearing themselves for this eventuality. Browne did not spare Lemass in his criticisms after he became Taoiseach, particularly for his involvement in the creation of the private enterprise economic system which had, he observed, failed the country so miserably.

He was less critical on the occasion of Lemass's election in the Dáil,[67] paying tribute to his understanding of the great need for the development of Irish industry in the early years of the State, and his successes as Minister for Supplies during the war. He criticised Lemass for what he described as 'his overall failure to create a plan whereby Irish industry could create the wealth which would give his colleagues in Social Welfare, Health and Education in particular the means whereby they might provide a modicum of social justice in society for the under-privileged'. But he welcomed his plan to create 100,000 new jobs (which Lemass had published four years earlier, when in opposition), expressing the hope that the only reason it had so far failed to materialise was due to the conservatism of his leader, or to the jealousies of his colleagues. And he wished him luck.

Few significant items of parliamentary business remained outstanding before the election. One of them, however, was the 1959 Broadcasting Authority Bill, which was to become the 1960 Broadcasting Act, and the foundation of what is now Radio Telefís Éireann as a semi-state company. Browne's view on these proposals was highly centralist;[68] one of his major criticisms was that the Bill did not give the Dáil 'direct control of this public corporation'. He was opposed to the idea of a licence fee, arguing that the new television service should be paid for out of taxation. And, in a number of comments, he indicated that he was to some extent out of sympathy with this new manifestation of contemporary culture. He feared that television would follow the example of Radio Éireann's sponsored programmes, 'practically 100 per cent canned music, jazz music or bebop music, practically continuously without any attempt at anything constructive, creative, or informative or educational'. He reserved special words of obloquy for advertisers, and their 'moronic standards'. Some of them, he thought, 'are such savages that they would be prepared to put their advertising into the mouth of an Othello or a Hamlet or wherever they think they could sell their stuff'.

It was a sombre and pessimistic enough introduction, on his part, to the sixties. It was to be a decade of extraordinary change which would see him take fresh tumbles off the political roundabout. At the same time, a generation which was in its childhood at the time of his controversial departure from government in 1951, and which hardly knew him except by distant reputation, would help to give him a new lease of political life, and in not just one but two more political parties.

CHAPTER EIGHT

In Labour,
In Vain

Two years into his first term of office, the new Fianna Fáil Taoiseach, Seán Lemass, called a general election for October 1961. There was a new array of leaders in the major parties. Lemass, although he was over sixty and had taken part in the 1916 Rising, was oriented towards the future. Richard Mulcahy had retired as leader of Fine Gael in 1959, and was succeeded not by John A. Costello, in spite of the fact that he had served twice as Taoiseach and was willing to stand, but by James Dillon, a parliamentarian of the old school and of independent spirit. William Norton had resigned the leadership of the Labour Party in 1960 (although he retained possession of the party leader's room in Leinster House, to the discomfiture of his successor), and Brendan Corish, son of another Labour TD and TD for his late father's Wexford constituency, had taken over at the age of forty-two, three years younger than Browne.

In the summer of 1961 Lemass had declared that it was government policy to join the Common Market, as the European Union was then known. Britain was also applying to join, and although the complex trade relationships between the two islands made it plain that Ireland could not exist outside the Common Market if Britain was inside, Lemass maintained at least a semblance of independence by ensuring that Ireland's application actually reached Brussels before that from London.

He focused the general election campaign almost entirely on this issue. Browne was opposed — indeed, most left-wing opinion at the time, and for a decade thereafter, was delighted at what it saw as a clear issue on which to campaign. It was, however, an issue which did not energise the electorate or the political parties generally, and the election was a dull affair. The absence of de Valera, now in Áras an Uachtaráin, was a distinct disadvantage for Fianna Fáil, which lost almost 5 per cent of the national vote and was three seats short of an overall majority, but Lemass was able to govern for the next three and a half years with a minority government supported solidly by a number of Independent deputies.

They did not, this time, include Noël Browne. In Dublin South-East, MacEntee topped the poll — the only time he ever did so — and what appears to have been an unsuccessful attempt at vote-splitting by the two Fine Gael candidates, John A. Costello and John O'Donovan, saw Browne take the third seat comparatively easily, although with a first preference total of 4,717, down more than 1,000 votes on his 1957 figure. If there is a trend to be discerned here, it seems to be that — the 1948 election apart — Browne appeared to be marginally more successful whenever he stood as an Independent, and less so when he stood as a member of a party — any party. It was, at the very least, a dilemma for a politician who was now in his third political party; who at one level perceived, as any intelligent person could, that membership of a group is almost a prerequisite for political effectiveness; but who found the constraints, compromises and disagreements that are an integral part of party political life distasteful at best, repellent at worst.

He and Jack McQuillan, re-elected in Roscommon at the head of the poll, remained the only two standard-bearers for the National Progressive Democrats, now more a flag than a party. Browne, however, still attracted a radical urban fringe element of support to his canvassing team. One of them was the young Cork lawyer Liam Hamilton, who had been called to the Bar five years earlier. Hamilton, who canvassed for Browne in Ringsend, was to follow him into the Labour Party, but abandoned politics eventually for the law, finally becoming Chief Justice in 1994.

Parliamentary politics, after the election, remained in the doldrums. There was, it seemed, no real alternative to Fianna Fáil. Labour, still smarting from the effects of participation in two inter-party governments whose main effect had apparently been to cost Dáil seats, had turned its back on government with a statement by its new leader that the party would not take part in a coalition. Fine Gael was therefore isolated, in that no foreseeable increase in its vote would be big enough to put it into government on its own. And the Independents who supported Lemass were rock-solid, even though some of them were later to pay the inevitable price for supporting his more unpopular measures, such as the 1963 turnover tax — the forerunner of VAT.

In these circumstances, there was little by way of real political opposition in the Dáil. Many senior Fine Gael figures, with the honourable exception of people like Liam Cosgrave, a future party leader, found it more congenial and appealing to spend time at their businesses or in the Law Library than in the unprofitable wasteland of the opposition benches in Leinster House. The political vacuum was filled by Noël Browne and Jack McQuillan, with a work rate that put many more experienced opposition deputies to shame.[1]

Labour was a party in transition. It had won sixteen seats — four more than in 1957 — and, although its vote was on an upswing, the new faces had yet to establish themselves. The increase in the Labour vote in Dublin was in fact lower than its increase nationally — a factor partly explicable by Lemass's appeal to the urban working-class vote. Although Sean Dunne was elected in Dublin County, he was an Independent Labour rather than a Labour candidate; Michael Mullen of the ITGWU, who was elected in Dublin North-West, was the only official Labour TD in the capital, as Denis Larkin had lost his seat in Dublin North-East. The remainder of the parliamentary party was made up by the so-called 'rural' TDs. They were not rural in the strict sense of the word — more non-metropolitan; in most cases they had strong trade union backgrounds and were based in larger towns. This background was not, however, a nursery for political radicalism. Mullen was derisive about his Parliamentary Labour Party colleagues, describing them to a researcher as 'a Party of individualists and drunken feckers'.[2]

The only positive note, prior to the election, was struck by the leader of the ITGWU, John Conroy, who had announced at the union's annual conference in July 1961 that since the Parliamentary Labour Party had shown an unambiguous willingness to support ICTU policy in the Dáil, this should be reciprocated by the union, although the union was not, as yet, formally affiliated with the party. An American Embassy official, who attended the ICTU conference in Cork in fact-gathering mode, noted the views of — among others — Jimmy Tully, chairman of the Labour Party, Brendan Corish, Jim Larkin junior, Michael McInerney of *The Irish Times*, and John Conroy himself. These conversations led him to the conclusion that the central organisation of the Labour Party was 'pitifully weak, particularly on the financial side'. To a large extent, he thought, the party and its adherents were living on hope, and on a feeling that because there was a trade union movement there ought to be a political expression of it. Evidently curious about what Labour thought of Browne and McQuillan, he recorded the leadership views in some detail.

> *The Labour Party maintains no association with the so-called National Progressive Democratic Party, consisting only of Dr Noël Browne and Mr Jack McQuillan in the Dáil, a group which has no constituency organisation, and does not expect to develop any. Various Labour Party leaders described these two eccentrics as 'crackpots' and 'screwballs' and stated that Dr Browne's basis of support in his fashionable Dublin constituency was largely confined to pseudo-intellectual liberals with whom Labour had no common interest.*[3]

In this post-election situation, the Browne-McQuillan axis was still a powerful one in the Dáil. Particularly at question time, they continued to harry the government mercilessly on a number of issues which would, in time, become more fully adopted by Labour. One of these was neutrality, an issue which had been dormant for years but which had suddenly gained new visibility with the prospect of Common Market membership.

Further momentum was supplied by the Cuban missile crisis of 1962, when the US president John F. Kennedy blockaded that country as part of a successful attempt to force the removal of Soviet missiles which had been stationed there. The confrontation between the two major Cold War powers engendered by this situation spilled over into many European countries. Irish interest was heightened by the fact that Pat Arrowsmith, a leading member of the British Campaign for Nuclear Disarmament, became so convinced of the imminence of nuclear war that she left London for west Cork, then pre-sumed to be one of the safest places in Europe in any such eventuality.

When the crisis was at its height, there were two protests on the same day — 23 October — at the US Embassy in Ballsbridge. In the afternoon, Noël Browne and a number of others, including a visiting member of the British Committee of 100 (an organisation in which Bertrand Russell was prominent) and a representative of Irish CND, called on the embassy and left in a protest note, without incident. In the evening, the same group led a demonstration march of between fifty and sixty people, many of them students, which was halted by Gardaí about fifty yards from the embassy, where it had hoped to deliver a further protest note.

The demonstrators then organised a sit-down on the street, and the Gardaí moved in to disperse them. Very unusually, they were using dogs. The following morning's *Irish Times* — seen with some alarm by Susan Browne, who had just come out of anaesthetic after a minor operation — printed a dramatic picture of one of these fearsome animals leaping at Noël Browne, its teeth firmly embedded in his coat. 'The assault, the strange animal sounds, the snarls, excited barks and whimpers, were all so unexpected and unthinkable that it was hard to know what was happening. There was the sudden realisation that a large and angry animal, with sharp teeth, was furiously tearing at your clothes, your body, your head, face and arms.'[4]

The Americans, who had apparently had an armed guard of Marines ready to defend US property, and who in any case had their attention more closely focused on Washington and Moscow, downplayed the incident. As the American Ambassador cabled home: 'Browne claimed that he and others bitten by police dogs and kicked shoved when sat and lay down on street in protest against inability deliver note to embassy. Scuffle received wide publicity and thus achieved presumed purpose organisers.'[5]

In Ireland, the incident had wider reverberations. The use of the dogs was discussed at cabinet, as the incident — or at the very least the unfavourable publicity it had generated — was of concern to Lemass. The

photograph itself almost instantly achieved iconic status; there can be few
people who came to political literacy in the 1960s who have not seen it,
and been affected by it. For many people it became emblematic of Browne
in his role as a lone and courageous voice protesting against the Establishment
— in this case, the most powerful Establishment in the world. Browne himself later came to the surprising conclusion that his participation in this
demonstration led to his defeat in the 1965 general election, because it had
given ammunition to his opponents to mount a red scare against him.[6]

Noël Browne's heightened political profile at this time obscured two
factors which were to have a significant effect on his future. One was his
health; the other his employment.

As far as his health was concerned, 1962 and 1963 saw a deterioration in
his physical condition that was apparent to those close to him. He had suffered at least two recurrences of his TB while a minister, and he experienced
a further relapse in 1963. On the employment front, his career as assistant
medical superintendent was drawing inexorably to a close. Progress in the
eradication of TB had made Newcastle, and a number of other similar sanatoria, redundant. When it closed, he would have to look for another job.

His illness was affecting his Dáil work. Jack McQuillan noted it.

> *There were a few times when it was important that he should have been well,*
> *and he wasn't. I was standing at the top of the stairs outside the chamber and*
> *saw Noël at the bottom. He came up, holding on to the stair rail; it took him*
> *ages. I said to him: 'We should join the Labour Party and take it over'.*[7]

In October 1963, the month in which his employment at Newcastle
ended, Noël Browne applied for membership of the Parliamentary Labour
Party with Jack McQuillan. Both were accepted, though not without a
struggle. William Norton, still a TD for Kildare (he died on 4 December
1963, and his son failed to win the resulting by-election for Labour in
February 1964) was opposed, as was Brendan Corish. Corish's ascendancy
over the party was, however, not complete as yet, and a determined effort
led by Tom Kyne, the Waterford TD, who was also a full-time official of the
ATGWU, Noël Browne's union, succeeded in overcoming these objections.
Jimmy Tully, the Meath TD who was to become Minister for Local
Government in 1973–7 and who was also secretary of the Federation of
Rural Workers, was another Browne supporter. The PLP drew the line at
describing what had happened as a 'merger' of the NPD and the Labour
Party, and it had a point; the NPD barely existed as an organisation. *The
Irish Times*, unaware of the undercurrents in the parliamentary party, reported
that there had been no opposition to Browne and McQuillan's entry; this
would almost certainly have been true of the party at large.[8]

Labour's Administrative Council formally accepted Browne and McQuillan — along with Sean Dunne — into membership of the party at its meeting on 27 November 1963.[9] Browne was to remain a member of the Labour Party until 1977 — almost fourteen years, the longest period by far he had remained in any political organisation — but the honeymoon, if this is what it was, effectively lasted only until the party's annual conference in 1970.

In the Dáil, Noël Browne was as active as any Labour TD, and more active than most. He could not, as a new member, be given a major responsibility immediately, but was eventually made spokesman on health in the summer of 1965, just before the election. His interest in education had grown, almost to the point where it had overtaken his traditional interest in health. It was supplemented by a deep suspicion of the government's foreign policy, particularly any development that might bring Ireland closer to NATO. He had an opportunity to support the call for legal adoption, when the government finally introduced the long overdue legislation.[10]

He also developed a passionate opposition to tobacco advertising, raising the matter on many occasions in the Dáil.[11] His views about smoking, although of long standing — he once chided his youngest sister, 'Why do you have to drag it down into your boots, Ruthie?'[12] — did not smooth his political path in a number of respects. The committee room in which the Parliamentary Labour Party met in Leinster House was long and narrow, and many PLP members smoked, creating a fug to which most of them had long become accustomed. Browne simply could not stand it, and would pointedly yank up one of the windows which, especially in winter, did almost as much to alienate him from his colleagues as anything he might have said.

It also on occasion affected his relationships with party workers. One of these, a devoted Labour Party constituency worker in Ringsend, had a job on the B & I ferry between Dublin and Liverpool, and had unlimited access to duty-free cigarettes. His wife had become a heavy smoker, and had seriously damaged her lungs. She had been used to getting some medication to relieve her condition from her local GP, but once when a visit to his surgery was not practicable, she asked Browne if he would give her a prescription for her regular drug. When he refused unless she promised to give up smoking, she, her husband and their entire extended family stopped voting and working for him and transferred their allegiance to Fianna Fáil.

This anecdote is interesting in itself because it is so unusual. The woman was not a patient of his, strictly speaking, but in general Noël Browne's patients worshipped him. He had an extraordinary way of making them feel special, and cared for, and they simply thought that there was nobody quite like him. Even when he was a minister, he had kept in touch with some of his former patients from Newcastle who lived in Dublin, and would call into their houses on his way to or from the Dáil, sometimes with presents of cream or other food to build up their health.[13]

In so far as issues generally were concerned, he was to some extent ahead of the general policy line in the party. Brendan Corish, although a comparatively young leader, was feeling his way slowly into more radical positions. The party's general secretary, Mary Davidson, had been in position for many years, and was powerful in her own right at head office because of this, but exercised little real initiative over the semi-feudal baronies which were the constituency organisations of the entrenched Labour TDs.

Browne's record, however, and his considerable political profile, was undoubtedly a major factor in awakening a younger generation to the political possibilities of Labour throughout the 1960s. These did not necessarily include newcomers like Michael O'Leary, Barry Desmond or Frank Cluskey, who were hacking out a route into the Dáil through the dense undergrowth of the organised trade union movement (O'Leary and Desmond were both at one stage employees of the Irish Congress of Trade Unions, and Cluskey was active in Larkin's union, the Workers' Union of Ireland). The union leadership had always had reservations about Browne. They did, however, include university students and other young radicals, who effectively had no other political vehicle for their idealism. Sinn Féin was a spent force after the end of the border campaign in 1962. Fianna Fáil still appeared to be to some extent in the grip of the old guard, at least until after 1966. Fine Gael's 'Just Society' initiative did not materialise until late in 1964, and the reluctance with which that party embraced it before the 1965 election was impossible to disguise. Michael D. Higgins, a young graduate, whose own political antecedents would more likely have been in Fianna Fáil, first encountered Browne at an off-campus political meeting in Galway, to which he had attracted a huge crowd, and joined Labour as a result.[14] Una Claffey, while a student at University College, Dublin, had a similarly decisive exposure to Browne's charisma at around the same time. 'He changed my life.'[15]

The loss of his job at Newcastle had devastating personal consequences. Chief among these was the forced sale of Roseville, the family home in Bray, as an unsympathetic bank manager believed that Browne could no longer service his £800 mortgage. The purchase of another house in Bray was frustrated when the local Catholic parish priest put pressure on the seller to withdraw before the contract had been signed.[16] Browne and his family, now reduced to his Dáil salary of £1,000 and ministerial pension of about £300 (a total of about £17,800 in 2000 terms), moved, with the help of a compensation payment for his loss of employment, to a small former national school building at Callary, on the southern side of the Sugarloaf mountain, with twenty acres. For some time Phyllis helped to make ends meet by market gardening, and by baking cakes which were sold in shops in Bray. As an experiment in modest self-sufficiency it was valiant, but ultimately non-viable.

Browne's search for a job was initially unsuccessful. He would not consider private practice, but public appointments — certainly those of any seniority — were for all practical purposes closed to him by his controversial past. In one case, he was even rejected for a lowly position whose duties would have chiefly consisted of distinguishing between normal and abnormal X-ray pictures.[17]

He was not the only doctor turned politician to pay a price like this. Michael ffrench-O'Carroll, his former colleague in both Clann na Poblachta and Fianna Fáil, also found it extremely difficult to get medical employment, not least because of his association with Noël Browne. His main source of income at the time he became involved in politics was a clinic he ran in Donnybrook. As a direct result of his involvement with Clann na Poblachta, this clinic — which operated, like other similar services, on a referral basis — was effectively boycotted by Dublin's Catholic doctors.

Complete disaster was averted only by the action of a number of the city's Protestant doctors who, hearing of what had happened, began to refer patients to him out of a sense of fairness, although many of them would have been as opposed to Browne as their Catholic counterparts would have been. While this eased the problem, it did not solve it, and ffrench-O'Carroll came to the conclusion that he had better resume his medical training. The clinic was sold, and he emigrated to the United States, where he did postgraduate work in very reduced circumstances.

On his return to Ireland, he found that although he went to interview after interview, he was for some unaccountable reason never selected for any post, despite his now impressive qualifications and experience — he had in fact turned down a substantial offer in the United States. When he enquired unofficially what the problem was, he was told that it was quite simple: at the important level at which senior appointments were made, he had been blacklisted.

He was advised to start at the bottom of the ladder again and did so, in a public health job in Co. Kerry where the salary and conditions were so unattractive that there had been, apparently, no other applicants. Subsequently, a position opened up in Cork, for which he successfully applied. He spent some two decades working there, especially with young people with problems of addiction. Though now retired, he still works in a similar field at Cluain Mhuire in Athy, Co. Kildare. He is one of the few remaining witnesses to the most turbulent episode in modern Irish political and medical history.

Mental health was one of the few areas in which, at the time, public appointments were easily available; it was not an area much pursued by the ambitious. After a number of fruitless enquiries, Browne ended up at St Brendan's Hospital in Dublin, which then had about 200 patients and was, as his autobiography testifies, a dim, Dickensian and at times deeply depressing institution in which to work.

In St Brendan's, Browne was working under the resident medical super-intendent, Dr John Dunne, whom he had last visited many years previously in his other incarnation as Minister for Health. Dunne was a larger than life figure. He had been educated in the European tradition of psychiatry, and studied in Vienna before World War II. This did not, however, mean that he had adopted continental methods. He was, in effect, a traditional psychiatrist of the old British school, who viewed psychiatric illness largely in organic, biochemical terms, treatable with drugs and ECT (electroconvulsive therapy). This was not necessarily out of line with what most of his contemporaries were doing, but it inevitably led to tensions with younger staff.

In St Brendan's, Dunne was master of all he surveyed. This was the source of problems as well as privileges. As RMS, he alone had the responsibility, and the authority, for signing involuntary patients into the hospital. Dublin medical folklore suggests that on one occasion he was absent at a play in the Gaiety when one such patient was admitted on the signature of an under-ling. The patient, unfortunately, happened to be a barrister, who researched the law and took an action for damages, necessitating the passage by the Oireachtas of a special mental treatment bill, one of whose real purposes — the indemnification of Dunne — was carefully concealed.

Dunne's managerial style was remote and authoritarian. He spent very little time in the hospital; one of his subordinate staff, wanting to see him, once had to wait outside his office for lengthy periods for three days. Dunne passed him on his way into the office and on his way out again without so much as acknowledging him. Finally, on the third day, he asked: 'Are you holding a gun to my head?'

Dunne was, however, a freethinker in Irish terms, and admired Browne, whom he viewed as possessing similar characteristics. His attitude to the younger man was one of encouragement and, to some extent, of protection. He offered him a position as house physician, because, as Browne described it later, 'there was a scarcity of domestics'.[18] Browne took up his new position in December 1963, therefore, two months after leaving Newcastle.

His sojourn there was to overlap in a significant way with that of Dr Ivor Browne, who had joined St Brendan's in 1962 after spending some time in the United States. Ivor Browne's experiences were a foretaste of what Noël was to experience the following year, and he was rebellious and critical. Eventually Dunne sent him to St Loman's, a subsidiary hospital opened for psychiatric patients in 1960. It had a history which was intimately connected with Noël Browne himself, who as Minister for Health had originally planned it as a 'preventorium', or hospital for young children at risk from TB. Quoted a building cost of £4,000 a bed, he discussed the matter with Michael ffrench-O'Carroll, who suggested that it could be done for less — probably for £2,000 a bed. Browne set up a small company under ffrench-O'Carroll's stewardship to get around the red tape, and gave him carte blanche. The hospital was built for £1,700 a bed.[19]

Now organisationally part of the St Brendan's complex, it was at first restricted to female patients; later there were admissions of both males and females. There was, however, no direct admission; Dunne decided who would be sent there from St Brendan's.

Despite being circumscribed in this way, Loman's became a haven for the younger and more liberal members of the State psychiatric service in Dublin — either because they were sent there or because they escaped to it from Brendan's. One of these, Vincent Crotty, had effectively managed to open Loman's in the first place only in the teeth of opposition from Dunne. He was to be joined by Ivor Browne, Dermot Walsh and others. So, bad and all as the prevailing regime was, there was also a small but dedicated group of psychiatrists who were attuned to the ideas that Browne himself was developing.

For two years after Noël Browne joined the staff, however, Dunne was still in charge. Possibly encouraged by Dunne, who in addition to his St Brendan's appointment was Professor of Psychiatry in UCD, Browne applied there at the beginning of the 1964 academic year for a place on the course leading to the award of the Diploma in Psychiatric Medicine. He paid the fee, but dropped out. There are no further records of his progress in the college.

Browne was surprised to find, among his new colleagues at this time, 'a similar pattern of really gullible credulousness' to that which he had discovered in his work with TB sufferers.[20] But whereas this led doctors involved in treating TB patients to the widespread practice of crushing the chest cage and cavity, which Browne had himself defended in an early paper read to the College of Physicians, it led their counterparts in psychiatric medicine to the widespread — and, in Browne's view — mistaken use of pharmacology and ECT. 'It occurs to me', he reflected many years later, 'that, as a member of the healing profession, violence and still more violence has been a distressingly important part of our armamentarium . . . As a doctor, the temptation to play the omniscient, omnipotent god figure is a heady brew.'[21] Michael D. Higgins, who had many long conversations with Browne on psychiatry and other topics, felt that he had been strongly influenced by Carl Jung and his idea of the unconscious.[22] During his work as a psychiatrist, he was to develop a particular interest in deviancy, and in the contested area of the relationship between psychiatric illness and societal conditions.

Noël Browne's psychiatric career was, however, still in its infancy when his political future — and his major source of income — was suddenly imperilled. Sixteen months after he had begun work at St Brendan's, Lemass dissolved the Dáil and called a general election for 7 April 1965. In January, Lemass had made his historic visit to Terence O'Neill at Stormont, and the economy was picking up under his policy of promoting industrial investment and exports. Browne was now a candidate for Labour in Dublin South-East and, given his previous record, would not seem to have been in any serious difficulty. There are, however, few sure bets in politics, and in 1965 Browne's position in South-East was less secure than it had been in previous elections. The recurrence of his TB, his temporary loss of employment and his house move all meant that his profile in the constituency was lower than usual. This was despite putting in an amount of constituency work that was regarded as satisfactory, certainly by John Kennedy, who was to be his running mate in 1969. 'In the period from 1963–1969, Browne regularly attended a fortnightly clinic in Ringsend. The volume of clinic work was quite heavy and Browne was hard-working, Everyone was satisfied with his attention to constituency work.'[23] But this was not enough, partly because there was too much neglected ground to be covered. In the two intervening elections since 1954, when the Labour candidate Vincent McDowell had picked up a derisory 1,455 votes (enough to deprive Browne of his own seat in that election, as it happened), Labour had not even troubled to run a candidate in the constituency, leaving the third seat to be fought over by Browne, Fianna Fáil and Fine Gael.

Browne increased his first preference votes by some 700 votes, but it was not enough. While his poor health and the state of the constituency organisation were contributory causes, there was also a skilful vote management campaign by Fianna Fáil to the benefit of its second candidate, Sean Moore, who had taken Browne's place on the Fianna Fáil ticket in 1957, and had been beavering away on the ground to evident effect. At the count in Bolton Street, emotions ran high. When the result was becoming clear, the door opened and C.J. Haughey, Fianna Fáil's director of elections, came in. He walked straight over to where Noël Browne was sitting on a ledge at the side of the hall with some of his supporters and told him: 'I've sought you out particularly — winning this seat was absolutely critical for us. There's nothing personal in it.' Browne jumped down and accepted the proffered hand, saying: 'That's OK, Charlie — that's politics.'

Browne's loyal supporters were overcome. One of them, his director of elections Niall Greene, felt the scales falling from his eyes; like the younger Browne who had spurned MacEntee's civility on the hustings in 1948, he simply did not understand how politicians who were so ideologically different from one another could engage in meaningless courtesies at a time like this, making it all look like some sort of game.[24] Another, Betty Dowling, who worked for years in the Labour Party's head office, instinctively drew back her foot to kick Haughey, was prevented from doing so by a fellow party worker, and promptly burst into tears.[25]

Nationally, the Fianna Fáil vote rose from 43.8 per cent to 47.8 per cent. The smaller parties effectively disappeared. The National Progressive Democrats had already done so; they were followed into oblivion by Clann na Talmhan, whose leader, Joe Blowick, had been a cabinet colleague of Browne in 1948–51. The four abstentionist Sinn Féin TDs were no more, and the Independents were reduced to two. Clann na Poblachta continued to hold one seat, in Cavan, but the party was dissolved later in the year.

Labour's vote jumped from 11.6 per cent to 15.4 per cent, and it emerged from the election with twenty-two seats, its highest total since 1927, not to be exceeded until the unprecedented tally in the election of 1992. In Dublin, the jump in Labour support was even more dramatic — from 8.4 per cent to 18.5 per cent — seeing the election of a number of newcomers, including Frank Cluskey, Dr John O'Connell and Sean Dunne, who had been Independent Labour in 1961.

Dublin South-East was out of step. The Fianna Fáil vote in the constituency rose from 44.3 per cent to 48.8 per cent. Moore's first preference vote, however, increased by some 2,500 as a result of the vote management strategy between himself and MacEntee. Now, instead of being 1,000 votes behind Browne on the first count, he was 1,000 votes ahead of him, and took the third seat comfortably. Noël Browne was out of the Dáil again.

His failure to retain his seat was a deep disappointment, not only to him but to many others in the party who — although not a few of them were later to cross swords with him — saw him as a potent force for attracting new members among young people. Ruairí Quinn, a UCD architecture student at the time, was, as he put it, 'an admirer, not a groupie', and remembers his contributions.[26] Browne's popularity with the rank and file was not mirrored in the upper reaches of the organisation. Although the party's annual report for that year recorded the loss of Browne's and McQuillan's seats as 'a great disappointment as both these members were valued Deputies',[27] he fared poorly in the tough intra-party struggle for nominations to the Seanad. Whereas Jack McQuillan was successful, Browne only secured a nomination on the (quite inappropriate) Agricultural Panel. He secured just thirty-three votes (the quota was sixty-eight) and was heavily defeated.

Browne and his family were now at a low ebb financially. He had the salary he received as a house physician, and his £300 ministerial pension (it was almost trebled to £875 after the radical recasting of Oireachtas salaries and pensions by C.J. Haughey in 1968). He still lacked formal psychiatric qualifications, and accordingly took to the academic trail again.

Although he was later to refer to his time in UCD in the course of a Dáil speech, he actually took his qualifying examination in psychiatry not in UCD but in Dublin University, where he was awarded the Diploma in Psychological Medicine in 1966. This was also the year in which he was elected a member of the Royal Medico-Psychological Association. Membership of the RMPA was open to any medically qualified person, subject to election and payment of a subscription, and there was no specific qualifying examination. The Association later became the Royal College of Psychiatrists, membership of which was automatically extended to members of its predecessor.

On a professional level, matters were improving. In 1966 Ivor Browne became head of St Brendan's, and began the long but urgently needed process of re-evaluation and reorganisation. In January of the same year Noël Browne secured a new appointment as assistant medical officer, the next step up the ladder from house physician, at an annual salary of £1,510, almost identical to the salary of a TD, which had been increased from £1,000 in 1960 to £1,500 (£17,800 in 2000 terms) in 1964. His ministerial pension was an additional £3,560 in 2000 terms. Plainly, neither TDs nor AMOs were the recipients of undue largesse from the community they served, but, curiously, Browne was to argue in January 1967 that TDs were 'overpaid surely'.[28] This suggests, at the least, that the medical salary he then enjoyed, modest though it may have been, was sufficient for his own and his family's needs at that time.

Browne continued to be involved in Dublin South-East and participated in the local elections of 1967, speaking at a few after-Mass meetings. His rhetorical style, developed in that bitter January of 1948, when electronic aids such as loudspeakers were in short supply, and shaped in part by his severely reduced lung capacity, was unique. He would start off — generally though not always without much in the way of notes — in a low voice, so low that his audience would have difficulty in hearing him. The benefit of that was that they would become, and remain, unusually silent, straining to catch his sibilant, understated voice. He would husband his physical resources until towards the end of his speech, when he would often begin to speak with more vigour, and more rapidly, in a crescendo which seemed to draw on hidden reserves and energised his audience, even as it frequently exhausted him. It was, nonetheless, an extremely effective technique.

Ruairí Quinn was becoming more active in constituency politics at around this time. His introduction to Leinster House, as it happened, had not been through Browne, but through Stephen Coughlan junior, son of the Labour TD (and ex-Clann na Poblachta candidate) from Limerick whose career was to be intertwined briefly with Browne's in a remarkable Labour Party controversy a few years later. During the local elections, Quinn ferried Browne about to after-Mass meetings in an old van he then owned. It was, he remembered years later, his first, pungent introduction to someone who had eaten a lot of garlic the previous evening.[29]

Whatever about Dublin South-East, Browne was already being encouraged by his supporters — who would have belonged to a variety of different constituency organisations — to raise his profile within the party as a whole. In the summer of 1967 it emerged that he was to seek the vice-presidency of the party at its annual conference, due in October; he was spoken of in the same breath as Barry Desmond (then still a research officer with the ICTU), Michael O'Leary TD and 'other radical candidates'.[30]

His candidacy was given a significant impetus by a major series of articles about him by Michael McInerney, based on extensive interviews with Browne himself. The seven *Irish Times* articles, which straddled two weeks, were not extraordinary in themselves, in that McInerney did similar series about other political figures, notably John A. Costello. They were, however, unusual to say the least in that the first of them appeared on 9 October 1967, in the immediate run-up to the Labour Party conference at which the leadership elections would be held, thus affording invaluable publicity to the prospective vice-president. They were illustrated, in part, by reprints of the newspaper advertisements which had been published by the Department of Health for the Mother and Child Scheme in 1951. Even more interestingly, they included a description by Browne of William Norton, who had died only four years previously, as 'shrewd, charming, able, and a great negotiator'. In his autobiography, Noël Browne reserved some of his harshest descriptions for the late leader of the Labour Party, and for his table manners in particular. Twenty years earlier, on the eve of presenting himself to Norton's party as a candidate for one of its most senior positions, the worst he could find to say about him was that he 'did not know how much power he had'.[31]

In point of fact he was elected unopposed, an evident sign of popularity among the rank and file. Barry Desmond won the chairmanship by 481 votes to 166 for Michael O'Leary.[32] Browne was now in the unusual position not only of having been a member of three political parties but of having held office in two of them. A profile published in *The Irish Times* the same weekend described him as now 'the complete strategist, adult and mature'.[33] The ever-present observer from the American Embassy in Dublin had a cooler view. Noting that Browne, 'something of a maverick', was 'now a convinced Socialist, although for idealist/intellectual reasons rather than for strictly political ones', he continued:

His current thinking places him on the Left Wing of the Labour Party; given his eloquence and the passion of his convictions it is to be expected that he will become its leader. The net result will be to add considerably to the stresses within the party . . . it is quite possible that the addition of the inherently conservative trade unionists on the party's right and Dr Browne on its left will again split the Labour Party. Even if this does not occur, Dr Browne's accession to the inner leadership may prove a godsend to the Fianna Fáil government. Dr Browne's views are so much more radical than the generality of the party that several members of the Government are positively looking forward to the prospect of using him as an Aunt Sally.[34]

The same observer found that the policy on coalition adopted by the party — that it would enter coalition only as a majority partner — was, in light of the fact that it would have to more than double its Dáil representation to have even a third of the Dáil seats, 'tying its hands needlessly'. Such considerations did not bother Noël Browne or, indeed, anyone else in Labour. The remainder of the year found him speaking at numerous party meetings around the country, focusing on criticism of the banks and the educational system,[35] and on his long-term ambition — the creation of a State scheme which would employ all doctors.[36]

Quite unexpectedly, a new political opportunity presented itself with the death of Jim Everett, the veteran Labour politician and a colleague of Browne's in the 1948–51 cabinet. He had then represented National Labour, a conservative offshoot from the original party, which rejoined forces with traditional Labour in 1950. A TD for Wicklow under one Labour banner or another since 1922, he was a stalwart of the ITGWU. The by-election was called for 16 March 1968.

Browne was interested. Dublin South-East had spurned him, nobody knew how far away the next election would be, and he had many links with the county — indeed, he still lived there. In addition, the Labour Party had an new, energetic, left-wing general secretary, Brendan Halligan, who was doing his utmost to refashion the party into a modern socialist organisation. A Browne candidacy, he thought, would not only focus attention on the party's new image — various committees were busily reworking its faded policy documents — but might even succeed in pulling off a victory.

There was, however, a snag — several snags, in fact. One of them was that Everett had been responsible for appointing one of his supporters to manage a sub-post office in the village of Baltinglass in 1950, touching off what became known as the Battle of Baltinglass, an intra-community and political controversy so intense that it was later the subject of a book. Worse, it had been one of the major issues on which Browne and Hartnett had challenged MacBride. Their party leader's failure to speak out against it, on the grounds that unsavoury things sometimes happened in politics,[37] led directly to Hartnett's resignation from the party and touched off the chain of events that was to result in the collapse of the inter-party government. Browne had a poor opinion of Everett, and didn't care who knew it.

Everett's nephew, Liam Kavanagh, a local government officer twenty years younger than Browne, felt that he had a reasonable chance himself — if not at the by-election, then at the succeeding general election. Deceptively soft-spoken, Kavanagh is a politician to his fingertips and, as the team from Labour's head office in Earlsfort Terrace discovered, dangerously easy to underestimate. When the team's blandishments looked like failing, Kavanagh was invited to come to Dublin himself with his brother Paddy, a key constituency figure, for a meeting with senior party officials, and asked if he would withdraw.[38] No, he said firmly, he wouldn't. If Browne was selected, he would get 4,000 votes and would lose at the general election. He — Liam Kavanagh — would get 6,000, and would win the seat at the next general election. Browne, he argued, simply did not have a chance.

The nomination was decided, as normal, by a vote of all the Labour branches in the constituency at a specially convened selection convention. Brendan Halligan and Barry Desmond scoured the constituency to drum up support for Browne. In Desmond's case, there was an additional incentive: if Browne could be persuaded to migrate to Wicklow, there would be the chance of a nomination in Dublin South-East for him. In his capacity as party chairman, Desmond sent a letter to the convention emphasising the wish of the party's ruling Administrative Council that Browne should get the nomination.[39] Browne's case was put in a passionate speech by Sean Dunne, the TD for Dublin County, who had deep and strong links with the constituency. He had, with Jim Larkin, helped to set up the Federation of Rural Workers, and had particular credibility in Wicklow, where he had worked as union organiser and had even helped to organise a strike by farm workers against employers who happened to be a community of nuns.

But Halligan, Desmond and Dunne were up against more firepower than they knew. The president of the ITGWU, John Conroy, was a Wicklow man, and helped to sway, in Kavanagh's favour, any delegates that were doubtful. When the vote came, it went for Kavanagh by 2:1. Browne delivered a gracious, pro forma speech, in which he made the traditional remarks about being prepared to do all that he could to get Kavanagh elected. He then went home to the house the family currently occupied in Greystones and was not to reappear for the remainder of the campaign, except at the very end, when he attended a meeting in Bray and spoke on Kavanagh's behalf. The most flattering portion of his remarks was rapidly printed up as a flyer and distributed as widely as possible across the constituency. Kavanagh, as he himself had predicted, got almost 6,000 votes, and was to win the seat at the following general election.

There was more to this particular campaign, however, than personalities. Fianna Fáil had been in power for more than a decade, and people in both the opposition parties were beginning to wonder whether they would be there for ever. Michael J. Higgins, the Fine Gael TD for the constituency, made a speech on behalf of his party's candidate, Godfrey Timmins, during the campaign suggesting that there should be a voting pact between Fine Gael and Labour on polling day, and discussing the possibility of another coalition. Muiris Mac Conghail, the young producer of the RTÉ 7 *Days* current affairs programme, invited Noël Browne, among others, to discuss it on air. He did so for a particular reason: having watched Browne closely, he knew that — unlike many of the party's senior members at that time — he was by no means a committed anti-coalitionist, certainly not in principle. To the astonishment and even alarm of the same senior figures, Browne made this clear in the television studio.

In his autobiography, Browne provides a different gloss on what happened, analysing it as part of what he saw as part of a joint strategy between Mac Conghail and David Thornley (then a presenter on the programme) to forward a pro-coalition agenda.

> *I was quite happy to collaborate with the Thornley-Mac Conghail plan until just before the conclusion . . . Asked about the true function of the minority in coalition, I replied 'just as soon as we achieve our political objectives in any coalition with a conservative party, it is the responsibility of a smaller radical party to pull the trap on the other parties.' . . . I hoped that the effect of my candid exposure of the reality of coalition politics would help at least to slow down the inevitable coalition which I saw ahead. I did not re-appear on* Seven Days *thereafter.*[40]

This later interpretation of the content of the programme can be contrasted with his reaction at the time; meeting Mac Conghail in the street the morning after the programme, he gave the producer a cheery 'thumbs-up' sign, plainly delighted with the outcome.[41] Tony Browne, then an economist in the Irish Sugar Company, a Labour activist and a close friend of Halligan (who had also worked in the Sugar Company as an economist before joining Labour in 1967), remembers Noël Browne driving him home after a party meeting at which the new series of policy statements was being prepared at about this time, and talking to him enthusiastically in the car parked outside his house about the positive aspects of coalition, and how to play parties off against each other.[42] He came to the conclusion that there was a deep antipathy on Browne's part towards Corish, and that his openness to the coalition idea, at least in principle, might be related partly to the fact that Corish had, both before and after the 1965 election, firmly ruled it out.

Indeed, at the Labour Party conference in 1968, when Noël Browne stood up to speak on electoral strategy and the audience applauded him to the echo, he warned them: 'I hope you will still be applauding when I've finished.' He went on to make the case for coalition — but coalition on specific terms. The terms he outlined may or may not have been realistic, but in point of fact, Noël Browne never declared opposition to coalition in principle, right up to and including his speech on this topic at the Labour Party conference in Limerick in 1976. His 1986 gloominess about the prospect of sharing political power is certainly not fully reflected in the recollections of those who knew him in the earlier period. For all that, he became a figurehead for many members of the party who were opposed to coalition at any time, at any price and with any party (but especially with Fine Gael). There were, in effect, significant differences on this issue between him and many of his supporters — differences which it was in both their interests occasionally to minimise or even conceal.

The rebuff for Browne in Wicklow gave him pause. Almost immediately, another option presented itself. This was a World Health Organization fellowship for North Africa, as part of which he would be advising a number of African governments, particularly on the eradication of TB. He accepted the offer with enthusiasm, taking leave of absence from his work at St Brendan's. There was a notable irony in this: the offer was mediated by none other than Dr James Deeny, Browne's old adversary in the Department of Health, who retained a liking for him despite all their battles, and who had maintained contacts with the WHO since his service there in the 1950s.[43] Accompanied by his daughter Susan, who had qualified as a nurse, Browne set off early in March of 1968.[44] Before leaving, he resigned his vice-presidency of the Labour Party 'due to professional reasons',[45] but he had not abandoned his political career. Within weeks of leaving, he had been readopted unanimously as a Labour candidate for the Dublin South-East constituency; Sheila Conroy, John Conroy's wife, was selected as the second candidate.[46] Part of the plan was that Phyllis would follow them when they had become established; the family car had been sold and other arrangements made.

The entire enterprise was a fiasco.[47] Noël and Susan had to surrender their passports on arriving in Libya, the first country in which they were to work, which meant that their movements were curtailed and that they could not leave the country without official permission. The political situation was unstable. Libya was entering the final phase of the rule of King Idris; Gaddafi was to capitalise on popular unrest and take over in 1969. Noël Browne found that the country, enriched by oil revenues, had acquired the most up-to-date medical equipment, but there was a complete lack of infrastructure.

These were not the only problems. Father and daughter alike felt anxious about and intimidated by the Islamic attitude towards women; Noël believed that they were being followed by plain-clothes police. Worse was to come. On St Patrick's Day, a Libyan with whom they had become friendly invited them to join him on a Yugoslav ship in the harbour for a small celebration, alcohol being generally banned in Libya. When they got back to the hotel Noël Browne, considerably agitated, suggested to his daughter that their drinks on board might have been spiked, and told her to lock her door securely from the inside.

The next day, he decided that it was all too much, and began making plans to abort his fellowship and go home. First of all, he pretended to the authorities that Susan was ill, so ill that she had to return immediately. Susan went home to put the second part of the plan into operation — this was to send a message to Noël to say that his wife was dying and that he, too, had to return urgently.

Once father and daughter were back in Dublin, Browne took matters further. According to a report by a civil servant in the National Archives:

> He rang the Minister for Health [Sean Flanagan] and told him about the conditions there: that foreigners are followed by police with guns, that all telephone calls are monitored and that women are mere chattels etc. Dr Browne would like the Minister to discourage Irish people from taking up appointments there and the Minister is wondering how he might do this. He is not anxious to make a public statement lest it would provoke undesirable discussion either in the newspapers or on television.[48]

Flanagan discussed the matter with the Taoiseach, Jack Lynch, after a cabinet meeting, but no further action appears to have been taken. The inference is that neither man took Browne's complaints seriously. The fact that he made no mention of this odd experience in his autobiography suggests that Browne, too, may subsequently have had second thoughts about his own reactions on this occasion.

Before and after the Libyan episode, Noël Browne had of course been continuing his psychiatric work. Ivor Browne had been making enormous changes in St Brendan's — knocking down walls, building new facilities, and encouraging new attitudes towards psychiatric illness on the part of staff and patients alike.[49] Ivor Browne recalls being told by a colleague around this time that the man concerned had been looking out a window with Noël Browne while the old walls were being demolished. Reflecting, as they watched, on James Joyce's fierce diatribe against his native country,

Noël observed thoughtfully: 'The old sow will never be the same again.'[50] This comment, however, suggests that Noël Browne's major criticisms of St Brendan's in *Against the Tide* essentially refer to the earlier period under John Dunne, something his colleagues from that time felt ought to have been made clearer.

Ivor Browne's approach to psychiatric medicine was radical, even for its time; in particular, the locked wards were, for the most part, opened up. This in turn created problems for many of the staff, who found the new regime disturbing and in some ways threatening. Noël Browne was one of the doctors who recognised that there was trauma among the staff as well as among the patients.

One of the newest developments, as it happened, was directly under Browne's control. This was a unit in St Brendan's, largely for homeless girls with psychiatric problems. Noël's way of dealing with them was — given the system which had operated under the old regime — extremely, and perhaps dangerously, liberal. He would take them into town, even to soccer matches, or send them on the bus out to his own house, where Phyllis would give them tea. But it was too much, too soon. Many of the girls, unprepared for any substantial measure of personal responsibility, needed limits as much as they needed freedom. A number of pregnancies ensued — so much so that the nurses in St Brendan's, frustrated and annoyed by what they saw as Noël Browne's over-indulgent approach, christened the unit 'Dr Browne's Baby Factory'. Matters came to a head, and the unit was closed down. In a society more conscious of individual rights and institutional responsibilities — as Ireland later became — the consequences of this sort of event for both doctor and hospital might have been considerably more serious. Noël Browne accepted the decision, but he was disappointed and angry.

For his views of the relationship between psychiatric illness and social conditions, we have the benefit of two formal contributions by Noël Browne to socio-medical debate, apparently the only two examples extant of his academic contributions in this area. This is undoubtedly a loss. A fellow member of the Labour Party who was also an academic, Michael D. Higgins, was often struck by what a good doctor he was — except in relation to himself — and by his strengths as a clinician and knowledge of recent developments.[51] The first is from 23 October 1968, when he read a paper to the autumn quarterly meeting of the Irish Division of the Royal Medico-Psychological Association. The second is his psychiatric analysis of the mind of John George Haigh, the British serial killer known as the 'Acid Bath Murderer' from his method of disposing of his victims, which was published in 1973, although written some time earlier.

Browne's paper to the RMPA was on 'Misfits in Society',[52] in which he gave an account of the work he was doing with adolescent psychopaths in

St Brendan's. His methodology was to collect them and isolate them from other patients to work out their problems of interpersonal relationships within their peer group and encourage them to 'evolve a society managed to a great extent by themselves'.

Progress towards maturity, he warned, was slow, with recurring risks of theft, misdemeanour, sexual aberrations and so on, so that, even when well settled in hospital, a minimum stay of five years would appear to be necessary.

He then identified four 'major causative elements' of juvenile psychopathy: broken homes, disturbed homes (e.g. alcoholic parents), rejection by parents, and isolation due to absence of parents. This final element, in the published synopsis of his paper, foreshadowed a speech he was to give in Seanad Éireann some years later. Adolescent psychopathy, he suggested, could be the result of parental absence, where the parents were fully involved in professional or working careers. He went on in his paper to 'question the wisdom of modern society diverting mothers from their primary and most important role to being members of a working community. The economic advantages would seem to be far outweighed by the degree and risk of psychopathy and neuroses in their children in later life.'

Arthur la Bern, the editor of the book on Haigh to which Noël Browne contributed a psychoanalytic chapter,[53] suggests that as a result of Browne's analysis, Haigh's character was no longer the enigma it had once been considered. Browne studied Haigh's numerous letters and a transcript of the trial — as Haigh had been executed, any closer examination was naturally out of the question — and came to the conclusion that the McNaghten Rules (devised in 1843) on the insanity of defendants in murder trials were 'archaic . . . and never justified'. His analysis of the inadequacies of the defence team's conduct of the case is pithy, his suggestion that they should have at least examined the possibility that Haigh was suffering from 'some macabre uncontrollable sado-masochistic sex drive' is at least arguable, and in general his demolition of the relevance of the McNaghten Rules is achieved with some panache. His overall conclusion, to the effect that when they hanged Haigh (the jury was out for only fifteen minutes) they hanged someone who was clinically insane, is compelling. All these, however, have to be set beside the throwaway manner in which he attacks his own profession ('If the law is an ass, then psychiatry is a jackass') and advances a general theory which would find acceptance only among its most extravagant practitioners: 'It is about time that criminality was accepted and treated as the product of emotional dysfunction that it is.'

His psychiatric colleagues, however much they might have disagreed with him on certain matters, came to respect one aspect of his character in particular: his professional solidarity and integrity. For some three years of the 1963–70 period, when he was working with the Dublin Health Authority in St Brendan's or, after the closure of the girls' unit, in Ballymun, he was a member of the Oireachtas. At no point did he blur the boundaries between his professional and his political lives. The temptation to make a political issue of the conditions he had encountered must have been substantial, but he recognised that this might only damage the advances that he and his colleagues were trying to achieve, and anything to do with his medical work was off-limits as far as his politics were concerned.

His relationship with Ivor Browne was good. In later years, Ivor Browne remembered it as being not particularly close, but then recalled two incidents which suggested otherwise. One was when he had a car accident near Lucan in the early 1960s, not long after Noël Browne had joined St Brendan's. Noël was the doctor who came to the scene and organised his emergency admission to Dr Steevens' Hospital. The second was some years later. Ivor had become interested in the use of newer drugs for the treatment of psychiatric illness, including LSD, and decided that he could not give this to his patients without testing it on himself. As this was unknown territory, he wanted another doctor present when he administered the dose to himself at home in Killiney. Noël was the person he asked, and Noël agreed — despite his own deep dislike of drug-based treatment for psychiatric patients. During the experiment, Noël cared for him with what Ivor Browne saw as his dominant mode as a doctor — great gentleness.

There was another side to Noël Browne which Ivor Browne and other colleagues at St Brendan's also witnessed from time to time. This was anger — a temper which rose, on occasion, to white heat, but which, in Ivor Browne's experience, was also unusually a 'controlled white heat'.[54] Sometimes there were occasions when the control had to be total. The two Brownes were once in London together, attending a psychiatric conference, when they went out for dinner to the home of a medical colleague. In the course of their dinner, the host began a tirade against black immigrants to Britain, and heaped praise on South Africa's apartheid regime. The tension was extraordinary. Ivor Browne saw Noël making a valiant, and ultimately successful, attempt to control his anger. Afterwards, outside, he became his normal self again.

The same issue, as it happened, was one which became a particular cause of Noël Browne's in politics. The late 1960s saw the rapid growth of the Irish Anti-Apartheid Association, an all-party organisation which focused in particular on visits by the Springboks, the all-white South African rugby team. Eamon de Valera, as president, pointedly declined invitations from the Irish Rugby Football Union to attend matches when they played in Dublin, but this did not dissuade thousands of rugby fans who regularly made their way into Lansdowne Road past anti-apartheid protesters. Browne was a regular member of these pickets, and on one occasion was put on duty beside the gate through which the most privileged members of the rugby fraternity entered the ground, fortified with hip flasks and protected by bulky sheepskin jackets. It was raining; the protesters had little money for placards and their small, sodden pieces of cardboard were therefore inscribed with the shortest message they could devise: 'Boks Go Home!' An attempt to engage the rugby fans in argument evoked the terse injunction to keep politics out of sport. One such exchange, his companion on the picket line noted, 'brought Noël as close as I have ever seen to uttering an expletive'.[55]

In politics, the Labour Party was in the process of moving up a gear, with a number of high-profile accessions. These included notably David Thornley, whose brilliant academic career had been supplemented by his incisive interviewing on RTE's flagship *7 Days*; Conor Cruise O'Brien, the former civil servant who had made a second career for himself as a radical journalist and was now Albert Schweitzer Professor of Humanities at New York University; and Justin Keating, the former communist, also a university lecturer and a noted broadcaster.

The party's 1969 annual conference was held in Dublin on 24–6 January. Throughout January, the newspapers were full of details of the new policy statements, which were carefully released at intervals to maximise publicity. A document on worker democracy was published on 8 January, which included a commitment to nationalise all banks, credit and insurance companies. Agricultural policy came next, on 13 January, with its proposals for the extension of farmers' control over production and marketing processes, the encouragement of group farming, and strict controls on the purchase of land by foreigners. Policy on land control was announced on 15 January, including State control of building land, and health, on 17 January, promised a wide range of free services.

Media reactions ranged from the startled to the hostile. *The Irish Times*, although it agreed that many of the proposals were a welcome contrast to the general run of 'makeshift, half-baked' party manifestos, described the new policies as 'openly socialist' and involving a massive invasion of individual rights. The worker democracy document attracted particular opprobrium; the *Cork Examiner* described it as 'communistic', and the *Irish Independent* said that it revealed 'a basic approach so drastic as to be unreal to most Irishmen'. The Federated Union of Employers dismissed it as a 'watered down version' of Russian ideas. More significantly, the new policies forced Fine Gael into a defensive posture, in which it retreated further from the prospect of ever sharing government with Labour — even if such an offer had been on the table — and Fianna Fáil, well attuned to the popular mood and aware of the likely limits of the electorate's appetite for radical change, licked its collective lips, waiting for the campaign to open.

At the conference, Brendan Corish carved out the party's position, and his own personal position, in terms of extraordinary clarity. There would be no coalition. The seventies would be socialist; and if the party ever decided to change its policy on the vexed question of participation in government, he would continue to serve it — but from the backbenches. Few in the party disagreed with him, certainly not many who were prepared to voice their opinions. From then until the election was called for June 1969, Labour staked out the socialist high ground.

Noël Browne paid a personal call on Jack McQuillan, urging him to rejoin Labour; McQuillan refused. Browne declared, 'You're not a socialist,' and stalked away (a few weeks later, he was back to renew their friendship).[56] In fact, McQuillan had become increasingly disillusioned with politics as such, and despite winning a Labour seat in the Seanad after the 1965 election (beating Barry Desmond's father in the process), he lost the party whip in 1967 in a row over internal discipline. Proinsias Mac Aonghusa was expelled from the party at this time, accused of attacking the leadership in an anony-mous newsletter. With him went his wife, Catherine McGuinness, who had been the Parliamentary Labour Party's able and hard-working research and policy officer for years. She turned full-time to a distinguished legal career, and was eventually appointed to the Supreme Court in January 2000.

McQuillan's disillusion had its origins in a deepening suspicion that his substantial electoral support had been due less to his socialism than to other, non-ideological factors, and towards the end of his life he felt that his old friend Browne was misinterpreting his electoral support as support for socialism, when he felt that it was due to other things, not least the strong residual memory of his work for TB sufferers, which had secured him the undying loyalty of countless families in every constituency.[57]

Ninety-nine Labour candidates took the field in June, in an atmosphere of unprecedented optimism. Brendan Halligan, who had officiated at the enthusiastic selection conference for Dublin South-East, held in the trad-itional venue — a meeting room above Margaret Gaj's restaurant in Baggot Street — got a telephone call from Noël Browne after the Labour Party's first party political broadcast on radio; Browne told him that it was the best he had ever heard.[58] The night before the election itself, Browne was so convinced that the Labour Party would do well that he did not hide, from one of his close associates, his belief that the party might even be in govern-ment after the election.[59] It was not a prospect which dismayed him. The Fianna Fáil vote went down by 2 per cent; Labour's went up by 1.6 per cent nationally, and by almost 10 per cent in Dublin. O'Brien, Thornley and Keating were all elected. So was Noël Browne, with a 5 per cent increase in the Labour vote in his constituency, where Fianna Fáil lost a seat because of Seán MacEntee's retirement. But Labour lost non-metropolitan seats, partly because of Jack Lynch's canny campaign, aimed at frightening rural voters with attacks on Labour's socialism.

Immediately after the election, in which Labour had managed simultaneously to lose seats while gaining votes, Browne wrote to Corish:

> *I hope you're not discouraged. You could not have done more than you did and we are all proud of you as Leader of the Labour Party. All I can do is promise you is that having done what I would do to win Dublin for Labour the rest of my political life will be dedicated to winning Ireland for Labour. Just tell me what you would wish me to do.*[60]

Noël Browne's return to the Dáil in 1969 was, however, at a high price. He was still working in St Brendan's and while on duty there one day after the election felt unwell and lay down on a daybed. When he didn't feel better, he suspected a heart attack, got up, drove himself to the Meath Hospital and had himself admitted, where his diagnosis proved correct.

Browne's latest brush with death (he received the sacrament of extreme unction on three occasions in his lifetime)[61] was accompanied by a strong sense of disenchantment with his work as a psychiatrist. He had for some time been working in the north-eastern area of the Eastern Health Board as a psychiatrist, chiefly in areas like Ballymun. What he saw there was to depress him profoundly, as he argued that the problems with which his patients were trying to cope were social and political, rather than personal and psychological, in origin. 'In psychiatry, I came across case after case which was beyond my powers to solve . . . I felt impotent and distressed . . . and over the years my political work has been affected by my disillusion with politics and by severe bouts of depression arising from my medical work.'[62]

Browne's success and that of others in 1969 masked major problems for the party. Many of the ninety-nine Labour candidates had had no realistic hope of election, so that the national increase in votes did not translate into seats. A canny Fianna Fáil campaign was aimed at frightening people about the radical changes envisaged by Labour; a newspaper advertisement just before the election warned: 'There are two Labour Parties — the traditional one . . . and a new group of extreme left-wing socialists preaching class warfare and who want total state control and all that goes with it.'[63] This was enhanced by a skilful redrawing of the constituency boundaries, which meant that although Fianna Fáil secured fewer votes, it won more seats. In Labour's case, it was the reverse — more votes but fewer seats, down to eighteen from their 1965 total of twenty-two, and listening to the tinkle of lost deposits all over the country.

While the newly elected high-profile candidates tore into their Dáil spokesmanships with enthusiasm, talent and commitment, other members of the party were beginning to re-evaluate the situation. They certainly would not have been in a majority, and few of them would even have had any clear idea about the direction in which they ought to travel, when a whole series of events changed the face of Irish politics. The North exploded in August 1969, even as the Seanad elections were taking place, and there was an attempt to import arms for Nationalists there. In April 1970 Jack Lynch sacked two of his ministers, C.J. Haughey and Neil Blaney, ostensibly because he was not convinced that they fully subscribed to government policy on Northern Ireland. A third minister, Kevin Boland, resigned. The two sacked ministers were charged with illegal arms importation. Blaney was never tried, as the case was thrown out in the District Court at the pre-liminary stage for want of evidence. Haughey, on the other hand, faced two trials. The first was aborted; in the second, he was acquitted.

Noël Browne, initially, gave Lynch a measure of support in the crisis. At a time when many opposition politicians were calling for an election to clear the air, he described such demands as 'illogical, inconsistent and emotionally opportunist'. The present time, he argued, was not the time 'in which we in the Labour Party should seek to exploit an internecine struggle in Fianna Fáil for our short term party gain . . . if Lynch is not in control, the armoured cars could take over'.[64]

As the public concentrated on events in the North and the government reaction to them, the whirlwind sequence of events was driving both Labour and Fianna Fáil into a reappraisal of their electoral strategies. Soon, it became apparent that Brendan Corish had changed or was in the process of changing his mind. Gossip within the party was widespread, and the move by Corish and other TDs towards a re-evaluation of electoral strategy was met by a regrouping of the anti-coalition forces, not least around Browne.

This was accompanied by a distinct hardening of his political rhetoric. Challenged by a reader of *The Irish Times* to name six Utopias where social-ism had been created, he replied: 'I can't. Six [sic] countries who, because they have used variants of Connolly's revolutionary socialism, are, I believe, making their way towards that objective in the broadest sense: Albania, China, Cuba, Hungary, Poland, USSR, Yugoslavia.'[65]

In September 1970, before the party had changed its position on coalition, but when it had become evident that a change was being contemplated, he made his endorsement of Marxism even more explicit, charging now that his own party, Labour 'corrupted over the years from the top, has become a con-servative party in its most precise sense'. Accusing the other Labour TDs of 'charlatanism', he argued that they now had to choose between 'social demo-cratic reformism' or — his own preference — 'the Marxist-based revolution-ary socialism of James Connolly'.[66] At the beginning of the following month, the party's Dublin Regional Council issued a statement supporting Browne.[67]

Even as the temperature rose, however, he did not abandon his view on coalition. Fianna Fáil and Fine Gael, he argued, should 'follow the logic of their conservative ideologies and join up to make a government'. If they failed to do this, 'then the Labour Party in the face of their intransigence where there is no single party with an overall majority becomes the kingmaker'.[68] The problem about this analysis, whether it was advanced by Noël Browne or anyone else, was that its real utility was to provide people who opposed coalition on principle with a substitute policy that looked less extreme. The prospect of Fianna Fáil and Fine Gael joining in government looks remote enough in 2000. In 1970, not only was this less likely, but putative supporters of the 'kingmaker' option would not, in practice, have been prepared to accept any terms likely to be agreed between Labour and a much larger party. They would also have had entirely unrealistic expectations about the prospects for Labour in any immediate general election caused by their unwillingness to accept terms based on electoral arithmetic rather than on socialist principles. Noël Browne's own, unrealistic benchmark — the possession of five key ministries — was not achievable even after Labour's extraordinary showing in 1994.

In March 1970, there was a by-election in Ballyfermot, caused by the death of Sean Dunne. Dunne, whose independence of spirit had something in common with that of Browne and McQuillan, had been elected for Labour in the constituency in 1969, along with Dr John O'Connell. It was the first time two Labour TDs had ever been elected in the same constituency; such a triumph was not to be repeated for many years. But Dunne died shortly after the election, even before formally taking his seat, and the by-election was an unseemly squabble. The Labour Party selected Mattie Merrigan as its candidate. Merrigan, general secretary of the Amalgamated Transport and General Workers Union, was a fiery trade unionist who was often on the opposing side to the Labour Party hierarchy, but who had a large and solid trade union following. He was also closely associated with Noël Browne in the party's Dublin Regional Council.

Unfortunately for him, Cora Dunne, Sean Dunne's widow, had been persuaded that she had a greater right to the seat, and a better chance of winning it. She ran as an Independent. Fianna Fáil wanted Dr Michael ffrench-O'Carroll to run in his old stamping ground, which would have brought about an odd situation in which he would have been campaigning against Noël Browne. In the end he declined, not for this reason but because by then he had taken an irrevocable decision to leave politics for medicine.

Cora Dunne's candidacy ruined Merrigan's chances. He almost won, in spite of her campaign. But the seat went to Noel Lemass, the Taoiseach's son. It was to be the last occasion on which Browne and the leaders of Labour campaigned on the same side in an election.

By late September 1970, it was evident that there was a mood for change within at least some sections of the party. A special conference was called for December in Cork to discuss electoral strategy, and the battle lines were drawn. Noël Browne's enthusiasm for Brendan Corish, forged in the white heat of the election only eighteen months earlier, had crumbled and vanished, never to reappear.

At the party conference Corish decided to lead from the front, abandoning the privilege of speaking from the platform and going, instead, to the podium on the floor of the hall from which rank-and-file members spoke. He talked frankly about how, and why, he had changed his views. As he outlined the circumstances involved — the national crisis caused by the Arms Trial and its ramifications — Noël Browne rose in his seat on the floor of the hall to cry 'Shame! Shame!' 'You will have an opportunity to cry "Shame" from this rostrum,' Corish retorted, before finishing his speech.[69]

Although the conference was tape-recorded, no viable record of the second half remains extant, and as the press were not admitted, there is no record of Noël Browne's speech. But he did speak against the leadership's resolution on electoral strategy, by all accounts passionately and, for many, convincingly. When the votes were taken at the end of the conference, however, there was a further development. Procedurally, the early votes were being taken on the anti-coalition resolutions, and the anti-coalition forces were losing, but not by a very substantial margin. After one vote, Browne suddenly stood up, and made as if to leave the hall. Delegates supporting the leadership of the party assumed that this had all been pre-arranged, but apparently this was not so. One of his supporters, Pat Carroll, shouted at him to sit down. Another supporter, Una Claffey, seated directly behind him, tried unsuccessfully to persuade him not to leave the hall, but when she failed to do so, decided that at least he should not be allowed to leave on his own, and got up to accompany him. When they saw this happening, quite a large number of anti-coalition delegates did the same. Of course this meant that the votes were no longer close, and led to a relatively easy acceptance of the leadership position at the end of the day.

If Browne had been doubtful about Corish's leadership, and antipathetic to it, even before December 1970, he was openly hostile to it afterwards. The next two and a half years were to see him launch an increasingly bitter series of broadsides, some against his party leader, others against the Catholic Church, which were to lead to his growing isolation within the parliamentary party, even as they raised his political profile outside it. The last occasion on which he sided with the Labour leadership at a party conference appears to have been in February 1971 when, at the party's annual conference, he moved the resolution against EEC entry.[70] He was in excellent company: Michael O'Leary, Conor Cruise O'Brien, Matt Merrigan and Jim Kemmy were all on the same side. Michael Pat Murphy TD, whose farming constituents in west Cork had other ideas, was one of the very few to speak in favour.

A number of things may be said about Browne's relationship with Corish, and by extension with the other members of the PLP who supported the change in electoral strategy. One is to underline the considerable evidence that the main difference between Noël Browne and the pro-coalitionists in the party (one may almost say the other pro-coalitionists) was on the question of tactics rather than objectives. The problem, and the source of the deep division on this issue, was Browne's apparent belief that fellow socialists who did not share his view of the appropriate tactics were, by virtue of this fact, also people who did not, or could not, share his objective. It is easy to see, in retrospect, why the gulf created by this mindset was so unbridgeable.

The second is in relation to Catholicism. Brendan Corish had, a few years earlier, created some comment by remarking that he was a Catholic first, an Irishman second and a socialist third. He spoke from the heart in this, as anyone who knew him could testify. In the Ireland of the 1960s and 1970s, however, where growing secularism and anticlericalism marched hand in hand, and where the institutional Catholic Church, in particular, was seen by some as behind the times and out of date, this admission had a curiously old-fashioned air about it. The assumption grew, although it was never articulated as such, that political convictions were — or ought to be — stronger than religious ones, which were seen as increasingly irrelevant to the real world.

This was the time at which Corish's credo was attacked, on more than one occasion, by Noël Browne, in a way which implied that Corish's Catholicism was effectively at odds with his socialism, and that by prioritising his religious commitment he was being a traitor to the cause. It can be argued, however, that Corish's position was perfectly defensible. History — including the history of many Catholic politicians and some 'Catholic' states — is all too replete with examples of what can go wrong when political leaders who profess religious values ignore or suppress these values when faced with the demands of ideology.

On a more personal level, it is difficult to understand how Noël Browne's position in 1951, when he accepted in public and in private the bishops' moral judgment on his Mother and Child Scheme, was in any essential way different from the position for which he was castigating Brendan Corish in the 1970s. Or, to put it another way, was his memory of what he himself had done in 1951, and his post factum rejection of it, in some way linked to the intensity of his repeated attacks on Corish on this issue?

One of the issues in this area was contraception, the legislation on which had been challenged for the first time in the Oireachtas by the newly elected Senator Mary Bourke (Robinson after December 1970), representing the Dublin University constituency. Almost immediately after her election in 1969, she made this one of her policy planks, and succeeded in embarrassing the government, which refused to give her time for a debate on a draft Bill, or even to allow it to be printed. This inevitably had echoes within the PLP, where the new faces — O'Brien, Keating and Thornley in particular — were in the middle of a period of adjustment with their longer-serving colleagues of a more conservative disposition. It was not even the case that these three acted or operated as a group; although they were subsequently lumped together in Noël Browne's catalogue of traitors to socialism, they differed profoundly on some issues (Northern Ireland, for example). It was not an easy process. It was also one in which the newcomers had perforce to make many more compromises than they wished, simply because the alternative would have been to split the party, and deeply embarrass Brendan Corish, for whom — in spite of his acknowledged and innate conservatism — they had a genuine affection and respect. Splitting the party would also, as conservatives and liberals alike were well aware, consign any hope of a governmental role to the dim and shadowy future.

Viewed from the perspective of the second millennium, these wrangles of the 1970s are barely credible, as is the evident readiness of the liberal members of the PLP to keep their heads down. The pace of change was painfully slow and, even excluding the wisdom conferred by hindsight, difficult to justify. But part of the problem was that Noël Browne's lack of a tactical sense made him the worst possible advocate of change in the smoke-filled party room, already riven by suspicion between its opposing groups, each of them conscious not only of the ideological demands of social democracy, but of the prospects of ministerial office.

Probably impelled in part by the publicity attaching to Mary Bourke's moves in the Seanad, Browne initiated a debate on contraception in the PLP. This, according to Browne himself, resulted in a five-hour meeting, in the course of which he was subjected to 'sustained abuse by all but a handful of members', some of whom called for his expulsion from the party. The result — surprisingly enough, given the composition of the PLP at the time — was a decision (which was not published) to support legislation if such were initiated. The subtext, however, was clear: the Labour Party itself, even in opposition, would not be in the business of initiating anything so risky; that was up to braver souls.[71]

In 1970, escaping from the grim wasteland of Ballymun, Browne was appointed by the Local Appointments Commission as senior psychiatrist in the Wicklow County Council area, and found himself back at Newcastle, where the former TB hospital had been turned into a psychiatric facility. This also involved an increase in income, which he received along with his ministerial pension, set at a quarter of the current rate for cabinet office-holders, and his TD's allowance. Even before this, it is somewhat difficult to reconcile what can be established about his income with the general sense, which he conveyed both to friends and to political supporters, that he was perennially short of money. His attitude to that commodity was described pithily but fondly by Phyllis, in terms which make him sound a little like James Joyce's father. What must it have been like to run the household in which he was the wage earner? 'Noël always believed that if one had money, one should invest it in property, but then he was a man who always felt that he had money, or would be lucky enough some day to inherit some, though from whom he never could tell.'[72] Indeed, he horrified some of his supporters by turning up to a party meeting in a working-class part of his constituency immediately after the 1969 election in a brand new sports car.

The constituency itself now began to suffer. After the 1969 election he promised his running mate, John Kennedy, that he would employ a part-time secretary and organise the constituency thoroughly, but then went absent for the best part of two years. Kennedy added:

> Noël became harder to contact and never attended branch meetings in order to explain his policies or discuss mutual problems. Branches weren't as active. Labour in South-East was in disarray in 1973 and this was due to Browne's inactivity. All the work of 1969 went to no avail. People called around to my house disillusioned, saying 'Where is Noël? We voted for him but we never see him.' On the canvass [in 1973] the slagging about Browne was disheartening, and he never lifted a finger to help Quinn.[73]

His disagreement with the party's strategy, or at least with what he conceived to be its implications, impelled Noël Browne to even greater heights of opposition. In October 1970 he had told the annual meeting of his own constituency council that Labour, as a party, was unworthy of support and that its leaders were 'using the word socialism to shoe-horn themselves into the back-seat of a ministerial Mercedes';[74] and in March 1971 he argued publicly that Labour, in common with all the main parties in the Republic, supported laissez-faire capitalism because it represented Catholic social and economic thinking. The Irish worker, he surprisingly declared, was better off under the Unionists in Stormont.[75]

His most controversial intervention, however, was in a speech to a Labour Party meeting in Tramore in April 1971, when he embarked on a sustained attack on the effects of the Catholic Church on Irish political life. It was a theme to which he been returning with increasing frequency. Like many others, he had been heartened and excited by the changes that were taking place in Catholicism in Ireland and elsewhere as a result of the reforming process initiated at the second Vatican Council. In 1967 he had called on the Labour Party 'to accept the implicit challenge of the new thinking in the Catholic Church and in the State and justify progressive views in fearless and imaginative terms'.[76] In 1968 he had written a speech for a meeting in Trinity College which contained a number of harsh criticisms of the Church, but had thought better of it and deleted them from the remarks he eventually delivered. The original speech, however, was published in *The Irish Times*, and for this he was mildly chastised by another speaker at the meeting, the radical Jesuit Fr Michael Sweetman.[77]

In Tramore, the Catholic Church came under attack under a number of different headings.[78] It was, he said, a sectarian, bigoted pressure group indistinguishable in its own way from the Orange order in Northern Ireland; it had absolute control of the Irish educational system, and through this controlled social and economic policy. It interfered in three principal ways: by overt interference, as in the Mother and Child Scheme; by preventing draft laws even being discussed, as in the case of legal adoption in 1948–51; and (a most unusual criticism) through the confessional.

The remarks which guaranteed his speech maximum visibility, however, had to do with sexuality. The context was the then current debate about contraception, and a recent speech in which Cardinal Conway had warned against changing the law on this subject in the Republic. Had Northern Ireland, he asked, been turned into a libertine Hibernian Sodom and Gomorrah because of the availability of contraceptives there?

> *It was true that in issues which closely concerned married couples and the human condition generally, [the hierarchy's] views were those of men who had deserted the field of battle as laymen knew it . . . Consciously or unconsciously, many of them have chosen their celibate lives because they find the whole subject of sex and heterosexual relationships threatening and embarrassing. Their judgement, then, cannot be trusted on these issues . . . they are not competent to advise the rest of us in the complex matters of our marriage relationships except in the narrowest of limits.*

When Noël Browne dealt with this controversy in his autobiography, he mentioned a number of other issues which, he said, his speech had addressed, but to which the published synopsis did not refer. These included co-education, interdenominational education, inter-church marriages, homosexuality, abortion, capital punishment, contraception, divorce, socialism and Marxism.

Discussing the meeting of the PLP on the Wednesday following his speech, he described the rural Labour deputies as 'shocked by my suggestion of sexual ambivalence among celibate clergy, and its consequences through clerical control of the schools'. His published remarks, however, link clerical control of schools not to sexual misdemeanours, but to the inculcation of a conservative political culture. He depicted David Thornley as uttering a tirade against him for creating *in the public mind the idea that these good ladies, with their brother and priest colleagues, were a band of homosexuals and lesbians who cavorted round their nunneries, convents and monasteries in wild orgies, not to mention what went on with their under-age pupils in the garden sheds of our national schools. All this tirade was because I had dared to refer to the possibility of ambivalent and confused attitudes among some of those who choose voluntary celibacy in religious orders, and had asked whether there might not be undesirable repercussions for our children.*[79]

The sexual or physical abuse of children, whether by members of religious orders or otherwise, did not become a public issue in any significant sense until some two decades later. Unfortunately, no full text of his remarks as delivered is available. If it were, it would provide an answer to one of the most intriguing questions still outstanding about this speech: did he, in 1971, actually relate the question of clerical celibacy directly to the then totally undiscussed issue of child abuse? If he did not, the possibility is that a number of issues, which were not seen as related until much later, were in some way telescoped in his memory when he was writing his book. If he did, it poses another question: what must Irish journalism have been like in 1971 if it ignored — or worse still suppressed — a charge of such magnitude made by someone who, as a practising psychiatrist dealing with many underprivileged young people, might have been expected to know what he was talking about?

Browne's second critique was so unusual that it also raises unanswered questions. It was based on his belief that the Catholic Church had used the confessional to inculcate social and economic conservatism. Again, this may well have been dealt with more fully in the complete text of his address, but as published it seems almost unique. In Catholic culture, especially where young males are concerned, the confessional is associated almost invariably not with the inculcation of social conservatism, but with the enumeration and description of the adolescent sins of the flesh in excruciating and ultimately mind-numbing detail. The confessionals at Beaumont must indeed have been different from those in Irish Catholic boys' schools.

There are two versions of what happened at the PLP meeting to address the furore his remarks had caused: one of them is Noël Browne's,[80] the other Conor Cruise O'Brien's.[81] In Browne's version, the main attack came from his erstwhile supporter David Thornley, aided and abetted by Conor Cruise O'Brien and Justin Keating, each of whom was signalling to Corish that he 'need have no fear of a revolt by the intellectuals or academics'. This *trahison des clercs*, as he saw it, left him in isolation.

Conor Cruise O'Brien's version of this critical meeting does not differ materially from Browne's in so far as the facts are concerned, but adds a number of significant details. One of them is that Thornley actually put down a motion to have the whip withdrawn from Browne (which would have effectively expelled him from the parliamentary party, though not necessarily from the party itself). The other is that O'Brien himself, despite the fact that he had come to regard Browne as 'half-mad and dangerous to know' (he had been sharing a Dáil office with him for some time), opposed Thornley's motion. In his view, removing the whip from Browne would have three undesirable consequences: it would help Browne to attain each of his two principal objectives — the embarrassment of Brendan Corish and the achievement of the crown of political martyrdom — and it would copperfasten what O'Brien believed to be the already excessive power of the Catholic Church.

The outcome of the discussion was an agreement that Corish would explain publicly that Browne had merely been expressing a personal opinion. Unwisely, however, this was backed up by a statement issued on behalf of the PLP. The statement, picking up on a derisive reference in Browne's speech to the availability of contraceptives in slot machines, contained the extraordinary and to all intents and purposes unasked-for commitment, redolent of the temper of the times, that 'Labour's policy does not advocate, and the party does not support, the availability of contraceptives to the unmarried, through slot machines or other such outlets.'[82] This gave Noël Browne a further opportunity to retaliate, in the course of which he repeated most of his original allegations.[83]

It would be another year before the internal and external pressure had built up to the point where the party felt it could make a move. When this happened, in February 1972, Browne and O'Connell were given permission to introduce a draft bill on family planning to the Dáil. It was only a gesture; they were permitted to move it not as representatives of the Labour Party but as individual TDs. Its fate was predictable and it really managed to satisfy nobody, as the party as a whole had obviously ducked the issue.

Noël Browne's criticism of the Catholic Church found a ready echo among many urban party members, particularly those who had been nominated by their constituencies to the Dublin Regional Council, which discussed the whole affair at a meeting shortly afterwards. At this meeting, which is not referred to in his autobiography, Browne gave an account of the parliamentary party session which had just taken place, and cast two of its members, O'Brien and Justin Keating, as the villains of the piece — O'Brien because he had suggested the compromise which Corish and others had accepted, Keating because he had allegedly voted for Browne's expulsion. It was true that O'Brien had suggested the compromise, but in order to depict him as hostile Browne had to conceal the fact that O'Brien had opposed the Thornley move. Equally, no vote had taken place on a resolution for his expulsion.

Both O'Brien and Keating were at the Regional Council meeting. Both challenged Browne's version of what had happened. Keating, in particular, challenged Browne either to substantiate the allegation that he had voted for Browne's expulsion, or withdraw it.[84] Browne said nothing but sat quietly in his place with his head in his hands. After a lengthy and increasingly embarrassed silence, the chairman moved on to the next business.

At a purely political level, few could have survived such an embarrassment in front of their peers. It did not, as it happened, appear to seriously affect Browne's credibility among some elements of the Dublin membership who were more and more disillusioned about what they saw as the party's loss of principle in its willingness to enter coalition. When his opponents thought about it later, however, their sense of the necessary political action they felt they had taken was, at least in Justin Keating's case, supplemented by a reflection on the elements in Noël Browne's traumatic life that had led him, willy-nilly, towards such a personal implosion.

Throughout this period, also, Noël Browne's attitude towards Brendan Corish had hardened and deepened. On at least one occasion, Browne made a point of sitting beside Corish at a parliamentary party meeting, one of the relatively few he attended. He then intervened in the discussion regardless of the agenda with a 'savagely hostile review of Corish's career', ending with a contemptuous reference to Corish's well-known declaration that he was a Catholic first, an Irishman second and a socialist third — before storming out. O'Brien saw it simply as hatred;[85] but, as Hermann Hesse once remarked, 'If you hate a person, you hate something in him that is part of yourself.'[86]

It is easy to underestimate the emotions engendered on such occasions. Corish's leadership was accepted by virtually all PLP members. He was liked by most, and held in evident affection by some. One of his most loyal lieutenants, Frank Cluskey, was so incensed by Browne's remarks on such an occasion that he pursued him out of the meeting, intent on settling the matter physically, but by the time he reached the corridor Browne had, luckily for both of them, disappeared.

The mercurial Thornley regretted his action soon enough — he defended Browne against one of his critics in public only a few weeks later[87] — but the two were no longer on speaking terms. Other Browne supporters were moved to chide him. One of them, Jack Dowling, an RTÉ producer who was a deeply committed Christian and a radical socialist,[88] urged Browne to 'realise the dangers of his role as well as its values'. Samson, he noted, had brought down the whole house around himself, but 'had this superiority to Noël Browne as a prophet: he used the jawbone of an ass as a weapon, not as a target'. Noël, he argued, could not cry havoc every six months.[89]

One of the few things on which Noël Browne and Conor Cruise O'Brien agreed was in relation to Northern Ireland. In a conversation before they became unfriendly, O'Brien once asked Browne a question: if he had to choose between the twin evils of Irish Republicanism and the Catholic Church, which would he choose? Browne's reply was unhesitating: he would prefer the embrace of the Church, for all its faults, to that of militant nationalism. Lenin, he once told the future Labour TD Eamon Gilmore in the course of a newspaper controversy, had been wrong to approve of James Connolly's participation in 1916.[90] Although he was moved by events in Northern Ireland, he abstained from open political involvement. At the same time, he was quick to take to task anyone who queried his credentials. When the journalist Nell McCafferty criticised him for not taking part in a protest march in Newry in February 1972, it seemed to touch a raw nerve. He retorted immediately that he had been there as a doctor and as part of a Knights of Malta medical team, not as a marcher. He went on, somewhat surprisingly in view of his past record, to criticise protesters:

> *How many houses have been built by the sitters-in? [a reference to the earlier campaign against the government's Forcible Entry and Occupation Act] Where are they now? Why did they give up? I am not interested in useless posturing. In parliament twenty years ago I was one of two ministers who spent £10 million on houses and hospitals. Since my childhood days I find that I can no longer get any real fun out of playing games.*[91]

Fr Enda McDonagh, then Professor of Theology at Maynooth, participated in the march, and exchanged glances with Noël as he passed the Knights of Malta post. Noël's expression, he thought, conveyed an amused sense of distance: 'He obviously thought we were being naive.'[92]

In the same year Browne responded, although in more measured tones, to the left-wing Republican activist Máirín de Burca.

> *If the choice is to be between the slow process of democratic political action with all its boring frustration and delays or yet another civil war, this time on sectarian lines, then she and those for whom she struggles must continue to suffer the agony of patience, because the alternative for all of us is too terrible.*[93]

His early support for Lynch on the North did not last long. By December 1972, writing for a British audience, he was of the opinion that 'once again the real enemy in Ireland is seen to be not simply Protestant Unionism, but Catholic, sectarian Republicanism. Led by Lynch or [Ruairí] Ó Brádaigh, there is no difference whatever.'[94] The years from 1948 to 1957, when his own Republicanism had flourished like the bay tree, were by now only a distant memory.

This issue apart, his relationships with the other members of the parliamentary party were going from bad to worse, if such were possible. Early in February 1972, he resigned as party spokesman on health 'because of the failure of the Parliamentary party to enumerate [sic] or seriously advocate a detailed socialist programme'.[95] He was replaced by Dr John O'Connell. It may be recalled that it was at this time the party had refused to allow Browne and John O'Connell to introduce their family planning bill — effectively a copy of the one introduced earlier in the Seanad by Mary Robinson, myself and Trevor West — other than as individual deputies. In June of the same year, he called on the party to declare that it did not wish to take part in a predominantly conservative government, or that it would do so only on condition that it was awarded 'the five power ministries of Finance, Industry and Commerce, Agriculture, Education and Justice'.[96] In October 1972 Browne told Brendan Corish, who was reshuffling front bench responsibilities, that he did not wish to have any front bench position.[97]

Nor were matters any more congenial in the party's Administrative Council, where an attack by Browne on Corish at the party's annual conference in the leader's home town of Wexford, and a further onslaught on the Catholic Church which he made in a lengthy interview in the *Sunday Press*,[98] evoked a sharp reaction. David Thornley, at this time chairman of the AC's organisation committee, put down a motion on 5 April 1972 for the AC's next meeting, urging that Browne be expelled for these stated reasons and 'because of his repeated and apparently irremediable refusal to accept discipline of any kind'.[99] Eight days later, his supporters counterattacked, with a similar motion from Des Bonass calling for the expulsion of the Limerick TD Stephen Coughlan, who had defended himself in a lengthy interview in the *Sunday Press* against charges of anti-Semitism and Fascism.[100] John O'Connell, it may be noted, was making speeches similarly critical of the leadership at this time.[101]

At the meeting of the AC on 13 April, David Thornley's resolution was withdrawn, and Des Bonass's one was lost by twenty votes to seven,[102] but this was not the end of the matter. Party discipline was becoming ragged overall as the country moved towards a general election and the defeated anti-coalition group continued to flex its muscles. Barry Desmond and David Thornley had been engaged in a public slanging match. Noël Browne had made another public attack on Corish. The West Galway Constituency Council had been airing party disagreements in public, in breach of a 1970 AC decision (which it must be said was widely flouted). The party officers, in an attempt to put manners on this unruly mob, presented a lengthy resolution to the September meeting of the AC castigating all the pugilists. There was an unsuccessful counter-move by Michael D. Higgins and others which implicitly criticised a speech on coalition by Brendan Corish, and the disciplinary motion was passed by sixteen votes to six.[103] Browne himself then circulated a letter to all members of the AC calling for disciplinary action to be taken against the party leader for this speech.[104]

Within Dublin South-East, things were also hotting up. Ruairí Quinn, who had qualified as an architect and had then left Ireland for some time, was back and had been active in the constituency since the autumn of 1971. He had been involved in a major structural reorganisation, in the course of which all the branches had been merged, as the existing ones were weak and ineffective. This branch — the central branch — subsequently spawned others in discrete geographical areas of the constituency. In his capacity as secretary of the Constituency Council, Quinn organised clinics at City Quay and Ringsend, but Noël attended these only rarely.

Quinn had been encouraged to put his name forward by Conor Cruise O'Brien and Justin Keating, both of whom had told him of their belief that Noël, because of his opposition to any coalition that might be proposed, would not stand again.[105] He did so, but on the basis, which he fully accepted, that he might be running as a second candidate, with Browne, and the constituency organisation committed itself to a two-candidate strategy.

Lynch then called a snap election for 28 February 1973, just ahead of the introduction of a new voters' register in March which Fianna Fáil feared would confer an advantage on the opposition parties, and relying on imminent good news from Europe (the country had voted by a huge majority in 1972 to enter the Common Market and there was an anticipation of major financial transfers from Europe, especially for farmers). He had also consolidated his position within the party after the Arms Trial and the crises associated with it.

Labour and Fine Gael, which had been preparing for such an eventuality psychologically, if not in negotiating terms, rapidly put together a fourteen-point programme for government, which on 9 February was accepted by Labour's Administrative Council by twenty-two votes to one.[106] It was, as even its supporters admitted, a rush job, short on specifics in some areas and dangerously open-ended in others. It caught the mood of the country, but not of Labour's dissidents. Both Browne and Thornley announced that they would not sign the party pledge which committed them to supporting it; Browne in particular declared that he could never forgive Brendan Corish, and that the fourteen-point plan 'represented the humane platitudes of public life everywhere'.[107] David Thornley later relented, and signed the party pledge a day late.

At the selection convention, Browne made it clear that he was immovable on this issue, to the consternation of at least some of his supporters, who had hoped that he would sign, stand, and continue to be a thorn in the flesh of the leadership.[108] A generally sympathetic study of Noël Browne's role in politics from 1948 to 1977 concluded that by February 1973 he had effectively deserted the Dublin South-East constituency for good, and thus 'avoided a popular court martial' which would have involved a punishing verdict at the polls.[109] Quinn was selected. The problem then was that the selection convention had already decided on a two-candidate strategy, which would have meant finding someone else to stand at short notice. This decision, however, was reversed after a brief adjournment, and Quinn stood on his own.

Quinn failed to be elected as the Labour vote in Dublin South-East plummeted by almost 50 per cent, from the 5,274 that Noël Browne got in 1969 to 2,927. Fine Gael took Noël Browne's former seat. In the country as a whole, the results were anomalous. Fianna Fáil increased its vote but lost seats; the Fine Gael and Labour candidates together lost votes but increased their seats, securing a majority in the Dáil to create the first non-Fianna Fáil government in sixteen years.

Not only was Noël Browne not part of it, he saw it as a final parting of the ways, and wrote tenderly to his wife:

My dear,

This is my last letter from Parliament. Thank you for having been such a wonderful wife, companion, secretary and political collaborator over all those 35 years. A remarkable woman.

Noël[110]

He did not know it but he would continue to be a member of the Oireachtas, in often extraordinary circumstances, for another decade.

CHAPTER NINE

The End of
the Affair

A s Noël Browne sat out the 1973 election on the sidelines, his sometime colleague David Thornley was re-elected in Dublin North-West, despite a fall in his vote from 8,500 to 5,000 first preferences. Thornley was being consumed by politics, his early idealism and ambition all but shattered by the grind of constituency work and the frustrations of opposition. His physical health was deteriorating, too, and his judgments were becoming erratic and self-centred. The new Coalition government was formed and he was not a member of it, not even in a junior capacity; he would now have to experience the even greater frustration of being a government backbencher. Before settling down to that penance, however, he was determined to show his party leader that he was still a force to be reckoned with, and refashion an old friendship into the bargain. As I sat on a bench outside Leinster House he came over to me bubbling with excitement, almost like a schoolboy. He had, he told me, just nominated Noël Browne for the Seanad — adding, with a hyperbole that was becoming all too frequent in his pronouncements — that it was one of the bravest things he had ever done in his life.

He may not have been fully aware of the fact that a number of other people had had the same idea, some time earlier. They had been active supporters of Noël Browne for a number of years, but did not necessarily live in the constituency he represented. They included David Neligan, a dentist, who had been closer to Browne than most, and had for years drafted many of his Dáil questions;[1] Dermot Boucher, then employed by the Irish National Productivity Centre; Brendan Scott, a teacher, a charismatic figure who attracted huge personal loyalty but who gave his own support selflessly to Browne; and Pat Carroll, another teacher, who ran unsuccessfully for Labour in the Cabra constituency (formerly Dublin North-West) in 1977, when Thornley lost his seat there. All were members of the Labour Party, increasingly disillusioned by what they saw as the drift towards passive participation in a Fine Gael-dominated coalition, and eager to support Browne in whatever stance he took. A number of them had joined different branches in Dublin South-East, where they could be of practical and organisational assistance to him, although Brendan Scott remained a member in the Dublin North-East constituency, in the same branch as Conor Cruise O'Brien, which was to lead to predictable conflicts.

It was not clear to many of them, coming up to the 1973 election, what Browne would actually do, and in fact he kept his intentions to himself until the night of the selection convention. This left them rudderless and uncertain about what to do next.

The idea that he might contest a Seanad seat in the TCD constituency evolved from discussions immediately after the selection conference. David Thornley, who heard about it later, did nominate Noël, but the main campaign to secure the requisite number of high-profile nominations — some fifteen are required — was organised by David Neligan. Candidates in the university constituencies generally use the names of their three nominators and ten assentors to draw attention to their support in a wide range of professional and academic fields, and, in this context, it was thought essential not to alienate voters by careless choices. Thornley's name in particular was regarded as highly doubtful, especially in the TCD constituency, given his apparent espousal of some Republican ideas.

In these circumstances, Neligan and others went to considerable lengths to attract names which would enhance Noël Browne's campaign in all the right quarters. Side-stepping David Thornley's efforts, they went after names which would attract support from a wide range of TCD graduates. Noël's rejection of Catholicism did not extend to all branches of the Christian religion, and Trinity's large Anglican constituency was expertly targeted. The Church of Ireland Archbishop of Cashel, Dr John Armstrong, who agreed over the telephone to be one of Noël's nominators, was a handy catch.[2]

The choice of Trinity was an inspired one. Noël was interested, but had to be talked into it; he was worried, in part, about the cost of the campaign. But the 1969 election had shown that winds of change were blowing through that august institution. Mary Robinson had made an extraordinary impact in her first term in the Oireachtas. Later, after the death of Senator Owen Sheehy Skeffington, to whom Noël himself had intermittently been close, the by-election had been won by Trevor West, another young Trinity staff member.

The third seat had been held for years by W.J.E. Jessop, a doctor and a professor in the TCD medical school. The medical school had a large block vote, and it was assumed that this would ensure his re-election for as long as

he wished to present himself to the electorate, comprised of all TCD graduates worldwide. As soon as he was nominated, however, Noël Browne
began to experience a bandwagon effect; he would not only attract a
Sheehy Skeffington vote but would secure at least some votes from younger
and more radical members of the medical profession. Even older members
of that profession, who might have had reason to resent his stance in 1951,
could be counted on to give him a preference after Jessop, on the grounds
that a left-wing doctor was better than no doctor at all.

From a standing start, Noël Browne came second on first preferences,
with almost 1,000 votes to Mary Robinson's 1,472, out of an electorate of
some 6,000. He had to wait until the fifth count for his election — on May
Day, as it happened — but the outcome was never really in doubt.

He was now in an anomalous situation. He was still a member of the
Labour Party, and of its constituency organisation in Dublin South-East —
although there were members of that organisation who felt, with some
bitterness, that had he campaigned for Ruairí Quinn, Labour might have
retained its seat there.[3] He was not, however, a member of the Parliamentary
Labour Party, because he had not signed the party pledge prior to the election and had not campaigned as a Labour candidate. Ruairí Quinn, as it
happened, had also succeeded in securing a Seanad seat subsequent to the
Dáil election.

The Labour Party sorted out this situation by a manoeuvre which was
not pretty but was effective, and was accomplished, in the end, with
Browne's possibly unwitting help. Initially it was simply a stand-off. Browne
insisted that, as a member of the Labour Party in good standing, he should
be automatically invited to meetings of the Parliamentary Labour Party. The
view within this organisation was that it did not invite anyone to become a
member but would consider the application of anyone who applied.

In either case the thorny question of the party pledge would have come
up, and this might have barred Browne. It is difficult to see how, having
refused to sign it before the election, he could sign it afterwards, unless he
were to adopt de Valera's strategy in relation to the oath in 1927, considering it to be no more than an empty formula. He and his supporters did not
in any case give the impression that he was seriously interested in membership, attacking as they did not only his sworn enemies in the PLP, but the
dwindling band who might under different circumstances have been his
friends. Corish, it was alleged, had allowed Cosgrave to dictate the exclusion
of Noël Browne as a precondition of the Coalition deal.[4] There is no evidence for this, and the possibility that Corish might have appointed Browne
to a Coalition cabinet was remote anyway, to say the least. The anti-Browne
feeling in Fine Gael surfaced only later in the lifetime of that government,
when an exasperated John Kelly, then Fine Gael chief whip, told Michael D.

Higgins that Fine Gael would never do another coalition deal with Labour unless Browne were not part of the equation.[5] The party leader was further dubbed 'Ramsay MacCorish', and accused of having 'joyously acquiesced' in Browne's 'political assassination'.[6] Browne himself made a speech within a week of polling day in which he attacked his former parliamentary colleagues — but by innuendo, and without giving any specific details which might be challenged or refuted. There were, he said, 'atheists, agnostics, good Marxists and liberals in the Parliamentary Labour Party who had told him privately that they agreed with what he had said [at Tramore in 1971] but that he should not have said it. These people were now members of the present government.'[7]

He had already, before the election, described his party's position on the North as 'sympathetic, sectarian, Catholic, pro-Provo'.[8] Now, while the controversy about his membership of the parliamentary grouping raged, he alienated some of his lifelong admirers not only by alleging that the Labour leadership had totally capitulated to Fine Gael, but by comparing the new government directly to that of Nazi Germany: 'We now have a truly blue, National Socialist government in Ireland.'[9]

How far should a political party tolerate dissent? There is no easy answer to this, certainly no answer which will stand for all times and circumstances and which is anything more than a platitude. It is also undeniable that, at this time, there was greater tolerance in the Labour Party for dissent on the right in matters which directly affected party policy and discipline. For some time before 1973, and indeed for some time after, the party had uncomfortably to continue to make room for conservatives such as Dan Spring, Stephen Coughlan and a few others who, although elected representatives, were widely known to oppose party policies on vexed matters like family planning, and pointedly absented themselves from the Dáil when these matters were voted on. The explanation — if not the excuse — for this was simple enough: the political centre of gravity in the parliamentary party was, and would remain for some considerable time, centre-right, just as the political centre of gravity among the activists was moving rapidly centre-left. In these circumstances, the threat of a split in the party, echoing that of the 1940s, was for many years enough to ensure that the widening cracks would be papered over, and repapered whenever necessary, in order to avoid consigning the Labour party to electoral oblivion once again. It was a practical motive, if not the highest one, and it did have the merits of keeping most of the dissidents, at both ends of the political spectrum, within the fold, and of ensuring that political representation of the conservative working class in the Dáil was not confined to Fianna Fáil.

The Browne affair came to a head on 25 July 1973 when the Parliamentary Labour Party received a letter from him asking that he be sent notifications of meetings. His case was initially supported by David Thornley and John O'Connell. Jimmy Tully argued that the Labour Party had not left Noël Browne — Browne had left the Labour Party by refusing to stand as a candidate of his own free will in the recent general election, and by sitting in the opposition benches in the Seanad. An amended motion, calling on the PLP to admit Noël Browne 'on condition that he accepts the party whip, signs the party pledge, and instructs his constituency to undertake the national collection', was then put to the meeting and defeated by thirteen votes to five.[10] (The 'national collection' consisted of sums collected locally and forwarded to headquarters to help pay the party's central expenses. By stitching this into the resolution, Browne's critics were serving notice on him that he would not be allowed to use the party as a political flag of convenience.) In the vote on this issue, Browne was supported by David Thornley, Stephen Coughlan, John O'Connell, Dan Spring and John Ryan. It was an odd coalition. Only O'Connell would have been likely to support Browne's views on the Church, and he was totally opposed to his view on Northern Ireland. Thornley and the other three would have been totally opposed to his views on the Church. It is easy to suppose that Thornley's vote was motivated primarily by a reawakening of the now fitful flame of his admiration for Browne. The motivation of the others was, more probably, a desire to embarrass or annoy the leadership for reasons unconnected with Browne — the refusal of preferment, for instance — in a situation in which they knew the majority would go safely the other way. And it did: the vote against Browne was by at least 3:1.

Browne responded by alleging that there was in fact a precedent for the situation in which he found himself — that of the former senator Jimmy Dunne — and that the ruling was mean and spiteful, unique to the Labour Party and himself. Echoing a criticism that Conor Cruise O'Brien had made (from the outside) of the Labour Party many years previously, he accused O'Brien and Keating of 'poltroonery', and added with heavy sarcasm: 'I feel flattered that my comrades in the Parliamentary Labour Party appear to be so insecure in their beliefs that they are unable to tolerate my humble criticism of their antics in government, even in the privacy of our committee rooms.'[11]

The resulting stalemate arguably suited both parties reasonably well. The Labour Party did not have to suffer the opprobrium of having expelled Browne from anything; technically, it was still waiting for his application. Equally, Browne was a senator without a party whip, free to speak and vote as he wished in the Oireachtas. He remained a member in good standing of the party, able to attend its annual conference and many other meetings at which he could continue to express his 'humble criticism'.

The Seanad was in some sense a liberation for him, especially as an

Independent, as he now effectively was. It was an ideal platform for his views. The pressure of Dáil-style divisions was absent, for the most part; it met less frequently; and the media spotlight on its activities was intermittent but benign. Although the Seanad salary was smaller than that of the Dáil, as an institution it laid less claim to his time.

None of this prevented the onset of what appears to have been quite a serious depression — so serious that he took unpaid leave from his local authority position for some ten months in 1974 and spent a great part of that time in Connemara. Jack McQuillan protested, 'They're all only Mongans and Bartleys down there,' identifying the two most prominent political dynasties in the area, one Fine Gael, the other Fianna Fáil.[12] But Browne would not be dissuaded and to the end of his life he maintained a deep attachment to that part of the country — Galway was his father's native county, it may be remembered. This was exemplified in a number of television documentaries made with and about him from the late 1970s to the 1990s, some of which reached extraordinary levels of semi-mystic intensity. He was to be found sitting in his new home, 'fishing line in his hands, accordion at his feet'.[13]

He would emerge at intervals from this craggy fastness to make a number of generally thoughtful speeches — on illegitimacy, natural resources, prisons, drug addiction and civil liberties (the 1976 Emergency Powers Bill, for instance)[14] — and occasionally to surprise even his supporters.

One of these was in a debate on a resolution sponsored by Mary Robinson and myself on the Report of the Committee on the Status of Women.[15] There now was, he warned, a preoccupation with the right of women to go out to work. Echoing his paper to the RMPS in 1968, he went on to suggest that

> the preoccupation with the right to go out to work represents a part of the manipulation which is carried on about the role of women in society. In fact, it appears to me that they are likely to be just as much manipulated by the new emphasis on the right of a woman to work outside the home as they ever have been manipulated into being restricted to being simply mothers in a family . . . The role of the mother is greatly undervalued. I sound very old-fashioned, no doubt, in speaking like this; but I suppose one deals with so much of the end-product of defective environmental factors which cause emotional stress of one kind or another that it becomes a rather more acute problem to me, simply because of my profession, than it might to other people . . . It seems to me that it represents a very ignorant — and I am using a crude word — misunderstanding of the role of the mother to her children if she thinks that having a baby is just like a cow dropping a calf in a field and going away and leaving it for someone else to rear . . . I do not think there is any doubt in the world that

children miss the working mother . . . A woman can follow any career she wishes . . . but once a mother has a child she has a role.[16]

Browne's growing attachment to the Seanad — despite his passionate earlier attempts to abolish that institution as an 'expensive pet' — was not entirely reciprocated; there were still a few flies in the parliamentary ointment. Mary Robinson was one of them. She had been doing pioneering work since 1969 on a number of issues in which Noël Browne felt that he had at least some proprietary interest, not least (because of his opposition to the Church) family planning. But Robinson's Bill (or Bills, there were several variants) was already on the order paper, signed by herself, by Senator Trevor West and by me. No further signatures were needed, and she did not invite Browne to add his. Browne felt discomfited by this,[17] but Robinson was not going to allow that bone to be taken away from her. He spoke in support of her Bill on a number of occasions, but on some others was absent for votes at times when the matter was very much in the public eye.

This occasionally drew comment, notably when he missed a procedural vote on the family planning bill on 14 November 1973. John Healy, writing as Backbencher in *The Irish Times*, drew attention to his absence;[18] this evoked a waspish reply which did not deny the charge, but attempted to turn it back on his accuser.[19] Hinting at Healy's Fianna Fáil sympathies, he quoted his mother's dictum: 'Tell me your company, and I'll tell you what you are,' and asked: 'Where has he been since 1951?'

It was February 1974 by the time Robinson finally got the agreement of the government to have her bill debated in the Seanad. It was tacitly understood that, after the debate, her bill would be withdrawn in favour of one which the government was going to introduce.[20] In this speech, Noël Browne became the first member of the Oireachtas publicly to advocate, in either House, the provision of therapeutic legal abortion — a position which he repeated from time to time, without doing any noticeable damage to his electoral success, until he retired from politics.

His rationale for this was twofold. Firstly, it was a question of minority rights — a denominational as much as a moral minority. Prefacing his remark with a rather unusually sweeping statement, he argued:

I do not believe that we have any right at all to deny any minority within our society. For this reason, I have interested myself in homosexuality, in therapeutic legal abortion and in contraception. I do not want any of these things for myself. But I believe that the Protestant minority in a society, where they are respected, is a measure of civilisation, the attitudes and standards and that sort of thing.[21]

Many members of the Protestant minority would without doubt have been happier with his second reason, advanced in the context of reducing the numbers of Irish girls going to the UK for abortions:

> *It is well established that contraception leads to a reduction in the incidence of therapeutic legal abortion. I consider therapeutic legal abortion to be a very distressing thing for the unfortunate girl herself, but there are circumstances in which I consider it should be permissible. Again, we have the rigidity of the Irish Catholic attitude on these matters when there are different Catholic attitudes on these matters. Catholic Austria will have an Abortion Act next year. Remember, therapeutic legal abortion is therapeutic, because it is going to help the lady from the point of view of her health, and legal because it has been passed by a responsible democratic society.*[22]

All in all, he made twenty-five speeches during his period in the Seanad. He participated in three of the six Seanad divisions in 1973, in three out of forty-seven in 1974 — the period when he was spending a lot of time in Connemara — in four out of twenty-seven in 1975, in six out of thirteen in 1976, and in four out of fourteen in 1977. He was not without support for his own causes when needed; I signed a motion with him in August 1973 on the vexed question of the Bula mineral deposits. In 1975, however, when I joined the Labour Party and applied for the whip, and in 1976 when Mary Robinson followed the same route, he was angry.[23]

Outside the Seanad, the temperature within the Labour Party continued to rise, fuelled from time to time by controversial decisions by the new Coalition government. It was an extraordinarily difficult time for any government. Violence in the North was increasing, and many people were being killed; ministers were subjected to repeated threats, involving the deployment of unheard-of levels of personal security; and the oil price shocks initiated by OPEC were putting the economy into a tailspin, as unemployment and inflation both rose dramatically, the latter up to a high of 26 per cent. Under these circumstances, government cohesion increased, just as the attacks, not least from disgruntled Labour anti-coalitionists, intensified.

At this time the Labour Party developed its own internal opposition, linked with, although not in any sense led by, Noël Browne. It was a loosely structured organisation called Liaison of the Left, and numbered among its ranks a number of prominent Browne supporters, including Mattie Merrigan, Dermot Boucher, Pat Carroll and Brendan Scott. It published occasional issues of a political magazine, *Labour Left*, and was particularly active in and around the fringes of the party's annual conference.

The first such conference after the general election, held in Cork in 1973, offered Noël Browne and his supporters within the party a tailor-made issue on which to embarrass the government and, in particular, the Labour minister Justin Keating. This was the so-called 'Bula Mines' affair, which revolved around the control of a large lead/zinc deposit in Co. Meath, some of which had been vested in the State under the land acts, the remainder of which was in private ownership. Left-wing delegates to the conference were determined to call for the nationalisation of the deposits and their exploitation by a publicly owned corporation. Keating, the Minister for Industry and Commerce, had limited room for manoeuvre. He could not expropriate the minerals in private ownership; the capital cost of an extraction plant was to all intents and purposes beyond the State's resources; and the most feasible strategy, in his view, was to facilitate the creation of a native Irish company which could develop the lead/zinc mine successfully and would contribute a reasonable amount to the State by way of mineral royalties.

To do this, however, he had to take responsibility for an arrangement under which the State acquired an interest in the privately owned part of the mineral deposit. The key issue was the valuation of the deposit. Inside the Dáil, Fianna Fáil TD Desmond O'Malley made a devastating attack on Keating, alleging that he had effectively squandered public money. Outside it, Noël Browne and his allies charged that, in addition, Keating had totally betrayed Labour Party policy on natural resources.

At the best of times, it would have been a sensitive issue, but in late 1973 it was given added significance by the overthrow of Salvador Allende in Chile. At the party conference, Browne led the attack on Keating. Clad in his trademark black leather jacket, he made one of the most effective political speeches of his life, invoking the shade of Allende, and ending, his arms outspread, with the dramatic exhortation: 'We only want the earth!'

The mood on the platform wavered between anxiety and consternation, as it appeared that Browne's speech had struck a chord in many uncommitted delegates. When the conference came to vote on the resolutions dealing with natural resources, the platform victories were being won by such narrow margins that scouts were sent out into all the neighbouring public houses to bring an abrupt end to the conviviality and summon delegates loyal to the leadership back into the City Hall to avert a political disaster.

In 1974, when the party met in Galway, it could have been a similar story, but for a miscalculation by Noël Browne which cost him dearly. Here, the issue was health. Brendan Corish, the party leader and Tánaiste, was Minister for Health and Social Welfare, and had been negotiating a new contract with hospital consultants which had become a confrontation. There were two diametrically opposed readings of the situation. Corish was under pressure from the consultants, who had begun to take industrial action by threatening the suspension of non-urgent procedures in hospitals, and engineered a deal. Browne and other critics of Corish within the party believed that the government had the consultants over a barrel[24] and could dictate terms.

Noël Browne was now a delegate associated with the Galway West constituency, and came to conference only on one day. He spoke in the same debate as David Thornley but, while both were critical of the record of the Coalition government, the reaction to the two from party delegates was markedly different. Thornley overran his time and had to curtail his remarks when the microphone on the speaker's podium was switched off; when he appealed for further time he was largely supported by delegates, but to no avail.

Noël Browne, when his turn came, criticised Keating, but reserved his strongest words for Brendan Corish. Right at the end, however, just when it looked as if he could sway uncommitted delegates to his point of view, he gestured angrily over at the party leader: 'He will do what he is told. He has always done it. He was a socialist once, then a conservative . . .'[25]

At this point the conference erupted — not, by and large, in favour of Browne, but against him. The boos and jeers which had greeted his attack on Corish were redoubled, and when he again attempted to make himself heard, they intensified. One delegate shouted: 'Go back to Fianna Fáil! Go back to Fianna Fáil!' Browne left the platform, but not before turning dramatically towards the platform party and, in a silent act of indictment, pointing an accusing finger at his party leader.

Even by the standards of political controversy, it was an ugly occasion. Labour's rank and file were not going to sit quietly and see Corish, who had led them into government for the first time in sixteen years, vilified by someone who, in their view, had abandoned a Labour seat at the previous general election. Their raucous objections, while they signified the fact that not all the strong emotions were on Noël Browne's side, were also an effective denial of his right to be heard. But Browne's own brand of personalised invective, and his opportunist use of the conference, evoked dismay among all but the most dedicated of his supporters. All that was left, at the end, was a black and bitter taste.

The 1975 Labour party conference was in Wexford. It does not seem that Browne either attended or spoke, but, on the outside, his critique was to be heard in other fora. Just before the conference, for instance, he made another attack on both Corish and the party general secretary, Brendan Halligan. Corish, he said, 'in the pursuit of his own petty self-advancement has defrauded the workers of their rightful heritage', but Halligan would 'manipulate a standing ovation for the leader'.[26] David Thornley was moved to reply.

Does he expect a new generation of young people to grow up every ten years in the belief that he is the Messiah? This . . . infuriatingly wayward and endlessly likeable man . . . has changed his mind so often that he baffles even me who has known him for twenty-five years . . . I do wish he would bury his vendettas against former colleagues and friends . . . Noël Browne is beginning to sound like a 78 record whose needle has got stuck in 1951.[27]

Thornley's carelessly easy prose style concealed mounting personal problems. As compensation for not getting ministerial office, he had been nominated as a Labour member of the Council of Europe, which inevitably involved much foreign travel, late nights and conviviality. It was one of the worst things that could have happened to him, although it was done for the best of reasons. He was at this stage an undiagnosed diabetic, and this combined with his political lifestyle was a recipe for disaster. When he mounted a Provisional Sinn Féin platform to defend freedom of speech (the meeting had been proscribed), this important issue was submerged by a rising tide of political embarrassment. At a lengthy parliamentary party meeting in April 1976, he suffered the fate which he had, some five years earlier, proposed for Noël Browne: withdrawal of the whip.[28]

His lifestyle and personality continued to deteriorate. At one stage, he collapsed in the Dáil and Dr John O'Connell, who attended to him and got him into hospital, suggested to his wife that she should seek professional help on his behalf. Petria, not knowing what to do, telephoned Noël Browne and asked him to meet her. He agreed, and they met close to Leinster House. To her dismay, Browne refused to accept that her husband had any real problem; David just liked his pint, he maintained. It was an extraordinarily dismissive end to their relationship.

In 1976 the Labour conference was in Limerick, and had to deal once again with the thorny question of coalition. Specifically, Brendan Corish and the parliamentary party had to secure, in advance, conference approval for an electoral strategy which would leave the possibility open for another coalition after the next election, whenever that might be.

Party and government alike were, by now, with their backs to the wall. Galloping inflation was ravaging the economy and leading to industrial unrest on an unprecedented scale. The ongoing crisis in the North threatened to destabilise politics in the Republic on almost a daily basis. If opinion polls had been taken — they did not effectively become part of the armoury of political parties until 1977 — they would have made distressing reading for the cabinet. Corish, nonetheless, made his position clear: he wanted the agreement of conference to a proposal which would leave the final decision on whether or not Labour should enter another coalition to a joint meeting of the parliamentary party and the Administrative Council.

The debate was a tense affair, lasting four hours and involving forty-six speakers. The leadership was concerned to defend its record in government; it was helped in this, to some extent, by the recent victory of Brendan Halligan in the Dublin South-West by-election occasioned by the death of Noel Lemass. Jimmy Tully, the party's deputy leader, led off the debate, arguing that nine points from the party's 1969 manifesto had been included in the 1973 programme for government. Managing briefly to take both sides of the road at once, he also pointed out that in the 1969 election the party had lost the deposits of forty-two of its ninety-nine candidates.

He identified the enemy plainly: the Liaison of the Left who, he said, had criticised Michael D. Higgins in the March 1975 by-election in Galway West. It is arguable that no intervention by Liaison of the Left would have materially influenced the result of that by-election in any way. Máire Geoghegan-Quinn, the successful Fianna Fáil candidate, had secured 45 per cent of the vote to Michael D. Higgins's 19 per cent. Noël Browne, however, had pointedly refused to endorse Higgins's candidature, saying that 'it would be an act of outrageous cynicism for me to ask for support for a Labour candidate, committed as Michael D. Higgins will certainly be to prolonging the lifetime of this government.'[29]

Justin Keating reinforced the attack, saying cuttingly that the anti-coalitionists had 'no brains, and no guts'.[30] Two of the most prominent members of Liaison, Pat Carroll and David Neligan, led for the opposition, followed by Mattie Merrigan. When Noël Browne rose to speak, however, there was a hush; he plainly carried most of the expectations of the opposition on his shoulders. When he started to speak, it was in a low, almost conversational tone, as he referred to his 'old friend' Seán MacEntee, and the difference between the Civil War generation and the modern generation in Irish politics.

Some, at least, of the anti-coalitionists were taken aback when he observed equably that he agreed with Frank Cluskey: coalition was not a principle.

> Remember, comrades, I spoke in favour of coalition and voted in favour of coalition in 1968. I have opposed the idea that we could go it alone, because I postulated the inevitability of multi-party government in the post-Civil War period as a transitional phase in Irish public life . . . I'm not so disappointed in what the coalition has failed to do — of course it has failed to do many things — I'm more disappointed that men of the quality of Conor O'Brien and Justin Keating and O'Leary and a few others have not bothered to examine why it is we have achieved so little in coalition.

The reason, he suggested to the conference, was Labour's failure to recognise that, in the absence of specific, binding, pre-governmental agreements, the

largest party would always dictate the terms. 'If there is to be another coalition, and I personally don't rule it out, then it should be a coalition in which
there are enforceable guarantees limited to some kind of timetable, with the
promise that we will break if these undertakings are not guaranteed.'

This less than overwhelming rejection of coalition was backed up by one
final suggestion: that the leadership should be authorised to negotiate the
best possible post-election agreement with another party, and should then
bring any such agreement back to conference 'to make the best decision in
the interests of the Labour movement'.

'Can you trust us to do this?' he concluded. 'Can you?'

There was one curious aspect to his argument, and one sense in which he
was, as it happened, too far ahead of his allies for them to comprehend the
subtlety of the position he had adopted. The curious aspect of his approach
was that he chose the issue of capital punishment to demonstrate the weak-
ness of the minority party in government. He might with more justice, and
more accuracy, have chosen the Mother and Child issue, which would
indeed have evoked a particularly positive response from his audience.

Although he was not specific in 1976 about the details of how this issue
had been dealt with in the 1948 cabinet, he was to write in 1986 that

> On a number of occasions both of us [i.e. Browne and MacBride] argued for
> clemency for men under sentence of death before the civil courts. Mulcahy . . .
> was curt . . . 'They must hang.' Blowick's comment, in his high-pitched
> squeak, was 'Hang them, hang them.' There was no attempt to argue or to
> rationalise their positions. With their majority they had no need to.[31]

The strong implication here is that this was an issue on which he and
MacBride were routinely defeated. In point of fact, however, only one man was
hanged during that government's period of office (one too many, no doubt, but
still only one). This was William Gambon, who was hanged in November
1948, after his appeal for clemency had been turned down by the cabinet.

But the five other people — four men and one woman — who were
condemned to death by the courts during that government's period of
office all had their sentences commuted by the cabinet.[32] The last one,
Patrick Heffernan, presents an anomaly in that his sentence was originally
confirmed by the cabinet in March 1951, while Browne was still a member,
but was commuted in April on the basis of a fresh affidavit, just after
Browne had resigned. The facts of cabinet policy on this issue, therefore,
reveal that Clann policy on the issue in fact prevailed far more frequently
than it was rejected. MacBride succeeded in saving five people out of the
six condemned — four of them with Noël Browne's support. Browne
remembered the one failure, and forgot the five successes.

Whatever about this particular argument and its validity, where he plainly outdistanced his supporters at the Limerick conference was in his attempt to deal with the question of coalition from the point of view of strategy rather than that of principle. Too many of the opponents of the leadership were bitterly opposed to coalition in principle, or at any time in the foreseeable future, for them to take on board the notion that a tactical approach to the question had the best chance of embarrassing the leadership, and perhaps even of defeating it.

There is a tangible irony in all of this. The position put forward by Noël Browne — that any coalition deal should be subject to ratification by a delegate conference of the party — was in some important respects the strategy adopted by Frank Cluskey when he succeeded Brendan Corish as leader in 1977, and which he successfully persuaded the party conference to adopt at its meeting in Killarney that year. The only substantial difference between the course of action urged by Browne in 1976 and that accepted by the party the following year (by which time he was no longer a member) would have been on the question of a fixed timetable.

Brendan Corish very probably had his own good reasons for rejecting this strategy when it was proposed by Noël Browne in 1976 — among them the fact that the party was then a partner in a uniquely unpopular government, and almost any deal that could be done with Fine Gael would evoke enough opposition to secure its defeat at conference. Under these circumstances, securing the agreement of a joint PLP-AC meeting was undoubtedly a far safer bet. But there was another, far simpler reason for not taking the Browne strategy on board at that point. For quite some time, the party officers and most of the parliamentary party had distrusted him deeply. His personal attacks on Corish, inside and outside the PLP, had exhausted any political capital he once had, and had turned him from an asset to the party — as he had been up to 1969 — into a liability. It was no time for fine distinctions; when political leadership is on the line, it never is.

One further policy matter deserves a brief mention at this stage: Northern Ireland. As has been seen, Noël Browne had, at least since the latter part of the 1950s, exchanged his earlier enthusiasm for traditional Irish Republicanism for an attitude of deep suspicion. Apart from a brief period when he supported Lynch against the dissidents in Fianna Fáil, he also tended to lump all Fianna Fáil leaders together, and associate them in an undifferentiated way with the activities of Sinn Féin and paramilitary Republican organisations.

In the autumn of 1976 Browne and other politicians, academics and journalists were invited by a US foundation to a conference in Amherst, Massachusetts, designed to give people of widely differing opinions an opportunity to meet and discuss the Northern Ireland problem away from the often constraining circumstances of their home environment. When he returned, Browne wrote an article on his experiences, in which he made two points in particular. One was to express his scorn for the journalists present who, he said, had been brave in attacking the Church when they were away from Ireland, but were noticeably quiet on this issue on their home turf. The other — much more surprising — was to express his admiration for the Republican leader Séamus Costello, whom he described as 'scintillating'.[33] Given Browne's known views about Republicanism, this was truly extraordinary. Costello led a breakaway movement from the IRA and Sinn Féin which was to turn into the Irish Republican Socialist Party and an associated military wing, the Irish National Liberation Army. Although his ideology was framed in a language which was a potent mixture of left-wing rhetoric and the terminology of national liberation, his paramilitary activities were widely known for their scope and ruthlessness. In 1977 he was shot dead sitting in his parked car in Dublin, in the course of a bitter feud within his own organisation. He was also, however, a remarkably charismatic individual on a purely personal level; and something in his personality evidently attracted Browne in a way he found impossible to resist. It was rarely, to put it mildly, that Noël Browne was attracted by another politician's charisma.

It was not long before Browne's credentials for writing about the conference were sharply attacked by Desmond Fennell, one of the journalists he had implicitly criticised. Fennell, rejecting Browne's overall summary of the proceedings, charged that, apart from his scheduled contribution, Noël Browne 'intervened in no debate and challenged no speaker'.[34] This observation, if true, mirrored the experiences of many who attended meetings at which Noël Browne spoke, in the Labour Party or in other organisations. He had a tendency to arrive just in time to make his own contribution, and then frequently left before any discussion of his own remarks, or the issues involved, could gather momentum.

His supporters in the party, who had never been disconcerted by this habit, were now actively looking around for a constituency which might return him to the Dáil. Dublin South-East was no longer an option; Ruairí Quinn, although unsuccessful in 1973, was now a member of the Seanad and actively campaigning in the constituency. Among the constituencies which attracted the attention of Noël Browne's supporters at this time were Dublin South and Dublin Artane, neither of which had a Labour TD. They were vastly different constituencies. Dublin South was a three-seater, and had the name of being one of the most Fine Gael-oriented constituencies in the country, with swathes of middle-class housing and small pockets of working-class voters. Browne addressed a meeting of the constituency council there in June 1975.[35] Artane, also a three-seater, was almost at the other end of the spectrum: acres of Dublin Corporation housing estates, with considerable social deprivation. It was also the constituency of C.J. Haughey who, from 1971 onwards, had been working his way back up the Fianna Fáil ladder from which he had so dramatically been pushed by the Arms Trial and the events surrounding it.

Coincidentally, I was also looking at that time for a constituency to fight on behalf of Labour, having become a member of the party in 1977, and had joined the Mount Merrion branch. Another member of the branch, Roger Cole, had been — and remained — close to Noël Browne for many years. I was soon told that Browne was interested in a nomination in the constituency, and asked for my reaction. I replied that I respected him, but did not believe that anyone had an automatic right to a nomination; that I would be quite happy to fight it out within the constituency, and would accept the result.

In the event, Browne's supporters soon began to concentrate on Artane instead. Here, the effects of the economic downturn had been particularly marked, and most voter hostility seemed to be directed against the junior partner in the Coalition. 'They were going to kick the Labour Party into the sea,' according to one activist.[36] This reaction was especially strong among younger working-class women, especially those married with small children. By November 1975, when he addressed a meeting in Donnycarney,[37] Artane had effectively been selected by Browne's supporters as the best option. This was formalised at the beginning of December 1976, when the Donnycarney branch — of which Des Bonass, an ATGWU official and a long-time supporter of his, was vice-chairman — nominated him formally to be the Labour candidate at the forthcoming election.[38]

This was not at all in accordance with the plans of the party leadership, which had assumed that there would be two Labour candidates in Artane — Paddy Dunne and Michael O'Halloran, the latter a former Lord Mayor, who between them would guarantee a seat in this populous working-class area. A pre-emptive strike was accordingly planned. At its meeting on 22 March 1977, the party's Administrative Council formally decided that it would not ratify the candidacy in the forthcoming election of any member of the party who, as a member of the Oireachtas, was not a member of the parliamentary party.[39] The general terms in which this decision was couched were disingenuous; the only person matching the description was Noël Browne.

At the selection conference itself, held on 23 March, things went seriously awry for the leadership. The first vote at a selection conference is on the number of candidates to be put forward, and the original plan had been for two, Dunne and O'Halloran. By now, however, Browne's allies were firmly in control of a majority of the branches in the constituency organisation.

The meeting voted by a majority for one candidate, and then Browne, who got twelve delegate votes as against four for each of the other two men, was selected as the official Dáil candidate. He immediately added to the embarrassment of the leadership by signing the party pledge — almost simultaneously attacking Corish in the course of a speech in the Seanad.[40]

The party bit the bullet. On 31 March it decided not to ratify Browne as the candidate by eighteen votes to three, and expelled one of his principal allies, Dermot Boucher.[41] At the end of April it rejected a petition signed by 250 party members to reinstate him. By the end of May the break was complete, when Browne, in Artane, and Mattie Merrigan, running in Finglas, launched an 'Independent Labour' campaign in both constituencies. David Neligan, who originally had been asked to run as Independent Labour in Crumlin, declined, and ended up as director of elections for Browne and Merrigan. A few days later, the two candidates issued a fifty-point manifesto,[42] and battle was joined. Browne announced during his campaign that if he was elected he would give up medical practice and would devote himself full-time to his constituents.[43] He retired from his position as senior psychiatrist on 30 June 1977, and in 1978, at the age of sixty-two, he withdrew his name from the medical register.

It was as bad-tempered and bitter a campaign as Labour had ever witnessed. Noël Browne's campaign in Artane attracted crowds of idealistic young left-wing activists, among them two of my current colleagues in Dublin City University, Brian Trench and Luke Gibbons; and a young teacher, Roddy Doyle.[44] On polling day on 16 June Browne swept to victory with more than 5,500 first preference votes, just half of Haughey's total, but more than twice the votes of the highest-placed official Labour candidate, Paddy Dunne. In Finglas, Merrigan was markedly less successful, polling only just over 1,500 votes, but his candidacy almost certainly spoiled the chances of Labour's former general secretary Brendan Halligan, who had transferred into that constituency from Ballyfermot, and was beaten by 824 votes on the last count by Fine Gael's Luke Belton.

It was a devastating result for Labour, not only in these two constituencies but across Dublin. Although Quinn was elected in Dublin South-East and I was elected in Dublin South, this was against the run of play. Conor Cruise O'Brien, Justin Keating and David Thornley all lost their seats; there were only five Labour TDs left in Dublin, not one of them on the north side of the Liffey. 'One key factor in the whole Dublin area', the Labour Party's annual report commented acidly and, as it happened, accurately, 'was the intervention of "Independent Labour" candidates in Artane and Finglas. One of these candidates, Dr Noël Browne, was successful in Artane, indicating that there was a Labour seat in the area.' The Independent Labour Campaign Committee, it added, 'conducted a vigorous, and at times virulent campaign against the Labour Party and unquestionably caused a lot of Labour Party voters to abstain or vote for other parties'.[45]

As the new Dáil prepared to meet, Noël Browne and his supporters immediately prepared to take the high ground. Browne retabled the bill on family planning, along with no fewer than sixteen Dáil motions on subjects from neutrality to natural resources.[46] This caused consternation among the established political parties, and not least in Labour, because no other party had as yet put down any motions for Private Members' Time. Under the standing orders of the House Noël Browne had the right to move each and every one of his motions in the first session of Private Members' Time, which would have forced all the major parties to vote them down in order to secure priority for their own, later-tabled resolutions. As the date for the first Private Members' Time debate approached, the trepidation was palpable; but Browne did not turn up to move his motions, and lost a unique opportunity hugely to embarrass each of his former parties, but more especially Labour.

For a month or two, there was a phoney war. Brendan Corish announced his resignation, and was succeeded by Frank Cluskey after an extraordinary election in which the parliamentary party votes were first tied at eight all in a contest between Cluskey and Michael O'Leary. Some time later, I wrote a lengthy letter to Cluskey suggesting that this was now the time to allow Browne back into the party, as a way of healing old sores.[47] This youthful enthusiasm on my part met with a stony silence. Eventually I asked Cluskey directly whether this could be done. 'It would split the party,' was his considered verdict; and that was the end of it.

On 29 September 1977 the Administrative Council performed the final act when it voted by sixteen votes to five in support of a resolution proposed by Brendan Corish stating that 'Noël Browne and Mattie Merrigan have ceased to be eligible for party membership and to take part in any activities of the Party at any level.'[48] Formally, their crime had been that they had stood in a general election against official party candidates. Matters were complicated by the controversy surrounding another Labour Party member who had also run an independent campaign. This was Mick Lipper, a train driver from Limerick, who had campaigned against — and beaten — the official Labour Party candidate, the controversial TD Stephen Coughlan. Coughlan's unscheduled departure was, if anything, a matter for quiet celebration; he had long been a thorn in the side of the parliamentary party's newer intake. So had Noël Browne, but of course for entirely different reasons. And whereas Coughlan had been replaced in his constituency by Lipper, a doughty trade unionist in the classic mould who shared Coughlan's Catholic allegiance but not his prejudices or his waywardness, Browne had not been replaced, but reinvented.

The problem, in a sense, was how to get Lipper into the parliamentary party, but to keep Browne (who was still a member of the party itself) out. In the event, Lipper solved the problem by applying formally for membership; Browne did not. At the same Administrative Council meeting, Mick Lipper was readmitted to the fold.[49]

It was already evident that Noël Browne had burned his boats. Less than two weeks after his formal expulsion from Labour, 300 people met in Dublin to form a new party — the Socialist Labour Party. Noël Browne and Jack McQuillan were among them. In yet another twist to the story, it was announced that Browne, although the only member of the party in the Oireachtas, would not hold any officership in the party, and would be merely an ordinary member.[50] This unusual arrangement — many party members evidently expected Noël Browne to advocate SLP party policies in the Dáil, even if he disagreed with them — reduced the possibility of open conflict between Browne and powerful groups within the party, but at the cost also of limiting the party's voice in the national parliament.

CHAPTER TEN

'How the Hell Did He Get into Irish Politics?'[1]

The Socialist Labour Party's foundation meeting was a euphoric affair, but one at which the nascent internal tensions were already evident, even to some committed observers and supporters. Noël Browne himself made a 'highly personalised, nearly meditative' contribution,[2] in which he expressed the view that the radical social change which was needed would not come through parliament. This was of a piece with a line of thought he had been developing earlier, and which had aroused no comment from either friends or enemies — the argument that parliament itself was outdated, a piece of nineteenth-century constitutional baggage of limited value, if indeed it had any value at all. Only three years earlier, in an attack on a federal plan for Northern Ireland jointly advanced by Conor Cruise O'Brien and Desmond Boal, a Northern MP and lawyer who reflected a radical streak in unionism which was prepared to consider some accommodation with the Republic provided that basic principles were left intact, Browne had told a Labour Party meeting, that 'the whole creaking, archaic system of parliamentary democracy . . . belongs to the scrapheap of history and . . . cannot be either modified or modernised'.[3] The global way in which he dismissed several centuries of parliamentary tradition was breathtaking. Equally, the absence of any controversy on foot of his remarks suggested that his opponents were no longer paying any serious attention to such flights of fancy, and that his supporters knew better than to question his pronouncements, even if they were just plain silly.

Not long afterwards, he rediscovered his enthusiasm for parliament, upbraiding *The Irish Times* for editorially criticising politicians. It was, he said, 'an impertinence that a journalist . . . should pontificate to us elected representatives, certainly to this one, from his pulpit in the intellectual bordello which is the world of peddling newspapers, about his concern with our unkindness to one another'.[4] These sudden changes of tack, and the prickly imperiousness of his terminology, did little to enhance his reputation, although they appeared to have little or no impact on his electoral success..

Mattie Merrigan, the new party's chairman, was taking an entirely different line, underlining his conviction that the SLP would not begin to be successful unless it contested elections and got members into the Dáil. In this he was echoed by many former members of the Labour Party who had followed him and Browne into the new party, and who tended to assume that a resurrection of Labour's 1969 policies, accompanied by hard con-stituency work, would put the new party on the right road. There was even a brief suggestion that former members of Labour should appeal their expulsions to the party's annual conference, as they had a right to do. This was finally abandoned after Dermot Boucher announced defiantly: 'I have gone down for the third time — I'm not coming up again!'[5] One of these former members, a high-profile politician now again reduced to the rank and file, was David Thornley, who joined the SLP's Dublin South-Central branch, of which he was elected an officer.[6] By May 1978, it was reported that the party had now established branches in thirty of the forty-four Dáil constituencies.[7] David Thornley, his last act of filial piety complete, died in June, aged forty-two.

All in all, however, electoral success did not seem to be a major priority for many members of the new party. This aspect of political organisation was frequently overtaken, and in some cases totally displaced, by intense internal ideological discussion. Early on, the party decreed that it would allow the maintenance of various 'tendencies' within its ranks and this, combined with the fact that it set about publishing not one but three separate journals — an internal party bulletin, a publication for the electorate at large, and a theoretical journal — sapped the energies of all but the most committed.

The president of the new party, David Neligan, had to keep the peace between members whose horizons were firmly fixed on the Dáil, and those whose preoccupations were more abstract, and more particularly between the party's chairman, Merrigan, and Browne, who did not get on well together. It was, however, only one of the tensions within the newborn SLP. Worse was to come, in the shape of potentially deep divisions on the questions of abortion, the North, and Noël Browne's role within the party.

Of these three, the abortion controversy was probably the least significant. Despite Noël Browne's continuing support for therapeutic legal abortion in certain circumstances, the SLP as a whole hesitated before finally taking an unambiguous stand on this issue. There were certainly many members in favour of it; but more cautious voices were heard to suggest that it be included only as a long-term goal, given its implications for the party's electoral hopes.

By far the biggest issue was that of the North. The SLP's first internal newsletter contained half a dozen statements on the national question, plain evidence of disagreement.[8] Its next issue criticised the organised Republican movement because it was 'elitist and militaristic and isolates itself from mass movement leading to demoralisation', but added that 'because Republican militants fight against British imperialism we defend them against repression'.[9] In May 1978 Noël Browne spoke on the Northern issue to a crowded meeting in the ATGWU hall in Dublin, when he criticised the 'bloody and undemocratic record of Irish republicanism, as interpreted by the leaders of all the republican parties in the Irish Republic', and criticised Connolly for having mistakenly taken part in 1916.[10] This gave rise to a wide-ranging controversy inside and outside the party.

Outside the party, participants in the debate included Cathal Goulding, Seán Garland and Danny Morrison, all of them hostile to Browne's position to one degree or another. Inside, a head of steam was building up; the safety valve finally blew at the party's conference at the end of January 1979. Something of the mood within the party can be gauged from a resolution submitted by the Derry/Donegal branch calling for an 'armed front of workers, socialists and republicans'. This was withdrawn only in favour of a composite resolution which called for Browne and Merrigan to lead a labour movement delegation to Long Kesh (later the Maze Prison). Merrigan made a passionately Republican speech about the North, in which he said that he abhorred the bombing of civilian targets, but that he understood the decision to take up arms. The following day, his speech was repudiated by Browne in a public statement (Browne did not address the conference itself). Simultaneously, Jack McQuillan resigned as an SLP trustee.[11] Within a week, Browne had resigned as the SLP parliamentary spokesperson.[12] The Long Kesh visit, unsurprisingly, did not take place; Browne was to disclose that he would have gone if the visit was extended to include other prisons, but this was rejected by his party.[13] Even his own rejection of militarism, however, was in some sense qualified. If he had himself been a Northern Catholic, he surmised some time later, 'it's very likely I would have ended up in one of the para-military movements because of the clear futility of parliamentary politics under the gerrymander'.[14]

Within the party, the wrangle continued, now extending to Browne's role itself. He had been appointed a trustee in December 1977, and had accepted the role of the SLP 'parliamentary spokesperson' in October 1978.[15] The ending of his three-month tenure of the latter position in the wake of the conference did not halt the controversy. The February meeting of the party's National Executive Committee recorded its view as follows:

> *The NEC wishes to advert to the media hysteria in connection with a gaffe by the party president at the annual conference and reiterates that the SLP is an independent political organisation and is not in any way sympathetic to the*

narrow nationalist aims or methods of the Provisional IRA, including the
bombing campaign which the party believes is counterproductive to the develop-
ment of a socialist united Ireland and a united anti-Imperialist campaign.[16]

It was not enough, not by a long shot. Jim Larragy, shortly to be
expelled from the party, tabled a resolution at this meeting recommending
that 'Noël Browne, as a TD, cannot remain as a member of the SLP while
refusing to act in the Dáil as an SLP spokesperson.'[17] Donncha Ó hÉalaithe
of the Galway West branch announced his intention of resigning from the
party, partly because of Noël Browne's conduct, and did so in March.[18]
Tony Gregory resigned in April.[19]

The Labour Party's deputy leader, Michael O'Leary, then issued an invitation which was unexpected, unwelcome and unsuccessful. It was to Noël
Browne, suggesting that he should, along with other former Labour Party
members who were now in the SLP, rejoin the larger organisation.[20] This idea
had not been discussed at any level within the Labour Party, as it happened,
and it is extremely doubtful that it would have secured any acceptance if it
had. O'Leary, the defeated candidate in the 1977 leadership election, was in
any case ploughing an increasingly lonely furrow, and the relationship
between him and Frank Cluskey ranged from poor to non-existent.

In any case, the SLP was still preoccupied with its own internal problems. The relationship between Browne (and McQuillan) and the party was
rapidly coming to a head. Mattie Merrigan fired a final shot at the retreating
McQuillan when he secured NEC support for a resolution recording that
the former trustee's resignation statement 'purported to assert that he was a
bona fide member of the party when in effect he never paid one penny in
accordance with our financial rules'.[21] The Browne problem was discussed
at an NEC meeting on 10 March, when it was recorded that the party's sole
member in the Oireachtas was against tabling amendments and questions
fed to him from within the party organisation — a salutary exercise of
caution on his part, it would appear. A delegation from the NEC was
appointed to discuss the matter with him,[22] but essentially there seems to
have been no change in the situation, as a similar approach was mooted a
few months later.[23]

By now, however, the new party was already deep in crisis. Three of the
largest branches, comprising 15–20 per cent of the entire membership, were
on the brink of disaffiliation, while a further 30 per cent of members were
actively considering departure. Dermot Boucher, as stern a critic of the
party he had just helped to found as he had been of the one from which he
had just been expelled, noted: 'The shambles of the party conference, with
its bitter divisive debates, had produced an atmosphere of gloom and
despondency [and] created an image of the SLP as an infantile debating

society, effectively controlled by a lunatic fringe with no conception what-ever of the realities of working class politics.'[24]

Noël Browne's focus, which had probably never been fully directed towards the SLP, was now firmly fixed on the Dáil itself. It was a Dáil which had, as a result of the election of 1977, a Fianna Fáil government with a majority of twenty, and in which Browne had total freedom to act and speak as he chose. His principal issues were marked out early: divorce and contraception, capital punishment, education, and prisons. They were to be supplemented by the fallout from an event which took place in 1979 — the replacement of Jack Lynch as Taoiseach and leader of the Fianna Fáil party by C.J. Haughey.

Before Lynch's resignation, the special cross that Haughey had to bear after his restoration to the cabinet as Minister for Health had been the belated attempt to legislate for family planning in the wake of the Supreme Court decision in the McGee case. This case, which dated back to 1973, was one in which a married woman had successfully challenged the constitutionality of a law which prevented her from importing contraceptives for her personal use. The dilemma facing the government was simply expressed: the McGee case had effectively struck down the old prohibitions, leaving nothing in their place, so legislation was essential to control the availability of contra-ceptives, now that they could not be banned outright. Any legislation which offended the Catholic Church, however, was virtually certain to run into serious difficulties within the Fianna Fáil parliamentary party, and by extension in the Dáil itself. The Haughey-engineered compromise was to legislate for the availability of contraceptives to married couples only, on the basis of a prescription from a medical practitioner. It was, even then, an Alice in Wonderland solution; twenty years later, it looks even more absurd — and yet it was patently the only law which that government felt it was within its power to enact.

Browne was in his element — all the more so because his former com-rades in the Labour Party, including deputies like Barry Desmond (who was to introduce infinitely more realistic legislation when he became Minister for Health in 1982) were in a position of deep embarrassment on this issue. Most Labour deputies, including myself, would have had little difficulty in uniting behind a series of liberalising amendments to the Haughey draft legislation, many of which would have been identical to those being drafted by Browne. There was, however, a hard core of Labour deputies who were unprepared to vote on family planning legislation in any shape or form, even if — as was the case here — the measures being proposed were effectively a modest restriction on the free-for-all which was a result of the McGee decision. Under these circumstances, the party had been forced to devise an escape hatch for itself. This was to announce that it already had a family planning bill on the stocks, which had not been subjected to the indignity (and possible intra-party hazards) of a Dáil vote. On these grounds, it declared that the Haughey bill was so fundamentally flawed as to be incapable of amendment, and that Labour therefore would not be submitting any amendments. Nor, it made clear, would its deputies be voting on amendments submitted by anyone else.

This strategy had the advantage of preventing a public display of disunity within the party, although few deputies seriously believed that the public was unaware of the real reason for this tactical retreat. Its disadvantage was that it permitted Noël Browne to make the running completely on the Haughey bill. Labour deputies could — and did — support many of his amendments verbally, but, when the Ceann Comhairle called for evidence that Browne had the necessary support to call a vote (ten deputies were required), we had to remain glued to our seats. On this occasion at least, Browne was more concerned to embarrass and attack Haughey than he was to pour scorn on the newfound Carthusianism of his former colleagues in the Labour Party.

By December 1979, Haughey had done his penance in Health. Lynch's star was waning fast, and poor results in the European and local elections that summer, compounded by the loss of two by-elections, one of them in his native city of Cork, hastened his already impending retirement. Haughey was elected leader of Fianna Fáil, and, on 11 December, Taoiseach.

Browne's speech on that occasion was scathing. Haughey, he argued, was not a Republican, because Republicans believed in a secular society, a pluralist society, and in a radical approach to politics. Those who had supported Haughey, on the other hand, were 'sectarian nationalists, crypto-provos'.[25] He saw the Fianna Fáil candidate for Taoiseach as a cross between Richard Nixon and the Portuguese dictator Salazar, someone who could not be trusted to hand over power if he failed to retain a parliamentary majority. 'I am afraid of Deputy Haughey. Curiously enough he is one of the two politicians I have been afraid of all my life. I am afraid of his potential with real power.'[26]

As deputies were leaving the chamber following the vote which elected Haughey, Ruairí Quinn, in his first term as a TD for Browne's old constituency, congratulated him on his speech and asked him who was the second politician of whom he had been afraid. Browne did not hesitate: 'MacBride.'[27]

Haughey's election might have produced something of a rapprochement between Browne and his organisation; equally, the departure of some disaffected members might have been a factor. Either way, Browne officially resumed his role as parliamentary spokesman for the SLP in March 1980, a little over a year after he had laid it down.[28] The party statement announcing this noted that he had assisted in the SLP's local election campaign the previous summer, although this, given the absence of any electoral success whatsoever, was not something to which attention might ordinarily have been drawn. It is difficult to discern any substantial change in Noël Browne's tactics thereafter as a result of this development, although there was a distinct increase in his level of activity. He was even suspended from the House on 26 June after getting involved in a major controversy about the revelations of the former secretary of the Department of Justice, Peter Berry, which had been published in *Magill*. (Berry implied that he had told Lynch about the importation of arms in 1970, but that Lynch had done nothing about it.). His suspension prompted widespread protests by opposition deputies and a walkout by Labour.[29]

Despite the apparent restoration of his relationship with the SLP, Browne was publicly musing about the role of Independent deputies in a context which suggests that he primarily saw himself as one of these. 'I don't agree with the concept of an independent deputy in the House. There is something elitist and crank about an independent. I am increasingly aware of his or her powerlessness. The role of a deputy is to change society, to be involved with a party . . .'[30]

Outside the Dáil, pressure was building up on the issue of divorce. The Divorce Action Group was founded on 15 April 1980, as opinion polls showed that more and more people were prepared to consider a constitutional change, although it was too early to say that there was a clear majority in favour. Within days, Noël Browne had tabled a bill for a simple constitutional amendment to delete the prohibition on divorce, and Mary Robinson had prepared a draft bill on the subject and presented it to the Parliamentary Labour Party. Noël Browne's bill put the Labour TDs in a particularly embarrassing position, because not all of them would vote for it, even on a free vote, and one or two might vote against it under any circumstances. As Cluskey attempted to push, pull or cajole the more reluctant members of his party into supporting a lowest common denominator policy — a resolution urging the establishment of an all-party committee to discuss the matter[31] — Noël Browne moved his own bill in June 1980.

Under standing orders, he was allocated five minutes to introduce it, and when he did so he referred specifically to Labour Party policy, to the public opinion polls, and to the possible effect of divorce on a rapprochement between North and South. When he had finished, the Minister for Justice, Gerry Collins, outlined the government's reasons for rejecting the bill: the majority of voters, he said bluntly, supported the existing prohibition, and it would be misleading to hold out prospects which were unlikely to materialise. When a vote was called, Browne alone rose to his feet and, when it appeared that he was the only one in support of the measure, enquired: 'Might I propose a further motion to the effect that this State be renamed the Irish holy Roman Catholic and apostolic republic?'[32]

The failure of Browne's motion, and pressure from the party's annual conference, now forced a reluctant PLP to revisit the issue. At the PLP meeting in November, Robinson suggested with considerable justice that the party was dragging its feet. The motion for an all-party committee was accordingly tabled, and debated in the Dáil in December. In an attempt to retrieve the initiative, Browne moved an amendment to the Labour Party motion, but it was one which exposed him to criticism on all sides in that it urged the establishment of divorce along the lines suggested by the previous all-party committee on the constitution, which had reported thirteen years earlier.

The problem here was that this committee, not over-endowed with constitutional or indeed religious knowledge, suggested that an answer might be found to the divorce problem by allowing divorce to those Irish citizens whose religions allowed this expedient. Even if it had been workable, this solution was technically sectarian, and Browne, in advancing it, was advancing a position which was in some respects less clear-cut, and certainly less defensible, than his own position earlier in the year. As the debate wore on, he was forced to admit that the previous committee's proposal, which he was now endorsing, was 'silly and unworkable [and] sectarian',[33] leaving him with no other grounds for opposing the motion other than its failure to put any time limit on the work of review that would be involved. His concern on this score, at least, was prescient; it was to be fifteen more years, and two constitutional referenda, before a majority of Dáil deputies and of the electorate finally agreed to the deletion of the anti-divorce provisions; by then they had lasted for more than forty years. Browne also, however — little realising what would happen within less than a year — suggested that Cluskey should make movement on divorce by Fine Gael a precondition for participation in any future coalition.[34]

The general election was closer than anyone suspected, and was to be called by Haughey for 11 June 1981, four years almost to the day since the previous election. In the interim, Noël Browne seemed to discover reserves of energy which many thought would by now have deserted him. He made powerful interventions on a number of his key subjects — the mental health services,[35] capital punishment,[36] a controversy involving the certification of a prisoner in Dundrum Central Mental Hospital,[37] and the ludicrousness of a criminal justice system which made it impossible to charge a man with rape if the victim was his wife.[38]

Even these issues, however, paled into relative insignificance beside another event which occurred in the heart of the constituency which the Taoiseach, Charles Haughey, shared with Noël Browne: the Stardust disaster. Early on the morning of 15 February 1981, a fire broke out in the Stardust ballroom in Artane. Forty-eight young people died either of smoke inhalation or of burns, and 160 were injured. It rapidly became public knowledge that the emergency exit doors to the ballroom had been locked. In the Dáil the following Tuesday, the House adjourned, as arrangements were made to set up a tribunal of inquiry. For the first time in many years, the Official Report of the day's proceedings was edged in black.[39] The Fianna Fáil Ard-Fheis, due to be held the following weekend, was cancelled.

The establishment of the tribunal prolonged rather than resolved the controversy. As it happened, Noël Browne had already been helping a family in his constituency — they lived within sight of the Stardust — whose children had been involved in a similar calamity in Donegal. It was an issue he was on top of from the start and, despite lacking the resources of the larger parties, he made much of the running on it with the help of David Neligan and others. The families of the victims were helped to set up an organisation. In the Dáil, Browne focused on one question extremely effectively: Where did responsibility lie, and what role had the statutory authorities — notably the fire authorities and the planning authorities — played? There was also a rumour, which Browne followed up to the maximum possible extent but for which he was never to get enough proof, that political pressure had been applied to ensure that certain conditions attaching to the planning permission for the ballroom would be waived. When the report of the tribunal was eventually published, on 5 July 1982, it concluded that the fire had probably been caused deliberately, and found fault with the owners, Dublin Corporation, and the Department of the Environment.

The Stardust Tribunal was eventually pushed into the background by an early general election, which took place in an atmosphere of some political instability created by the then current hunger strike in the Maze Prison, in the course of which ten Republican prisoners were to die. Four of the hunger strikers won Dáil seats, eating into the Fianna Fáil vote, which went down by more than 5 per cent. It was also the first election in which abortion became an issue. The recently formed Pro-Life Campaign, after an intensive and skilful campaign, secured commitments, first from Haughey and subsequently from Garret FitzGerald (who had succeeded Liam Cosgrave as Fine Gael leader in 1977), to introduce an anti-abortion amendment into the Constitution. Three referenda and several Supreme Court judgments later, that particular issue has still not been resolved.

Although Haughey nearly pulled it off — an additional 260 votes in two constituencies would have given him two extra seats — Fianna Fáil emerged from the election with a combined total of two seats less than a Fine Gael alliance, and there was a cluster of four Independents (eight including the H-Block TDs), most of whom were unfavourable to Haughey or distrusted him deeply.

They included Browne, who had easily retained his seat in the newly drawn and renamed constituency of Dublin North-Central, now a four-seater which he shared with Haughey. His first preference vote total was almost three times the combined votes of the two Labour candidates. Interestingly, in view of his public antipathy to the Fianna Fáil leader, he was the only candidate — apart from the second and third Fianna Fáil candidates — to benefit to any degree from the redistribution of Haughey's enormous surplus. Other newcomers included the veteran socialist from Limerick, Jim Kemmy, elected as an Independent, and Joe Sherlock from Cork East, representing Sinn Féin the Workers' Party. They were welcomed by Browne as the only socialists — with himself — in the new Dáil. Almost unnoticed in the fuss was the election of a future leader of the Labour Party, the new deputy for Kerry North, Dick Spring.

It was a hung Dáil. Fianna Fáil TDs were resigned to opposition, more or less; the critical question was whether Garrett FitzGerald would be able to put together a stable government. The odds favoured him, even if they were primarily driven up by the anti-Haughey factor. Browne's intentions were the subject of much speculation, as it quickly became evident that his was one of the couple of swing votes which would determine the formation of the next government. He appeared to waver, immediately after the election, suggesting that there was no difference between Haughey and FitzGerald in policy terms.[40] He even allowed himself a brief fantasy, suggesting he could exert power over Fianna Fáil, and might vote for that party — a rerun of 1951 — if Haughey were not its leader.[41] He blew hot and cold about Labour, threatening at one stage to vote against the nomination of any Labour ministers 'unless they renounce their claim to represent Socialism'.[42] This, as it happened, was within ten days of a declaration that he 'would vote for a Labour Taoiseach, and I would vote a thousand times for Michael D. Higgins'.[43]

The powerful position he now held brought about a sea change in Noël Browne's relationship with the SLP, and was effectively the death knell for the organisation itself. Noël had always been uncomfortable with the thought of being under the discipline of any party, regardless of its size. The prospect of being driven, in his future relations with government, by an undisciplined group of enthusiastic, unrealistic and quarrelsome followers was too much to contemplate. Even as the last bundles of votes were being counted in Bolton Street in the early hours of 12 June, the enthusiasm of Browne's SLP party workers was sharply tempered by a sense that the end was nigh. One campaigner, realising that although Browne had been re-elected, the SLP would hardly rise again, told a journalist: 'Noël demands everything. It's all or nothing for him. How the hell did he get into Irish politics?'[44]

Noël himself, simultaneously, was shrugging off the SLP the way a snake sloughs off an old skin. 'I was never really enthusiastic about the establishment of a small party. I never had any function or office in it whatever.'[45] It took some time, but the protracted funeral rites eventually came to a predictably bitter end. In November, he confirmed that he had ended his relationship with the SLP 'after a series of disagreements, most recently about the raising of the school leaving age'.[46] The issue in fact was probably not the raising of school leaving age but the FitzGerald government's plan to save money in primary education by raising the age at which children were eligible to enter primary school. Browne's support for this plan, which was fiercely resisted by the INTO, had been acquired in return for a governmental commitment to support pre-school education in socially deprived areas. The following day, the SLP, with its dying breath, claimed that Noël Browne had 'never been a bona fide member of the party [and] made no financial contribution to the party even though he used the party's certificate during the last election. The party did make a financial contribution to his campaign.'[47] The SLP was formally wound up in August 1982.[48]

With that inconvenience out of the way, it was a time for doing deals. FitzGerald, understandably, was not prepared to enter a formal relationship with anyone except Labour, under its new leader, Michael O'Leary (Cluskey had lost his seat as the result of an intra-party dispute with John O'Connell, now an Independent). The potential new government could, however, give some general assurances to individual deputies that its heart was in the right place. Browne's shopping list was unique in that the issues which concerned him were not budgetary, and included the possibility of some action on capital punishment, divorce, and physical punishment in schools.[49] On these issues FitzGerald, for all that Browne retained a distrust of him, was obviously credible. In the Dáil votes on the nominations for Taoiseach, however, Browne now adopted a different strategy. The lesson of the inter-party government, he declared, had not been the failure of the Mother and Child Scheme, but the way in which coalitions had led to the ultimate disappearance of the smaller parties — a fate he suspected also awaited Labour. In light of this, he was now suggesting, not that Labour should insist on retaining the power ministries in any coalition deal, but that the party should 'decide to negotiate either with Fianna Fáil or Fine Gael to get the best bargain they could and stay out of office'[50] — in other words, to support a minority government, an expedient which had not been adopted by anyone, for obvious reasons, since Seán MacBride in 1954–7. Neither Fianna Fáil nor Fine Gael could reform the capitalist system, and accordingly he would abstain in the vote for FitzGerald. Both he and Kemmy — who told the House that 'I found my foot in some strange doors last week and my foot will stay inside those doors'[51] — voted against Haughey. Kemmy voted for FitzGerald.

In the event, FitzGerald won by eighty-one votes to seventy-eight. Abstention, however, was not a long-term option; the Dáil voting figures were too tightly balanced for that. Increasingly, both Browne and Kemmy were pulled into a position of supporting the administration, although initially there was no indication that this was causing them much grief, and indeed some indications that their support was being given more and more willingly.

There was rapid movement on corporal punishment in schools, despite a rearguard action by some teachers. It was eventually banned by John Boland, FitzGerald's Minister for Education, after the following general election but while the cabinet was operating on a caretaker basis. In October 1981 the government was opposing a Fianna Fáil motion to move the writ for an early by-election in Cavan-Monaghan (whose hunger striker TD Kieran Doherty had died in the Maze). When Browne rose to defend the government's decision he made his position totally clear. Throughout most of his political life, he argued, there were a number of issues which he had failed to get Fianna Fáil to support. FitzGerald's government was now making 'courageous decisions' on these issues: capital punishment, corporal punishment, divorce and family planning, and tax reform. On these grounds, he had no hesitation whatsoever in supporting the government.[52] On one occasion, he told a surprised Garret FitzGerald privately that, on contentious matters of personal morality such as contraception and divorce, he would be wise to take the views and concerns of the hierarchy into account.[53] He gave no reason for offering this unusual advice, but he may well have been reflecting, at the end of his political career, on what his own stand in 1951 had cost him in terms of his ability to create government policy in the intervening decades, forcing him to remain a critic on the sidelines.

He was still prepared to fire a warning shot across the government's bows on occasion. When the Fianna Fáil leader pressed FitzGerald for a policy statement on the question of the abortion amendment, Browne intervened: 'In view of the fact that none of the women Members of the House is pre-pared to refute the suggestion that women have not the right to choose in this matter let me as a male member of this House say that I believe they have a right to choose on this issue.'[54] This potentially explosive issue was, however, overtaken almost immediately by an unplanned series of events, focusing on budgetary matters, which eventually brought down the government less than a year after it had been voted into office.

FitzGerald and O'Leary had determined that a central plank of government policy would be a major increase in social welfare payments, and wrote into the Budget a provision for an increase which was to be the largest, in real terms, for many years. The problem arose when it came to deciding how it would be paid for. Two options emerged: finding it through taxation, including putting value added tax on certain items of clothing, or eliminating food subsidies. In the negotiations around this issue, both

Browne and Kemmy indicated firmly to FitzGerald that they were opposed to removing the food subsidies; Kemmy was 'vaguer' on the issue of taxation,[55] so the taxation route was the one taken. Browne's supporters argued furiously against it,[56] but he was not persuadable. He had already taken, and announced, his decision not to stand in the next election, whenever it came.[57] Although he was to describe the VAT element of the taxation package four years later as 'particularly silly proposals',[58] all the elements of that package were inevitably tied in with each other, and with the proposed increases in social spending. Browne was therefore evidently prepared to vote for them when the necessary financial resolutions were put to the House on 27 January 1982.

What actually happened created a situation in which the Dáil had only one vote on the Budget, instead of the multiplicity of votes which are a normal feature of the debate. As is normal on Budget night, the taxation changes, which come into effect immediately, are voted on in a series of financial resolutions. The first such resolution was to increase the excise duty on beer, and this would have been followed in the normal course of events by the votes on VAT and other elements of the taxation package. It was clear all round that the fate of the first vote would determine the fate of the others. Then, to the obvious surprise of the government, Kemmy, Sherlock and Independent Seán Dublin Bay Loftus moved to vote against the first resolution, despite some last-minute private pleas by FitzGerald. Noël Browne voted with the government, which lost the division by one vote.[59] The Dáil was dissolved before any other votes could be called — effectively there was no point — and the election called for 18 February.

Browne now found himself, flatteringly, the focus of extraordinary entreaties from representatives of the party which had expelled him, and also from the party which had helped to terminate his appointment as Minister for Health in 1951. Michael O'Leary's invitation for him to rejoin Labour, issued at the time when he said he would not contest the next election, had already been turned down.[60] Garret FitzGerald tried next, reasoning that Browne would almost certainly secure re-election as an Independent in Artane, and thus deprive Fianna Fáil of a seat. Browne received FitzGerald's request courteously, said he would consider it overnight, and then declined.[61] At Labour's selection conference in Dublin North-Central, a last-minute attempt to draft Browne (who may not even have been aware of it) was made by some delegates, who were told by the conference chairperson, Senator Evelyn Owens, that the proposal could not be entertained because Browne was not a member of the party.[62]

He was tempted, however, on one final occasion. As a result of the unscheduled 18 February 1982 election, Charles Haughey now became Taoiseach, with a minority administration. Immediately after the election he sought to increase his voting strength by inviting Richard Burke, the Fine Gael TD, former Minister for Education (1973–6) and EEC Commissioner, to vacate his seat in the Dublin West constituency in return for nomination back to the Commission, assuming that Fianna Fáil would win the resulting by-election. Burke accepted his invitation, and resigned at the end of March. In the event, Haughey's plan misfired, and Liam Skelly, the Fine Gael candidate, was victorious in the by-election. Before Skelly's selection, however, Fine Gael had carried out market research which told them that if Noël Browne stood, he would win the seat, and went to Labour with this information. Labour accordingly approached Browne, who said that he would be interested in standing, but only if he had the unanimous support of the Labour organisation in the constituency. This was difficult — indeed impossible — to arrange, as that organisation had, by and large, fallen into the hands of the so-called Militant Tendency, an entryist group of young Trotskyists who were later expelled from the party. The Militants (or 'Millies' as they were known within the party) were intent on running a no-hope candidate, and eventually succeeded in doing so.[63]

Undeterred by this, Labour made one final attempt, when the Haughey government collapsed prematurely and a fresh general election was called for 24 November 1982, the third election in eighteen months. Dick Spring, who had been elected leader of the party following Michael O'Leary's sudden resignation (he had been defeated on electoral policy at the party's Galway conference after the first 1982 election), asked Noël Browne to run again in Dublin North-East. Browne's response was double-edged: he would do anything he could to help Dick Spring — but only if the party was led by him, and not by the 'rump' behind him.[64] It was, for all his goodwill towards Spring, a response which embodied an unusual view of the appropriate relationship between a party and its leader; and it was definitely a farewell.

CHAPTER ELEVEN

Still Against
the Tide

Noël Browne was aged sixty-six when he finally retired from active politics. His retirement lasted some fifteen years. It was, by and large, a time for children and grandchildren, who visited him and Phyllis frequently at their home in Connemara or in the grace and favour cottage they enjoyed in Malahide on their visits to Dublin. In Connemara, there was a routine: the daily paper, reading, talking — above all, talking with Phyllis — and walks in the wild countryside he had adopted as his own.[1] The child of a family which had been ravaged by TB, whose parents and three of his siblings had all died of the disease, he was, by any standards, beating the odds.

The Brownes now had an element of financial security, which essentially dated from the late 1960s when his former ally and later nemesis, C.J. Haughey, had as Minister for Finance sharply increased TDs' emoluments to a more reasonable level. As of September 1983, shortly after he retired, he now had more than twenty years' Dáil service, entitling him to a full Dáil pension of half a TD's current salary of £16,413. In addition, he had his ministerial pension, equivalent to a quarter of the additional £15,456 then payable to a member of the cabinet. Finally, there was his pension from his employment with the Eastern Health Board, where he had served a total of some fourteen years in different capacities, ending up as Senior Psychiatrist.

Anyone who expected him to decline into the sear and yellow leaf would, however, have been disappointed. This was not Noël Browne's style. There were, it is true, elements of reflection and repose. Journalists beat a path to his Connemara door from time to time, finding their way with difficulty down the narrow, twisting lanes to Cloughmore, hidden at the end of a rocky peninsula. He and Phyllis met them and entertained them with a slightly old-world graciousness, as he patiently answered questions — some of them no doubt for the hundredth time — and reminisced (not always accurately, it must be said, but memory plays tricks on the best of us) about his life in politics and the controversies in which he had been involved. Academic researchers also travelled to see him.

Television developed a particular fascination with him, treating him almost as an icon. The RTÉ Irish-language series *Cúrsaí* devoted a complete programme to him in 1987; the station's archive notes on this programme comment: 'Mainly ag caint faoi droch staid na tíre.'[2] The third programme in the RTÉ series *The War Years and After*, transmitted in May 1995, was very largely about Noël Browne, Noel Hartnett and Clann na Poblachta, and featured the Liam Ó Laoghaire film *Our Country*, the first party political film ever produced in Ireland.[3] *Radharc* made a documentary called 'Medics, Mitres and Ministers',[4] which was broadcast in December 1991; and the elegiac *Requiem for a Civilisation*,[5] written by Browne himself and transmitted in 1992, recorded his fascination with the people and landscapes of the west of Ireland. Another programme, consisting mainly of interaction between Browne and Michael D. Higgins, was filmed partly on the Galway–Dublin train, and featured a sequence which was cut from the final version. It occurred as Higgins talked to Browne about his relationship with his wife. They had had a marriage of almost five decades and, as Higgins noted, had become to all intents and purposes one person; what would happen when one of them died? Noël Browne said nothing, and seemed to go into a long reverie which — had it been shown — would itself have had an extraordinary impact.

This reflective period of Noël Browne's life was punctuated, as might have been expected, by episodes of controversy and disputation, his occasionally emollient and optimistic phrases set off by black and bitter words. What he said and wrote still made headlines, from time to time. He seemed increasingly to blame the Catholic Church for the ills of Irish society. The State, he suggested in 1994, was 'the increasingly decadent rump of the once great, now extinct Pan-European Holy Roman Empire'. The North of Ireland, he suggested by contrast (in phraseology which would have embarrassed all but the most hardbitten Unionists), 'with all its warts . . . represents Europe of the Reformation, the Enlightenment, the Renaissance, the French Revolution, the Industrial Revolution, and much else'.[6] But even at that he was not immune to a certain wistfulness, as *Irish Times* journalist John Waters remembered him writing some years earlier: 'I often wonder if the Church wasn't so powerful, would we have a better socialist movement, because you'd get more thoughtful people into socialism, if this great organisation wasn't assimilating a whole lot of very kindly, good people.'[7] A rare compliment, indeed.

His admiration for Séamus Costello long evaporated, the Republicanism of his youth only a distant memory, if even that, he turned an increasingly critical eye not just on Republicanism but on nationalism. In a ferocious attack on John Hume and his party in 1990, written in collaboration with Jack McQuillan, he asked rhetorically: 'Is his hand and that of his deputy Seamus Mallon not also on the Armalite, and their hearts with the Provos?'[8]

Three episodes in particular, however, acted as milestones in this last decade of his life. The first was the publication of his autobiography in 1986; the second was a visit he made to the Soviet Union shortly afterwards; and the third was the presidential election of 1990.

His autobiography, *Against the Tide* (the phrase was one he had used about himself in a Dáil debate), had a difficult enough birth. Michael Gill, the publisher, wrote to him on his retirement in 1982 suggesting that he put pen to paper. It was to be four years, and a number of major revisions later, before the autobiography finally reached the bookshops. The difficulty resided partly in the fact that the very act of writing it was cathartic, stirring such emotions that at times Browne would simply have to stop and let the tears come. It was also related to the fact that he saw his manuscript very much as his testament, and took poorly to attempts by editors and others to query facts or references or establish a coherent chronology. Michael D. Higgins was an essential midwife to the project, reassuring him that the publishers, Gill & Macmillan, would deal fairly by him and his book. At one point, Browne took the manuscript to Jack and Angela McQuillan. Jack was hesitant, no doubt feeling that some of the portraits were too sharply drawn; Angela, on the other hand, found that once she had started it, she simply could not tear herself away from the pages, and urged him strongly to publish it.[9] The complexity, and occasional asperity, of the process is hinted at in his preface to *Against the Tide*, where he thanks Deirdre Rennison of Gill & Macmillan 'for keeping the peace between myself, Michael Gill, and others'.

The reader's report on the first draft noted perceptively:

> *Many people regard Noël Browne as a bit of a nuisance and wish he would shut up or go away; yet at the same time they have an uneasy feeling that he has been deplorably treated and that it would be worth finding out more about his life and opinions. He is the thorn that pricks the Irish conscience and touches the sense of decency and fair play that is part of the Irish psyche.*[10]

The book's 'burning flow of passionate rage', the reader concluded, was its prime ingredient, one which he would not like to see checked or stunted. The author had a novelist's eye, but seemed totally unaware that he possessed this great and rare gift. At the same time, there were problems which needed to be dealt with: the 'great gush of bile' on the author's enemies, some of which needed to be replaced by more careful characterisation; a 'rather slapdash attitude to the truth', which called for thorough checking of facts; and a number of 'long, formless harangues which are clearly self-oriented rather than reader-oriented'.

A later report, in March 1985, indicated that substantial work had been done. The author had replaced the bludgeon with the surgeon's probe, particularly in his portrait of MacBride, who was no longer 'an almost incredible monster of iniquity [but] a full delineated human being'. Problems remained, notably with chronology, accuracy and style, but the reader recommended that this be accepted as the final version as, 'if we insist on further overall revision, the work may become irksome to him, with undesirable effects on the text'.

No version of the original text is extant, but notes of the editing process, contain among other things lists of people who might be expected to sue for libel if Noël Browne's comments about them were published.[11] They included, as might be expected, Seán MacBride, Barry Desmond, May and Justin Keating (two pages about Justin Keating were eventually excised), C.J. Haughey, Garret FitzGerald and Dan Morrissey. As Noël acknowledged in his foreword, Phyllis contributed enormously to the process; at a time when word processing was only for initiates, she undertook the work of typing and retyping with a patience and dedication which, as he pointed out, made her in a sense part-author.

The book was a publishing sensation when it appeared in November 1986. The publishers printed an initial run of 3,000 copies; it was sold out in a week. By the middle of January 1987 a further 35,000 copies had been sold, as *Against the Tide* challenged for the title of Ireland's fastest-selling book ever.[12] Midway through the following year, it had sold more than 53,000 copies.[13] The total was to rise to more than 80,000, and the book is still in print, selling approximately 1,000 copies a year.

Two elements of *Against the Tide*, in particular, caught the public's imagination and attention, and demonstrated two sides of the author's character which made him such an extraordinary, and at the same time difficult, public man. One was the vividness of his childhood recollections, happy and unhappy, from the idyll of Athlone to the trauma of his father's death and the family's journey to Mayo. Here there are word-paintings with all the intensity of Victorian melodrama, all the more disarming because written by a participant, not by a novelist. We are with him in the sickroom in which his infant sister died, with him in the trap that took them through the cold January weather to their first exile in Ballinrobe, with him as he kisses his dying mother's clammy forehead. The quality of empathy, of emotional intelligence, which he possessed in such abundance and exercised to such effect not only with his patients and those close to him but with his political audiences, is here astonishingly translated into print.

The second is the section entitled 'Cabinet Portraits', towards the end of the book, which has an intensity of quite a different kind, eighteenth- rather than nineteenth-century in its pitiless evocation of political opponents. Even in a country which mines, on occasion, some rich veins of political hatred, it quite took the breath away. Most if not all of these portraits were of people who had opposed Browne or frustrated his plans. Only two of them — Paddy McGilligan, the Fine Gael Minister for Finance, and T.J. Murphy, the Labour Minister for Local Government, emerge with any credit at all. William Norton, the object of his most savage attack, had by then been dead for over twenty years. The intervening years, it appeared, had honed rather than softened the edges of that sharp resentment Browne had felt in the cabinet room in early 1951, but not even that can fully explain the ferocity of the indictment, the way in which its barbs tear through the flesh of political reputations half-forgotten at this stage. To understand that, we have to go much further back, to something in the author's childhood and youth which alone can explain the laser-like intensity with which Noël Browne's anger was focused on former enemies and, indeed, sometimes on former friends.

Ivor Browne, Noël Browne's colleague for many years in psychiatric medicine, who witnessed his anger directly on occasion, suggests that it is no longer enough to say that the reaction to traumatic experience is to repress the memory of it. More modern thinking suggests that this is quite incorrect. To get into long-term memory the experience has to go through the primitive brain. What actually happens in circumstances involving extreme trauma — such as Noël's mother's death, or the circumstances of his move from Ireland to England — is that the experience gets, as it were, locked in the primitive brain. In effect the trauma is shut off prior to being experienced — it never yet actually happened to the person. It is the 'frozen present'. What this means is that subsequent emotions or circumstances trigger not a memory of the trauma, but the actual psychic enactment of the experience which caused it. This is what accounts for the intensity of the anger and other emotions involved.[14] In this context, it is interesting that what may well have been one of the most traumatic experiences of all — the journey to a foreign country in the company of his terminally ill mother, an almost equally ill brother and his sisters — is dealt with in his book only in a few, offhand lines, without any of the evocative detail that attaches to other, possibly less significant events.

We have the evidence of his book that he experienced his mother's illness and death as a rejection by Ireland of her and, by extension, of Browne himself. No less significant was his memory of his crippled older brother Jody, by which he was to some degree obsessed,[15] and which may have been in part responsible for his hostility towards many members of his own profession. To the end of his life, he believed that Jody's death had been the result of experimental surgery carried out without much heed of the consequences by a London doctor on a misshapen little Irish immigrant of no social significance.

Reaction to the book was little short of ecstatic. Part of this was due to the sort of qualities identified by the publisher's reader; part of it, equally, was due to the fact that this was in many ways a unique publishing event — the first detailed memoir by any Irish cabinet minister of his time in government. In that respect, at least, it had the field to itself. Professor John A. Murphy of University College, Cork said that the book revealed a bleak, melancholy and increasingly bitter temperament, but that his comments were 'fair game and historically informative' (*Sunday Independent*); Dick Walsh described it as a 'powerful . . . fine book' (*The Irish Times*); the historian Ronan Fanning thought it 'painful and passionate' (*Sunday Independent*); and Michael D. Higgins believed it was 'of major importance historically' (*Hot Press*).[16] Breandán Ó hEithir, who had already written to some degree critically about Noël Browne in *The Begrudger's Guide to Irish Politics*, was swimming across, rather than with, the tide. In particular, he asked whether there was any real difference between John A. Costello's submission to the hierarchy in 1951 and Noël Browne's own final response to the bishops, which had been couched in almost identical language. But Browne, he suggested, might take such comments in good part: 'One who has written so critically of former friends and colleagues would scarcely be pleased by further applications of balm to his national record.'[17]

The book, about which Noël Browne spoke on *The Late Late Show* with a piercing sense of self-belief that was mesmerising in its effect, won him arts awards from two national newspapers, the *Sunday Tribune* and the *Sunday Independent*. And the literary success which suddenly surrounded his twilight years was accompanied by invitations to visit Moscow, where he went in 1988 and 1990. On each occasion he addressed Soviet audiences with, it must be said, a somewhat oversimplified view of twentieth-century Irish history. The reason he was defeated at the 1965 general election, he told the Forum for Peace, was 'because a minuscule group of us had protested publicly at the US attitude to the Cuban Revolution of the time'.[18] At one of his meetings, he told his audience that the Irish Republic was ruled from Rome;[19] at another, that 'it is our political leaders, and not the Church of Rome, who is [*sic*] to blame for our misfortunes'.[20]

He was fascinated by his Moscow visits. In particular, he approved of the official policy towards culture and the arts, involving the subsidisation of music and ballet to the extent that they remained accessible to many social classes. He was a passionate devotee of late Classical music and Romantic music himself — of Brahms and Mahler, among others[21] — and warmed to that element in Soviet life in a way which made him uncritical of other aspects of it. Some of those who had fought the long fight with him back in Dublin were less than enamoured of the enthusiasm he evinced for the Soviet Union;[22] but he was not to be deflected, and indeed carried his support into the political sphere, deriding opponents of the Soviet invasion of Afghanistan.

In January 1988, his former friend and latterly bitter opponent, Seán MacBride, died. Browne attended his funeral in the Pro-Cathedral on 18 January. The attendance, reflecting MacBride's many-coloured career, included not only the president, Dr Patrick Hillery, and the Taoiseach, C.J. Haughey, but the American Ambassador and Gerry Adams. During the funeral service, Michael D. Higgins, who was also present, noted a tall man approaching Noël Browne and speaking briefly to him.[23] This man told Browne that he wished to discuss a matter of some importance with him, and, as the funeral was hardly the appropriate venue, offered to come down to Galway and see him afterwards. He did so by arrangement, and met Browne in the Great Southern Hotel in Eyre Square, where they had a lengthy conversation about Archbishop John Charles McQuaid.

That much is certain. What happened afterwards is overlaid by rumour and speculation to such an extent that it is difficult to draw any firm conclusions whatsoever from the episode. Dr Browne's interlocutor, who said he was a school inspector, wrote down his name on a piece of paper at the end of the conversation and gave it to Browne as an aide-mémoire. Browne put it into a pocket of his jacket, which had a hole in it; by the time he went to retrieve it, the piece of paper had fallen out — and Browne could not remember the man's name.[24] He remembered enough of the conversation, however, to write a story which blended, in semi-fictional form, known elements of the life of McQuaid with another story depicting the late archbishop as making pederastic advances to a young boy in a Dublin public house.[25]

The format in which he wrote it requires some elucidation. Encouraged by Michael D. Higgins,[26] who thought that the earlier sections of his auto-biography had considerable literary promise, Browne had begun to readdress some elements of his childhood experience in semi-fictional form. Some of these works in progress have already been referred to — notably the story, involving an amalgamation of at least two separate incidents, from his days as a protégé of the Chance family. The treatment of what his visitor said to him about Archbishop McQuaid took the form that it did precisely because this was the mode in which Browne was writing at the time; but it has the special disadvantage that it makes it next to impossible to distinguish fact, alleged fact, and fiction. This is all the more so since the participants are either dead or untraceable. All that Noël Browne could remember was that his interlocutor was tall, grey-haired and distinguished-looking, and had a special interest in the Irish language (a description which is almost an identikit of any senior Department of Education inspector).

Mike Mellotte, an RTÉ researcher who was interviewing Browne after this event, was apparently the first person outside his immediate family to whom Browne mentioned the incident. Browne asked him if it would be possible for him to trace the inspector on the basis of the scanty information available. Mellotte tried, but failed. Subsequently, when he asked Browne whether he believed what he had been told, Browne said nothing, but shrugged his shoulders. He had apparently not written it in anticipation of publication — although this raises the question of why he wrote (and rewrote) it at all — and it came to light only much later when Phyllis made it available to Archbishop McQuaid's biographer, John Cooney. It would be foolhardy indeed to draw any conclusions from it about McQuaid, although it says a great deal about Browne's attitude to his late adversary, whom he at one point described *tout court*, and in an offhand way hardly consonant with his own medical or psychological training, as 'a pederast'.[27]

None of this was to emerge until after Browne's death. In the wake of his book's success, however, one final political prize was to materialise tantalisingly in front of him, only to be snatched away. This was the prospect of a nomination for the presidency by his own and other parties, for the election due to take place in November 1990 to find a successor for Paddy Hillery, now at the end of his second term of office.

Dick Spring, the Labour Party leader, had made clear early in January of 1990 his conviction that there should be a contest for the presidency, and even offered to stand himself if no other candidate was forthcoming. At the suggestion of his friend John Rogers, his attention focused on Mary Robinson, but even as he began a lengthy period of political courtship — the engagement was nearly broken off on the issue of Robinson's refusal to rejoin the Labour Party — it became evident that some members of his party had other ideas. Almost as soon as Spring had floated the idea of an election, Noël Browne's supporters were in action.[28] They included people like Emmet Stagg, who had lately been worsted by Spring in the Labour Party's internal battles, Michael D. Higgins, David Neligan, and others like Jack McQuillan, a political outsider for many years but still close to Browne. It was a group which also embodied the remains of the Liaison of the Left, which had its origins in the Browne Independent Labour campaign of 1977, and included supporters from a range of constituencies.

It was not difficult for this group to come to a consensus that Noël Browne would make an ideal candidate, and Michael D. Higgins was deputed to approach him directly and ask for a response. As time passed, however, and no word came back from Browne, some of them began to wonder whether Michael D. had actually managed to make contact. Jack McQuillan impishly suggested that it might be because Michael D. himself would not be averse to the idea of becoming a presidential candidate (indeed, he was being spoken of as such at the time). In the event, the process was short-circuited when a small group went to see Noël Browne in Malahide and, in great good humour, he readily agreed to allow his name to be put forward, although he did not then or at any time prior to the nomination make any public statement on the issue.

When the Labour Party was officially asked what it thought of a Browne candidacy, its (anonymous) reply was calculated to damn his chances without naming him. Whoever the party nominated, the spokesman said (this was early days, before the Robinson/Spring stand-off), would be a Labour Party member and a Labour Party candidate.[29] The same report indicated that Browne might run if he were a united left candidate, and would campaign for the idea of radical change in society. At the end of January 1990, the Workers' Party held an inconclusive meeting with Browne,[30] and for a time newspaper publicity concentrated heavily on Browne's chances, almost to the exclusion of Mary Robinson. On 26 March, he even secured the backing of the Labour Women's National Council, an organisation in which Robinson, during her time in the party, had played a prominent role.

Spring, however, was moving quickly, and got the Parliamentary Labour Party to endorse his proposal of Robinson at its meeting on 4 April. Despite a last-minute plea on his behalf by Emmet Stagg,[31] Browne's candidacy was defeated at a joint meeting of the PLP and Labour's Administrative Council on 26 April by at least 4:1. After the vote, Spring rang Browne to inform him, as a courtesy, of the result. It was not, he observed later, a long conversation.[32] Browne's quondam supporters then moved wholeheartedly behind Mary Robinson, and played a substantial part in her extraordinary victory.

Browne's views of the presidency, and of the woman who won it without having to compromise her political independence, were ambivalent at best. Not long before he died, he told an interviewer that it would have been 'a fantastic honour' to have been offered the candidacy; but maintained, almost in the same breath, that it was an 'impotent, titular post'.[33] In March 1997 he was simultaneously suggesting that Mary Robinson had 'squandered . . her undoubted talents' on seven years in the presidency, and asking why she did not stay on to clear out the Augean stables.[34]

By far his most bitter words, however, were reserved for a letter after he and Phyllis had seen Susan off to Malta, where she lives, after a visit she had made to them in Connemara. Criticising what he described as 'President Robinson's roseate, black-tie, Waldorf-Astoria diaspora', he went on, in words which echoed something far older and deeper than the recent parting with his daughter:

May one grieving Irish family, among those bidding farewell and those left behind, tell our roving President her fatuous, low-watt, low-powered 'cheapest available, warmly welcoming electrical' candle brought no comfort to our diaspora and could now, permanently, be switched off.[35]

The silence which greeted this attack was evidence that it was a broadside which — like some others he had delivered — damaged the reputation of its author more than that of its object. It is impossible, at this remove in time, to guess at its deep source, or sources. One analysis would suggest that it was a combination of genuine emotion about emigration infused with personal pique; but even this runs the risk of underestimating the depth of the wellsprings of Browne's emotional life, and in particular the effect of that harrowing journey from Mayo to London sixty-five years before.

In an earlier interview, in a rare moment which combined his unshakeable, almost grandiloquent belief in his own mission with a confession that he was himself at a loss to understand some elements of his political behaviour, he had observed:

I confess that there is something Messianic about me . . . You would have to go back, I suppose, into the whole of my life to wonder why it is that I can't disengage myself . . . I have been unable to get any kind of emotional peace, any kind of emotional satisfaction. If that is a Messianic complex then I suppose I have it. I can't help it, it is part of my personality . . . I have been unable when I see what I feel is human suffering or degradation, humiliation or pain or avoidable unhappiness . . . to pass by on the other side. As a psychiatrist, I should know more about myself as a person . . . I unfortunately haven't been able to do it.[36]

His death was now only months away. He was taken to hospital in the middle of the 1997 general election campaign, and it was soon clear that he was dying. His doctor telephoned Michael D. Higgins; Michael D's telephone answering machine had — unknown to the doctor and to many others who left messages on that particularly busy day — just run out of tape, and Michael D. never got the message, or indeed even knew that it had been left for him.

Noël Browne died in the Regional Hospital in Galway on 22 May, as the campaign entered its final stages. His frail lungs had finally given up the fight. He was buried in a small, beautiful graveyard within walking distance of his last home in Baile na hAbhann — the house to which, after Roseville in Bray, he was more attached than any other. He had left a note asking that no religious service should be held for him. Phyllis, who was aware of the existence of the note but not of its precise location, decided to exercise her rights as Noël's widow to effect a modest compromise: she decided not to search for the note. A local priest, Fr Hughie Loftus, said the Lord's Prayer as the burial took place. The grave is marked by a simple, irregular stone carrying only his name and dates.

Four years after his death, Phyllis was still answering letters from admirers of Noël Browne who wanted to sympathise or share their experiences with her. As the millennium turned, she got a letter from a nun, enclosing five pounds to put daffodils on his grave.

Epilogue

Noël Browne's life and character have been so controversial that they invite a verdict; Browne himself had little time for people whose view of him and his mission was in any way *nuancé* or provisional. A balance sheet, however, is a better and a fairer way of making an assessment, not least because — especially in the case of a man who saw things in such stark, black and white terms — it allows for the necessary complexities of human character. The critic, while rejecting Browne's self-assessment as the tragic hero, can nonetheless perceive elements of real significance and social and political importance in his story. The loyalist, although he may deride the small-minded and self-interested opponents who put obstacle after obstacle in his way and watched gleefully as he tripped over them, can come to accept that Noël Browne's hubris was real, or that he had, at the very least, the defects of his virtues.

His career suggests assessment both on the personal and on the institutional or political level. On the personal level, was the Noël Browne who presented himself to us the real Noël Browne, and what made him the kind of man he was? The early pages of this book are an attempt to answer that question. They show a person whose childhood was emotionally scarred in ways we can hardly guess at, and in ways of which Browne himself was only dimly aware. He hints at it in his autobiography, where he refers in particular to the steadfast and vital role played by his wife, Phyllis. The uniqueness of this role, he suggests, is because his childhood experiences of loss — especially the loss of his parents and his elder brother — had made him wary of forming close relationships with anyone. His own immediate family apart, he tended to reject intimacy because of this fear that its immense benefits would be snatched away as soon as he had begun to enjoy them.

This in turn had an important, possibly even central, and certainly negative effect on many of his political relationships. At a superficial level, the way in which his history is littered with the corpses of such relationships can be put down simply to the belief that he was difficult or, in some cases, impossible to get on with for very long; at a deeper level, it speaks of the way in which he was capable of refusing to accept what he most needed, precisely because of his fear that he would subsequently lose it. This made him distrustful of people, almost incapable of forming equal alliances except with a very small number of individuals, and prone to turning off, wiping out and walking away. Had he moved from psychiatry into psychoanalysis, he would have had to construct a case history for himself in which these characteristics and tendencies would have been further explored; in a sense, *Against the Tide* was a rough first draft of that case history.

That deep trauma which affected so many of his interpersonal and political relationships had, however, another and more beneficent set of effects. People who have been damaged themselves are often among those who have an extraordinary ability to care for others. In this context, he was cut out for medicine. He had a genuine doctor's passion, as healer and carer. When people who had been his patients responded to him, as they did, it was not to any professional bedside manner, but to something authentic and rooted deep in his own sense of self.

This translated onto the political level too. His passion to redress injustices was real, his passion for equality unmistakable. And he had a genius for self-dramatisation which, at its best, evoked from those who voted for him and supported him the feeling that he could articulate, in a way that they could not, the truth that human problems were capable of political solutions, and that the need for these solutions was real and pressing. His political power — and at times it was considerable — came not least from his ability to project undeniable human needs as a basis for legitimate, positive and creative public emotion. Without doubt, he became an icon for many of his generation, not least because it was a generation which, without being able to formulate it in any very distinct way, was struggling to emerge from a chrysalis of political, religious and social tutelage that had encased it for too long.

Why then, for thirty years of a thirty-five-year political career, was so much passion and ability channelled increasingly into one organisational cul-de-sac after another? It cannot all be put down to the machinations of his opponents, or to the deviousness of his enemies, not least because so many of them had been, if only for a time, his friends. There is no simple answer to this, any more than there is a simple answer to the question of why he exercised such political appeal for so many. Part of the explanation, however, is that the self-dramatisation which was such a powerful weapon in his hands could so easily turn against the man who wielded it. It made it difficult — and in the end impossible — for him to build the intra-government and intra-party coalitions on the basis of which political progress inches forward in democratic societies. He had an intolerance of the pragmatists and the conciliators, especially of those who shared his objectives but questioned his choice of means. He could retreat from challenges and confrontations into an interior monologue which was so intense that it all but blotted out the world outside. And all of this evoked an understandable and occasionally regretful intolerance, among many of those who might have been his allies, of his wayward, headstrong, often self-contradictory and self-indulgent but sometimes prophetic voice.

Noël Browne believed that the defeat of the Mother and Child Scheme, and the increasingly malign influence, as he saw it, of the Catholic Church in Ireland, were prime examples of the root and branch problems which would have to be solved if the country's political needs were ever to be met. This analysis, as powerful as it is simplistic, should now be seen as the part of his legacy we can best do without. But even as they reject — as they must — the Samson-like genius for self-immolation which brought the pillars of not one but many temples crashing about his own head in the later years, those of the generation which he helped to energise should not forget the fire that burned within.

Notes

Notes to Chapter One (pp. 1–34)

1. McGirr (1997), p. 280.
2. *Connaught Sentinel*, 17 April 1951.
3. Information from Mrs Biddy Kelly, Loughrea, a cousin of Noël Browne's.
4. Browne (1986), pp. 1–2.
5. Interview with Galway Bay FM, 1996; tape in the possession of Dr Harry Hitchcock, Galway, an old friend of Noël Browne's.
6. Note from the editor to Noël Browne, with annotation as described. Correspondence in the possession of Gill & Macmillan.
7. This is discussed in more detail in chapter 3.
8. Browne (1986), p. 126.
9. 'Get', in this case, standing for illegitimate offspring.
10. DD, vol. 111, col. 2531, 8 July 1948.
11. DD, vol. 111, col. 1967, 1 July 1948.
12. DD, vol. 117, cols. 269–70, 6 July 1949.
13. DD, vol. 172, col. 587, 14 January 1959.
14. NAI, 1911 Census returns for Waterford City.
15. In Browne (1986), Noël names her as Mary Therese Browne (p. 3), but Theresa is the name on her baptismal certificate.
16. Interview, Phyllis Browne.
17. NAI, cabinet minutes for 4 March 1949, G 3/15.
18. NAI, RIC records, MFA 24/10: Record no. 54 738.
19. Browne (1986), p. 3.
20. Information from Lt.-Col. Michael Magoris, a contemporary of Noël Browne's at Beaumont.
21. Interview, Phyllis Browne.
22. Browne (1986), pp. 27–8.
23. Eileen died in 1937; Jody *c.* 1930; Kitty in 1981; Noël in 1997; Martha in 1989; Una in 1976. Ruth Wick Browne lives with her husband, David, in Tennessee.

24. Albert (1980), pp. 87–95. I am indebted to my colleague John Hurley, Professor of Psychology, DCU, for this reference.

25. Sulloway (1996), *passim.*

26. TCD MSS, 11067-25.

27. McInerney (1968), p. 174.

28. Interview, Phyllis Browne.

29. Interview, Phyllis Browne.

30. Interview, T.C.J. O'Connell, RBP.

31. Interview, James Deeny, RBP.

32. Interview, Conor Cruise O'Brien.

33. Interview, Owen Dudley Edwards.

34. Spollen, p. 53.

35. Noël Browne to Michael Gill, 7 June 1986.

36. Browne (1986), p. 12.

37. Browne (1986), pp. 3–24.

38. TCD MSS, 11069-108.

39. Interview, Galway Bay FM.

40. NSPCC, London, p. 2.

41. Letter to author from NSPCC archivist, Nicholas Malton, 31 March 1998. Joseph Browne's service record card is still closed to the public, along with others from this era, on the grounds that they may contain sensitive personal information.

42. Spollen (n.d.), p. 51. Copy in the author's possession. Mr Spollen died in 1997.

43. Information from NSPCC, 17 April 1998.

44. *The Irish School Weekly*, 2 July 1927, p. 826. Information courtesy of Senator Joe O'Toole, INTO.

45. It is probable that Browne's RIC pension had also increased over this period.

46. Browne (1986), facing p. 116.

47. See *infra*, opposite p. 00.

48. Interview, Phyllis Browne.

49. Browne (1986), p. 44.

50. 'The Republican Enigma', speech by Noël Browne at the Mercy Convent, Galway, 3 December 1988. Copy in author's possession. The TCD papers include MSS with a number of similar references.

51. TCD MSS, 11097-108.

52. Spollen, pp. 50–51.

53. Spollen, p. 52.

54. Cooney (1999), pp. 285–7.

55. Information from Mr John Bracken, courtesy of Rev. Brother Brian O'Halloran, Marist Brothers, Athlone.

56. Interview, Galway Bay FM.

57. (1986), p. 25.

58. (1986), p. 26.
59. Browne MS. The pages of the manuscript are not consistently numbered, and so no page references are given.
60. Interview, Galway Bay FM.
61. Browne (1986), p. 13.
62. Browne MS.
63. Browne MS.
64. Browne (1986), p. 33.
65. Browne (1986), p. 8.
66. Browne (1986), p. 9.
67. TCD MSS, 11067-108.
68. Browne MS.
69. The inadvertent substitution in this first draft MS of his mother's Christian name for that of his sister, Annie, is noteworthy. A possible year for Annie's birth and death is 1925.
70. Noël Browne, undated, unpublished MS, McQP.
71. Browne MS.
72. Information from NSPCC archivist, Nicholas Malton.
73. Browne (1986), p. 26.
74. *Westmeath Examiner*, 17 September 1927.
75. Spollen, p. 53.
76. NAI, Wills Register for 1927, no. 75.
77. Browne (1986), p. 3.
78. Browne (1986), pp. 28–9.
79. Browne (1986), p. 29.
80. TCD MSS, 11097-108.
81. TCD MSS, 11097-103.
82. For this and related information I am indebted to Mgr Tom Shannon, PP, Ballinrobe, Co. Mayo.
83. Browne (1986), p. 35.
84. *Dublin Opinion*, May 1946.
85. Browne (1986), p. 29.
86. Information from Mrs Biddy Kelly, Loughrea. I am grateful to Mrs Kelly and to her nephew, Clem Walsh, for much valuable information in this chapter.
87. Browne (1986), p. 35.
88. Cited in Little (1999), p. 81.
89. The address given on Mary Theresa Browne's death certificate.
90. He mistakenly says twelve in his autobiography.
91. Noël Browne's recollection, as told to his wife. Interview, Phyllis Browne.
92. Information from Mrs Biddy Kelly, Loughrea.
93. Browne MS.
94. Information from Ruth Wick Browne, Noël's sister.
95. Interview, Phyllis Browne.

96. Interview, David Neligan.

97. MS of speech by Dr Noël Browne at candlelight memorial service, St Patrick's Cathedral, 21 May 1995, McQP.

98. Little (1999), p. 197. The sentence preceding the quotation is a paraphrase from the psychologist Michael Friedman, quoted by Little.

99. Cited in Little (1999), p. 93.

100. Nuala O'Faolain's account in *The Irish Times*, 4 July 1994.

101. Noël Browne recounts this piece of folklore in his autobiography.

102. March 1932.

103. Interview, T.C.J. O'Connell, RBP.

104. *Beaumont Review*, December 1932, JAL.

105. *Beaumont Review*, December 1933, JAL.

106. *Beaumont Review*, July 1934.

107. Browne (1986), p. 61.

108. Browne MS.

109. *Beaumont Review*, December 1932.

110. Information from Dr Andrew Doughty, Surrey.

111. Browne MS.

112. Browne (1986), p. 82.

113. Information from Mrs Biddy Kelly.

114. Browne (1986) says 1933, but the TCD records are specific on this point. In any case he was still in Beaumont in 1933.

115. Information from Mrs Biddy Kelly.

116. Michael D. Higgins, who discussed this story with Browne, suggests that it is probably an amalgam of two separate incidents from his youth.

117. Information from Mr Douglas Gageby, who was a Trinity student in the pre-war years.

118. Information from Dr Anne Towell (née Dowds), a classmate of Noël Browne's.

119. Information from Mrs Peter Denham.

120. DD, vol. 328, cols. 220–21, 25 March 1981.

121. Browne MS.

122. Interview, William Pike; interview, Bunty Pike (Mrs Pike); letters from Drs Anne Towell (née Dowds) and Moira Woodgate (née Mallagh), TCD contemporaries.

123. Interview, Bunty Pike (Mrs William Pike).

124. Interview, William Pike.

125. Browne (1998), p. 23.

126. Browne (1998), pp. 61–4.

127. Interview, Phyllis Browne.

128. Browne MS.

129. Interview, William Pike, from which other details of this journey are also taken.

130. University of Dublin records.
131. Information from Dr Frank Rogers.
132. Interview, William Pike.
133. Interview, William Pike.
134. Details of Noël Browne's employment record 1941–77 are as supplied by the Eastern Health Board's records.
135. Browne (1986), pp. 71–6.
136. Interview, Michael ffrench-O'Carroll.
137. TCD MSS, 11067-5.
138. Hitchcock (1995), pp. 40 et seq.
139. Interview, Phyllis Browne.
140. TCD MSS, 11067-11. The text is fragmentary and undated.
141. Interview, Phyllis Browne.
142. Interview, Phyllis Browne.
143. Browne (1986), p. 75.

Notes to Chapter Two (pp. 35–58)

1. Health Embarkation Scheme, Fifth Monthly Report, March 1944. DDA, AB8/B/XVII.
2. Cooney (1999), p. 154.
3. 26 May 1944, DDA, AB8/B/XVII.
4. McDowell memorandum, p. 2.
5. DDA, 8 March 1943.
6. Dr Muiris Houston, *Sunday Business Post*, 28 March 1999.
7. Detailed documentation for this controversy can be found in DDA, AB8/B/XVII.
8. 22 November 1943, DDA, AB8/B/XVII.
9. Noël Browne's Eastern Health Board employment records indicate that he returned in October 1943 but this is plainly wrong. The most likely date seems to be 1946.
10. O'Connor is the author of *The Fight Against TB in Ireland in the 1940s*.
11. Interview of Dr E.G.T. MacWeeney by John Whyte, RBP.
12. Interview, James Deeny, RBP.
13. Interview, Louie O'Brien.
14. Statement by P.J. Little, Minister for Posts and Telegraphs, cited in MacDermott (1998), p. 16.
15. Deeny (1989), p. 128.
16. Deeny (1989), p. 162.
17. Public Health Bill, 1945, Sections 19 (3) and 29.
18. *Journal of the Medical Association of Éire*, May 1946, quoted in O'Connor (1994), p. 79. This privately published book is an invaluable source of documentation on the period.

19. 'TB and its defeat', paper read by Noël Browne to the University College, Galway, Medical School, 1 February 1989. TCD MSS, 11067-4.

20. This is certainly the view of Dr Michael ffrench-O'Carroll, a Clann member in the late 1940s who joined Fianna Fáil with Noël Browne in 1953 when both were Independent TDs.

21. 6 February 1946, DDA, AB8/B/XVII.

22. 12 April 1946, quoted in O'Connor (1994), p. 68.

23. Deeny (1989), p. 128.

24. *The Irish Times*, 30 April 1946.

25. *Sunday Independent*, 7 April 1946, quoted in O'Connor (1994), p. 69.

26. *The Irish Times*, 20 April 1946, quoted in O'Connor (1994), p. 77.

27. Interview, Ruth Wick Browne.

28. McDowell memorandum, p. 2. McDowell later acted as Browne's solicitor when Noël and Phyllis bought and sold houses, and in some other matters.

29. McDowell memorandum, pp. 2–3.

30. O'Connor (1994), p. 87.

31. (1986), p. 119.

32. MacDermott (1998), pp. 38–43.

33. MacBride to de Valera, 14 May 1945, NAI D/T S 14 544A.

34. Interview of Seán MacBride by Martin McGovern, McGovern (1979), p. 21.

35. 18 January 1948, quoted in Cronin (1987), p. 186.

36. Interview, Ruth Wick Browne.

37. Interview, Phyllis Browne.

38. Interview, Ruth Wick Browne.

39. For this necessarily brief outline of the history of this Act I am indebted to Ruth Barrington's definitive account (1987), pp. 176–93.

40. Barrington (1987), p. 176.

41. Browne (1986), p. 152.

42. Information from Charles Flanagan, TD.

43. P. 89.

44. Interview of Noël Browne by Gerry Gregg, cited in McGovern (1979), note 64, chapter VI.

45. *Irish People*, 3 January 1948, cited in McGovern (1979), p. 33.

46. Interview, Dr Harry Hitchcock. Dr Hitchcock worked under Dr Cullen when he became Noël Browne's locum in 1948.

47. Deeny (1989), p. 163.

48. Letter to editor, *Journal of the Medical Association of Éire*, vol. 22 (1948), no. 128, pp. 26–7.

49. Seán MacBride, *Irish Press*, 16 March 1987.

50. O'Connor (1994), pp. 115–17.

51. O'Connor (1994), p. 116.

52. *The Clann*, 28 December 1947, NAI, JUS 8/942.

53. Interview, Phyllis Browne.

54. Interview, Ruth Wick Browne.
55. *The Irish Times*, 5 January 1948 (speech at Kilmallock).
56. *The Irish Times*, 15 January 1948.
57. *The Irish Times*, 16 January 1948.
58. *The Irish Times*, 17 January 1948. The other Clann candidates included seventeen farmers, thirteen teachers, four barristers, two joiners, a dentist, a labourer, a student — and 'a woman of independent means'.
59. *The Irish Times*, 27 January 1948.
60. *The Irish Times*, 3 January 1948.
61. O'Connor (1994), pp. 119–20.
62. O'Connor (1994), p. 120.
63. *The Irish Times*, 2 February 1948.
64. *Irish Independent*, 17 January 1948.
65. *Clann*, 6 January 1948, cited in McGovern (1979), p. 41.
66. Browne (1986), p. 103.
67. McGovern (1979), note 19 to chapter VII.
68. *The Irish Times*, 15 January 1948.
69. *The Irish Times*, 21 January 1948.
70. McDowell memorandum, p. 3.
71. Cf. *Irish Press*, 3 February 1948.
72. *The Irish Times*, 4 February 1948.
73. 31 January 1948.
74. Yeats (1999), p. 49.
75. O'Connor (1994), p. 47.
76. Rugby to Machtig, 5 March 1948, PRO, DO 130/90.
77. Interview, Louie O'Brien.
78. McGovern (1979), pp. 103–4.
79. Interview, Michael ffrench-O'Carroll.
80. Information from Pádraig McCartan, SC.
81. Interview, Louie O'Brien.
82. 19 February 1948.
83. *Sunday Express*, 23 May 1948.
84. Interview, Louie O'Brien.

Notes to Chapter Three (pp. 59–90)

1. Noël Browne to his colleague, Dr Michael ffrench-O'Carroll, repeatedly. Interview, Michael ffrench-O'Carroll.
2. Interview, Dr Harry Hitchcock.
3. Interview, Phyllis Browne.
4. Interview, Phyllis Browne.
5. He also at one stage owned an Adler, a powerful sports car renowned for winning the Circuit of Ireland rally. Interview, Ruth Wick Browne.
6. See fifth page of first photograph section.

7. Interview, Marje Cooney.
8. Interview of Dr McQuaid by John Whyte, 14 August 1969, RBP.
9. McQuaid interview.
10. See Cooney (1999), *passim*.
11. Rugby to Machtig, Dominions Office, 17 August 1948, PRO, DO 130/90.
12. MacBride to McQuaid, 7 February 1948, DDA, MCS.
13. Interview of Seán MacBride by John Whyte: letter from John Whyte to author, 13 June 1969.
14. DDA, MCS.
15. DD, vol. 113, col. 312, 24 November 1948. The reference was to an unscripted speech by Seán MacBride.
16. Review Body on Higher Remuneration in the Public Sector, Dublin, Stationery Office, Prl. 2674, pp. 107–8.
17. Interview, Dr Harry Hitchcock.
18. DD, vol. 111, cols. 2530–31, 8 July 1948.
19. DD, vol. 111, col. 2581, 8 July 1948.
20. DD, vol. 112, col. 20, 13 July 1948.
21. Income tax was not applied to parliamentary allowances until 1960.
22. DD, vol. 117, cols. 269–70, 6 July 1949.
23. Cf. *Irish Press*, 9 January 1951, contrasting the expedition of this project with the delay attending the other.
24. DD, vol. 117, col. 315, 6 July 1949.
25. DD, vol. 117, col. 275, 6 July 1949.
26. DD, vol. 117, cols. 290–301, 6 July 1949.
27. DD, vol. 111, cols. 225–39, 8 July 1948.
28. Dr C. Byrne, *Irish Press*, 22 January 1948, cited in McGovern (1979), p. 80.
29. *Irish Press*, 22 November 1948.
30. McDowell memorandum, pp. 3–5.
31. McDowell memorandum, p. 5.
32. Deeny (1989), p. 165.
33. DD, vol. 103, col. 1134, 20 November 1946.
34. I am indebted to Charles Lysaght, whose father, Dr Charles Lysaght, was responsible for the hospital building programme in the department at this time, for this insight.
35. The word was actually used by James Deeny in a post-retirement conversation with Professor Tom Garvin of UCD. Information from Professor Garvin.
36. Interview, Michael Mulvihill, RBP.
37. Interview, James Deeny, 29 November 1983, RBP.
38. Deeny interview cited.
39. Information from Tom O'Higgins.
40. DD, vol. 111, col. 1979, 15 June 1948.
41. Interview, Tony Browne, son of Victor Browne. Tony Browne, an economist, later became international secretary of the Labour Party. In 1997 he was appointed a director of the European Bank for Reconstruction and Development.

42. Deeny (1989) p. 172.
43. *Irish Independent*, 2 October 1948.
44. *Irish Independent*, 3 February 1949.
45. Cited in Horgan (1986), p. 65.
46. McGovern (1979), note 38 to chapter VI, interview with MacBride.
47. Browne MS.
48. Interview, Phyllis Browne.
49. DD, vol. 110, cols. 13872–3, 12 May 1948.
50. Barrington (1987), especially pp. 195–221. Any figures not otherwise sourced are from this work.
51. DD, vol. 111, cols. 2261–86, 6 July 1948. Any quotations from Dr Browne not otherwise referenced are from this speech.
52. DD, vol. 111, col. 2261, 6 July 1948.
53. This view was expressed privately by Costello to Dr Patrick McCartan, who enjoyed the confidence of many significant figures in the 1948–51 government. Information from Pádraig McCartan, SC.
54. Article by Seán MacBride, *Sunday Press*, 16 March 1987: 'I had already had a number of discussions with Joe McGrath, who was strongly in favour of the hospital building programme.'
55. Documents relating to this Council's work are in NAI, Department of Health, M 100/91.
56. NAI, Department of Health, A8/164.
57. NAI, Department of Health, D 112/349.
58. Deeny (1989), p. 166.
59. Deeny (1989), p. 169.
60. Dr Barry O'Donnell in Lyons (1999), p. 3.
61. Lyons (1999), p. 156.
62. Deeny (1989), p. 170.
63. *Journal of the Medical Association of Éire*, vol. 23, no. 36, October 1948, p. 63, cited in Barrington (1987), p. 205.
64. Interview, Dr Harry Hitchcock.
65. DD, vol. 116, col. 887, 21 June 1949.
66. DD, vol. 116, col. 887, 21 June 1949.
67. DD, vol. 116, col. 1796 ff, 1 July 1949.
68. *Irish Press*, 22 September 1949.
69. DD, vol. 111, col. 2540, 8 July 1948.
70. Interview, Ted Russell.
71. DD, vol. 116, col. 1803, 1 July 1949.
72. Browne (1986), p. 124.
73. Barrington (1987), p. 200.
74. Maguire (1998), p. 139.
75. The best treatment to date of this episode is in McCullagh (1998), pp. 72–108.

76. (1986), p. 129.
77. Information from Nicholas Harman, Sir Charles Harman's son.
78. Letter from Caitriona Lawlor, Mount Merrion, to the editor, *The Irish Times*, 8 February 1994. Caitriona Lawlor, a former secretary to Seán MacBride, has the late Clann leader's papers.
79. DD, vol. 117, col. 270, 6 July 1949.
80. DD, vol. 114, col. 2524, 7 April 1949.
81. Speech at Clonakilty, 10 June 1949. Typescript in NAI, GIS 1/48.
82. *Irish Press*, 10 September 1949.
83. *Irish Press*, 13 September 1949.
84. *Irish Independent*, 2 February 1950.
85. *Irish Independent*, 23 February 1920.
86. Noël Browne to Ruth Browne (undated), May 1950, RWB.
87. Noël Browne to Ruth Browne (undated), May 1950, RWB.
88. Noël Browne to Ruth Browne, 12 December 1950, RWB.

Notes to Chapter Four (pp. 91–119)

1. Browne (1986), p. 153.
2. See especially Whyte (1971), McKee (1986), Barrington (1987), Deeny (1989), McCullagh (1998), McDermott (1998) and Cooney (1999).
3. This is the view of Ruth Barrington (1987).
4. *The Irish Times*, 4 June 1947. Cutting in Norton papers, ILHS. Fr Leo McCann, CC, who also spoke at the meeting, did not raise any objection to the proposed scheme.
5. Interview, James Deeny, RBP.
6. Quoted in Browne (1986), p. 152.
7. Interview of James Deeny by John Whyte, 23 August 1966, RBP.
8. P. 153.
9. DD, vol. 125, col. 947, 12 April 1951 (emphasis added).
10. Unless otherwise sourced, quotations are from NAI, D/T, S 13444 G; emphasis added.
11. Browne MS.
12. Cited in Barrington (1987), p. 202.
13. DD, vol. 111, col. 2289, 15 June 1948.
14. Browne MS.
15. Information from Professor Ronan Fanning. Dr Fanning's wife, in contrast, thought Noël Browne marvellous — he was the first person for whom she ever voted in a general election.
16. Interview of Dr Paddy Fanning by John Whyte, 24 August 1966, RBP.
17. Cited in Morgan (1984), p. 159.
18. Browne MS.
19. Browne MS.

20. The word is actually used as a description of the cabinet's action, by Deeny (1989), p. 178.
21. Ó Cinnéide to Delaney, 19 August 1948. Copy in DDA, MCS, AB8/B/XVIII.
22. 8 July 1949.
23. Cited in Davies (1980), p. 291.
24. The quotation, cited in McKee (1986), p. 166, dates from 1944! The detailed account of the negotiations between Health and Finance on the system by which the medical profession would be remunerated for the new scheme is in NAI, Department of Finance S72/5/49, from which further references on the issue in this chapter are also drawn.
25. EO'C to Almond, Department of Health, 24 March 1949.
26. Interview of John Darby, Department of Health, by John Whyte, 14 August 1967, RBP.
27. The Council's papers and agendas are in NAI, Department of Health, M100 series.
28. Memo on neonatal scheme in Dublin maternity hospitals, 21 April 1951, NAI D/Health M 100/119.
29. DD, vol. 125, col. 316, 6 July 1949.
30. Memorandum on Mother and Child Service, Department of the Taoiseach, 2 April 1951. NAI, D/T S 13444 G.
31. Browne to McQuaid, 14 December 1949. DDA, AB8/B/XVIII.
32. DD, vol. 118, col. 1722, 1 December 1949.
33. Browne to Costello, 13 February 1950, NAI, S 14 997A.
34. *The Irish Times*, 29 May 1950.
35. Interview, Dr Michael ffrench-O'Carroll.
36. Rugby to Machtig, 24 February 1948, PRO, DO 130/90.
37. Garrett and Beaudry to State Department, 8 March 1948 and 29 July 1948, USNA, 800-872, Box 16.
38. Garrett to State Department, 22 December 1948, USNA, 800-872, Box 16.
39. Clann *Bulletin*, vol. 1, no. 1, October 1949, McQP.
40. Rugby to Dominions Office, 1 June 1950, PRO, DO 130/110.
41. William Norton papers, ILHS.
42. Barrington (1987), p. 313.
43. DD, vol. 125, col. 749, 12 April 1951.
44. DD, vol. 122, col. 1217, 11 July 1950.
45. McKee (1986), p. 190.
46. NAI, D/T S 14470A. The note on the file adds: 'Seen by Taoiseach before today's government meeting 25/8/50.'
47. McGovern (1979), p. 75.
48. (1986), p. 181.
49. *Irish Press*, 17 March 1987.
50. (1998), p. 148.

51. (1986), p. 138.
52. McKee (1986), p. 170.
53. Browne MS.
54. Copy in DDA, MCS, AB8/B/XVIII.
55. Department of Health memorandum, p. 1.
56. Interview of Seán MacBride, *Sunday Press*, 7 December 1986.
57. Memorandum and letter, 9 November 1950, LOB.
58. (1986), pp. 180–81.
59. Memorandum and letter, 9 November 1950, LOB.
60. MacBride to O'Donoghue, 9 November 1950, p. 7.
61. Interview of Seán MacBride, *Sunday Press*, 7 December 1986.
62. Information from Brian Murphy, a former member of the Clann executive.
63. Interview, Phyllis Browne, December 1999.
64. Aodh de Blacam papers; courtesy of Mrs Nora de Blacam.

Notes to Chapter Five (pp. 120–49)

1. Excerpts from minutes of meetings: LOB.
2. Ard-Chomhairle minutes, meeting of 6/7 January 1951. LOB.
3. McQuaid memorandum, 15 January 1951, prepared for meeting of Standing Committee of Hierarchy on 16 January. DDA, MCS.
4. Copy of document in William Norton papers, Irish Labour History Society Archives.
5. *Sunday Press*, 11 February 1951.
6. Interview, T.C.J. O'Connell, RBP.
7. Interview, T.C.J. O'Connell, RBP.
8. Interview, T.C.J. O'Connell, RBP. The identity of the 'Offaly solicitor' remains unknown to this day.
9. 'Medics, Mitres and Ministers', *Radharc* documentary, RTÉ 1991.
10. MacBride review of situation, Clann na Poblachta Ard-Chomhairle Meeting, 31 March 1951. LOB.
11. William H. Christensen, American Embassy, Dublin, to State Department, 23 February 1951. USNA, 740A.00/2-2351.
12. Interview, T.C.J. O'Connell, RBP.
13. It was later reversed, by the same government, when the appointee was asked to resign.
14. Browne to Chair, Standing Committee, 8 February 1951. LOB.
15. MacBride to Smyllie, 21 February 1951. LOB.
16. MacBride to Browne, 26 February 1951. LOB.
17. (1986), p. 138.
18. Correspondence between Hartnett and MacBride re meeting on the evening of 28 February 1951, LOB.
19. Christensen to State Department, 9 March 1951. USNA, 740A.00/4.
20. *Sunday Independent*, 11 February 1951, p. 2: 'May Lose My Job, Doctor Says'.

21. Interview of James Deeny by John Whyte, RBP.
22. Interview of Cardinal Conway by John Whyte; information from John Whyte to author, 15 March 1969.
23. McQuaid note on events surrounding the Mother and Child Scheme, DDA, MCS, AB8/B/XVIII.
24. Letter to author from John Whyte, 15 March 1969.
25. Letter to author from John Whyte, 15 March 1969.
26. Private source.
27. Report to Standing Committee, 3 March 1951. DDA, MCS, AB8/B/XVIII.
28. Cited in Manning (1999), p. 266.
29. *Irish Independent*, 6 March 1951.
30. Cf. IMA response to the minister's letter, *Irish Independent*, 17 March 1951.
31. McQuaid report to Standing Committee of Hierarchy, 3 March 1951. DDA, MCS, AB8/B/XVIII.
32. MacBride to Browne, 8 March 1951. LOB.
33. Interview, Louie O'Brien.
34. Seán MacBride, minute of meeting with Noel Hartnett, 19 November 1951. LOB.
35. In his autobiography, Noël Browne mentions (p. 176) that the letter was handed to him on 6 April, just before the fateful cabinet meeting. He seems, however, to have inadvertently telescoped the two occasions, and the two episcopal communications, one from McQuaid personally on 8 March, and the other from McQuaid on behalf of the hierarchy, which was given to Costello on 5 April. He was definitely shown McQuaid's first letter on 8 March, and made his radio broadcast on the same date.
36. Department of Finance to secretary, Department of Health, 8 March 1951. NAI, Department of Finance S72/5/49.
37. McGilligan to Browne, 14 March 1951. NAI, Department of Finance S72/5/49.
38. Quoted by Costello, DD, vol. 125, cols. 757–8, 12 April 1951.
39. Internal Department of Finance memorandum, 8 March 1951. NAI, Department of Finance S72/5/49.
40. 12 September 1949. Full text in NAI, GIS 1/49.
41. McQuaid note of conversation with Costello, 5 April 1951. DDA, MCS, AB8/B/XVIII.
42. McKee (1986), p. 182.
43. Interview of James Dillon by John Whyte, 17 May 1966, RBP.
44. 'Conversations with James Dillon', *Sunday Independent*, 29 November 1987.
45. McQuaid note of conversation with Costello on that day, 'Notes on Events in March 1951', DDA, MCS.
46. Walsh to McQuaid, 14 April 1951, DDA, MCS, AB8/B/XVIII.
47. Dillon interview, RBP.
48. Dillon interview, RBP. See also Manning (1999), pp. 266–72.

49. I am indebted to Professor Dermot Keogh for this clarification.

50. 'Mother and Child Scheme', memorandum. DDA MCS, AB8/B/XVIII.

51. Undated notes on events in March 1951, DDA, MCS, AB8/B/XVIII. McQuaid's note of his meeting with Browne is headed '3.15 p.m., 21 March 1951. Interview sought by Dr Browne.' This, however, must be an error: the entry for Holy Thursday, 22 March, notes that at 1 p.m. McQuaid learned that Dr Browne wished to see him, and that the interview was arranged for the same afternoon at 3.15 p.m.

52. Staunton to McQuaid, 31 March 1951, DDA, MCS, AB8/B/XVIII.

53. Resolutions forwarded to Noël Browne on 2 April 1951 by secretary, Ard-Chomhairle. LOB.

54. Interview, Jack McQuillan.

55. 'Mother and Child Scheme' memorandum, DDA, MCS, AB8/B/XVIII.

56. Undated MS memorandum by Dr McQuaid of events from 4 to 10 April (probably written on 11 April), DDA, MCS.

57. 'Mother and Child Scheme' memorandum, DDA, MCS, AB8/B/XVIII.

58. McQuaid undated memorandum, probably 10 or 11 April 1951. DDA, MCS, AB8/B/XVIII. Brendan Corish was later to become leader of the Labour Party just as it decided to admit Noël Browne as a member.

59. Draft minute of Special Ard-Chomhairle meeting, 8 April 1951. LOB.

60. Browne (1986), p. 186.

61. Information from Brian Murphy, a Clann member and confidant of Kevin White.

62. Quoted contemporaneously in *The Irish Times*, 7 May 1971.

63. Minutes of National Executive meeting, 8 April 1951, pp. 2–17. LOB.

64. Browne to Ard-Rúnaidhe, Clann na Poblachta, 11 April 1951. LOB.

65. Browne (1986), p. 75; *Hot Press*, interview with John Waters, 1986.

66. *The Irish Times*, 10 January 1984.

67. Interview, Ruth Wick Browne.

68. Information from Charles Lysaght, BL.

69. Interview, Phyllis and Susan Browne.

70. McInerney (1968), pp. 204–5.

71. Mgr Cremin's role is briefly mentioned in unpublished papers in the possession of Gill & Macmillan.

72. Interview with Mgr Frank Cremin, 6 May 1999.

73. McQuaid to Felici, 15 April 1951, DDA, MCS, AB8/B/XVIII.

74. Dr McQuaid's MS report to Standing Committee of Hierarchy, 3 March 1951, DDA, MCS, AB8/B/XVIII.

75. McQuaid to Staunton, 1 April 1951, DDA, MCS.

76. Cooney (1999), pp. 94–106.

77. Rugby to Machtig, 24 February 1948, PRO, DO 130/90.

78. See *infra*, chapter 6.

79. Review of *Against the Tide*, *The Furrow*, Maynooth, vol. 38, no. 2, February 1987, p. 104.
80. Keogh (1998), p. 213.
81. DDA, MCS, AB8/B/XVIII.
82. DDA, MCS, AB8/B/XVIII.
83. 25 April 1951.
84. Interview with Michael Mulvihill, RBP.

Notes to Chapter Six (pp. 150–86)

1. Information from Dr Paddy Lynch.
2. (1984), pp. 453–4.
3. Christensen to State Department, 23 October 1950, USNA, 840A.55/10-2350.
4. Christensen to State Department, 13 April 1951, USNA, 740A.00/4-1351.
5. McQuaid to Felici, 15 April 1951, DDA, MCS.
6. 12 April 1951.
7. 14 April 1951.
8. 14 April 1951. The writer was most probably Barbara Dixon, the daughter of a prominent Dublin doctor, Charles Dixon, who was a political radical and a historian of the 1798 period.
9. *The Irish Times*, 19 April 1951.
10. 20 April 1951.
11. *The Irish Times*, 14 April 1951.
12. 'Why He Chose the Name Pius', *Irish Independent*, 12 April 1951.
13. *Irish Independent*, 31 December 1954.
14. Information from Jilly Howarth (née Chance) and Francis Chance.
15. I am indebted, for some of this information, to a term paper by DCU student Ian Kilroy (1968) on 'The Mother and Child Scheme and the Press'.
16. DD, vol. 125, col. 673, 12 April 1951.
17. DD, vol. 125, col. 667, 12 April 1951.
18. DD, vol. 125, col. 802, 12 April 1951.
19. DD. vol. 125, cols. 907–9, 17 April 1951.
20. (1986), p. 188.
21. *The Irish Times*, 13 April 1951.
22. Information from Donal Nevin.
23. 17 April 1951.
24. 21 April 1951.
25. 21 April 1951.
26. 21 April 1951.
27. 21 April 1951.
28. 21 April 1951.
29. 21 April 1951.
30. 21 April 1951.

31. *The Irish Times*, 24 April 1951.
32. Reported in *The Irish Times*, 23 April 1951.
33. *The Irish Times*, 23 April 1951.
34. DD, vol. 126, col. 1231, 10 July 1951.
35. Information from Charles Lysaght, BL.
36. Memorandum to secretary, Department of Health, 16 April 1951. NAI, Department of Health, M100/119.
37. 'Summary of 1950 Proposals for a Mother and Child Health Service', Department of Health, 21 April 1951. NAI, Department of Health, M100/119.
38. *The Irish Times*, 5 May 1951.
39. Cited in McDermott (1998), p. 162.
40. *The Irish Times*, 25 May 1951.
41. Information from Dr Michael ffrench-O'Carroll.
42. *The Irish Times*, 24 April 1951.
43. *The Irish Times*, 23 May and 12 June 1951.
44. Browne (1986), p. 208. Interview, Dr Michael ffrench-O'Carroll.
45. *The Irish Times*, 19 May 1951 (emphasis added).
46. *The Irish Times*, 23 May 1951.
47. *The Irish Times*, 1 May 1951.
48. *The Irish Times*, 1 May 1951.
49. *The Irish Times*, 28 May 1951.
50. Information from Pádraig McCartan, SC.
51. *The Irish Times*, 18 and 25 May 1951.
52. *The Irish Times*, 17 May 1951.
53. *The Irish Times*, 12 May 1951.
54. Donal Nevin's recollection.
55. Editorial, 30 May 1951.
56. Little (1999).
57. Cited in Little (1999), p. 154.
58. *The Irish Times*, 9 June 1951.
59. Editorial, 2 June 1951.
60. *Sunday Independent*, 3 June 1951.
61. Browne (1986), p. 210.
62. Noël Browne to author, 26 June 1996.
63. Interview, Noël Browne with Ciaran Carty, 1985, courtesy of Ciaran Carty.
64. Interview, Michael ffrench-O'Carroll.
65. DD, vol. 126, col. 38, 13 June 1951.
66. DD, vol. 126, col. 40, 13 June 1951.
67. DD, vol. 126, col. 65, 13 June 1951.
68. DD, vol. 126, col. 44, 13 June 1951.
69. DD, vol. 126, col. 58, 13 June 1951.
70. DD, vol. 126, col. 951, 5 July 1951.

71. DD, vol. 130, cols. 1003–11, 1 July 1951.
72. Lee (1989), pp. 322–5.
73. (1989), p. 324.
74. (1986), p. 211.
75. DD, vol. 131, col. 196, 23 April 1952.
76. DD, vol. 131, col. 205, 23 April 1952.
77. DD, vol. 126, col. 1228, 10 July 1951.
78. DD, vol. 126, col. 1250, 10 July 1951.
79. Browne (1998), pp. 124–5.
80. DD, vol. 134, col. 1529, 13 November 1952.
81. E.g. DD, vol. 137, col. 6005, 18 March 1953.
82. DD, vol. 122, col. 253, 11 July 1950.
83. DD, vol. 139, col. 886, 9 June 1953.
84. DD, vol. 138, col. 91, 15 April 1953.
85. DD, vol. 139, col. 1905, 24 June 1953.
86. DD, vol. 141, cols. 1131 and 1133, 30 July 1953.
87. *The Irish Times*, 4 June 1983.
88. *The Irish Times*, 4 June 1983.
89. DDA, MCS.
90. Interview, T.C.J. O'Connell. Barrington papers.
91. McQuaid to Ryan, 30 January 1953; Ryan to McQuaid, 2 February 1953; Lucey to McQuaid, 30 January 1953. DDA, MCS.
92. McQuaid to Mgr Alibrandi (later Nuncio to Ireland), 2 May 1956. DDA, MCS.
93. Interview, Phyllis Browne.
94. McInerney (1968), p. 205.
95. Interview, Donal Nevin.
96. Interview, Sam Nolan.
97. Copy of typescript of article in Cork Consulate's dispatch to State Department, 18 July 1952, USNA, 740A.00/10-2152. The anonymous correspondent of *The Round Table* in the Republic was the author's grandfather, Cork solicitor John J. Horgan. The editors of the journal continued to publish his contributions for many years after Ireland had left the Commonwealth.
98. Edney, US Embassy, Dublin, to State Department, USNA, FW-740A.00 (W)/9-1952.
99. *The Irish Times*, 1 September 1952.
100. *The Irish Times*, 9 September 1952.
101. Lindholm (1990), p. 66.
102. *The Irish Times*, 2 October 1953.
103. FF 344.
104. Interview, Dr Michael ffrench-O'Carroll.
105. Interview, Jack McQuillan.

106. Interview, Phyllis Browne.
107. *The Irish Times*, 29 October 1953.
108. 29 October 1953.
109. Randolph Roberts, US Embassy, to State Department, 29 October 1953, USNA, 740A.00/10-2953.
110. Chargé d'affaires, Dublin, to Dominions Office, 9 November 1953. PRO, DO 35/7940.
111. Yeats (1999), p. 58.
112. *The Irish Times*, 25 January 1954.
113. FF 344.
114. Information from Dr Michael ffrench-O'Carroll.
115. Dr O'Connell (Archbishop McQuaid's secretary) to MacBride, 25 May 1954, DDA, MCS.
116. FF 894.
117. *The Irish Times*, 20 May 1954.
118. *Irish Press*, 14 October 1954.
119. Interview, Phyllis Browne.
120. FF 344, from which all references to the National Executive in 1954 and 1955 are also drawn.
121. (1986), p. 226.
122. (1999), p. 60.
123. Report on branches, Dublin SE Constituency, FF 281.
124. Minutes of Dublin SE Comhairle Ceanntar, FF 281.
125. Family source.
126. Interview, Phyllis Browne.
127. Ó Cléirigh to Lemass, 9 February 1955, FF 281.
128. Interview, Petria Thornley.
129. Interview, Petria Thornley.
130. FF 315.
131. 14 November 1954, FF 281.
132. Irish Cruising Club Annual, 1956. I am indebted to W.M. Nixon, an inexhaustible source of information on all matters connected with sailing, for details of Noël Browne's sailing activities.
133. FF 723.
134. Information from Dr Michael ffrench-O'Carroll, who discussed Browne with MacEntee at around this time.
135. *Irish Press*, 21 November 1956.
136. McCann, White and FitzGerald to Clarke, 30 November 1956. Copy in FF 281.
137. Undated memorandum, FF 281.
138. Miss Kathleen Lynch to general secretary, 7 February 1957, FF 281.
139. Alexander Clutterbuck (British Ambassador in Dublin) to Dominions Office, London, 4 March 1957. PRO, DO 35/5195.

140. Private source.
141. Yeats (1999), p. 61.
142. Information from Máire Mhac an tSaoi.
143. Interview, David Neligan.
144. (1999), p. 62.
145. Lemass's version of this meeting was recounted by him to Brian Lenihan. Author's interview with Brian Lenihan, May 1994.
146. Minutes of Ard-Chomhairle meeting, FF 344.
147. (1986), p. 226. For a replication of the error see, e.g., Horgan (1986), p. 66, and Yeats (1999), p. 62.

Notes to Chapter Seven (pp. 187–208)

1. Interview, Owen Dudley Edwards.
2. Interview, Owen Dudley Edwards.
3. Interview, Owen Dudley Edwards, from which other insights into the National Progressive Democrat Party and the 1913 Club are also drawn.
4. Interview, Owen Dudley Edwards.
5. Interview, Owen Dudley Edwards.
6. Alexander Clutterbuck (British Ambassador in Dublin) to Marquess of Salisbury, 23 March 1957. PRO, DO 35/5195.
7. DD, vol. 161, col. 23, 20 March 1957.
8. Interview, Proinsias Mac Aonghusa.
9. Interview, Owen Dudley Edwards.
10. Interview, Petria Thornley.
11. J.A. la Freniere to State Department, 19 March 1957. USNA, 740A.00/3-1957.
12. (1986), p. 250.
13. Information from Justin Keating.
14. The Irish Times, 2 November 1957.
15. Browne (1986), p. 250.
16. Obituary of Professor Laurence Roche, The Irish Times, 4 December 1999.
17. Information from Dr Trevor West, FTCD, a contemporary of Laurence Roche.
18. The Irish Times, 17 May 1958.
19. Report to London for 9–22 May 1958. PRO, CON 298/9/1.
20. 19 May 1958.
21. The Irish Times, 22 May 1958.
22. 17 May 1958.
23. Cf. Cooney (1999), p. 321.
24. Gregg (1981), p. 95.
25. (1986), p. 253.
26. National Progressive Democrats: 'Draft notes for canvassers'. Proinsias Mac Aonghusa papers.
27. New Statesman, 14 June 1958.

28. 25 June 1958.
29. Editorial, *The Irish Times*, 27 June 1958.
30. Interview of David Thornley by Paul Hickey, cited in Gregg (1981), note 47 to chapter II.
31. Interview of Noël Browne by Gerry Gregg, cited in Gregg (1981), note 47 to chapter II.
32. 'Portrait from a Poisoned Pen', Edward Thornley, *Irish Independent,* 15 November 1986.
33. *Daily Mail*, 5 July 1958.
34. Interview, Owen Dudley Edwards.
35. *Daily Mail*, 5 July 1958.
36. 1913 Club statement, Proinsias Mac Aonghusa papers.
37. 5 July 1958.
38. Letter from 'Ex-NPD Supporter', *Evening Mail*, 14 July 1958.
39. Letter from 'Democrat', *Evening Mail*, 15 July 1958.
40. Letter from '1913 Club Member', *Evening Mail*, 17 July 1958.
41. *The Plough*, June 1958, cited in Gregg (1981), note 47 to chapter II.
42. DD, vol. 162, col. 344, 5 June 1957.
43. DD, vol. 162, col. 352, 5 June 1957.
44. DD, vol. 163, cols. 47–8, 26 June 1957.
45. DD, vol. 163, col. 50, 26 June 1957.
46. DD, vol. 162, col. 309, 5 June 1957.
47. DD, vol. 173, col. 946, 11 March 1959.
48. DD, vol. 167, cols. 202–4, 10 April 1958.
49. DD, vol. 163, cols. 730–31, 4 July 1957.
50. P. Hickey and J.C. McGrath, 'The National Progressive Democrats', unpublished seminar paper, UCD, *c.* 1978, p. 103, cited in Gregg (1981), note 48 to chapter II.
51. DD, vol. 165, col. 323, 19 February 1958.
52. DD, vol. 168, cols. 997–1002, 29 May 1958.
53. DD, vol. 179, cols. 546–1154, 17 February–2 March 1960.
54. Sheldon was an Independent Protestant deputy from Donegal, and subsequently a senator. He died in 1999.
55. DD, vol. 164, cols. 835–49, 20 November 1957; cols. 1131–50, 27 November 1957; and cols. 1456–7, 4 December 1957.
56. DD, vol. 171, cols. 1667–707, 4 December 1958.
57. DD, vol. 171, col. 1705, 4 December 1958.
58. DD, vol. 171, col. 1667, 4 December 1958.
59. DD, vol. 174, col. 1546, 5 May 1959.
60. For this debate, cf. DD, vol. 171 and 172, *passim*, and Coogan (1993), pp. 674–5.
61. Curran (1992), *passim*.
62. Coogan (1993), p. 734.

63. Browne (1986), p. 236.
64. Interview, Phyllis Browne.
65. Interview, Phyllis Browne.
66. Susan Browne, *Sunday Tribune*, 26 May 1985.
67. DD, vol. 176, cols. 13–16, 23 June 1959.
68. DD, vol. 179, cols. 774–88, 24 February 1960.

Notes to Chapter Eight (pp. 209–47)

1. P. Hickey and J.C. McGrath, 'The National Progressive Democrats', unpublished seminar paper, UCD, c. 1978, p. 103, cited in Gregg (1981), note 48 to chapter II.
2. McGovern (1979), note 51 to chapter II.
3. Edward R. O'Connor, US Embassy, Dublin, to State Department, 4 August 1961. USNA, 740A.00/8-461.
4. Browne (1986), p. 255.
5. McCloskey, US Ambassador, to State Department, 24 October 1962. USNA, 740A.00/10-2462.
6. (1986), p. 256.
7. Interview, Jack McQuillan.
8. 23 November 1963.
9. Minutes, Labour Party Administrative Council. LPA.
10. DD, vol. 206, cols. 899–910, 10 December 1963.
11. Cf. for example DD, vol. 207, col. 286, 30 January 1964 and col. 1786, 27 February 1964.
12. Interview, Ruth Wick Browne.
13. Interview, Tony Browne.
14. Interview, Michael D. Higgins.
15. Interview, Una Claffey.
16. Interview, Phyllis Browne.
17. Browne (1986), p. 239.
18. Profile, *The Irish Times*, 14 October 1967.
19. Information from Dr Michael ffrench-O'Carroll.
20. 'TB and its Defeat', paper read by Noël Browne to UCG Medical School, 1 February 1989. TCD MSS, 11067, 4–5.
21. TCD MSS, 11067-5.
22. Interview, Michael D. Higgins.
23. McGovern (1979), p. 116.
24. Interview, Niall Greene.
25. Interview, Betty Dowling.
26. Interview, Ruairí Quinn.
27. Labour Party, Annual Report 1964–5. LPA.
28. Speech in Galway, *The Irish Times*, 23 January 1967.
29. Interview, Ruairí Quinn.

30. *The Irish Times*, 9 July 1967.
31. *The Irish Times*, 9 October 1967.
32. Labour Party Annual Report 1967–8. LPA.
33. 14 October 1967.
34. Raymond Guest to State Department, 2 November 1967. USNA, POL 12-3 IRE.
35. *The Irish Times*, 30 October 1967.
36. *The Irish Times*, 30 November 1967.
37. Browne (1986), pp. 138–9.
38. Interview, Liam Kavanagh.
39. Interview, Brendan Halligan.
40. (1986), pp. 265–6.
41. Information from Muiris Mac Conghail.
42. Interview, Tony Browne.
43. Information from Professor Tom Garvin, UCD, who interviewed Dr Deeny on this and other topics.
44. *The Irish Times*, 16 March 1968.
45. Labour Party Annual Report, 1967–8. LPA.
46. *The Irish Times*, 23 March 1968. Sheila Conroy withdrew later, and was replaced as a candidate by J.P. Kennedy.
47. Interview, Susan Browne.
48. NAI, D/T 98/6/446.
49. Interview, Ivor Browne.
50. Interview, Ivor Browne.
51. Interview, Michael D. Higgins.
52. Supplement to *The British Journal of Psychiatry*, October 1969, p. 28.
53. (1973), pp. 158–74.
54. Interview, Ivor Browne.
55. Interview, Michael D. Higgins.
56. Interview, Jack McQuillan.
57. Interview, Jack McQuillan.
58. Interview, Brendan Halligan.
59. Interview, David Neligan.
60. Browne to Corish, 25 June 1969. Letter courtesy of Brendan Halligan.
61. Information from Phyllis Browne.
62. Interview, Noël Browne, cited in McGovern (1979), p. 117.
63. *Evening Press*, 17 June 1969, cited in McGovern (1979), p. 106.
64. *The Irish Times*, 2 June 1970.
65. *The Irish Times*, 2 September 1970.
66. *The Irish Times*, 21 September 1970.
67. Michael McInerney, *The Irish Times*, 3 October 1970.
68. *The Irish Times*, 28 October 1970.
69. Tape recording of early part of conference, LPA.

70. RTÉ Archive tape 97D00936, 26 February 1971.
71. Noël Browne, *The Irish Times*, 3 May 1971. The only extant account of this meeting is Browne's. The minutes of the PLP for this period are missing, but his account was not subsequently denied.
72. Browne (1999), p. 153.
73. Cited in Gregg (1981), p. 116.
74. *This Week*, 1 October 1970.
75. *This Week*, 5 March 1971.
76. *The Irish Times*, 23 January 1967. This may be the speech which persuaded Michael D. Higgins to join the Labour Party.
77. *The Irish Times*, 6 December 1968.
78. *The Irish Times*, 24 April 1971.
79. (1986), p. 263.
80. (1986), pp. 261–4. In the course of this, he mistakenly attributes a quotation from Nietzche to O'Brien.
81. (1999), pp. 323–4.
82. *The Irish Times*, 30 April 1971.
83. *The Irish Times*, 3 May 1971.
84. O'Brien (1999), p. 324. Interview, Justin Keating.
85. (1999), p. 325.
86. From *Demian* (1919), cited in 'The Last Word on Hate', A.C. Grayling, *Guardian*, 12 February 2000.
87. Letter to the editor, *The Irish Times*, 13 May 1971.
88. He was also a co-author of the seminal book about internal RTÉ politics in the 1960s, *Sit Down and Be Counted*.
89. *The Irish Times*, 14 May 1971 (the second of two articles on this topic by Dowling).
90. *The Irish Times*, 9 September 1971.
91. *The Irish Times*, 11 February 1972.
92. Information from Fr Enda McDonagh.
93. *The Irish Times*, 6 June 1972.
94. Article in the British Labour weekly *Tribune*, reported in *The Irish Times*, 19 December 1972.
95. Noël Browne, letter to the editor, *The Irish Times*, 6 March 1972.
96. Noël Browne, article in the *Sunday Press*, 25 June 1972.
97. AC minutes of meeting on 7 September 1972. NGP.
98. 2 April 1972.
99. Documentation for AC meeting of 13 April 1972. NGP.
100. Interview by Emer O'Kelly, *Sunday Press*, 26 March 1972.
101. *The Irish Times*, 25 March 1972.
102. Minutes of AC meeting of 13 April 1972. NGP.
103. Minutes of AC meeting of 11 September 1972. NGP.
104. Minutes of AC meeting of 12 October 1972. NGP.

105. Interview, Ruairí Quinn.
106. Labour Party Annual Report 1972–3. LPA.
107. *The Irish Times*, 9 February 1973.
108. Interview, David Neligan.
109. McGovern (1979), p. 116.
110. Noël to Phyllis Browne, 7 February 1973. Phyllis Browne personal papers.

Notes to Chapter Nine (pp. 248–66)

1. Interview, David Neligan.
2. Interview, David Neligan.
3. *The Irish Times*, 27 July 1973.
4. Letter from Pat Carroll, *The Irish Times*, 19 February 1973.
5. Interview, Michael D. Higgins.
6. Letter from Dermot Boucher, *The Irish Times*, 16 February 1973. James Ramsay MacDonald (1866–1937), the British Labour leader, participated in an all-party government, which resulted in substantial electoral losses for his own party.
7. *The Irish Times*, 26 March 1973.
8. *The Irish Times*, 19 December 1972, quoting his article in the British Labour weekly *Tribune*.
9. Letter from Noël Browne to editor, *The Irish Times*, 2 June 1973; letter from Pat Dempsey, former supporter, to editor, *The Irish Times*, 5 June 1973.
10. Minutes, PLP, 25 July 1973. LPA.
11. *The Irish Times*, 31 July 1973.
12. Interview, Jack McQuillan.
13. Interview of Noël Browne by Cormac O'Connell, *Sunday Press*, 26 May 1974.
14. Cf. SD, vol. 85, cols. 318–607, 14, 15 and 16 September 1976.
15. SD, vol. 75, cols. 629–35, 25 July 1973.
16. SD, vol. 75, cols. 632–5, 25 July 1973.
17. Interview, David Neligan.
18. 14 November 1973.
19. Letter to the editor, 19 November 1973.
20. It did so in 1976 in the Dáil, when, on a free vote, it was unexpectedly defeated, the Taoiseach, Liam Cosgrave, and other government deputies voting against the Minister for Justice's measure.
21. SD, vol. 77, col. 351, 21 February 1974.
22. SD, vol. 77, col. 356, 21 February 1974.
23. Information from former Senator Trevor West, who discussed this with him at the time.
24. Interview, David Neligan.
25. *The Irish Times*, 21 October 1974.
26. *Hibernia*, 31 October 1975.

27. *Hibernia*, 14 November 1975, cited in Gregg (1981), p. 121.

28. The whip was restored to him just before the 1977 election, but to no avail: he lost his seat.

29. *The Irish Times*, 13 January 1975. See also 'Backbencher', *The Irish Times*, 11 January 1975.

30. References to this debate are from the tape-recordings for Session 4 of the 1976 Labour Party Conference, tapes 1, 2 and 3. LPA. I was present for this debate.

31. Browne (1986), pp. 128–9.

32. Cabinet minutes for 29 October 1948, NAI, G 3/15; cabinet minutes for 3 May 1949, NAI, G 3/15; cabinet minutes for 22 December 1949, NAI, G 3/15; cabinet minutes for 11/12 May 1951, NAI, G 5/219.

33. *The Irish Times*, 6 September 1976.

34. *The Irish Times*, 13 September 1976.

35. *The Irish Times*, 26 June 1975.

36. Interview, David Neligan.

37. *The Irish Times*, 8 November 1975.

38. *The Irish Times*, 3 March 1977.

39. *The Irish Times*, 23 March 1977.

40. *The Irish Times*, 24 March, 26 March and 31 March 1977.

41. *The Irish Times*, 1 April 1977.

42. *The Irish Times*, 4 June 1977.

43. Noël Browne election leaflet, Dublin Artane (undated). BTP.

44. Interview, David Neligan.

45. Annual Report, 1976–8, Labour Party, p. 43. LPA.

46. *The Irish Times*, 26 July 1977.

47. No copy of this letter survives; Cluskey, notoriously, did not keep much in the way of correspondence.

48. Minutes, Labour Party Administrative Council, 29 September 1977. LPA.

49. *The Irish Times*, 30 September 1977.

50. *The Irish Times*, 10 October 1977.

Notes to Chapter Ten (pp. 267–80)

1. Anonymous SLP party worker, 12 June 1981, quoted in Maire Crowe's article on Noël Browne, *Irish Press*, 19 June 1981.

2. Brian Trench in *Hibernia*, 14 October 1977. BTP.

3. *The Irish Times*, 8 March 1974.

4. *The Irish Times*, 31 December 1977.

5. Brian Trench in *Hibernia*, 14 October 1977. BTP.

6. 'David Thornley: An Appreciation' by David Boucher, SLP internal *Bulletin* no. 1, July 1978. BTP.

7. *Socialist Labour*, vol. 1, no. 1, 6 May 1978. BTP.

8. SLP internal *Bulletin* no. 1, *c.* February 1978. BTP.

9. SLP internal *Bulletin* no. 2, June 1979, BTP.
10. Excerpted in SLP *Bulletin* no. 2, June 1978. BTP.
11. *The Irish Times*, 30 January 1979.
12. *The Irish Times*, 7 February 1979.
13. Noël Browne to editor, *The Irish Times*, 16 July 1981, when he said that this had happened 'over a year ago'.
14. Interview with Jim Downey, *The Irish Times*, 7 July 1981.
15. Letter to *The Irish Times* from Carol Louthe, SLP headquarters, 9 Parnell Square, 21 October 1978.
16. SLP NEC minutes, 10 February 1979. BTP.
17. SLP NEC minutes, 10 February 1979. BTP.
18. SLP NEC minutes, 10 March 1979. BTP.
19. SLP NEC minutes, 21 April 1979. BTP.
20. *The Irish Times*, 2 February 1979.
21. SLP NEC agenda for 10 February 1979. BTP.
22. SLP NEC minutes, 10 March 1979. BTP.
23. SLP NEC minutes, 14 July 1979. BTP.
24. Undated memorandum (probably February/March 1979). BTP.
25. DD, vol. 317, col. 1371, 11 December 1979.
26. DD, vol. 317, cols. 1374–5, 11 December 1979.
27. Interview, Ruairí Quinn.
28. *The Irish Times*, 15 March 1980.
29. *The Irish Times*, 30 June 1980.
30. Interview with Jacqui Dunne, *Sunday Independent*, 29 June 1980.
31. Horgan (1997a), pp. 95–8.
32. DD, vol. 321, col. 1474, 3 June 1980.
33. DD, vol. 323, col. 1470, 4 November 1980.
34. DD, vol. 323, col. 1471, 4 November 1980.
35. DD, vol. 324, cols. 771–88, 19 November 1980.
36. DD, vol. 325, cols. 1068–9, 11 December 1981.
37. DD, vol. 326, col. 981, 4 February 1981.
38. DD, vol. 327, cols. 326–39, 25 February 1981.
39. DD, vol. 326, cols. 1831–4, 17 February 1981.
40. Interview with Maire Crowe, *Irish Press*, 19 June 1981.
41. Interview with Olivia O'Leary, *The Irish Times*, 15 June 1981.
42. *The Irish Times*, 24 June 1981.
43. Interview with Olivia O'Leary, *The Irish Times*, 15 June 1981.
44. See note 1 above.
45. Interview with Maire Crowe, *Irish Press*, 19 June 1981.
46. *The Irish Times*, 9 November 1981.
47. *The Irish Times*, 10 November 1981.
48. *The Irish Times*, 27 August 1982.
49. Interview, Michael D. Higgins.

50. DD, vol. 329, cols. 19–20, 30 June 1981.

51. DD, vol. 329, col. 22, 30 June 1981.

52. DD, vol. 330, cols. 226–9, 21 October 1981.

53. Information from Garret FitzGerald.

54. DD, vol. 332, col. 7, 26 January 1982.

55. Information from Dr Garret FitzGerald.

56. Interview, David Neligan.

57. *The Irish Times*, 1 February 1982.

58. Browne (1986), p. 269.

59. Division list in DD, vol. 331, col. 411, 27 January 1982.

60. *The Irish Times*, 1 February 1982.

61. Information from Dr Garret FitzGerald. Fine Gael actually picked up Noël Browne's old seat in North-Central.

62. *The Irish Times*, 24 April 1982.

63. Interview, Ruairí Quinn.

64. *The Irish Times*, 6 November 1982.

Notes to Chapter Eleven (pp. 281–91)

1. Interview, Phyllis Browne.

2. RTÉ Accession no. BA902.

3. RTÉ Accession no. HX90/7099.

4. RTÉ Accession no. HX60/2736.

5. RTÉ Accession no. HX60/3712.

6. Letter to the editor, *The Irish Times*, 10 November 1994.

7. Quoted by Waters, *The Irish Times*, 10 June 1997.

8. *The Irish Times*, 17 December 1990.

9. Interview, Angela McQuillan.

10. Gill & Macmillan files.

11. Gill & Macmillan files.

12. Eoghan Corry, *Sunday Press*, 18 January 1987.

13. *Business and Finance*, 18 June 1987.

14. Interview, Ivor Browne.

15. Interview, David Neligan.

16. Undated review extracts, Gill & Macmillan files.

17. *Sunday Press*, 30 November 1986.

18. Speech to the Forum for Peace, Moscow, TCD MSS, 11067-76.

19. Speech in Moscow, 1988, TCD MSS, 11067-29.

20. Speech in Moscow, 1990, TCD MSS, 11067-97.

21. Interview, Phyllis Browne.

22. Interview, David Neligan.

23. Interview, Michael D. Higgins.

24. Interview, Phyllis Browne.

25. TCD MSS, 11067 164, 181–3, 197, 198.

26. Interview, Michael D. Higgins.
27. Ref. Cooney.
28. Interview, David Neligan.
29. *The Irish Times*, 19 January 1990.
30. *The Irish Times*, 29 January 1990.
31. *The Irish Times*, 23 April 1990.
32. Information from Dick Spring.
33. *The Irish Times*, 20 November 1996.
34. *The Irish Times*, 20 March 1997.
35. *The Irish Times*, 13 January 1996.
36. Interview with Gerry Gregg, cited in Gregg (1981), p. 125.

Sources

Abbreviations

Public archives

NAI   National Archives of Ireland
PRO   Public Records Office, Kew
PRONI   Public Records Office of Northern Ireland
USNA   United States National Archives, Washington

Other archives

DDA   Dublin Diocesan Archives
JAL   Jesuit Archives, Mount Street, London
LPA   Labour Party Archives
MBA   Marist Brothers Archives, Athlone
RSPCC   Royal Society for the Prevention of Cruelty to Children Archives
RTÉ   Radio Telefís Éireann Archives
TCD MSS   Noël Browne papers, TCD Manuscript Library

Oireachtas debates

DD   Debates, Dáil Éireann
SD   Debates, Seanad Éireann

Private papers

Browne MS   Material excised from *Against the Tide* during editing
BTP   Papers, mostly relating to the Socialist Labour Party, in the posses-
             sion of Brian Trench
deBP   Papers of the late Aodh de Blacam, courtesy of Mrs de Blacam
LOB   Personal papers of Louie O'Brien, former secretary to Seán
             MacBride
McQP   Personal papers of the late Jack McQuillan, courtesy of Angela
             McQuillan
NGP   Labour Party papers in the possession of Niall Greene

PB   Personal papers, Phyllis Browne
PMcA   Personal papers, including press cuttings, of Proinsias Mac
            Aonghusa
RBP   Personal papers of Ruth Barrington, including interviews by her
            and the late John Whyte of Archbishop J.C. McQuaid and others
RWB   Personal papers of Ruth Wick Browne

Bibliography

Albert, R.S. (1980), 'Family Positions and the Attainment of Eminence', in *Gifted Child Quarterly* (1980), no. 24, pp. 87–95.

Barrington, Ruth (1987), *Health, Medicine and Politics in Ireland 1900–1970*, Dublin, Institute of Public Administration.

Browne, Noël (1948), 'The Spread of Tuberculosis', in *Journal of the Medical Association of Éire*, vol. 22 (1948), no. 128, pp. 26–7.

Browne, Noël (1973), 'Psychiatric analysis by Dr Noël Browne', in *Haigh: The Mind of a Murderer* (ed. Arthur la Bern), London, W.H. Allen.

Browne, Noël (1986), *Against the Tide*, Dublin, Gill & Macmillan.

Browne, Phyllis (1998), *Thanks for the Tea, Mrs Browne: My Life with Noël*, Dublin, New Island Books.

Browne, Vincent (1981) (ed.), *The Magill Book of Irish Politics*, Dublin, Magill Books.

Coogan, Tim Pat (1993), *De Valera: Long Fellow, Long Shadow*, London, Hutchinson.

Cooney, John (1999), *John Charles McQuaid, Ruler of Catholic Ireland*, Dublin, O'Brien Press.

Cronin, Sean (1987), *Washington's Irish Policy 1916–1986*, Tralee, Anvil Books.

Curran, Catherine (1992), 'The *Irish Press* and Fianna Fáil', Ph.D. thesis, Dublin City University.

Davies, A.F. (1980), *Skills, Outlooks and Passions: A Psychoanalytic Contribution to the Study of Politics*, Cambridge University Press.

de Brún, Nollaig (Noël Browne) (1952), 'Dualgas Orainn Tionscail Mhóra a Bhunú sa Ghaeltacht', *Comhar*, Meán Fomhair.

Deeny, James (1987), 'Towards balancing a distorted record', review of *Against the Tide* in *Journal of the Irish Medical Association*, vol. 80, no. 8, August 1987, pp. 222–5.

Deeny, James (1989), *To Care and to Cure: Memoirs of a Chief Medical Officer*, Dublin, Glendale Press.

Deeny, James (1998), *The End of an Epidemic: Essays in Irish Public Health 1935–65*, Dublin, A.&A. Farmar.

Department of Health and Department of Local Government (1950), *Tá Éire ag Forbairt — Ireland is Building*, Dublin.

Dormandy, Thomas (1999), *The White Death: A History of Tuberculosis*, London, Hambledon Press.

Gregg, Gerry (1981), 'Dr Noël Browne: Irish Political Maverick 1948–1977', MA thesis, University College, Dublin.

Hitchcock, Harry (1995), *T.B. or not TB.?*, Galway, Centre for Health Promotion Studies.

Horgan, John (1986), *Labour: The Price of Power*, Dublin, Gill & Macmillan.

Horgan, John (1997a), *Mary Robinson: An Independent Voice*, Dublin, O'Brien Press.

Horgan, John (1997b), *Lemass: The Enigmatic Patriot*, Dublin, Gill & Macmillan.

Kavanagh, James (1987), 'Against the Tide' (review) in *The Furrow*, vol. 38, no. 2, February 1987, pp. 97–108.

Keogh, Dermot (1994), *Twentieth-Century Ireland: Nation and State*, Dublin, Gill & Macmillan.

Lee, J.J. (1989), *Ireland 1912–1985: Politics and Society*, Cambridge University Press.

Lindholm, Charles (1990), *Charisma,* London, Basil Blackwell.

Little, Graham (1999), *The Public Emotions: From Mourning to Hope*, Sydney, The Australian Broadcasting Corporation.

Lyons, J.B. (1999), *A Pride of Professors*, Dublin, A. & A. Farmar.

McCullagh, David (1998), *A Makeshift Majority: The First Inter-Party Government, 1948–51*, Dublin, Institute of Public Administration.

MacDermott, Eithne (1998), *Clann na Poblachta*, Cork University Press.

McGirr, Michael (1997), 'At Home in Memory', in *The Oxford Book of Australian Essays*, Melbourne, Oxford University Press, pp. 279–301.

McGovern, Martin (1979), 'The Emergence and Development of Clann na Poblachta', MA thesis, University College Dublin.

McKee, Eamonn C. (1986), 'Church–State Relations and the Development of Irish Health Policy: The Mother and Child Scheme 1944–53', in *Irish Historical Studies*, vol. XXV, no. 98 (Nov. 1986), pp. 159–94.

McInerney, Michael (1968), 'Church and State', *University Review*, vol. 5 (1968), no. 2, pp. 171–215.

McRedmond, Louis (1996), (ed.), *Modern Irish Lives*, Dublin, Gill & Macmillan.

Macy, Chris (ed.) (1999), *Rehab News: Celebrating 50 Years of the Rehab Group*, Dublin, The Rehabilitation Institute.

Maguire, Martin (1998), *Servants to the Public: A History of the Local Government and Public Services Union 1901–1990*, Dublin, Institute of Public Administration for IMPACT.

Manning, Maurice (1999), *James Dillon: A Biography*, Dublin, Wolfhound Press.

Morgan, Kenneth (1984), *Labour in Power 1948–1951*, Oxford, Clarendon Press.

NSPCC (n.d.), *A Short History: The foundation of the NSPCC and its Role Today*, London, NSPCC.

O'Boyle, Michael and Benbow, Camilla (1990), 'Handedness and its Relationship to Ability and Talent', in *Left-Handedness: Behavioural Implications and Anomalies*, S. Coren (ed.), pp. 343–71, Holland, Elsevier.

O'Brien, Conor Cruise (1998), *Memoir: My Life and Times*, Dublin, Poolbeg.

O'Connor, Charles (1994), *The Fight Against TB in Ireland in the 1940s*, Cape Town.

Review Body on Higher Remuneration in the Public Sector (n.d.), Dublin, Stationery Office, Prl. 2674.

Spollen, James A. (n.d.), *What a Press . . . What a People*, Athlone.

Sulloway, Frank (1996), *Born to Rebel: Birth Order, Family Dynamics, and Creative Lives*, London, Little Brown.

Whyte, John (1971), *Church and State in Modern Ireland 1923–1970*, Dublin, Gill & Macmillan.

Yeats, Michael (1999), *Cast a Cold Eye: Memories of a Poet's Son and Politician*, Dublin, Blackwater Press.

Newspapers and Periodicals

Beaumont Review
Bulletin (Socialist Labour Party)
Clann
Connaught Sentinel
Daily Mail
Evening Mail
Guardian
Hibernia
Hot Press
Irish Independent
Irish Press
Irish Times
Journal of the Medical Association of Éire
New Statesman
Plough
Socialist Labour
Sunday Business Post
Sunday Express
Sunday Independent
Sunday Press
Sunday Tribune
Westmeath Examiner

Index